MW00874852

The Geneva Bible 1560 with Apocrypha

The Complete Version of the Bible 1560
Includes ALL of these Apocryphal Texts.

Jeremy Copson

Disclaimer

The Apocryphal texts included in this edition have historical significance but are not recognized as canonical scripture by all Christian denominations. These texts are provided for their historical and literary value and are not intended to represent doctrinal authority.

Any acknowledgments to contributors or sources are made with gratitude and do not imply endorsement of the contents or conclusions of this edition.

Index of Apocryphal Books

THE BOOK OF TOBIT

1

1 The book of the words of Tobit, the son of Tobiel, the son of Ananiel, the son of Aduel, the son of Gabael, of the seed of Asiel, of the tribe of Naphtali; 2 who in the days of Enemessar king of the Assyrians was carried away captive out of Thisbe, which is on the right hand of Kedesh Naphtali in Galilee above Asher. 3 I, Tobit walked in the ways of truth and righteousness all the days of my life, and I did many alms deeds to my kindred and my nation, who went with me into the land of the Assyrians, to Nineveh.4 When I was in my own country, in the land of Israel, while I was yet young, all the tribe of Naphtali my father fell away from the house of Jerusalem, which was chosen out of all the tribes of Israel, that all the tribes should sacrifice there, and the temple of the habitation of the Most High was hallowed and built therein for all ages.5 All the tribes which fell away together sacrificed to the heifer Baal, and so did the house of Naphtali my father.6 I alone went often to Jerusalem at the feasts, as it has been ordained to all Israel by an everlasting decree, having the first fruits and the tenths of my increase, and that which was first shorn; and I gave them at the altar to the priests the sons of Aaron.7 I gave a tenth part of all my increase to the sons of Levi, who ministered at Jerusalem. A second tenth part I sold away, and went, and spent it each year at Jerusalem. 8 A third tenth I gave to them to whom it was appropriate, as Deborah my father's mother had commanded me, because I was left an orphan by my father.

9 When I became a man, I took as wife Anna of the seed of our own family. With her, I became the father of Tobias. 10 When I was carried away captive to Nineveh, all my kindred and my relatives ate of the bread of the Gentiles;11 but I kept myself from eating, 12 because I remembered God with all my soul. 13 So the Most High gave me grace and favor in the sight of Enemessar, and I was his purchasing agent. 14 And I went into Media, and left ten talents of silver in trust with Gabael, the brother of Gabrias, at Rages of Media.15 And when Enemessar was dead, Sennacherib his son reigned in his place. In his time, the highways were troubled, and I could no longer go into Media. 16 In the days of Enemessar, I did many alms deeds to my kindred: I gave my bread to the hungry, 17 and my garments to the naked. If I saw any of my race dead, and thrown out on the wall of Ninevah, I buried him. 18 If Sennacherib the king killed any, when he came fleeing from Judea, I buried them privately; for in his wrath he killed many; and the bodies were sought for by the king, and were not found. 19 But one of the Ninevites went and showed to the king concerning me, how I buried them, and hid myself; and when I knew that I was sought for to be put to death, I withdrew myself for fear. 20 And all my goods were

forcibly taken away, and there was nothing left to me, save my wife Anna and my son Tobias. 21 No more than fifty five days passed before two of his sons killed him, and they fled into the mountains of Ararat. And Sarchedonus his son reigned in his place; and he appointed Achiacharus my brother Anael's son over all the accounts of his kingdom, and over all his affairs. 22 Achiacharus requested me, and I came to Nineveh. Now Achiacharus was cupbearer, keeper of the signet, steward, and overseer of the accounts. Sarchedonus appointed him next to himself, but he was my brother's son.

2

1 Now when I had come home again, and my wife Anna was restored to me, and my son Tobias, in the feast of Pentecost, which is the holy feast of the seven weeks, there was a good dinner prepared for me, and I sat down to eat. 2 I saw abundance of meat, and I said to my son, "Go and bring whatever poor man you find of our kindred, who is mindful of the Lord. Behold, I wait for you." 3 Then he came, and said, "Father, one of our race is strangled, and has been cast out in the marketplace."4 Before I had tasted anything, I sprang up, and took him up into a chamber until the sun had set.5 Then I returned, washed myself, ate my bread in heaviness, 6 and remembered the prophecy of Amos, as he said, "Your feasts will be turned into mourning, and all your mirth into lamentation. 7So I wept: and when the sun had set, I went and dug a grave, and buried him. 8 My neighbors mocked me, and said, "He is no longer afraid to be put to death for this matter; and yet he fled away. Behold, he buries the dead again."9 The same night I returned from burying him, and slept by the wall of my courtyard, being polluted; and my face was uncovered.

10 I didn't know that there were sparrows in the wall. My eyes were open and the sparrows dropped warm dung into my eyes, and white films came over my eyes. I went to the physicians, and they didn't help me; but Achiacharus nourished me, until I went into Elymais. 11 My wife Anna wove cloth in the women's chambers, 12 and sent the work back to the owners. They on their part paid her wages, and also gave her a kid. 13 But when it came to my house, it began to cry, and I said to her, "Where did this kid come from? Is it stolen? Give it back to the owners; for it is not lawful to eat anything that is stolen." 14 But she said, "It has been given to me for a gift more than the wages."I didn't believe her, and I asked her to return it to the owners; and I was ashamed of her.But she answered and said to me, "Where are your alms and your righteous deeds? Behold, you and all your works are known."

3

1 I was grieved and wept, and prayed in sorrow, saying,2 "O Lord, you are righteous, and all your

works and all your ways are mercy and truth, and you judge true and righteous judgment forever.3 Remember me, and look at me. Don't take vengeance on me for my sins and my ignorances, and the sins of my fathers who sinned before you. 4 For they disobeyed your commandments. You gave us as plunder, for captivity, for death, and for a proverb of reproach to all the nations among whom we are dispersed.

5 Now your judgments are many and true, that you should deal with me according to my sins and the sins of my fathers, because we didn't keep your commandments, for we didn't walk in truth before you.6 Now deal with me according to that which is pleasing in your sight. Command my spirit to be taken from me, that I may be released, and become earth. For it is more profitable for me to die rather than to live, because I have heard false reproaches, and there is much sorrow in me. Command that I be released from my distress, now, and go to the everlasting place. Don't turn your face away from me." 7 The same day it happened to Sarah the daughter of Raguel in Ecbatana of Media, that she also was reproached by her father's maidservants; 8 because that she had been given to seven husbands, and Asmodaeus the evil spirit killed them, before they had lain with her. And they said to her, "Do you not know that you strangle your husbands? You have had already seven husbands, and you haven't borne the name of any one of them. 9 Why do you scourge us? If they are dead, go your ways with them. Let us never see either son or daughter from you." 10 When she heard these things, she was grieved exceedingly, so that she thought about hanging herself. Then she said, "I am the only daughter of my father. If I do this, it will be a reproach to him, and I will bring down his old age with sorrow to the grave." 11 Then she prayed by the window, and said, "Blessed are you, O Lord my God, and blessed is your holy and honorable name forever! Let all your works praise you forever! 12 And now, Lord, I have set my eyes and my face toward you.13 Command that I be released from the earth, and that I no longer hear reproach. 14 You know, Lord, that I am pure from all sin with man, 15 and that I never polluted my name or the name of my father in the land of my captivity. I am the only daughter of my father, and he has no child that will be his heir, nor brother near him, nor son belonging to him, that I should keep myself for a wife to him. Seven husbands of mine are dead already. Why should I live? If it doesn't please you to kill me, command some regard to be had of me, and pity taken of me, and that I hear no more reproach."16 The prayer of both was heard before the glory of the great God. 17 Raphael also was sent to heal them both, to scale away the white films from Tobit's eyes, and to give Sarah the daughter of Raguel for a wife to Tobias the son of Tobit; and to bind Asmodaeus the evil spirit; because

it belonged to Tobias that he should inherit her. At that very time, Tobit returned and entered into his house, and Sarah the daughter of Raguel came down from her upper chamber.

4

1 In that day Tobit remembered the money which he had left in trust with Gabael in Rages of Media, 2 and he said to himself, I have asked for death; why do I not call my son Tobias, that I may explain to him about the money before I die? 3 And he called him, and said,"My child, if I die, bury me. Don't despise your mother. Honor her all the days of your life, and do that which is pleasing to her, and don't grieve her. 4 Remember, my child, that she has seen many dangers for you, when you were in her womb. When she is dead, bury her by me in one grave. 5 My child, be mindful of the Lord our God all your days, and don't let your will be set to sin and to transgress his commandments: do righteousness all the days of your life, and don't follow the ways of unrighteousness. 6 For if you do what is true, your deeds will prosperously succeed for you, and for all those who do righteousness. 7 Give alms from your possessions. When you give alms, don't let your eye be envious. Don't turn away your face from any poor man, and the face of God won't be turned away from you. 8 As your possessions are, give alms of it according to your abundance. If you have little, don't be afraid to give alms according to that little; 9 for you lay up a good treasure for yourself against the day of necessity; 10 because alms-giving delivers from death, and doesn't allow you to come into darkness. 11 Alms is a good gift in the sight of the Most High for all that give it. 12 Beware, my child, of all fornication, and take first a wife of the seed of your fathers. Don't take a strange wife, who is not of your father's tribe; for we are the descendants of the prophets. Remember, my child, that Noah, Abraham, Isaac, and Jacob, our fathers of old time, all took wives of their kindred, and were blessed in their children, and their seed will inherit the land. 13 And now, my child, love your kindred, and don't scorn your kindred and the sons and the daughters of your people in your heart, to take a wife of them; for in scornfulness is destruction and much trouble, and in idleness is decay and great lack; for idleness is the mother of famine. 14 Don't let the wages of any man who works for you wait with you, but give it to him out of hand. If you serve God, you will be rewarded. Take heed to yourself, my child, in all your works, and be discreet in all your behavior. 15 And what you yourself hate, do to no man. Don't drink wine to drunkenness, and don't let drunkenness go with you on your way. 16 Give of your bread to the hungry, and of your garments to those who are naked. Give alms from all your abundance. Don't let your eye be envious when you give alms. 17 Pour out your bread on the burial of the just, and give nothing

to sinners. 18 Ask counsel of every man who is wise, and don't despise any counsel that is profitable. 19 Bless the Lord your God at all times, and ask of him that your ways may be made straight, and that all your paths and counsels may prosper; for every nation has no counsel; but the Lord himself gives all good things, and he humbles whom he will, as he will. And now, my child, remember my commandments, and let them not be blotted out of your mind. 20 And now I explain to you about the ten talents of silver, which I left in trust with Gabael the son of Gabrias at Rages of Media. 21 And fear not, my child, because we are made poor. You have much wealth, if you fear God,and depart from all sin, and do that which is pleasing in his sight."

5

1 Then Tobias answered and said to him, "Father, I will do all things, whatever you have commanded me. 2 But how could I receive the money, since I don't know him?"3 He gave him the handwriting, and said to him, "Seek a man who will go with you, and I will give him wages, while I still live; and go and receive the money."4 He went to seek a man, and found
Raphael who was an angel; 5 and he didn't know it. He said to him, "Can I go with you to Rages of Media? Do you know those places well?"6 The angel said to him, "I will go with you. I know the way well. I have lodged with our brother Gabael."7 Tobias said to him, "Wait for me, and I will tell my father."8 He said to him, "Go, and don't wait. And he went in and said to his father, "Behold, I have found someone who will go with me."But he said, "Call him to me, that I may know of what tribe he is, and whether he be a trustworthy man to go with you."9 So he called him, and he came in, and they saluted one another.10 And Tobit said to him, "Brother, of what tribe and of what family are you? Tell me."11 He said to him, "Do you seek a tribe and a family, or a hired man which will go with your son?"And Tobit said to him, "I want to know, brother, your kindred and your name."12 And he said, "I am Azarias, the son of Ananias the great, of your kindred."13 And he said to him, "Welcome, brother. Don't be angry with me, because I sought to know your tribe and family. You are my brother, of an honest and good lineage; for I knew Ananias and Jathan, the sons of Shemaiah the great, when we went together to Jerusalem to worship, and offered the firstborn, and the tenths of our increase; and they didn't go astray in the error of our kindred. My brother, you are of a great stock. 14 But tell me, what wages shall I give you? A drachma a day, and those things that be necessary for you, as to my son? 15 And moreover, if you both return safe and sound, I will add something to your wages."16 And so they agreed. And he said to Tobias, "Prepare yourself for the journey. May God prosper you." So his son prepared what was needful for the journey, and his father said

to him, "Go with this man; but God, who dwells in heaven, will prosper your journey. May his angel go with you." Then they both departed, and the young man's dog went with them. 17 But Anna his mother wept, and said to Tobit, "Why have you sent away our child? Isn't he the staff of our hand, in going in and out before us? 18 Don't be greedy to add money to money; but let it be as refuse compared to our child. 19 For what the Lord has given us to live is enough for us."20 Tobit said to her, "Don't worry, my sister. He will return safe and sound, and your eyes will see him. 21 For a good angel will go with him. His journey will be prospered, and he will return safe and sound."22 So she stopped weeping.

6

1 Now as they went on their journey, they came at evening to the river Tigris, and they lodged there. 2 But the young man went down to wash himself, and a fish leaped out of the river, and would have swallowed up the young man. 3 But the angel said to him, "Grab the fish!"So the young man grabbed the fish, and hauled it up onto the land.4 And the angel said to him, "Cut the fish open, and take the heart, the liver, and the bile, and keep them with you." 5 And the young man did as the angel commanded him; but they roasted the fish, and ate it. And they both went on their way, till they drew near to Ecbatana. 6 The young man said to the angel, "Brother Azarias, of what use is the heart, the liver, and the bile of the fish?" 7 He said to him, "About the heart and the liver: If a demon or an evil spirit troubles anyone, we must burn those and make smoke of them before the man or the woman, and the affliction will flee. 8 But as for the bile, it is good to anoint a man that has white films in his eyes, and he will be healed." 9 But when they drew near to Rages, 10 the angel said to the young man, "Brother, today we will lodge with Raguel. He is your kinsman. He has an only daughter named Sarah. I will speak about her, that she should be given to you for a wife. 11 For her inheritance belongs to you, and you only are of her kindred.12 The maid is fair and wise. And now hear me, and I will speak to her father. When we return from Rages we will celebrate the marriage; for I know that Raguel may in no way marry her to another according to the law of Moses, or else he would be liable to death, because it belongs to you to take the inheritance, rather than any other."13 Then the young man said to the angel, "Brother Azarias, I have heard that this maid has been given to seven men, and that they all perished in the bride-chamber.14 Now I am the only son of my father, and I am afraid, lest I go in and die, even as those before me. For a demon loves her, which harms no man, but those which come to her. Now I fear lest I die, and bring my father's and my mother's life to the grave with sorrow because of me. They have no other son to bury them." 15 But the angel said to him, "Don't you

remember the words which your father commanded you, that you should take a wife of your own kindred? Now hear me, brother; for she will be your wife. Don't worry about the demon; for this night she will be given you as wife.16 And when you come into the bride-chamber, you shall take the ashes of incense, and shall lay upon them some of the heart and liver of the fish, and shall make smoke with them.17 The demon will smell it, and flee away, and never come again any more. But when you go near to her, both of you rise up, and cry to God who is merciful. He will save you, and have mercy on you. Don't be afraid, for she was prepared for you from the beginning; and you will save her, and she will go with you. And I suppose that you will have children with her."When Tobias heard these things, he loved her, and his soul was strongly joined to her.

7

1 They came to Ecbatana, and arrived at the house of Raguel. But Sarah met them; and she greeted them, and they her. Then she brought them into the house. 2 Raguel said to Edna his wife, "This young man really resembles Tobit my cousin!" 3 And Raguel asked them, "Where are you two from, kindred?"They said to him, "We are of the sons of Naphtali, who are captives in Nineveh."4 He said to them, "Do you know Tobit our brother? They said, "We know him."Then he said to them, "Is he in good health?"5 They said, "He is both alive, and in good health." Tobias said, "He is my father." 6 And Raguel sprang up, and kissed him, wept, 7 blessed him, and said to him, "You are the son of an honest and good man." When he had heard that Tobit had lost his sight, he was grieved, and wept; 8 and Edna his wife and Sarah his daughter wept. They received them gladly; and they killed a ram of the flock, and served them meat.But Tobias said to Raphael, "Brother Azarias, speak of those things of which you talked about in the way, and let the matter be finished." 9 So he communicated the thing to Raguel. Raguel said to Tobias, "Eat, drink, and make merry: 10 for it belongs to you to take my child. However I will tell you the truth. 11 I have given my child to seven men of our relatives, and whenever they came in to her, they died in the night. But for the present be merry."And Tobias said, "I will taste nothing here, until you all make a covenant and enter into that covenant with me." 12 Raguel said, "Take her to yourself from now on according to custom. You are her relative, and she is yours. The merciful God will give all good success to you." 13 And he called his daughter Sarah, and took her by the hand, and gave her to be wife of Tobias, and said, "Behold, take her to yourself after the law of Moses, and lead her away to your father." And he blessed them. 14 He called Edna his wife, then took a book, wrote a contract, and sealed it. 15 Then they began to eat. 16 And Raguel called his wife Edna, and

said to her, "Sister, prepare the other chamber, and bring her in there." 17 She did as he asked her, and brought her in there. She wept, and she received the tears of her daughter, and said to her,18 "Be comforted, my child. May the Lord of heaven and earth give you favor for this your sorrow. Be comforted, my daughter."

8

1 When they had finished their supper, they brought Tobias in to her. 2 But as he went, he remembered the words of Raphael, and took the ashes of the incense, and put the heart and the liver of the fish on them, and made smoke with them. 3 When the demon smelled that smell, it fled into the uppermost parts of Egypt, and the angel bound him. 4 But after they were both shut in together, Tobias rose up from the bed, and said, "Sister, arise, and let's pray that the Lord may have mercy on us." 5 And Tobias began to say, "Blessed are you, O God of our fathers, and blessed is your holy and glorious name forever. Let the heavens bless you, and all your creatures. 6 You made Adam, and gave him Eve his wife for a helper and support. From them came the seed of men. You said, it is not good that the man should be alone. Let's make him a helper like him.7 And now, O Lord, I take not this my sister for lust, but in truth. Command that I may find mercy and grow old with her."8 She said with him, "Amen." And they both slept that night.9 Raguel arose, and went and dug a grave, 10 saying, "Lest he also should die." 11 And Raguel came into his house, 12 and said to Edna his wife, "Send one of the maidservants, and let them see if he is alive. If not, we will bury him, and no man will know it." 13 So the maidservant opened the door, and went in, and found them both sleeping, 14 and came out, and told them that he was alive. 15 Then Raguel blessed God, saying, "Blessed are you, O God, with all pure and holy blessing! Let your saints bless you, and all your creatures! Let all your angels and your elect bless you forever! 16 Blessed are you, because you have made me glad; and it has not happened to me as I suspected; but you have dealt with us according to your great mercy. 17 Blessed are you, because you have had mercy on two that were the only begotten children of their
parents. Show them mercy, O Lord. Fulfill their life in health with gladness and mercy.18 He commanded his servants to fill the grave. 19 He kept the wedding feast for them fourteen days. 20 Before the days of the wedding feast were finished, Raguel sware to him, that he should not depart till the fourteen days of the wedding feast were fulfilled; 21 and that then he should take half of his goods, and go in safety to his father; and the rest, said he, when my wife and I die.

9

1 And Tobias called Raphael, and said to him, 2 "Brother Azarias, take with you a servant and two camels,

and go to Rages of Media to Gabael, and receive the money for me, and bring him to the wedding feast, 3 because Raguel has sworn that I must not depart. 4 My father counts the days; and if I wait long, he will be very grieved. 5 So Raphael went on his way, and lodged with Gabael, and gave him the handwriting; so he brought forth the bags with their seals, and gave them to him. 6 Then they rose up early in the morning together, and came to the wedding feast. Tobias blessed his wife.

10

1 Tobit his father counted every day. When the days of the journey were expired, and they didn't come, 2 he said, "Is he perchance detained? Or is Gabael perchance dead, and there is no one to give him the money?" 3 He was very grieved. 4 But his wife said to him, "The child has perished, seeing he waits long." She began to bewail him, and said, 5 "I care about nothing, my child, since I have let you go, the light of my eyes." 6 Tobit said to her, "Hold your peace. Don't worry. He is in good health." 7 And she said to him, "Hold your peace. Don't deceive me. My child has perished." And she went out every day into the way by which they went, and ate no bread in the day-time, and didn't stop bewailing her son Tobias for whole nights, until the fourteen days of the wedding feast were expired, which Raguel had sworn that he should spend there. Then Tobias said to Raguel, "Send me away, for my father and my mother look no more to see me." 8 But his father-in-law said to him, "Stay with me, and I will send to your father, and they will declare to him how things go with you." 9 Tobias said, "No. Send me away to my father." 10 Raguel arose, and gave him Sarah his wife, and half his goods, servants and cattle and money; 11 and he blessed them, and sent them away, saying, "The God of heaven will prosper you, my children, before I die." 12 And he said to his daughter, "Honor your father-in-law and your mother-in-law. They are now your parents. Let me hear a good report of you." Then he kissed her. Edna said to Tobias, "May the Lord of heaven restore you, dear brother, and grant to me that I may see your children of my daughter Sarah, that I may rejoice before the Lord. Behold, I commit my daughter to you in special trust. Don't cause her grief.

11

1 After these things Tobias also went his way, blessing God because he had prospered his journey; and he blessed Raguel and Edna his wife. Then he went on his way until they drew near to Nineveh. 2 Raphael said to Tobias, "Don't you know, brother, how you left your father? 3 Let's run forward before your wife, and prepare the house. 4 But take in your hand the bile of the fish." So they went their way, and the dog went after them. 5 Anna sat looking around toward the path for her son. 6 She saw him coming, and said to his father,

"Behold, your son is coming with the man that went with him!"
7 Raphael said, "I know, Tobias, that your father will open his eyes. 8 Therefore anoint his eyes with the bile, and being pricked with it, he will rub, and will make the white films fall away. Then he will see you."9 Anna ran to him, and fell upon the neck of her son, and said to him, "I have seen you, my child! I am ready to die." They both wept.
10 Tobit went
toward the door and stumbled; but his son ran to him, 11 and took hold of his
father. He rubbed the bile on his father's eyes, saying, "Cheer up, my father." 12 When his eyes began to hurt, he rubbed them. 13 Then the white films peeled away from the corners of his eyes; and he saw his son, and fell upon his neck. 14 He wept, and said, "Blessed are you, O God, and blessed is your name forever! Blessed are all your holy angels! 15 For you scourged, and had mercy on me. Behold, I see my son Tobias." And his son went in rejoicing, and told his father the great things that had happened to him in Media. 16 Tobit went out to meet his daughter-in-law at the gate of Nineveh, rejoicing and blessing God. Those who saw him go marveled, because he had received his sight. 17 Tobit gave thanks before them, because God had shown mercy on him. When Tobit came near to Sarah his daughter-in-law, he blessed her, saying, "Welcome, daughter! Blessed is God who has brought you to us, and blessed are your father and your mother." And there was joy among all his kindred who were at Nineveh. 18 Achiacharus and Nasbas his brother's son came. 19 Tobias' wedding feast was kept seven days with great gladness.

12

1 And Tobit called his son Tobias, and said to him, "See, my child, that the man which went with you have his wages, and you must give him more." 2 And he said to him, "Father, it is no harm to me to give him the half of those things which I have brought; 3 for he has led me for you in safety, and he cured my wife, and brought my money, and likewise cured you." 4 The old man said, "It is due to him."5 And he called the angel, and said to him, "Take half of all that you have brought."6 Then he called them both privately, and said to them, "Bless God, and give him thanks, and magnify him, and give him thanks in the sight of all that live, for the things which he has done with you. It is good to bless God and exalt his name, showing forth with honor the works of God. Don't be slack to give him thanks. 7 It is good to conceal the secret of a king, but to reveal gloriously the works of God. Do good, and evil won't find you. 8 Good is prayer with fasting, alms, and righteousness. A little with righteousness is better than much with unrighteousness. It is better to give alms than to lay up gold. 9 Alms delivers from death, and it purges away all sin. Those who give alms and do

righteousness will be filled with life; 10 but those who sin are enemies to their own life. 11 Surely I will conceal nothing from you. I have said, 'It is good to conceal the secret of a king, but to reveal gloriously the works of God.' 12 And now, when you prayed, and Sarah your daughter-in-law, I brought the memorial of your prayer before the Holy One. When you buried the dead, I was with you likewise. 13 And when you didn't delay to rise up, and leave your dinner, that you might go and cover the dead, your good deed was not hidden from me. I was with you. 14 And now God sent me to heal you and Sarah your daughter-in-law. 15 I am Raphael, one of the seven holy angels which present the prayers of the saints and go in before the glory of the Holy One." 16 And they were both troubled, and fell upon their faces; for they were afraid. 17 And he said to them, "Don't be afraid. You will all have peace; but bless God forever. 18 For I came not of any favor of my own, but by the will of your God. Therefore bless him forever. 19 All these days I appeared to you. I didn't eat or drink, but you all saw a vision. 20 Now give God thanks, because I ascend to him who sent me. Write in a book all the things which have been done." 21 Then they rose up, and saw him no more. 22 They confessed the great and wonderful works of God, and how the angel of the Lord had appeared to them.

13

1 And Tobit wrote a prayer for rejoicing, and said,"Blessed is God who lives forever! Blessed is his kingdom!2 For he scourges, and shows mercy. He leads down to the grave, and brings up again. There is no one who will escape his hand. 3 Give thanks to him before the Gentiles, all you children of Israel!For he has scattered us among them. 4 Declare his greatness, there. Extol him before all the living,because he is our Lord,and God is our Father forever. 5 He will scourge us for our iniquities, and will again show mercy, and will gather us out of all the nations among whom you are all scattered. 6 If you turn to him with your whole heart and with your whole soul,to do truth before him, then he will turn to you,and won't hide his face from you. See what he will do with you.Give him thanks with your whole mouth. Bless the Lord of righteousness. Exalt the everlasting King. I give him thanks in the land of my captivity, and show his strength and majesty to a nation of sinners. Turn, you sinners, and do righteousness before him. Who can tell if he will accept you and have mercy on you? 7 I exalt my God. My soul exalts the King of heaven,and rejoices in his greatness. 8 Let all men speak, and let them give him thanks in Jerusalem. 9 O Jerusalem, the holy city, he will scourge you for the works of your sons, and will again have mercy on the sons of the righteous. 10 Give thanks to the Lord with goodness, and bless the everlasting King,that his tabernacle

may be built in you again with joy, and that he may make glad in you those who are captives,and love in you forever those who are miserable. 11 Many nations will come from afar to the name of the Lord Godwith gifts in their hands, even gifts to the King of heaven. Generations of generations will praise you, and sing songs of rejoicing. 12 All those who hate you are cursed. All those who love you forever will be blessed. 13 Rejoice and be exceedingly glad for the sons of the righteous; for they will be gathered together and will bless the Lord of the righteous. 14 Oh blessed are those who love you. They will rejoice for your peace.Blessed are all those who mourned for all your scourges; because they will rejoice for you when they have seen all your glory. They will be made glad forever. 15 Let my soul bless God the great King. 16 For Jerusalem will be built with sapphires, emeralds, and precious stones;your walls and towers and battlements with pure gold. 17 The streets of Jerusalem will be paved with beryl, carbuncle, and stones of Ophir. 18 All her streets will say, "Hallelujah!"and give praise, saying, "Blessed be God, who has exalted you forever!"

14

1 Then Tobit finished giving thanks.2 He was fifty-eight years old when he lost his sight. After eight years, he received it again. He gave alms and he feared the Lord God more and more, and gave thanks to him. 3 Now he grew very old; and he called his son with the six sons of his son, and said to him, "My child, take your sons. Behold, I have grown old, and am ready to depart out of this life.4 Go into Media, my child, for I surely believe all the things which Jonah the prophet spoke of Nineveh, that it will be overthrown, but in Media there will rather be peace for a season. Our kindred will be scattered in the earth from the good land. Jerusalem will be desolate, and the house of God in it will be burned up, and will be desolate for a time.5 God will again have mercy on them, and bring them back into the land, and they will build
the house, but not like to the former house, until the times of that age are fulfilled. Afterward they will return from the places of their captivity, and build up Jerusalem with honor. The house of God will be built in it forever with a glorious building, even as the prophets spoke concerning it.6 And all the nations will turn to fear the Lord God truly, and will bury their idols.7 All the nations will bless the Lord, and his people will give thanks to God, and the Lord will exalt his people; and all those who love the Lord God in truth and righteousness will rejoice, showing mercy to our kindred. 8 And now, my child, depart from Nineveh, because those things which the prophet Jonah spoke will surely come to pass. 9 But you must keep the law and the ordinances, and show yourself merciful and righteous, that it may be well with you.10 Bury me decently, and your

mother with me. Don't stay at Nineveh. See, my child, what Aman did to Achiacharus who nourished him, how out of light he brought him into darkness, and all the recompense that he made him. Achiacharus was saved, but the other had his recompense, and he went down into darkness. Manasses gave alms, and escaped the snare of death which he set for him; but Aman fell into the snare, and perished. 11 And now, my children, consider what alms does, and how righteousness delivers."While he was saying these things, he gave up the ghost in the bed; but he was one hundred fifty eight years old. Tobias buried him magnificently.12 When Anna died, he buried her with his father. But Tobias departed with his wife and his sons to Ecbatana to Raguel his father-in- law,13 and he grew old in honor, and he buried his father-in-law and mother- in-law magnificently, and he inherited their possessions, and his father Tobit's.14 He died at Ecbatana of Media, being one hundred twenty seven years old. 15 Before he died, he heard of the destruction of Nineveh, which Nebuchadnezzar and Ahasuerus took captive. Before his death, he rejoiced over Nineveh.

THE BOOK OF JUDITH

1

1 In the twelfth year of the reign of Nebuchadnezzar, who reigned over the Assyrians in Nineveh, the great city, in the days of Arphaxad, who reigned over the Medes in Ecbatana,2 and built around Ecbatana walls of hewn stones three cubits broad and six cubits long, and made the height of the

wall seventy cubits, and its breadth fifty cubits, 3 and set its towers at its gates one hundred cubits high, and its breadth in the foundation was sixty cubits,4 and made its gates, even gates that were raised to the height of seventy cubits, and their breadth forty cubits, for his mighty army to go out of, and the setting in array of his footmen— 5 in those days King Nebuchadnezzar made war with King Arphaxad in the great plain. This plain is on the borders of Ragau.6 There came to meet him all that lived in the hill country, and all that lived by Euphrates, Tigris, and Hydaspes, and in the plain of Arioch the king of the Elymaeans. Many nations of the sons of Chelod assembled themselves to the battle. 7 And Nebuchadnezzar king of the Assyrians sent to all who lived in Persia, and to all who lived westward, to those who lived in Cilicia, Damascus, Libanus, Antilibanus, and to all who lived along the sea coast, 8 and to those among the nations that were of Carmel and Gilead, and to the higher Galilee and the great plain of Esdraelon, 9 and to all who were in Samaria and its cities,

and beyond Jordan to Jerusalem, Betane, Chellus, Kadesh, the river of Egypt, Tahpanhes, Rameses, and all the land of Goshen, 10 until you come above Tanis and Memphis, and to all that lived in Egypt, until you come to the borders of Ethiopia.11 All those who lived in all the land made light of the commandment of Nebuchadnezzar king of the Assyrians, and didn't go with him to the war; for they were not afraid of him, but he was before them as one man. They turned away his messengers from their presence without effect, and with disgrace. 12 And Nebuchadnezzar was exceedingly angry with all this land, and he swore by his throne and kingdom that he would surely be avenged upon all the coasts of Cilicia, Damascus, and Syria, that he would kill with his sword all the inhabitants of the land of Moab, the children of Ammon, all Judea, and all who were in Egypt, until you come to the borders of the two seas.13 And he set the battle in array with his army against King Arphaxad in the seventeenth year; and he prevailed in his battle, and turned to flight all the army of Arphaxad, with all his horses and all his chariots.14 He took possession of his cities. He came to Ecbatana and took the towers, plundered its streets, and turned its beauty into shame. 15 He took Arphaxad in the mountains of Ragau, struck him through with his darts, and utterly destroyed him to this day. 16 He returned with them to Nineveh, he and all his company of sundry nations an exceedingly great multitude of men of war. There he took his ease and banqueted, he and his army, for one hundred twenty days.

2

1 In the eighteenth year, the twenty-second day of the first month, there was talk in the house of Nebuchadnezzar king of the

Assyrians that he should be avenged on all the land, even as he spoke. 2 He called together all his servants and all his great men, and communicated with them his secret counsel, and with his own mouth, recounted the wickedness of all the land. 3 They decreed to destroy all flesh which didn't follow the word of his mouth. 4 It came to pass, when he had ended his counsel, Nebuchadnezzar king of the Assyrians called Holofernes the chief captain of his army, who was second to himself, and said to him, 5 "The great king, the lord of all the earth, says: 'Behold, you shall go out from my presence, and take with you men who trust in their strength, to one hundred twenty thousand footmen and twelve thousand horses with their riders. 6 And you shall go out against all the west country, because they disobeyed the commandment of my mouth. 7 You shall declare to them that they should prepare earth and water, because I will go out in my wrath against them, and will cover the whole face of the earth with the feet of my army, who will plunder them. 8 Their slain will fill their valleys and brooks, and the river will be filled with their dead until it overflows. 9 I will lead them as captives to the utmost parts of all the earth. 10 But you shall go forth, and take all their coasts for me first. If they will yield themselves to you, then you must reserve them for me until the day of their reproof. 11 As for those who resist, your eye shall not spare; but you shall give them up to be slain and to be plundered in all your land. 12 For as I live, and by the power of my kingdom, I have spoken, and I will do this with my hand. 13 Moreover, you shall not transgress anything of the commandments of your lord, but you shall surely accomplish them, as I have commanded you. You shall not defer to do them.'14 So Holofernes went out from the presence of his lord, and called all the governors, the captains, and officers of the army of Asshur. 15 He counted chosen men for the battle, as his lord had commanded him, to one hundred twenty thousand, with twelve thousand archers on horseback. 16 He arranged them as a great multitude is ordered for the war. 17 He took camels, donkeys, and mules for their baggage, an exceedingly great multitude, and sheep, oxen, and goats without number for their provision, 18 and a large supply of rations for every man, and a huge amount of gold and silver out of the king's house. 19 He went out, he and all his army, on their journey, to go before King Nebuchadnezzar, and to cover all the face of the earth westward with their chariots, horsemen, and chosen footmen. 20 A great company of various nations went out with them like locusts and like the sand of the earth. For they could not be counted by reason of their multitude. 21 And they departed out of Nineveh three days' journey toward the plain of Bectileth, and encamped from Bectileth near the mountain which is at the left hand of the Upper Cilicia. 22 And he took all his army, his footmen, horsemen, and chariots, and went away from there into the hill country, 23 and destroyed Put and Lud, and plundered all the children of Rasses and the children of Ishmael, which were along the wilderness to the south of the land of the Chellians. 24 And he went over Euphrates, and went through Mesopotamia, and broke down all the high cities that were upon the river Arbonai, until you come to the sea. 25 And he took possession of the borders of Cilicia, and killed all who resisted him, and came to the borders of Japheth, which were toward the south, opposite Arabia.26 He surrounded all the children of Midian, and set their tents on fire, and plundered their sheepfolds.27 He went down into the plain of Damascus in the days of wheat harvest, and set all their fields on fire, and utterly destroyed their flocks and herds, plundered their cities, laid their plains waste, and struck all their young men with the edge of the sword. 28 And the fear and the dread of him fell upon those who lived on the sea coast, upon those who were in Sidon and Tyre, those who lived in Sur and Ocina, and all who lived in Jemnaan. Those who lived in Azotus and Ascalon feared him exceedingly.

3

1 And they sent to him messengers with words of peace, saying, 2 "Behold, we the servants of Nebuchadnezzar the great king lie before you. Use us as it is pleasing in your sight. 3 Behold, our dwellings, and all our country, and all our fields of wheat, and our flocks and herds, and all the sheepfolds of our tents, lie before your face. Use them as it may please you. 4 Behold, even our cities and those who dwell in them are your servants. Come and deal with them as it is good in your eyes." 5 So the men came to Holofernes, and declared to him according to these words. 6 He came down toward the sea coast, he and his army, and set garrisons in the high cities, and took out of them chosen men for allies.7 They received him, they and all the country round about them, with garlands and dances and timbrels. 8 He cast down all their borders, and cut down their sacred groves. It had been given to him to destroy all the gods of the land, that all the nations would worship Nebuchadnezzar only, and that all their tongues and their tribes would call upon him as a god. 9 Then he came toward Esdraelon near to Dotaea, which is opposite the great ridge of Judea. 10 He encamped between Geba and Scythopolis. He was there a whole month, that he might gather together all the baggage of his army.

4

1 The children of Israel who lived in Judea heard all that Holofernes the chief captain of Nebuchadnezzar king of the Assyrians had done to the nations, and how he had plundered all their temples and destroyed them utterly. 2 They were exceedingly afraid at his approach,

and were troubled for Jerusalem and for the temple of the Lord their God;3 because they had newly come up from the captivity, and all the people of Judea were recently gathered together; and the vessels, the altar, and the house were sanctified after being profaned. 4 And they sent into every coast of Samaria, to Konae, to Beth-horon, Belmaim, Jericho, to Choba, Aesora, and to the valley of Salem;5 and they occupied beforehand all the tops of the high mountains, fortified the villages that were in them, and stored supplies for the provision of war, for their fields were newly reaped. 6 Joakim the high priest, who was in those days at Jerusalem, wrote to those who lived in Bethulia and Betomesthaim, which is opposite Esdraelon toward the plain that is near to Dothaim, 7 charging them to seize upon the ascents of the hill country; because by them was the entrance into Judea, and it was easy to stop them from approaching, inasmuch as the approach was narrow, with space for two men at the most. 8 And the children of Israel did as Joakim the high priest had commanded them, as did the senate of all the people of Israel, which was in session at Jerusalem. 9 And every man of Israel cried to God with great earnestness, and with great earnestness they humbled their souls.10 They, their wives, their children, their cattle, and every sojourner, hireling, and servant bought with their money put sackcloth on their loins.11 Every man and woman of Israel, including the little children and the inhabitants of Jerusalem, fellprostrate before the temple, cast ashes upon their heads, and spread out their sackcloth before the Lord. They put sackcloth around the altar. 12 They cried to the God of Israel earnestly with one consent, that he would not give their children as prey, their wives as plunder, the cities of their inheritance to destruction, and the sanctuary to being profaned and being made a reproach, for the nations to rejoice at. 13 The Lord heard their voice, and looked at their affliction. The people continued fasting many days in all Judea and Jerusalem before the sanctuary of the Lord Almighty. 14 And Joakim the high priest, and all the priests who stood before the Lord, and those who ministered to the Lord, had their loins dressed in sackcloth and offered the continual burnt offering, the vows, and the free gifts of the people. 15 They had ashes on their turbans. They cried to the Lord with all their power, that he would look upon all the house of Israel for good.

5

1 Holofernes, the chief captain of the army of Asshur, was told that the children of Israel had prepared for war, had shut up the passages of the hill country, had fortified all the tops of the high hills, and had set up barricades in the plains.2 Then he was exceedingly angry, and he called all the princes of Moab, the captains of Ammon, and

all the governors of the sea coast, 3 and he said to them, "Tell me now, you sons of Canaan, who are these people who dwell in the hill country? What are the cities that they inhabit? How large is their army? Where is their power and their strength? What king is set over them, to be the leader of their army? 4 Why have they turned their backs, that they should not come and meet me, more than all who dwell in the west?" 5 Then Achior, the leader of all the children of Ammon, said to him, "Let my lord now hear a word from the mouth of your servant, and I will tell you the truth concerning these people who dwell in this hill country, near to the place where you dwell. No lie will come out of the mouth of your servant.6 These people are descended from the Chaldeans. 7 They sojourned before this in Mesopotamia, because they didn't want to follow the gods of their fathers,which were in the land of the Chaldeans. 8 They departed from the way of their parents, and worshiped the God of heaven, the God whom they knew. Their parents cast them out from the face of their gods, and they fled into Mesopotamia and sojourned there many days. 9 Then their God commandedthem to depart from the place where they sojourned, and to go into the land of Canaan. They lived there, and prospered with gold and silver, and with exceedingly much cattle. 10 Then they went down into Egypt, for a famine covered all the land of Canaan. They sojourned there until they had grown up. They became a great multitude there, so that one could not count the population of their nation. 11 Then the king of Egypt rose up against them, and dealt subtly with them, and brought them low, making them labor in brick, and made them slaves. 12 They cried to their God, and he struck all the land of Egypt with incurable plagues; so the Egyptians cast them out of their sight.13 God dried up the Red sea before them, 14 and brought them into the way of Sinai Kadesh-Barnea and they cast out all that lived in the wilderness. 15 They lived in the land of the Amorites, and they destroyed by their strength everyone in Heshbon. Passing over Jordan, they possessed all the hill country. 16 They cast out before them the Canaanite, the Perizzite, the Jebusite, the Shechemite, and all the Girgashites, and they lived in that country many days. 17 And while they didn't sin before their God, they prospered, because God who hates iniquity was with them.18 But when they departed from the way which he appointed them, they were destroyed in many severe battles, and were led captives into a land that was not theirs. The temple of their God was razed to the ground, and their cities were taken by their adversaries. 19 And now they have returned to their God, and have come up from the dispersion where they were dispersed, and have possessed Jerusalem, where their sanctuary is, and are settled in the hill country; for it was desolate. 20 And now, my lord and master, if there is any error in this people, and they sin against their God, we will find out what this thing is in which they stumble, and we will go up and overcome them. 21 But if there is no lawlessness in their nation, let my lord now pass by, lest their Lord defend them, and their God be for them, and we will be a reproach before all the earth." 22 It came to pass, when Achior had finished speaking these words, all the people standing around the tent complained. The great men of Holofernes, and all who lived by the sea side and in Moab, said that he should be cut to pieces.23 For, they said, "We will not be afraid of the children of Israel, because, behold, they are a people that has no power nor might to make the battle strong. 24 Therefore now we will go up, and they will be a prey to be devoured by all your army, Lord Holofernes."

6

1 And when the disturbance of the men that were around the council had ceased, Holofernes the chief captain of the army of Asshur said to Achior and to all the children of Moab before all the people of the foreigners: 2 "And who are you, Achior, and the mercenaries of Ephraim, that you have prophesied among us as today, and have said that we should not make war with the race of Israel, because their God will defend them? And who is God but Nebuchadnezzar?3 He will send forth his might, and will destroy them from the face of the earth, and their God will not deliver them; but we his servants will strike them as one man. They will not sustain the might of our cavalry. 4 For with them we will burn them up. Their mountains will be drunken with their blood. Their plains will be filled with their dead bodies. Their footsteps will not stand before us, but they will surely perish, says King Nebuchadnezzar, lord of all the earth; for he said, 'The words that I have spoken will not be in vain.' 5 But you, Achior, hireling of Ammon, who have spoken these words in the day of your iniquity, will see my face no more from this day, until I am avenged of the race of those that came out of Egypt.6 And then the sword of my army, and the multitude of those who serve me, will pass through your sides, and you will fall among their slain when I return.7 Then my servants will bring you back into the hill country, and will set you in one of the cities by the passes. 8 You will not perish until you are destroyed with them. 9 And if you hope in your heart that they will not be taken, don't let your countenance fall. I have spoken it, and none of my words will fall to the ground." 10 Then Holofernes commanded his servants who waited in his tent to take Achior, and bring him back to Bethulia, and deliver him into the hands of the children of Israel.11 So his servants took him, and brought him out of the camp into the plain, and they moved from the midst of the plains into the hill country, and came to the springs that were under Bethulia. 12 When the men of the city saw them on the top of the hill, they took up their weapons, and went out of

the city against them to the top of the hill. Every man that used a sling kept them from coming up, and threw stones at them. 13 They took cover under the hill, bound Achior, cast him down, left him at the foot of the hill, and went away to their lord. 14 But the children of Israel descended from their city, and came to him, untied him, led him away into Bethulia, and presented him to the rulers of their city, 15 which were in those days Ozias the son of Micah, of the tribe of Simeon, and Chabris the son of Gothoniel, and Charmis the son of Melchiel. 16 Then they called together all the elders of the city; and all their young men ran together, with their women, to the assembly. They set Achior in the midst of all their people. Then Ozias asked him what had happened.17 He answered and declared to them the words of the council of Holofernes, and all the words that he had spoken in the midst of the princes of the children of Asshur, and all the great words that Holofernes had spoken against the house of Israel.18 Then the people fell down and worshiped God, and cried, saying,19 "O Lord God of heaven, behold their arrogance, and pity the low estate of our race. Look upon the face of those who are sanctified to you this day." 20 They comforted Achior, and praised him exceedingly. 21 Then Ozias took him out of the assembly into his house, and made a feast for the elders. They called on the God of Israel for help all that night.

7

1 The next day Holofernes commanded all his army and all the people who had come to be his allies, that they should move their camp toward Bethulia, seize the passes of the hill country, and make war against the children of Israel.2 Every mighty man of them moved that day. The army of their men of war was one hundred seventy thousand footmen, plus twelve thousand horsemen, besides the baggage and the men who were on foot among them— an exceedingly great multitude. 3 They encamped in the valley near Bethulia, by the fountain. They spread themselves in breadth over Dothaim even to Belmaim, and in length from Bethulia to Cyamon, which is near Esdraelon. 4 But the children of Israel, when they saw the multitude of them, were terrified, and everyone said to his neighbor, "Now these men will lick up the face of all the earth. Neither the high mountains, nor the valleys, nor the hills will be able to bear their weight. 5 Every man took up his weapons of war,and when they had kindled fires upon their towers, they remained and watched all that night. 6 But on the second day Holofernes led out all his cavalry in the sight of the children of Israel which were in Bethulia, 7 viewed the ascents to their city, and searched out the springs of the waters, seized upon them, and set garrisons of men of war over them. Then he departed back to his people. 8 All the rulers of the

children of Esau, all the leaders of the people of Moab, and the captains of the sea coast came to him and said,9 "Let our lord now hear a word, that there not be losses in your army. 10 For this people of the children of Israel do not trust in their spears, but in the height of the mountains wherein they dwell, for it is not easy to come up to the tops of their mountains.11 And now, my lord, don't fight against them as men fight who join battle, and there will not so much as one man of your people perish.12 Remain in your camp, and keep every man of your army safe. Let your servants get possession of the water spring, which flows from the foot of the mountain, 13 because all the inhabitants of Bethulia get their water from there. Then thirst will kill them, and they will give up their city. Then we and our people will go up to the tops of the mountains that are near, and will camp upon them, to watch that not one man gets out of the city. 14 They will be consumed with famine—they, their wives, and their children. Before the sword comes against them they will be laid low in the streets where they dwell. 15 And you will pay them back with evil, because they rebelled, and didn't meet your face in peace." 16 Their words were pleasing in the sight of Holofernes and in the sight of all his servants; and he ordered them to do as they had spoken. 17 And the army of the children of Ammon moved, and with them five thousand of the children of Asshur, and they encamped in the valley. They seized the waters and the springs of the waters of the children of Israel. 18 The children of Esau went up with the children of Ammon, and encamped in the hill country near Dothaim. They sent some of them toward the south, and toward the east, near Ekrebel, which is near Chusi, that is upon the brook Mochmur. The rest of the army of the Assyrians encamped in the plain, and covered all the face of the land. Their tents and baggage were pitched upon it in a great crowd. They were an exceedingly great multitude. 19 The children of Israel cried to the Lord their God, for their spirit fainted; for all their enemies had surrounded them. There was no way to escape out from among them. 20 All the army of Asshur remained around them, their footmen and their chariots and their horsemen, for thirty-four days. All their vessels of water ran dry for all the inhabitants of Bethulia. 21 The cisterns were emptied, and they had no water to drink their fill for one day; for they rationed drink by measure. 22 Their young children were discouraged. The women and the young men fainted for thirst. They fell down in the streets of the city, and in the passages of the gates. There was no longer any strength in them. 23 All the people, including the young men, the women, and the children, were gathered together against Ozias, and against the rulers of the city. They cried with a loud voice, and said before all the elders, 24 "God be judge between all of you and us, because you have done us great wrong, in that you have not spoken words of peace with the children of Asshur. 25 Now we have no helper; but God has sold us into their hands, that we should be laid low before them with thirst and great destruction. 26 And now summon them, and deliver up the whole city as prey to the people of Holofernes, and to all his army. 27 For it is better for us to be captured by them. For we will be servants, and our souls will live, and we will not see the death of our babies before our eyes, and our wives and our children fainting in death. 28 We take to witness against you the heaven and the earth, and our God and the Lord of our fathers, who punishes us according to our sins and the sins of our fathers. Do what we have said today!"

29 And there was great weeping of all with one consent in the midst of the assembly; and they cried to the Lord God with a loud voice. 30 And Ozias said to them, "Brethren, be of good courage! Let us endure five more days, during which the Lord our God will turn his mercy toward us; for he will not forsake us utterly. 31 But if these days pass, and no help comes to us, I will do what you say." 32 Then he dispersed the people, every man to his own camp; and they went away to the walls and towers of their city. He sent the women and children into their houses. They were brought very low in the city.

8

1 In those days Judith heard about this. She was the daughter of Merari, the son of Ox, the son of Joseph, the son of Oziel, the son of Elkiah, the son of Ananias, the son of Gideon, the son of Raphaim, the son of Ahitub, the son of Elihu, the son of Eliab, the son of Nathanael, the son of Salamiel, the son of Salasadai, the son of Israel.2 Her husband was Manasses, of her tribe and of her family. He died in the days of barley harvest. 3 For he stood over those who bound sheaves in the field, and was overcome by the burning heat, and he fell on his bed, and died in his city Bethulia. So they buried him with his fathers in the field which is between Dothaim and Balamon. 4 Judith was a widow in her house three years and four months.5 She made herself a tent upon the roof of her house, and put on sackcloth upon her loins. The garments of her widowhood were upon her. 6 And she fasted all the days of her widowhood, except the eves of the Sabbaths, the Sabbaths, the eves of the new moons, the new moons, and the feasts and joyful days of the house of Israel. 7 She was beautiful in appearance, and lovely to behold. Her husband Manasses had left her gold, silver, menservants, maidservants, cattle, and lands. She remained on those lands. 8 No one said anything evil about her, for she feared God exceedingly. 9 She heard the evil words of the people against the governor, because they fainted for lack of water; and Judith heard all the words that Ozias spoke to them, how he swore to them that he would deliver the city to the Assyrians

after five days. 10 So she sent her maid, who was over all things that she had, to summon Ozias, Chabris, and Charmis, the elders of her city. 11 They came to her, and she said to them, “Hear me now, O you rulers of the inhabitants of Bethulia! For your word that you have spoken before the people this day is not right. You have set the oath which you have pronounced between God and you, and have promised to deliver the city to our enemies, unless within these days the Lord turns to help you. 12 Now who are you that you have tested God this day, and stand in the place of God among the children of men? 13 Now try the Lord Almighty, and you will never know anything. 14 For you will not find the depth of the heart of man, and you will not perceive the things that he thinks. How will you search out God, who has made all these things, and know his mind, and comprehend his purpose? No, my kindred, don’t provoke the Lord our God to anger!15 For if he has not decided to help us within these five days, he has power to defend us in such time as he will, or to destroy us before the face of our enemies.16 But don’t you pledge the counsels of the Lord our God! For God is not like a human being, that he should be threatened, neither is he like a son of man, that he should be won over by pleading. 17 Therefore let’s wait for the salvation that comes from him, and call upon him to help us. He will hear our voice, if it pleases him.18 For there arose none in our age, neither is there any of us today, tribe, or kindred, or family, or city, which worship gods made with hands, as it was in the former days;19 for which cause our fathers were given to the sword, and for plunder, and fell with a great destruction before our enemies. 20 But we know no other god beside him. Therefore we hope that he will not despise us, nor any of our race.21 For if we are captured, all Judea will be captured and our sanctuary will be plundered; and he will require our blood for profaning it. 22 The slaughter of our kindred, the captivity of the land, and the desolation of our inheritance, he will bring on our heads among the Gentiles, wherever we will be in bondage. We will be an offense and a reproach to those who take us for a possession. 23 For our bondage will not be ordered to favor; but the Lord our God will turn it to dishonor. 24 And now, kindred, let’s show an example to our kindred, because their soul depends on us, and the sanctuary, the house, and the altar depend on us. 25 Besides all this let’s give thanks to the Lord our God, who tries us, even as he did our fathers also. 26 Remember all the things which he did to Abraham, and all the things in which he tried Isaac, and all the things which happened to Jacob in Mesopotamia of Syria, when he kept the sheep of Laban his mother’s brother. 27 For he has not tried us in the fire, as he did them, to search out their hearts, neither has he taken vengeance on us; but the Lord scourges those who come near to him, to admonish them.” 28 And Ozias said to her, “All that you have spoken, you have spoken with a good heart. There is no one who will deny your words. 29 For this is not the first day wherein your wisdom is manifested; but from the beginning of your days all the people have known your understanding, because the disposition of your heart is good. 30 But the people were exceedingly thirsty, and compelled us to do as we spoke to them, and to bring an oath upon ourselves, which we will not break. 31 And now pray for us, because you are a godly woman, and the Lord will send us rain to fill our cisterns, and we will faint no more." 32 Then Judith said to them, "Hear me, and I will do a thing, which will go down to all generations among the children of our race.33 You shall all stand at the gate tonight. I will go out with my maid. Within the days after which you said that you would deliver the city to our enemies, the Lord will deliver Israel by my hand.34 But you shall not inquire of my act; for I will not tell you until the things are finished that I will do."35 Then Ozias and the rulers said to her, "Go in peace. May the Lord God be before you, to take vengeance on our enemies." 36 So they returned from the tent, and went to their stations.

9

1 But Judith fell upon her face, and put ashes upon her head, and uncovered the sackcloth with which she was clothed. The incense of that evening was now being offered at Jerusalem in the house of God, and Judith cried to the Lord with a loud voice, and said, 2 "O Lord God of my father Simeon, into whose hand you gave a sword to take vengeance on the strangers who loosened the belt of a virgin to defile her, uncovered her thigh to her shame, and profaned her womb to her reproach; for you said, 'It shall not be so;' and they did so.3 Therefore you gave their rulers to be slain, and their bed, which was ashamed for her who was deceived, to be dyed in blood, and struck the servants with their masters, and the masters upon their thrones; 4 and gave their wives for a prey, and their daughters to be captives, and all their spoils to be divided among your dear children; which were moved with zeal for you, and abhorred the pollution of their blood, and called upon you for aid. O God, O my God, hear me also who am a widow. 5 For you did the things that were before those things, and those things, and such as come after; and you planned the things which are now, and the things which are to come. The things which you planned came to pass. 6 Yes, the things which you determined stood before you, and said, 'Behold, we are here; for all your ways are prepared, and your judgment is with foreknowledge.'7 For, behold, the Assyrians are multiplied in their power. They are exalted with horse and rider. They were proud of the strength of their footmen. They have trusted in shield, spear, bow, and sling. They don't know that you are the Lord

who breaks the battles. 'The Lord' is your name.8 Break their strength in your power, and bring down their force in your wrath; for they intend to profane your sanctuary, and to defile the tabernacle where your glorious name rests, and to destroy the horn of your altar with the sword. 9 Look at their pride, and send your wrath upon their heads. Give into my hand, which am a widow, the might that I have conceived. 10 Strike by the deceit of my lips the servant with the prince, and the prince with his servant. Break down their arrogance by the hand of a woman. 11 For your power stands not in numbers, nor your might in strong men, but you are a God of the afflicted. You are a helper of the oppressed, a helper of the weak, a protector of the forsaken, a savior of those who are without hope. 12 Please, please, God of my father, and God of the inheritance of Israel, Lord of the heavens and of the earth, Creator of the waters, King of all your creation, hear my prayer.13 Make my speech and deceit to be their wound and bruise, who intend hard things against your covenant, your holy house, the top of Zion, and the house of the possession of your children. 14 Make every nation and tribe of yours to know that you are God, the God of all power and might, and that there is no other who protects the race of Israel but you."

10

1 It came to pass, when she had ceased to cry to the God of Israel, and had finished saying all these words, 2 that she rose up where she had fallen down, called her maid, and went down into the house that she lived on the Sabbath days and on her feast days. 3 She pulled off the sackcloth which she had put on, took off the garments of her widowhood, washed her body all over with water, anointed herself with rich ointment, braided the hair of her head, and put a tiara upon it. She put on her garments of gladness, which she used to wear in the days of the life of Manasses her husband. 4 She took sandals for her feet, and put on her anklet, bracelets, rings, earrings, and all her jewelry. She made herself very beautiful to deceive the eyes of all men who would see her. 5 She gave her maid a leather container of wine and a flask of oil, and filled a bag with roasted grain, lumps of figs, and fine bread. She packed all her vessels together, and laid them upon her. 6 They went out to the gate of the city of Bethulia, and found Ozias and the elders of the city, Chabris and Charmis standing by it. 7 But when they saw her, that her countenance was altered and her apparel was changed, they were greatly astonished by her beauty and said to her,8 "May the God of our fathers give you favor, and accomplish your purposes to the glory of the children of Israel, and to the exaltation of Jerusalem." Then she worshiped God,9 and said to them, "Command that they open the gate of the city for me, and I will go out to accomplish the things you spoke with me about." And they

commanded the young men to open to her, as she had spoken;10 and they did so. Then Judith went out, she, and her handmaid with her. The men of the city watched her until she had gone down the mountain, until she had passed the valley, and they could see her no more.11 They went straight onward in the valley. The watch of the Assyrians met her;12 and they took her, and asked her, "Of what people are you? Where are you coming from? Where are you going?" She said, "I am a daughter of the Hebrews. I am fleeing away from their presence, because they are about to be given you to be consumed. 13 I am coming into the presence of Holofernes the chief captain of your army, to declare words of truth. I will show him a way that he can go and win all the hill country, and there will not be lacking of his men one person, nor one life." 14 Now when the men heard her words, and considered her countenance, the beauty thereof was exceedingly marvelous in their eyes. They said to her, 15 "You have saved your life, in that you have hurried to come down to the presence of our master. Now come to his tent. Some of us will guide you until they deliver you into his hands.16 But when you stand before him, don't be afraid in your heart, but declare to him what you just said, and he will treat you well."17 They chose out of them a hundred men, and appointed them to accompany her and her maid; and they brought them to the tent of Holofernes. 18 And there was great excitement throughout all the camp, for her coming was reported among the tents. They came and surrounded her as she stood outside Holofernes' tent, until they told him about her.19 They marveled at her beauty, and marveled at the children of Israel because of her. Each one said to his neighbor, "Who would despise these people, who have among them such women? For it is not good that one man of them be left, seeing that, if they are let go, they will be able to deceive the whole earth. 20 Then the guards of Holofernes and all his servants came out and brought her into the tent. 21 And Holofernes was resting upon his bed under the canopy, which was woven with purple, gold, emeralds, and precious stones. 22 And they told him about her; and he came out into the space before his tent, with silver lamps going before him.23 But when Judith had come before him and his servants, they all marveled at the beauty of her countenance. She fell down upon her face and bowed down to him, but his servants raised her up.

11

1 Holofernes said to her, "Woman, take courage. Don't be afraid in your heart; for I never hurt anyone who has chosen to serve Nebuchadnezzar, the king of all the earth.2 And now, if your people who dwell in the hill country had not slighted me, I would not have lifted up my spear against them; but they have done these things to themselves.3 And now tell me why

you fled from them and came to us; for you have come to save yourself. Take courage! You will live tonight, and hereafter;4 for there is no one that will wrong you, but all will treat you well, as is done to the servants of King Nebuchadnezzar my lord." 5 And Judith said to him, "Receive the words of your servant, and let your handmaid speak in your presence, and I won't lie to my lord tonight.6 If you will follow the words of your handmaid, God will bring the thing to pass perfectly with you; and my lord will not fail to accomplish his purposes.7 As Nebuchadnezzar king of all the earth lives, and as his power lives, who has sent you for the preservation of every living thing, not only do men serve him by you, but also the beasts of the field, the cattle, and the birds of the sky will live through your strength, in the time of Nebuchadnezzar and of all his house.8 For we have heard of your wisdom and the subtle plans of your soul. It has been reported in all the earth that you only are brave in all the kingdom, mighty in knowledge, and wonderful in feats of war.9 And now as concerning the matter which Achior spoke in your council, we have heard his words; for the men of Bethulia saved him, and he declared to them all that he had spoken before you.10 Therefore, O lord and master, don't neglect his word, but lay it up in your heart, for it is true; for our race will not be punished, neither will the sword prevail against them, unless they sin against their God.11 And now, that my lord may not be defeated and frustrated in his purpose, and that death may fall upon them, their sin has overtaken them, wherewith they will provoke their God to anger, whenever they do wickedness.12 Since their food failed them, and all their water was scant, they took counsel to kill their livestock, and determined to consume all those things which God charged them by his laws that they should not eat.13 They are resolved to spend the first fruits of the grain and the tithes of the wine and the oil, which they had sanctified and reserved for the priests who stand before the face of our God in Jerusalem, which it is not fitting for any of the people so much as to touch with their hands.14 They have sent some to Jerusalem, because they also that dwell there have done this thing, to bring them permission from the council of elders.15 When these instructions come to them and they do it, they will be given to you to be destroyed the same day.16 Therefore I your servant, knowing all this, fled away from their presence. God sent me to work things with you, at which all the earth will be astonished, even as many as hear it.17 For your servant is religious, and serves the God of heaven day and night. Now, my lord, I will stay with you; and your servant will go out by night into the valley. I will pray to God, and he will tell me when they have committed their sins.18 Then I will come and tell you. Then you can go out with all your army, and there will be none of them that will resist you.19 And I will lead you through the midst of Judea, until you come to Jerusalem. I will set your throne in the midst of it. You will drive them as sheep that have no shepherd, and a dog will not so much as open his mouth before you; for these things were told me according to my foreknowledge, and were declared to me, and I was sent to tell you."20 Her words were pleasing in the sight of Holofernes and of all his servants. They marveled at her wisdom, and said,21 "There is not such a woman from one end of the earth to the other, for beauty of face and wisdom of words."22 Holofernes said to her, "God did well to send you before the people, that might would be in our hands, and destruction among those who slighted my lord.23 And now you are beautiful in your countenance, and wise in your words. If you will do as you have spoken, your God will be my God, and you will dwell in the palace of King Nebuchadnezzar, and will be renowned through the whole earth."

12

1 He commanded that she should be brought in where his silver vessels were set, and asked that his servants should prepare some of his own delicacies for her, and that she should drink from his own wine.2 And Judith said, "I can't eat of it, lest there be an occasion of stumbling; but provision will be made for me from the things that have come with me."3 And Holofernes said to her, "But if the things that are with you should run out, from where will we be able to give you more like it? For there is none of your race with us."4 And Judith said to him, "As your soul lives, my lord, your servant will not use up those things that are with me until the Lord works by my hand the things that he has determined."5 Then Holofernes' servants brought her into the tent, and she slept until midnight. Then she rose up toward the morning watch,6 and sent to Holofernes, saying, "Let my lord now command that they allow your servant to go out to pray."7 Holofernes commanded his guards that they should not stop her. She stayed in the camp three days, and went out every night into the valley of Bethulia and washed herself at the fountain of water in the camp.8 And when she came up, she implored the Lord God of Israel to direct her way to the triumph of the children of his people.9 She came in clean and remained in the tent until she ate her food toward evening.10 It came to pass on the fourth day, that Holofernes made a feast for his own servants only, and called none of the officers to the banquet.11 And he said to Bagoas the eunuch, who had charge over all that he had, "Go now, and persuade this Hebrew woman who is with you that she come to us, and eat and drink with us.12 For behold, it would be a disgrace if we shall let such a woman go, not having had her company; for if we don't draw her to ourselves, she will laugh us to scorn."13 Bagoas went from the

presence of Holofernes, and came in to her, and said, "Let this fair lady not fear to come to my lord, and to be honored in his presence, and to drink wine and be merry with us, and to be made this day as one of the daughters of the children of Asshur who serve in Nebuchadnezzar's palace."14 Judith said to him, "Who am I, that I should contradict my lord? For whatever would be pleasing in his eyes, I will do speedily, and this will be my joy to the day of my death."15 She arose, and decked herself with her apparel and all her woman's attire; and her servant went and laid fleeces on the ground for her next to Holofernes, which she had received from Bagoas for her daily use, that she might sit and eat upon them.16 Judith came in and sat down, and Holofernes' heart was ravished with her. His passion was aroused, and he exceedingly desired her company. He was watching for a time to deceive her from the day that he had seen her.17 Holofernes said to her, "Drink now, and be merry with us."18 Judith said, "I will drink now, my lord, because my life is magnified in me this day more than all the days since I was born."19 Then she took and ate and drank before him what her servant had prepared.20 Holofernes took great delight in her, and drank exceedingly much wine, more than he had drunk at any time in one day since he was born.

13

1 But when the evening had come, his servants hurried to depart. Bagoas shut the tent outside, and dismissed those who waited from the presence of his lord. They went away to their beds; for they were all weary, because the feast had been long.2 But Judith was left alone in the tent, with Holofernes lying along upon his bed; for he was drunk with wine.3 Judith had said to her servant that she should stand outside her bedchamber, and wait for her to come out, as she did daily; for she said she would go out to her prayer. She spoke to Bagoas according to the same words.4 All went away from her presence, and none was left in the bedchamber, small or great. Judith, standing by his bed, said in her heart, O Lord God of all power, look in this hour upon the works of my hands for the exaltation of Jerusalem.5 For now is the time to help your inheritance, and to do the thing that I have purposed to the destruction of the enemies which have risen up against us.6 She came to the bedpost which was at Holofernes' head, and took down his sword from there.7 She drew near to the bed, took hold of the hair of his head, and said, "Strengthen me, O Lord God of Israel, this day."8 She struck twice upon his neck with all her might and cut off his head,9 tumbled his body down from the bed, and took down the canopy from the posts. After a little while she went out, and gave Holofernes' head to her maid;10 and she put it in her bag of food. They both went out together to prayer, according to

their custom. They passed through the camp, circled around that valley, and went up to the mountain of Bethulia, and came to its gates.11 Judith said afar off to the watchmen at the gates, "Open, open the gate, now. God is with us, even our God, to show his power yet in Israel, and his might against the enemy, as he has done even this day."12 It came to pass, when the men of her city heard her voice, they made haste to go down to the gate of their city, and they called together the elders of the city.13 They all ran together, both small and great, for it seemed unbelievable to them that she had come. They opened the gate and received them, making a fire to give light, and surrounded them.14 She said to them with a loud voice, "Praise God! Praise him! Praise God, who has not taken away his mercy from the house of Israel, but has destroyed our enemies by my hand tonight!"15 Then she took the head out of the bag and showed it, and said to them, "Behold, the head of Holofernes, the chief captain of the army of Asshur, and behold, the canopy under which he laid in his drunkenness. The Lord struck him by the hand of a woman.16 And as the Lord lives, who preserved me in my way that I went, my countenance deceived him to his destruction, and he didn't commit sin with me, to defile and shame me."17 All the people were exceedingly amazed, and bowed themselves, and worshiped God, and said with one accord, "Blessed are you, O our God, who have this day humiliated the enemies of your people."18 Ozias said to her, "Blessed are you, daughter, in the sight of the Most High God, above all the women upon the earth; and blessed is the Lord God, who created the heavens and the earth, who directed you to cut off the head of the prince of our enemies.19 For your hope will not depart from the heart of men that remember the strength of God forever.20 May God turn these things to you for a perpetual praise, to visit you with good things, because you didn't spare your life by reason of the affliction of our race, but prevented our ruin, walking a straight way before our God." And all the people said, "Amen! Amen!"

14

1 Judith said to them, "Hear me now, my kindred, and take this head, and hang it upon the battlement of your wall.2 It will be, so soon as the morning appears, and the sun comes up on the earth, you shall each take up his weapons of war, and every valiant man of you go out of the city. You shall set a captain over them, as though you would go down to the plain toward the watch of the children of Asshur; but you men shall not go down.3 These will take up their full armor, and shall go into their camp and rouse up the captains of the army of Asshur. They will run together to Holofernes' tent. They won't find him. Fear will fall upon them, and they will flee before your face.4 You men, and all that inhabit every border of Israel, shall pursue them

and overthrow them as they go.5 But before you do these things, summon Achior the Ammonite to me, that he may see and know him that despised the house of Israel, and that sent him to us, as it were to death.6 And they called Achior out of the house of Ozias; but when he came, and saw the head of Holofernes in a man's hand in the assembly of the people, he fell upon his face, and his spirit failed.7 But when they had recovered him, he fell at Judith's feet, bowed down to her, and said, "Blessed are you in every tent of Judah! In every nation, those who hear your name will be troubled.8 Now tell me all the things that you have done in these days."And Judith declared to him in the midst of the people all the things that she had done, from the day that she went out until the time that she spoke to them.9 But when she finished speaking, the people shouted with a loud voice, and made a joyful noise in their city.10 But when Achior saw all the things that the God of Israel had done, he believed in God exceedingly, and circumcised the flesh of his foreskin, and was joined to the house of Israel, to this day.11 But as soon as the morning arose, they hanged the head of Holofernes upon the wall, and every man took up his weapons, and they went forth by bands to the ascents of the mountain.12 But when the children of Asshur saw them, they sent word to their leaders, and they went to their captains and tribunes, and to every one of their rulers.13 They came to Holofernes' tent, and said to him that was over all that he had, "Wake our lord up, now, for the slaves have been bold to come down against us to battle, that they may be utterly destroyed."14 Bagoas went in, and knocked at the outer door of the tent; for he supposed that Holofernes was sleeping with Judith.15 But when no one answered, he opened it, went into the bedchamber, and found him cast upon the threshold dead; and his head had been taken from him.16 He cried with a loud voice, with weeping, groaning, and shouting, and tore his garments.17 He entered into the tent where Judith lodged, and he didn't find her. He leaped out to the people, and cried aloud,18 "The slaves have dealt treacherously! One woman of the Hebrews has brought shame upon the house of King Nebuchadnezzar; for, behold, Holofernes lies upon the ground, and his head is not on him!"19 But when the rulers of the army of Asshur heard this, they tore their tunics, and their souls were troubled exceedingly. There were cries and an exceedingly great noise in the midst of the camp.

15

1 When those who were in the tents heard, they were amazed at what happened.2 Trembling and fear fell upon them, and no man dared stay any more in the sight of his neighbor, but rushing out with one accord, they fled into every way of the plain and of the hill country.3 Those who had encamped in the hill country round about Bethulia

fled away. And then the children of Israel, every one who was a warrior among them, rushed out upon them.4 Ozias sent to Betomasthaim, Bebai, Chobai, and Chola, and to every border of Israel, to tell about the things that had been accomplished, and that all should rush upon their enemies to destroy them.5 But when the children of Israel heard this, they all fell upon them with one accord, and struck them to Chobai. Yes, and in like manner also, people from Jerusalem and from all the hill country came (for men had told them about what happened in their enemies' camp), and those who were in Gilead and in Galilee fell upon their flank with a great slaughter, until they were past Damascus and its borders. 6 The rest of the people who lived at Bethulia fell upon the camp of Asshur, and plundered them, and were enriched exceedingly. 7 The children of Israel returned from the slaughter, and got possession of that which remained. The villages and the cities that were in the hill country and in the plain country took many spoils; for there was an exceedingly great supply. 8 Joakim the high priest, and the elders of the children of Israel who lived in Jerusalem, came to see the good things which the Lord had showed to Israel, and to see Judith and to greet her. 9 When they came to her, they all blessed her with one accord, and said to her, "You are the exaltation of Jerusalem! You are the great glory of Israel! You are the great rejoicing of our race! 10 You have done all these things by your hand. You have done with Israel the things that are good, and God is pleased with it. May you be blessed by the Almighty Lord forever!"And all the people said, "Amen!"11 And the people plundered the camp for thirty days; and they gave Holofernes' tent to Judith, along with all his silver cups, his beds, his bowls, and all his furniture. She took them, placed them on her mule, prepared her wagons, and piled them on it. 12 And all the women of Israel ran together to see her; and they blessed her, and made a dance among them for her. She took branches in her hand, and distributed them to the women who were with her. 13 Then they made themselves garlands of olive, she and those who were with her, and she went before all the people in the dance, leading all the women. All the men of Israel followed in their armor with garlands, and with songs in their mouths.

16

1 And Judith began to sing this song of thanksgiving in all Israel, and all the people sang with loud voices this song of praise.2 Judith said, "Begin a song to my God with timbrels. Sing to my Lord with cymbals. Make melody to him with psalm and praise. Exalt him, and call upon his name. 3 For the Lord is the God that crushes battles. For in his armies in the midst of the people, he delivered me out of the hand of those who persecuted me. 4 Asshur came out of the mountains from the north. He came

with ten thousands of his army. Its multitude stopped the torrents. Their horsemen covered the hills. 5 He said that he would burn up my borders, kill my young men with the sword, throw my nursing children to the ground, give my infants up as prey, and make my virgins a plunder.6 "The Almighty Lord brought them to nothing by the hand of a woman. 7 For their mighty one didn't fall by young men, neither did sons of the Titans strike him. Tall giants didn't attack him, but Judith the daughter of Merari made him weak with the beauty of her countenance. 8 "For she put off the apparel of her widowhood for the exaltation of those who were distressed in Israel. She anointed her face with ointment, bound her hair in a tiara, and took a linen garment to deceive him.9 Her sandal ravished his eye. Her beauty took his soul prisoner The sword passed through his neck.10 "The Persians quaked at her daring. The Medes were daunted at her boldness.11 "Then my lowly ones shouted aloud. My oppressed people were terrified and trembled for fear. They lifted up their voices and the enemy fled. 12 The children of slave-girls pierced them through, and wounded them as fugitives' children. They perished by the army of my Lord.13 "I will sing to my God a new song: O Lord, you are great and glorious, marvelous in strength, invincible. 14 Let all your creation serve you; for you spoke, and they were made. You sent out your spirit, and it built them. There is no one who can resist your voice. 15 For the mountains will be moved from their foundations with the waters, and the rocks will melt as wax at your presence: But you are yet merciful to those who fear you. 16 For all sacrifice is little for a sweet savor, and all the fat is very little for a whole burnt offering to you; but he who fears the Lord is great continually.17 "Woe to the nations who rise up against my race! The Lord Almighty will take vengeance on them in the day of judgment and put fire and worms in their flesh; and they will weep and feel their pain forever." 18 Now when they came to Jerusalem, they worshiped God. When the people were purified, they offered their whole burnt offerings, their free will offerings, and their gifts.19 Judith dedicated all Holofernes' stuff, which the people had given her, and gave the canopy, which she had taken for herself out of his bedchamber, for a gift to the Lord.20 And the people continued feasting in Jerusalem before the sanctuary for three months, and Judith remained with them. 21 After these days, everyone departed to his own inheritance. Judith went away to Bethulia, and remained in her own possession, and was honorable in her time in all the land.22 Many desired her, but no man knew her all the days of her life from the day that Manasses her husband died and was gathered to his people.23 She increased in greatness exceedingly; and she grew old in her husband's house, to one hundred five years. She let her maid go free. Then she died in

Bethulia. They buried her in the cave of her husband Manasses.24 The house of Israel mourned for her seven days. She distributed her goods before she died to all those who were nearest of kin to Manasses her husband, and to those who were nearest of her own kindred. 25 There was no one who made the children of Israel afraid any more in the days of Judith, nor for a long time after her death.

THE BOOK OF ESTHER (WITH ADDITIONS)

1

1 [In the second year of the reign of Ahasuerus the great king, on the first day of Nisan, Mordecai the son of Jair, the son of Shimei, the son of Kish, of the tribe of Benjamin, a Jew dwelling in the city Susa, a great man, serving in the king's palace, saw a vision. Now he was one of the captives whom Nebuchadnezzar king of Babylon had carried captive from Jerusalem with Jeconiah the king of Judea. This was his dream: Behold, voices and a noise, thunders and earthquake, tumult upon the earth. And, behold, two great serpents came out, both ready for conflict. A great voice came from them. Every nation was prepared for battle by their voice, even to fight against the nation of the just. Behold, a day of darkness and blackness, suffering and anguish, affection and tumult upon the earth. And all the righteous nation was troubled, fearing their own afflictions. They prepared to die, and cried to God. Something like a great river from a little spring with much water, came from their cry. Light and the sun arose, and the lowly were exalted, and devoured the honorable.Mordecai, who had seen this vision and what God desired to do, having arisen, kept it in his heart, and desired by all means to interpret it, even until night. Mordecai rested quietly in the palace with Gabatha and Tharrha the king's two chamberlains, eunuchs who guarded the palace. He heard their conversation and searched out their plans. He learned that they were preparing to lay hands on King Ahasuerus; and he informed the king concerning them. The king examined the two chamberlains. They confessed, and were led away and executed. The king wrote these things for a record. Mordecai also wrote concerning these matters. The king commanded Mordecai to serve in the palace, and gave gifts for this service. But Haman the son of Hammedatha the Bougean was honored in the sight of the king, and he endeavored to harm Mordecai and his people, because of the king's two chamberlains.] And it came to pass after these things in the days of Ahasuerus, (this Ahasuerus ruled over one hundred twenty-seven provinces from India) 2 in those days, when King Ahasuerus was on the throne in the city of Susa, 3 in the third year of his reign, he made a feast for his

friends, for people from the rest of the nations, for the nobles of the Persians and Medes, and for the chief of the local governors. 4 After this— after he had shown them the wealth of his kingdom and the abundant glory of his wealth during one hundred eighty days 5 when the days of the wedding feast were completed, the king made a banquet lasting six days for the people of the nations who were present in the city, in the court of the king's house,6 which was adorned with fine linen and flax on cords of fine linen and purple, fastened to golden and silver studs on pillars of white marble and stone. There were golden and silver couches on a pavement of emerald stone, and of mother-of-pearl, and of white marble, with transparent coverings variously flowered, having roses arranged around it.7 There were gold and silver cups, and a small cup of carbuncle set out, of the value of thirty thousand talents, with abundant and sweet wine, which the king himself drank.8 This banquet was not according to the appointed law, but as the king desired to have it. He charged the stewards to perform his will and that of the company. 9 Also Vashti the queen made a banquet for the women in the palace where King Ahasuerus lived. 10 Now on the seventh day, the king, being merry, told Haman, Bazan, Tharrha, Baraze, Zatholtha, Abataza, and Tharaba, the seven chamberlains, servants of King Ahasuerus,11 to bring in the queen to him, to enthrone her, and crown her with the diadem, and to show her to the princes, and her beauty to the nations, for she was beautiful. 12 But queen Vashti refused to come with the chamberlains; so the king was grieved and angered. 13 And he said to his friends, "This is what Vashti said. Therefore pronounce your legal judgment on this case." 14 So Arkesaeus, Sarsathaeus, and Malisear, the princes of the Persians and Medes, who were near the king, who sat chief in rank by the king, drew near to him, 15 and reported to him according to the laws what it was proper to do to queen Vashti, because she had not done the things commanded by the king through the chamberlains. 16 And Memucan said to the king and to the princes, "Queen Vashti has not wronged the king only, but also all the king's rulers and princes; 17 for he has told them the words of the queen, and how she disobeyed the king. As she then refused to obey King Ahasuerus, 18 so this day the other wives of the chiefs of the Persians and Medes, having heard what she said to the king, will dare in the same way to dishonor their husbands. 19 If then it seems good to the king, let him make a royal decree, and let it be written according to the laws of the Medes and Persians, and let him not alter it: 'Don't allow the queen to come in to him any more. Let the king give her royalty to a woman better than she.' 20 Let the law of the king which he will have made be widely proclaimed in his kingdom. Then all the women will give honor to their husbands, from the poor even to the rich." 21 This advice pleased the king and the princes; and the king did as Memucan had said, 22 and sent into all his kingdom through the several provinces, according to their language, so that men might be feared in their own houses.

2

1 After this, the king's anger was pacified, and he no more mentioned Vashti, bearing in mind what she had said, and how he had condemned her.2 Then the servants of the king said, "Let chaste, beautiful young virgins be sought for the king. 3 Let the king appoint local governors in all the provinces of his kingdom, and let them select beautiful, chaste young ladies and bring them to the city Susa, into the women's apartment. Let them be consigned to the king's chamberlain, the keeper of the women. Then let things for purification and other needs be given to them.4 Let the woman who pleases the king be queen instead of Vashti." This thing pleased the king; and he did so.5 Now there was a Jew in the city Susa, and his name was Mordecai, the son of Jairus, the son of Shimei, the son of Kish, of the tribe of Benjamin. 6 He had been brought as a prisoner from Jerusalem, whom Nebuchadnezzar king of Babylon had carried into captivity. 7 He had a foster child, daughter of Aminadab his father's brother. Her name was Esther. When her parents died, he brought her up to womanhood as his own. This lady was beautiful. 8 And because the king's ordinance was published, many ladies were gathered to the city of Susa under the hand of Hegai; and Esther was brought to Hegai, the keeper of the women. 9 The lady pleased him, and she found favor in his sight. He hurried to give her the things for purification, her portion, and the seven maidens appointed her out of the palace. He treated her and her maidens well in the women's apartment. 10 But Esther didn't reveal her family or her kindred, for Mordecai had charged her not to tell. 11 But Mordecai used to walk every day by the women's court, to see what would become of Esther. 12 Now this was the time for a virgin to go into the king, when she had completed twelve months; for so are the days of purification fulfilled, six months while they are anointing themselves with oil of myrrh, and six months with spices and women's purifications. 13 And then the lady goes in to the king. The officer that he commands to do so will bring her to come in with him from the women's apartment to the king's chamber.14 She enters in the evening, and in the morning she departs to the second women's apartment, where Hegai the king's chamberlain is keeper of the women. She doesn't go in to the king again, unless she is called by name. 15 And when the time was fulfilled for Esther the daughter of Aminadab the brother of Mordecai's father to go in to the king, she neglected nothing which the chamberlain, the women's keeper,

commanded; for Esther found grace in the sight of all who looked at her. 16 So Esther went in to King Ahasuerus in the twelfth month, which is Adar, in the seventh year of his reign. 17 The king loved Esther, and she found favor beyond all the other virgins. He put the queen's crown on her. 18 The king made a banquet for all his friends and great men for seven days, and he highly celebrated the marriage of Esther; and he granted a remission of taxes to those who were under his dominion.19 Meanwhile, Mordecai served in the courtyard. 20 Now Esther had not revealed her country, for so Mordecai commanded her, to fear God, and perform his commandments, as when she was with him. Esther didn't change her manner of life. 21 Two chamberlains of the king, the chiefs of the body- guard, were grieved, because Mordecai was promoted; and they sought to kill King Ahasuerus. 22 And the matter was discovered by Mordecai, and he made it known to Esther, and she declared to the king the matter of the conspiracy.23 And the king examined the two chamberlains and hanged them. Then the king gave orders to make a note for a memorial in the royal library of the goodwill shown by Mordecai, as a commendation.

3

1 After this, King Ahasuerus highly honored Haman the son of Hammedatha, the Bugaean. He exalted him and set his seat above all his friends.2 All in the palace bowed down to him, for so the king had given orders to do; but Mordecai didn't bow down to him. 3 And they in the king's palace said to Mordecai, "Mordecai, why do you transgress the commands of the king?" 4 They questioned him daily, but he didn't listen to them; so they reported to Haman that Mordecai resisted the commands of the king; and Mordecai had shown to them that he was a Jew. 5 When Haman understood that Mordecai didn't bow down to him, he was greatly enraged, 6 and plotted to utterly destroy all the Jews who were under the rule of Ahasuerus. 7 In the twelfth year of the reign of Ahasuerus, Haman made a decision by casting lots by day and month, to kill the race of Mordecai in one day. The lot fell on the fourteenth day of the month of Adar.8 So he spoke to King Ahasuerus, saying, "There is a nation scattered among the nations in all your kingdom, and their laws differ from all the other nations. They disobey the king's laws. It is not expedient for the king to tolerate them. 9 If it seem good to the king, let him make a decree to destroy them, and I will remit into the king's treasury ten thousand talents of silver."10 So the king took off his ring, and gave it into the hands of Haman to seal the decrees against the Jews. 11 The king said to Haman, "Keep the silver, and treat the nation as you will." 12 So the king's recorders were called in the first month, on the thirteenth day, and they wrote as Haman

commanded to the captains and governors in every province, from India even to Ethiopia, to one hundred twenty-seven provinces; and to the rulers of the nations according to their languages, in the name of King Ahasuerus. 13 The message was sent by couriers throughout the kingdom of Ahasuerus, to utterly destroy the race of the Jews on the first day of the twelfth month, which is Adar, and to plunder their goods. [The following is the copy of the letter. "From the great King Ahasuerus to the rulers and the governors under them of one hundred twenty-seven provinces, from India even to Ethiopia, who hold authority under him: "Ruling over many nations and having obtained dominion over the whole world, I was determined (not elated by the confidence of power, but ever conducting myself with great moderation and gentleness) to make the lives of my subjects continually tranquil, desiring both to maintain the kingdom quiet and orderly to its utmost limits, and to restore the peace desired by all men. When I had asked my counselors how this should be brought to pass, Haman, who excels in soundness of judgment among us, and has been manifestly well inclined without wavering and with unshaken fidelity, and had obtained the second post in the kingdom, informed us that a certain ill-disposed people is scattered among all the tribes throughout the world, opposed in their law to every other nation, and continually neglecting the commands of the king, so that the united government blamelessly administered by us is not quietly established. Having then conceived that this nation is continually set in opposition to every man, introducing as a change a foreign code of laws, and injuriously plotting to accomplish the worst of evils against our interests, and against the happy establishment of the monarchy, we instruct you in the letter written by Haman, who is set over the public affairs and is our second governor, to destroy them all utterly with their wives and children by the swords of the enemies, without pitying or sparing any, on the fourteenth day of the twelfth month Adar, of the present year; that the people aforetime and now ill-disposed to us having been violently consigned to death in one day, may hereafter secure to us continually a well constituted and quiet state of affairs."14 Copies of the letters were published in every province; and an order was given to all the nations to be ready for that day. 15 This business was hastened also in Susa. The king and Haman began to drink, but the city was confused.

4

1 But Mordecai, having perceived what was done, tore his garments, put on sackcloth, and sprinkled dust upon himself. Having rushed forth through the open street of the city, he cried with a loud voice, "A nation that has done no wrong is going to be destroyed!" 2 He came to the king's gate, and stood; for it was not lawful for him to enter into the

palace wearing sackcloth and ashes. 3 And in every province where the letters were published, there was crying, lamentation, and great mourning on the part of the Jews. They wore sackcloth and ashes. 4 The queen's maids and chamberlains went in and told her; and when she had heard what was done, she was deeply troubled. She sent clothes to Mordecai to replace his sackcloth, but he refused. 5 So Esther called for her chamberlain Hathach, who waited upon her; and she sent to learn the truth from Mordecai. 7 Mordecai showed him what was done, and the promise which Haman had made the king of ten thousand talents to be paid into the treasury, that he might destroy the Jews. 8 And he gave him the copy of what was published in Susa concerning their destruction to show to Esther; and told him to charge her to go in and entreat the king, and to beg him for the people. "Remember, he said, the days of your humble condition, how you were nursed by my hand; because Haman, who holds the next place to the king, has spoken against us to cause our death. Call upon the Lord, and speak to the king concerning us, to deliver us from death." 9 So Hathach went in and told her all these words. 10 Esther said to Hathach, "Go to Mordecai, and say, 11 'All the nations of the empire know than any man or woman who goes in to the king into the inner court without being called, that person must die, unless the king stretches out his golden sceptre; then he shall live. I haven't been called to go into the king for thirty days.' 12 So Hathach reported to Mordecai all the words of Esther. 13 Then Mordecai said to Hathach, "Go, and say to her, 'Esther, don't say to yourself that you alone will escape in the kingdom, more than all the other Jews. 14 For if you keep quiet on this occasion, help and protection will come to the Jews from another place; but you and your father's house will perish. Who knows if you have been made queen for this occasion?' "15 And Esther sent the messenger who came to her to Mordecai, saying, 16 "Go and assemble the Jews that are in Susa, and all of you fast for me. Don't eat or drink for three days, night and day. My maidens and I will also fast. Then I will go in to the king contrary to the law, even if I must die." 17 So Mordecai went and did all that Esther commanded him. 18 [He prayed to the Lord, making mention of all the works of the Lord. 19 He said, "Lord God, you are king ruling over all, for all things are in your power, and there is no one who can oppose you in your purpose to save Israel; 20 for you have made the heaven and the earth and every wonderful thing under heaven. 21 You are Lord of all, and there is no one who can resist you, Lord. 22 You know all things. You know, Lord, that it is not in insolence, nor arrogance, nor love of glory, that I have done this, to refuse to bow down to the arrogant Haman. 23 For I would gladly have kissed the soles of his feet for the safety of Israel. 24 But I have done this that I might not set the glory of man above the glory of God. I will not worship anyone except you, my Lord, and I will not do these things in arrogance. 25 And now, O Lord God, the King, the God of Abraham, spare your people, for our enemies are planning our destruction, and they have desired to destroy your ancient inheritance. 26 Do not overlook your people, whom you have redeemed for yourself out of the land of Egypt. 27 Listen to my prayer. Have mercy on your inheritance and turn our mourning into gladness, that we may live and sing praise to your name, O Lord. Don't utterly destroy the mouth of those who praise you, O Lord."28 All Israel cried with all their might, for death was before their eyes. 29 And queen Esther took refuge in the Lord, being taken as it were in the agony of death. 30 Having taken off her glorious apparel, she put on garments of distress and mourning. Instead of grand perfumes she filled her head with ashes and dung. She greatly humbled her body, and she filled every place of her glad adorning with her tangled hair.31 She implored the Lord God of Israel, and said, "O my Lord, you alone are our king. Help me. I am destitute, and have no helper but you, 32 for my danger is near at hand. 33 I have heard from my birth in the tribe of my kindred that you, Lord, took Israel out of all the nations, and our fathers out of all their kindred for a perpetual inheritance, and have done for them all that you have said. 34 And now we have sinned before you, and you have delivered us into the hands of our enemies, 35 because we honored their gods. You are righteous, O Lord. 36 But now they have not been content with the bitterness of our slavery, but have laid their hands on the hands of their idols 37 to abolish the decree of your mouth, and utterly to destroy your inheritance, and to stop the mouth of those who praise you, and to extinguish the glory of your house and your altar, 38 and to open the mouth of the Gentiles to speak the praises of vanities, and that a mortal king should be admired forever. 39 O Lord, don't surrender your sceptre to those who don't exist, and don't let them laugh at our fall, but turn their counsel against themselves, and make an example of him who has begun to injure us. 40 Remember us, O Lord! Manifest yourself in the time of our affliction. Encourage me, O King of gods, and ruler of all dominion! 41 Put harmonious speech into my mouth before the lion, and turn his heart to hate him who fights against us, to the utter destruction of those who agree with him. 42 But deliver us by your hand, and help me who am alone and have no one but you, O Lord. 43 You know all things, and know that I hate the glory of transgressors, and that I abhor the bed of the uncircumcised and of every stranger.44 You know my necessity, for I abhor the symbol of my proud station, which is upon my head in the days of my splendor. I abhor it as a menstruous cloth, and I don't wear it in the days of my tranquility. 45 Your handmaid has not eaten at Haman's table, and I have not honored the banquet of the king, neither have I drunk wine of libations. 46 Neither has your handmaid rejoiced since the day of my promotion until now, except in you, O Lord God of Abraham. 47 O god, who has power over all, listen to the voice of the desperate, and deliver us from the hand of those who devise mischief. Deliver me from my fear.]

5

1 It came to pass on the third day, when she had ceased praying, that she took off her servant's dress and put on her glorious apparel. Being splendidly dressed and having called upon God the Overseer and Preserver of all things, she took her two maids, and she leaned upon one, as a delicate female, and the other followed bearing her train. She was blooming in the perfection of her beauty. Her face was cheerful and looked lovely, but her heart was filled with fear. Having passed through all the doors, she stood before the king. He was sitting on his royal throne. He had put on all his glorious apparel, covered all over with gold and precious stones, and was very terrifying. And having raised his face resplendent with glory, he looked with intense anger. The queen fell, and changed her color as she fainted. She bowed herself upon the head of the maid who went before her. But God changed the spirit of the king to gentleness, and in intense feeling, he sprang from off his throne, and took her into his arms, until she recovered. He comforted her with peaceful words, and said to her, "What is the matter, Esther? I am your relative. Cheer up! You shall not die, for our command is openly declared to you: 'Draw near.' "2 And having raised the golden sceptre, he laid it upon her neck, and embraced her. He said, "Speak to me."So she said to him, "I saw you, my lord, as an angel of God, and my heart was troubled for fear of your glory; for you, my lord, are to be wondered at, and your face is full of grace." While she was speaking, she fainted and fell.Then the king was troubled, and all his servants comforted her. 3 The king said, "What do you desire, Esther? What is your request? Ask even to the half of my kingdom, and it shall be yours." 4 Esther said, "Today is a special day. So if it seems good to the king, let both him and Haman come to the feast which I will prepare this day." 5 The king said, "Hurry and bring Haman here, that we may do as Esther said." So they both came to the feast about which Esther had spoken. 6 At the banquet, the king said to Esther, "What is your request, queen Esther? You shall have all that you require." 7 She said, "My request and my petition is:8 if I have found favor in the king's sight, let the king and Haman come again tomorrow to the feast which I shall prepare for them, and tomorrow I will do as I have done today."9 So Haman went out from the king very glad and merry; but when Haman saw Mordecai the Jew in the court, he

was greatly enraged. 10 Having gone into his own house, he called his friends, and his wife Zeresh. 11 He showed them his wealth and the glory with which the king had invested him, and how he had promoted him to be chief ruler in the kingdom.12 Haman said, "The queen has called no one to the feast with the king but me, and I am invited tomorrow. 13 But these things don't please me while I see Mordecai the Jew in the court. 14 Then Zeresh his wife and his friends said to him, "Let a fifty cubit tall gallows be made for you. In the morning you speak to the king, and let Mordecai be hanged on the gallows; but you go in to the feast with the king, and be merry."The saying pleased Haman, and the gallows was prepared.

6

1 The Lord removed sleep from the king that night; so he told his servant to bring in the books, the registers of daily events, to read to him. 2 And he found the records written concerning Mordecai, how he had told the king about the king's two chamberlains, when they were keeping guard, and sought to lay hands on Ahasuerus. 3 The king said, "What honor or favor have we done for Mordecai?"The king's servants said, "You haven't done anything for him." 4 And while the king was enquiring about the kindness of Mordecai, behold, Haman was in the court. The king said, "Who is in the court? Now Haman had come in to speak to the king about hanging Mordecai on the gallows which he had prepared. 5 The king's servants said, "Behold, Haman stands in the court."And the king said, "Call him!" 6 The king said to Haman, "What should I do for the man whom I wish to honor?"Haman said within himself, "Whom would the king honor but myself?" 7 He said to the king, "As for the man whom the king wishes to honor, 8 let the king's servants bring the robe of fine linen which the king puts on, and the horse on which the king rides, 9 and let him give it to one of the king's noble friends, and let him dress the man whom the king loves. Let him mount him on the horse, and proclaim through the streets of the city, saying, "This is what will be done for every man whom the king honors!" 10 Then the king said to Haman, "You have spoken well. Do so for Mordecai the Jew, who waits in the palace, and let not a word of what you have spoken be neglected!"11 So Haman took the robe and the horse, dressed Mordecai, mounted him on the horse, and went through the streets of the city, proclaiming, "This is what will be done for every man whom the king wishes to honor."12 Then Mordecai returned to the palace; but Haman went home mourning, with his head covered. 13 Haman related the events that had happened to him to Zeresh his wife and to his friends. His friends and his wife said to him, "If Mordecai is of the race of the Jews, and you have begun to be humbled before him, you will assuredly fall; and you will not be able to

withstand him, for the living God is with him."14 While they were still speaking, the chamberlains arrived to rush Haman to the banquet which Esther had prepared.

7

1 So the king and Haman went in to drink with the queen. 2 The king said to Esther at the banquet on the second day, "What is it, queen Esther? What is your request? What is your petition? It shall be done for you, up to half of my kingdom." 3 She answered and said, "If I have found favor in the sight of the king, let my life be granted as my petition, and my people as my request.4 For both I and my people are sold for destruction, pillage, and genocide. If both we and our children were sold for male and female slaves, I would not have bothered you, for this isn't worthy of the king's palace." 5 The king said, "Who has dared to do this thing?"6 Esther said, "The enemy is Haman, this wicked man!"Then Haman was terrified in the presence of the king and the queen.7 The king rose up from the banquet to go into the garden. Haman began to beg the queen for mercy, for he saw that he was in serious trouble. 8 The king returned from the garden; and Haman had fallen upon the couch, begging the queen for mercy. The king said, "Will you even assault my wife in my house?"And when Haman heard it, he changed countenance. 9 And Bugathan, one of the chamberlains, said to the king, "Behold, Haman has also prepared a gallows for Mordecai, who spoke concerning the king, and a fifty cubit high gallows has been set up on Haman's property."The king said, "Let him be hanged on it!" 10 So Haman was hanged on the gallows that had been prepared for Mordecai. Then the king's wrath was abated.

8

1 On that day, King Ahasuerus gave to Esther all that belonged to Haman the slanderer. The king called Mordecai, for Esther had told that he was related to her. 2 The king took the ring which he had taken away from Haman and gave it to Mordecai. Esther appointed Mordecai over all that had been Haman's. 3 She spoke yet again to the king, and fell at his feet, and implored him to undo Haman's mischief and all that he had done against the Jews.

4 Then the king extended the golden sceptre to Esther; and Esther arose to stand near the king. 5 Esther said, "If it seems good to you, and I have found favor in your sight, let an order be sent that the letters sent by Haman may be reversed—letters that were written for the destruction of the Jews who are in your kingdom. 6 For how could I see the affliction of my people, and how could I survive the destruction of my kindred?" 7 Then the king said to Esther, "If I have given and freely granted you all that was Haman's, and hanged him on a gallows because he laid his hands upon the Jews, what more

do you seek?8 Write in my name whatever seems good to you, and seal it with my ring; for whatever is written at the command of the king, and sealed with my ring, cannot be countermanded.9 So the scribes were called in the first month, which is Nisan, on the twenty-third day of the same year; and orders were written to the Jews, whatever the king had commanded to the local governors and chiefs of the local governors, from India even to Ethiopia one hundred twenty-seven local governors, according to the several provinces, in their own languages. 10 They were written by order of the king, sealed with his ring, and the letters were sent by the couriers.11 In them, he charged them to use their own laws in every city, to help each other, and to treat their adversaries and those who attacked them as they pleased, 12 on one day in all the kingdom of Ahasuerus, on the thirteenth day of the twelfth month, which is Adar.13 Let the copies be posted in conspicuous places throughout the kingdom. Let all the Jews be ready against this day, to fight against their enemies. The following is a copy of the letter containing orders:[The great King Ahasuerus sends greetings to the rulers of provinces in one hundred twenty-seven local governance regions, from India to Ethiopia, even to those who are faithful to our interests. Many who have been frequently honored by the most abundant kindness of their benefactors have conceived ambitious designs, and not only endeavor to hurt our subjects, but moreover, not being able to bear prosperity, they also endeavor to plot against their own benefactors. They not only would utterly abolish gratitude from among men, but also, elated by the boastings of men who are strangers to all that is good, they supposed that they would escape the sin-hating vengeance of the ever- seeing God. And oftentimes evil exhortation has made partakers of the guilt of shedding innocent blood, and has involved in irremediable calamities many of those who had been appointed to offices of authority, who had been entrusted with the management of their friends' affairs; while men, by the false sophistry of an evil disposition, have deceived the simple goodwill of the ruling powers. And it is possible to see this, not so much from more ancient traditional accounts, as it is immediately in your power to see it by examining what things have been wickedly perpetrated by the baseness of men unworthily holding power. It is right to take heed with regard to the future, that we may maintain the government in undisturbed peace for all men, adopting needful changes, and ever judging those cases which come under our notice with truly equitable decisions. For whereas Haman, a Macedonian, the son of Hammedatha, in reality an alien from the blood of the Persians, and differing widely from our mild course of government, having been hospitably entertained by us, obtained so large a share of our universal kindness as to be called our father, and to continue the person next to the royal throne, reverenced of all; he however, overcome by pride, endeavored to deprive us of our dominion, and our life; having by various and subtle artifices demanded for destruction both Mordecai our deliverer and perpetual benefactor, and Esther the blameless consort of our kingdom, along with their whole nation. For by these methods he thought, having surprised us in a defenseless state, to transfer the dominion of the Persians to the Macedonians. But we find that the Jews, who have been consigned to destruction by the most abominable of men, are not malefactors, but living according to the most just laws, and being the sons of the living God, the most high and mighty, who maintains the kingdom, to us as well as to our forefathers, in the most excellent order. You will therefore do well in refusing to obey the letter sent by Haman the son of Hammedatha, because he who has done these things has been hanged with his whole family at the gates of Susa, Almighty God having swiftly returned to him a worthy punishment. We enjoin you then, having openly published a copy of this letter in every place, to give the Jews permission to use their own lawful customs and to strengthen them, that on the thirteenth of the twelfth month Adar, on the self-same day, they may defend themselves against those who attack them in a time of affliction. For in the place of the destruction of the chosen race, Almighty God has granted them this time of gladness. Therefore you also, among your notable feasts, must keep a distinct day with all festivity, that both now and hereafter it may be a day of deliverance to us and who are well disposed toward the Persians, but to those that plotted against us a memorial of destruction. And every city and province collectively, which shall not do accordingly, shall be consumed with vengeance by spear and fire. It shall be made not only inaccessible to men, but most hateful to wild beasts and birds forever.] Let the copies be posted in conspicuous places throughout the kingdom and let all the Jews be ready against this day, to fight against their enemies.14 So the horsemen went forth with haste to perform the king's commands. The ordinance was also published in Susa.

15 Mordecai went out robed in royal apparel, wearing a golden crown and a diadem of fine purple linen. The people in Susa saw it and rejoiced. 16 The Jews had light and gladness 17 in every city and province where the ordinance was published. Wherever the proclamation took place, the Jews had joy and gladness, feasting and mirth. Many of the Gentiles were circumcised and became Jews for fear of the Jews.

9

1 Now in the twelfth month, on the thirteenth day of the month, which is Adar, the letters written by the

king arrived. 2 In that day, the adversaries of the Jews perished; for no one resisted, through fear of them. 3 For the chiefs of the local governors, and the princes and the royal scribes, honored the Jews; for the fear of Mordecai was upon them. 4 For the order of the king was in force, that he should be celebrated in all the kingdom. 6 In the city Susa the Jews killed five hundred men,7 including Pharsannes, Delphon, Phasga,8 Pharadatha, Barea, Sarbaca, 9 Marmasima, Ruphaeus, Arsaeus, and Zabuthaeus, 10 the ten sons of Haman the son of Hammedatha the Bugaean, the enemy of the Jews; and they plundered their property on the same day.11 The number of those who perished in Susa was reported to the king. 12 Then the king said to Esther, "The Jews have slain five hundred men in the city Susa. What do you think they have done in the rest of the country? What more do you ask, that it may be done for you?" 13 Esther said to the king, "Let it be granted to the Jews to do the same to them tomorrow. Also, hang the bodies of the ten sons of Haman."14 He permitted it to be done; and he gave up to the Jews of the city the bodies of the sons of Haman to hang.15 The Jews assembled in Susa on the fourteenth day of Adar and killed three hundred men, but plundered no property. 16 The rest of the Jews who were in the kingdom assembled, and helped one another, and obtained rest from their enemies; for they destroyed fifteen thousand of them on the thirteenth day of Adar, but took no spoil. 17 They rested on the fourteenth of the same month, and kept it as a day of rest with joy and gladness. 18 The Jews in the city of Susa assembled also on the fourteenth day and rested; and they also observed the fifteenth with joy and gladness. 19 On this account then, the Jews dispersed in every foreign land keep the fourteenth of Adar as a holy day with joy, each sending gifts of food to his neighbor. 20 Mordecai wrote these things in a book and sent them to the Jews, as many as were in the kingdom of Ahasuerus, both those who were near and those who were far away, 21 to establish these as joyful days and to keep the fourteenth and fifteenth of Adar;22 for on these days the Jews obtained rest from their enemies; and in that month, which was Adar, in which a change was made for them from mourning to joy, and from sorrow to a holiday, to spend the whole of it in good days of feasting and gladness, sending portions to their friends and to the poor.23 And the Jews consented to this as Mordecai wrote to them,24showing how Haman the son of Hammedatha the Macedonian fought against them, how he made a decree and cast lots to destroy them utterly; 25 also how he went in to the king, telling him to hang Mordecai; but all the calamities he tried to bring upon the Jews came upon himself, and he was hanged, along with his children. 26 Therefore these days were called Purim, because of the lots (for in their language they are called Purim) because of the words of this letter, and because of all they suffered on this account, and all that happened to them. 27 Mordecai established it, and the Jews took upon themselves, upon their offspring, and upon those who were joined to them to observe it, neither would they on any account behave differently; but these days were to be a memorial kept in every generation, city, family, and province. 28 These days of Purim shall be kept forever, and their memorial shall not fail in any generation.29 Queen Esther the daughter of Aminadab and Mordecai the Jew wrote all that they had done, and gave the confirmation of the letter about Purim. 31 Mordecai and Esther the queen established this decision on their own, pledging their own well-being to their plan.32 And Esther established it by a command forever, and it was written for a memorial.

10

1 The king levied a tax upon his kingdom both by land and sea. 2 As for his strength and valour, and the wealth and glory of his kingdom, behold, they are written in the book of the Persians and Medes for a memorial.3 Mordecai was viceroy to King Ahasuerus, and was a great man in the kingdom, honored by the Jews, and lived his life loved by all his nation. 4 [Mordecai said, "These things have come from God.5 For I remember the dream which I had concerning these matters; for not one detail of them has failed.6 There was the little spring which became a river, and there was light, and the sun and much water. The river is Esther, whom the king married and made queen. 7 The two serpents are Haman and me. 8 The nations are those which combined to destroy the name of the Jews.9 But as for my nation, this is Israel, even those who cried to God and were delivered; for the Lord delivered his people. The Lord rescued us out of all these calamities; and God worked such signs and great wonders as have not been done among the nations. 10 Therefore he ordained two lots. One for the people of God, and one for all the other nations. 11 And these two lots came for an appointed season, and for a day of judgment, before God, and for all the nations. 12 God remembered his people and vindicated his inheritance. 13 They shall observe these days in the month Adar, on the fourteenth and on the fifteenth day of the month, with an assembly, joy, and gladness before God, throughout the generations forever among his people Israel. 14 In the fourth year of the reign of Ptolemeus and Cleopatra, Dositheus, who said he was a priest and Levite, and Ptolemeus his son brought this letter of Purim, which they said was authentic, and that Lysimachus the son of Ptolemeus, who was in Jerusalem, had interpreted.]

THE PRAYER OF AZARIAH AND THE SONG OF THE THREE HOLY CHILDREN

24 They walked in the midst of the fire, praising God, and blessing the Lord. 25 Then Azarias stood, and prayed like this. Opening his mouth in the midst of the fire he said, 26 "Blessed are you, O Lord, you God of our fathers! Your name is worthy to be praised and glorified for evermore;27 for you are righteous in all the things that you have done. Yes, all your works are true. Your ways are right, and all your judgments are truth. 28 In all the things that you have brought upon us, and upon the holy city of our fathers, Jerusalem, you have executed true judgments. For according to truth and justice you have brought all these things upon us because of our sins. 29 For we have sinned and committed iniquity in departing from you.30 In all things we have trespassed, and not obeyed your commandments or kept them. We haven't done as you have commanded us, that it might go well with us. 31 Therefore all that you have brought upon us, and everything that you have done to us, you have done in true judgment. 32 You delivered us into the hands of lawless enemies, most hateful rebels, and to an unjust king who is the most wicked in all the world. 33 And now we can't open our mouth. Shame and reproach have come on your servants and those who worship you. 34 Don't utterly deliver us up, for your name's sake. Don't annul your covenant. 35 Don't cause your mercy to depart from us, for the sake of Abraham who is loved by you, and for the sake of Isaac your servant, and Israel your holy one, 36 to whom you promised that you would multiply their offspring as the stars of the sky, and as the sand that is on the sea shore. 37 For we, O Lord, have become less than any nation, and are brought low this day in all the world because of our sins. 38 There isn't at this time prince, or prophet, or leader, or burnt offering, or sacrifice, or oblation, or incense, or place to offer before you, and to find mercy. 39 Nevertheless in a contrite heart and a humble spirit let us be accepted, 40 like the burnt offerings of rams and bullocks, and like ten thousands of fat lambs. So let our sacrifice be in your sight this day, that we may wholly go after you, for they shall not be ashamed who put their trust in you. 41 And now we follow you with all our heart. We fear you, and seek your face. 42 Put us not to shame; but deal with us after your kindness, and according to the multitude of your mercy. 43 Deliver us also according to your marvelous works, and give glory to your name, O Lord. Let all those who harm your servants be confounded. 44 Let them be ashamed of all their power and might, and let their strength be broken. 45 Let them know that you are the Lord, the only God, and

glorious over the whole world." 46 The king's servants who put them in didn't stop making the furnace hot with naphtha, pitch, tinder, and small wood, 47 so that the flame streamed out forty nine cubits above the furnace. 48 It spread and burned those Chaldeans whom it found around the furnace. 49 But the angel of the Lord came down into the furnace together with Azarias and his fellows, and he struck the flame of the fire out of the furnace, 50 and made the midst of the furnace as it had been a moist whistling wind, so that the fire didn't touch them at all. It neither hurt nor troubled them. 51 Then the three, as out of one mouth, praised, glorified, and blessed God in the furnace, saying, 52 "Blessed are you, O Lord, you God of our fathers, to be praised and exalted above all forever! 53 Blessed is your glorious and holy name, to be praised and exalted above all forever! 54 Blessed are you in the temple of your holy glory, to be praised and glorified above all forever! 55 Blessed are you who see the depths and sit upon the cherubim, to be praised and exalted above all forever.56 Blessed are you on the throne of your kingdom, to be praised and extolled above all forever! 57 Blessed are you in the firmament of heaven, to be praised and glorified forever! 58 O all you works of the Lord, bless the Lord! Praise and exalt him above all forever!59 O you heavens, bless the Lord! Praise and exalt him above all for ever! 60 O you angels of the Lord, bless the Lord! Praise and exalt him above all forever! 61 O all you waters that are above the sky, bless the Lord! Praise and exalt him above all forever! 62 O all you powers of the Lord, bless the Lord! Praise and exalt him above all forever! 63 O you sun and moon, bless the Lord! Praise and exalt him above all forever! 64 O you stars of heaven, bless the Lord! Praise and exalt him above all forever! 65 O every shower and dew, bless the Lord! Praise and exalt him above all forever! 66 O all you winds, bless the Lord! Praise and exalt him above all forever! 67 O you fire and heat, bless the Lord! Praise and exalt him above all forever! 68 O you dews and storms of snow, bless the Lord! Praise and exalt him above all forever! 69 O you nights and days, bless the Lord! Praise and exalt him above all forever! 70 O you light and darkness, bless the Lord! Praise and exalt him above all forever! 71 O you cold and heat, bless the Lord! Praise and exalt him above all forever! 72 O you frost and snow, bless the Lord! Praise and exalt him above all forever! 73 O you lightnings and clouds, bless the Lord! Praise and exalt him above all forever! 74 O let the earth bless the Lord! Let it praise and exalt him above all forever! 75 O you mountains and hills, bless the Lord! Praise and exalt him above all forever! 76 O all you things that grow on the earth, bless the Lord! Praise and exalt him above all forever! 77O sea and rivers, bless the Lord! Praise and exalt him above all forever! 78 O you springs, bless the Lord! Praise and exalt him above all forever! 79 O you whales and all that move in the waters, bless the Lord! Praise and exalt him above all forever! 80 O all you birds of the air, bless the Lord! Praise and exalt him above all forever! 81 O all you beasts and cattle, bless the Lord! Praise and exalt him above all forever! 82 O you children of men, bless the Lord! Praise and exalt him above all forever! 83 O let Israel bless the Lord! Praise and exalt him above all forever. 84 O you priests of the Lord, bless the Lord! Praise and exalt him above all forever! 85 O you servants of the Lord, bless the Lord! Praise and exalt him above all forever! 86 O you spirits and souls of the righteous, bless the Lord! Praise and exalt him above all forever! 87 O you who are holy and humble of heart, bless the Lord! Praise and exalt him above all forever!88 O Hananiah, Mishael, and Azariah, bless the Lord! Praise and exalt him above all forever; for he has rescued us from Hades, and saved us from the hand of death! He has delivered us out of the midst of the furnace and burning flame. He has delivered us out of the midst of the fire.89 O give thanks to the Lord, for he is good; for his mercy is forever. 90 O all you who worship the Lord, bless the God of gods, praise him, and give him thanks; for his mercy is forever!"

THE HISTORY OF SUSANNA

1A man lived in Babylon, and his name was Joakim. 2 He took a wife, whose name was Susanna, the daughter of Helkias, a very fair woman, and one who feared the Lord. 3 Her parents were also righteous, and taught their daughter according to the law of Moses. 4 Now Joakim was a great rich man, and had a beautiful garden next to his house. The Jews used to come to him, because he was more honorable than all others. 5 The same year, two of the elders of the people were appointed to be judges, such as the Lord spoke of, that wickedness came from Babylon from elders who were judges, who were supposed to govern the people. 6 These were often at Joakim's house. All that had any lawsuits came to them. 7 When the people departed away at noon, Susanna went into her husband's garden to walk. 8 The two elders saw her going in every day and walking; and they were inflamed with lust for her. 9 They perverted their own mind and turned away their eyes, that they might not look to heaven, nor remember just judgments. 10 And although they both were wounded with lust for her, yet dared not show the other his grief. 11 For they were ashamed to declare their lust, what they desired to do with her. 12 Yet they watched eagerly from day to day to see her. 13 The one said to the other, "Let's go home, now; for it is dinner time." 14 So when they had gone out, they parted company, and turning back again, they came to the same place. After they had asked one another the cause, they acknowledged their lust. Then they appointed a time both together, when they might find her alone. 15 It happened, as they watched on an opportune day, she went in as before with only two maids, and she desired to wash herself in the garden; for it was hot. 16 There was nobody there except the two elders who had hid themselves and watched her. 17 Then she said to her maids, “Bring me olive oil and ointment, and shut the garden doors, that I may wash myself.” 18 They did as she asked them and shut the garden doors, and went out themselves at the side doors to fetch the things that she had commanded them. They didn’t see the elders, because they were hidden. 19 Now when the maids had gone out, the two elders rose up and ran to her, saying, 20 “Behold, the garden doors are shut, that no man can see us, and we are in love with you. Therefore consent to us, and lie with us. 21 If you will not, we will testify against you, that a young man was with you; therefore you sent your maids away from you.” 22 Then Susanna sighed, and said, “I am trapped; for if I do this thing, it is death to me. If I don’t do it, I can’t escape your hands. 23 It is better for me to fall into your hands, and not do it, than to sin in the sight of the Lord.” 24 With that Susanna cried with a loud voice; and the two elders cried out against her. 25 Then one of them ran and opened the garden doors. 26 So when the servants of the house heard the cry in the garden, they rushed in at the side door to see what had happened to her. 27 But when the elders had told their tale, the servants were greatly ashamed; for there was never such a report made of Susanna. 28 It came to pass on the next day, when the people assembled to her husband Joakim, the two elders came full of their wicked intent against Susanna to put her to death, 29 and said before the people, “Send for Susanna, the daughter of Helkias, Joakim’s wife.” So they sent; 30 and she came with her father and mother, her children, and all her kindred. 31 Now Susanna was a very delicate woman, and beautiful to behold. 32 These wicked men commanded her to be unveiled, for she was veiled, that they might be filled with her beauty. 33 Therefore her friends and all who saw her wept. 34 Then the two elders stood up in the midst of the people and laid their hands upon her head. 35 She, weeping, looked up toward heaven; for her heart trusted in the Lord. 36 The elders said, “As we walked in the garden alone, this woman came in with two maids, shut the garden doors, and sent the maids away. 37 Then a young man who was hidden there came to her and lay with her. 38 And we, being in a corner of the garden, saw this wickedness and ran to them. 39 And when we saw them together, we couldn’t hold the man; for he was stronger than we, and opened the doors, and leaped out. 40 But having taken this woman, we asked who the young man was, but she would not tell us.

We testify these things. 41 Then the assembly believed them, as those who were elders of the people and judges; so they condemned her to death. 42 Then Susanna cried out with a loud voice, and said, “O everlasting God, you know the secrets, and know all things before they happen. 43 You know that they have testified falsely against me. Behold, I must die, even though I never did such things as these men have maliciously invented against me.” 44 The Lord heard her voice. 45 Therefore when she was led away to be put to death, God raised up the holy spirit of a young youth, whose name was Daniel. 46 He cried with a loud voice, “I am clear from the blood of this woman!”47 Then all the people turned them toward him, and said, “What do these words that you have spoken mean?” 48 So he, standing in the midst of them, said, “Are you all such fools, you sons of Israel, that without examination or knowledge of the truth you have condemned a daughter of Israel? 49 Return again to the place of judgment; for these have testified falsely against her.”50 Therefore all the people turned again in haste, and the elders said to him, “Come, sit down among us, and show it to us, seeing God has given you the honor of an elder.” 51 Then Daniel said to them, “Put them far apart from each another, and I will examine them.” 52 So when they were put apart one from another, he called one of them, and said to him, “O you who have become old in wickedness, now your sins have returned which you have committed before, 53 in pronouncing unjust judgment, condemning the innocent, and letting the guilty go free; although the Lord says, ‘You shall not kill the innocent and righteous.’ 54 Now then, if you saw her, tell me, under which tree did you see them companying together?” He answered, “Under a mastick tree.” 55 And Daniel said, “You have certainly lied against your own head; for even now the angel of God has received the sentence of God and will cut you in two.” 56 So he put him aside, and commanded to bring the other, and said to him, “O you seed of Canaan, and not of Judah, beauty has deceived you, and lust has perverted your heart. 57 Thus you have dealt with the daughters of Israel, and they for fear were intimate with you; but the daughter of Judah would not tolerate your wickedness. 58 Now therefore tell me, under which tree did you take them being intimate together?” He answered, “Under an evergreen oak tree.” 59 Then Daniel said to him, “You have also certainly lied against your own head; for the angel of God waits with the sword to cut you in two, that he may destroy you.” 60 With that, all the assembly cried out with a loud voice, and blessed God, who saves those who hope in him. 61 Then they arose against the two elders, for Daniel had convicted them of false testimony out of their own mouth. 62 According to the law of Moses they did to them what they maliciously intended to do to their neighbor. They put them to death, and the innocent blood was saved the same day. 63 Therefore Helkias and his wife praised God for their daughter Susanna, with Joakim her husband, and all the kindred, because there was no dishonesty found in her. 64 And from that day forth, Daniel had a great reputation in the sight of the people.

BEL AND THE DRAGON

1King Astyages was gathered to his fathers, and Cyrus the Persian received his kingdom. 2 Daniel lived with the king, and was honored above all his friends. 3 Now the Babylonians had an idol called Bel, and every day twelve great measures of fine flour, forty sheep, and six firkins of wine were spent on it. 4 The king honored it and went daily to worship it; but Daniel worshiped his own God. The king said to him, "Why don't you worship Bel?" 5 He said, "Because I may not honor idols made with hands, but only the living God, who has created the sky and the earth, and has sovereignty over all flesh." 6 Then the king said to him, "Don't you think that Bel is a living god? Don't you see how much he eats and drinks every day?" 7 Then Daniel laughed, and said, "O king, don't be deceived; for this is just clay inside, and brass outside, and never ate or drank anything." 8 So the king was angry, and called for his priests, and said to them, "If you don't tell me who this is who devours these expenses, you shall die. 9 But if you can show me that Bel devours them, then Daniel shall die; for he has spoken blasphemy against Bel." Daniel said to the king, "Let it be according to your word." 10 Now there were seventy priests of Bel, besides their wives and children. The king went with Daniel into Bel's temple. 11 So Bel's priests said, "Behold, we will leave; but you, O king, set out the food, and mix the wine and set it out, shut the door securely, and seal it with your own signet. 12 When you come in the morning, if you don't find that Bel has eaten everything, we will suffer death, or else Daniel, who speaks falsely against us." 13 They weren't concerned, for under the table they had made a secret entrance, by which they entered in continually, and consumed those things. 14 It happened, when they had gone out, the king set the food before Bel. Now Daniel had commanded his servants to bring ashes, and they scattered them all over the temple in the presence of the king alone. Then they went out, shut the door, sealed it with the king's signet, and so departed. 15 Now in the night, the priests came with their wives and children, as they usually did, and ate and drank it all. 16 In the morning, the king arose, and Daniel with him. 17 The king said, "Daniel, are the seals whole?" He said, "Yes, O king, they are whole." 18 And as soon as he had opened the door, the king looked at the table, and cried with a loud voice, "You are great, O Bel, and with you is no deceit at all!" 19 Then Daniel laughed, and held the king that he should not go in, and said, "Behold now the pavement, and mark well whose footsteps these are." 20 The king said, "I see the footsteps of men, women, and children." Then the king was angry, 21 and took the priests with their wives and children, who showed him the secret doors, where they came in and consumed the things that were on the table. 22 Therefore the king killed them, and delivered Bel into Daniel's power, who overthrew it and its temple. 23 In that same place there was a great dragon which the people of Babylon worshiped. 24 The king said to Daniel, "Will you also say that this is of brass? Behold, he lives, eats and drinks. You can't say that he is no living god. Therefore worship him." 25 Then Daniel said, "I will worship the Lord my God; for he is a living God. 26 But allow me, O king, and I will kill this dragon without sword or staff." The king said, "I allow you." 27 Then Daniel took pitch, fat, and hair, and melted them together, and made lumps of them. He put these in the dragon's mouth, so the dragon ate and burst apart. Daniel said, "Behold, these are the gods you all worship." 28 When the people of Babylon heard that, they took great indignation, and conspired against the king, saying, "The king has become a Jew. He has pulled down Bel, slain the dragon, and put the priests to the sword." 29 So they came to the king, and said, "Deliver Daniel to us, or else we will destroy you and your house." 30 Now when the king saw that they trapped him, being constrained, the king delivered Daniel to them. 31 They cast him into the lion's den, where he was six days. 32 There were seven lions in the den, and they had been giving them two carcasses and two sheep every day, which then were not given to them, intending that they would devour Daniel. 33 Now there was in Jewry the prophet Habakkuk, who had made stew, and had broken bread into a bowl. He was going into the field to bring it to the reapers. 34 But the angel of the Lord said to Habakkuk, "Go carry the dinner that you have into Babylon to Daniel, in the lions' den." 35 Habakkuk said, "Lord, I never saw Babylon. I don't know where the den is." 36 Then the angel of the Lord took him by the crown, and lifted him up by the hair of his head, and with the blast of his breath set him in Babylon over the den. 37 Habakkuk cried, saying, "O Daniel, Daniel, take the dinner which God has sent you." 38 Daniel said, "You have remembered me, O God! You haven't forsaken those who love you!" 39 So Daniel arose and ate; and the angel of God set Habakkuk in his own place again immediately. 40 On the seventh day, the king came to mourn for Daniel. When he came to the den, he looked in, and, behold, Daniel was sitting. 41 Then the king cried with a loud voice, saying, "Great are you, O Lord, you God of Daniel, and there is none other beside you!" 42 So he drew him out, and cast those that were the cause of his destruction into the den; and they were devoured in a moment before his face.

THE WISDOM OF SOLOMON

1

1 Love righteousness, all you who are judges of the earth. Think of the Lord with a good mind. Seek him in singleness of heart, 2 because he is found by those who don't put him to the test, and is manifested to those who trust him. 3 for crooked thoughts separate from God. His Power convicts when it is tested, and exposes the foolish; 4 because wisdom will not enter into a soul that devises evil, nor dwell in a body that is enslaved by sin. 5 For a holy spirit of discipline will flee deceit, and will depart from thoughts that are without understanding, and will be ashamed when unrighteousness has come in. 6 For wisdom is a spirit who loves man, and she will not hold a blasphemer guiltless for his lips, because God is witness of his inmost self, and is a true overseer of his heart, and a hearer of his tongue. 7 Because the spirit of the Lord has filled the world, and that which holds all things together knows what is said. 8 Therefore no one who utters unrighteous things will be unseen; neither will Justice, when it convicts, pass him by. 9 For in his counsels the ungodly will be searched out, and the sound of his words will come to the Lord to bring his lawless deeds to conviction; 10 because a jealous ear listens to all things, and the noise of murmurings is not hidden. 11 Beware then of unprofitable murmuring,and keep your tongue from slander; because no secret utterance will go on its way void,and a lying mouth destroys a soul. 12 Don't court death in the error of your life.Don't draw destruction upon yourselves by the works of your hands; 13 because God didn't make death, neither does he delight when the living perish.14 For he created all things that they might have being.The generative powers of the world are wholesome, and there is no poison of destruction in them, nor has Hades royal dominion upon earth; 15 for righteousness is immortal, 16 but ungodly men by their hands and their words summon death; deeming him a friend they pined away. They made a covenant with him, because they are worthy to belong with him.

2

1 For they said within themselves, with unsound reasoning, "Our life is short and sorrowful. There is no healing when a man comes to his end, and no one was ever known who was released from Hades. 2 Because we were born by mere chance,and hereafter we will be as though we had never been, because the breath in our nostrils is smoke, and reason is a spark kindled by the beating of our heart,

3 which being extinguished, the body will be turned into ashes, and the spirit will be dispersed as thin air. 4 Our name will be forgotten in time. No one will remember our works. Our life will pass away as the traces of a cloud, and will be scattered as is a mist, when it is chased by the rays of the sun, and overcome by its heat. 5 For our allotted time is the passing of a shadow, and our end doesn't retreat, because it is securely sealed, and no one turns it back. 6 "Come therefore and let's enjoy the good things that exist. Let's use the creation earnestly as in our youth. 7 Let's fill ourselves with costly wine and perfumes,and let no spring flower pass us by. 8 Let's crown ourselves with rosebuds before they wither. 9 Let none of us go without his share in our proud revelry. Let's leave tokens of mirth everywhere,because this is our portion, and this is our lot. 10 Let's oppress the righteous poor. Let's not spare the widow, nor regard the gray hair of the old man. 11 But let our strength be a law of righteousness; for that which is weak is proven useless. 12 But let's lie in wait for the righteous man, because he annoys us, is contrary to our works, reproaches us with sins against the law,and charges us with sins against our training. 13 He professes to have knowledge of God, and calls himself a child of the Lord. 14 He became to us a reproof of our thoughts. 15 He is grievous to us even to look at, because his life is unlike other men's, and his paths are strange. 16 We were regarded by him as something worthless, and he abstains from our ways as from uncleanness. He calls the latter end of the righteous happy. He boasts that God is his father. 17 Let's see if his words are true. Let's test what will happen at the end of his life. 18 For if the righteous man is God's son, he will uphold him, and he will deliver him out of the hand of his adversaries. 19 Let's test him with insult and torture, that we may find out how gentle he is, and test his patience. 20 Let's condemn him to a shameful death, for he will be protected, according to his words." 21 Thus they reasoned, and they were led astray; for their wickedness blinded them, 22 and they didn't know the mysteries of God, neither did they hope for wages of holiness, nor did they discern that there is a prize for blameless souls. 23 Because God created man for incorruption, and made him an image of his own everlastingness; 24 but death entered into the world by the envy of the devil, and those who belong to him experience it.

3

1 But the souls of the righteous are in the hand of God, and no torment will touch them. 2 In the eyes of the foolish they seemed to have died. Their departure was considered a disaster, 3 and their travel away from us ruin, but they are in peace. 4 For even if in the sight of men they are punished, their hope is full of immortality. 5 Having borne a little chastening, they will receive

great good; because God tested them, and found them worthy of himself.

6 He tested them like gold in the furnace, and he accepted them as a whole burnt offering. 7 In the time of their visitation they will shine. They will run back and forth like sparks among stubble. 8 They will judge nations and have dominion over peoples. The Lord will reign over them forever. 9 Those who trust him will understand truth. The faithful will live with him in love,because grace and mercy are with his chosen ones. 10 But the ungodly will be punished even as their reasoning deserves,those who neglected righteousness and revolted from the Lord; 11 for he who despises wisdom and discipline is miserable. Their hope is void and their toils unprofitable. Their works are useless. 12 Their wives are foolish and their children are wicked. 13 Their descendants are cursed.For the barren woman who is undefiled is happy, she who has not conceived in transgression. She will have fruit when God examines souls. 14 So is the eunuch which has done no lawless deed with his hands, nor imagined wicked things against the Lord; for a precious gift will be given to him for his faithfulness, and a delightful inheritance in the Lord's sanctuary. 15 For good labors have fruit of great renown. The root of understanding can't fail. 16 But children of adulterers will not come to maturity. The seed of an unlawful union will vanish away. 17 For if they live long, they will not be esteemed, and in the end, their old age will be without honor. 18 If they die young, they will have no hope, nor consolation in the day of judgment. 19 For the end of an unrighteous generation is always grievous.

4

1 It is better to be childless with virtue, for immortality is in the memory of virtue,because it is recognized both before God and before men. 2 When it is present, people imitate it. They long after it when it has departed. Throughout all time it marches, crowned in triumph, victorious in the competition for the prizes that are undefiled. 3 But the multiplying brood of the ungodly will be of no profit, and their illegitimate offshoots won't take deep root,nor will they establish a sure hold. 4 For even if they grow branches and flourish for a season, standing unsure, they will be shaken by the wind. They will be uprooted by the violence of winds. 5 Their branches will be broken off before they come to maturity. Their fruit will be useless, never ripe to eat, and fit for nothing. 6 For unlawfully conceived children are witnesses of wickedness against parents when they are investigated. 7 But a righteous man, even if he dies before his time, will be at rest. 8 For honorable old age is not that which stands in length of time, nor is its measure given by number of years, 9 but understanding is gray hair to men, and an unspotted life is ripe old age. 10 Being found well-

pleasing to God, someone was loved. While living among sinners he was transported. 11 He was caught away, lest evil should change his understanding, or guile deceive his soul. 12 For the fascination of wickedness obscures the things which are good, and the whirl of desire perverts an innocent mind. 13 Being made perfect quickly, he filled a long time; 14 for his soul was pleasing to the Lord. Therefore he hurried out of the midst of wickedness. 15 But the peoples saw and didn't understand, not considering this, that grace and mercy are with his chosen, and that he visits his holy ones; 16 but a righteous man who is dead will condemn the ungodly who are living, and youth who is quickly perfected will condemn the many years of an unrighteous man's old age.

17 For the ungodly will see a wise man's end,and won't understand what the Lord planned for him, and why he safely kept him. 18 They will see, and they will despise; but the Lord will laugh them to scorn. After this, they will become a dishonored carcass and a reproach among the dead forever; 19 because he will dash them speechless to the ground, and will shake them from the foundations. They will lie utterly waste. They will be in anguish and their memory will perish. 20 They will come with coward fear when their sins are counted. Their lawless deeds will convict them to their face.

5

1 Then the righteous man will stand in great boldness before the face of those who afflicted him, and those who make his labors of no account. 2 When they see him, they will be troubled with terrible fear, and will be amazed at the marvel of salvation. 3 They will speak among themselves repenting, and for distress of spirit they will groan,"This was he whom we used to hold in derision, as a parable of reproach. 4 We fools considered his life madness, and his end without honor. 5 How was he counted among sons of God? How is his lot among saints? 6 Truly we went astray from the way of truth. The light of righteousness didn't shine for us. The sun didn't rise for us. 7 We took our fill of the paths of lawlessness and destruction. We traveled through trackless deserts, but we didn't know the Lord's way. 8 What did our arrogance profit us? What good have riches and boasting brought us? 9 Those things all passed away as a shadow, like a rumor that runs by, 10 like a ship passing through the billowy water, which, when it has gone by, there is no trace to be found, no pathway of its keel in the waves. 11 Or it is like when a bird flies through the air, no evidence of its passage is found, but the light wind, lashed with the stroke of its pinions, and torn apart with the violent rush of the moving wings, is passed through. Afterwards no sign of its coming remains. 12 Or it is like when an arrow is shot at a mark, the air it divided closes up again immediately, so that men don't

know where it passed through. 13 So we also, as soon as we were born, ceased to be; and we had no sign of virtue to show, but we were utterly consumed in our wickedness." 14 Because the hope of the ungodly man is like chaff carried by the wind, and as foam vanishing before a tempest; and is scattered like smoke by the wind, and passes by as the remembrance of a guest who stays just a day. 15 But the righteous live forever. Their reward is in the Lord, and the care for them with the Most High. 16 Therefore they will receive the crown of royal dignity and the diadem of beauty from the Lord's hand, because he will cover them with his right hand, and he will shield them with his arm. 17 He will take his zeal as complete armor, and will make the whole creation his weapons to punish his enemies: 18 He will put on righteousness as a breastplate, and will wear impartial judgment as a helmet. 19 He will take holiness as an invincible shield. 20 He will sharpen stern wrath for a sword. The universe will go with him to fight against his frenzied foes. 21 Shafts of lightning will fly with true aim. They will leap to the mark from the clouds, as from a well-drawn bow. 22 Hailstones full of wrath will be hurled as from a catapult. The water of the sea will be angered against them. Rivers will sternly overwhelm them. 23 A mighty wind will encounter them. It will winnow them away like a tempest. So lawlessness will make all the land desolate.Their evil-doing will overturn the thrones of princes.

6

1 Hear therefore, you kings, and understand. Learn, you judges of the ends of the earth. 2 Give ear, you rulers who have dominion over many people, and make your boast in multitudes of nations, 3 because your dominion was given to you from the Lord, and your sovereignty from the Most High. He will search out your works, and will inquire about your plans, 4 because being officers of his kingdom, you didn't judge rightly, nor did you keep the law, nor did you walk according to God's counsel. 5 He will come upon you awfully and swiftly, because a stern judgment comes on those who are in high places. 6 For the man of low estate may be pardoned in mercy, but mighty men will be mightily tested. 7 For the Sovereign Lord of all will not be impressed with anyone, neither will he show deference to greatness; because it is he who made both small and great, and cares about them all; 8 but the scrutiny that comes upon the powerful is strict. 9 Therefore, my words are to you, O princes, that you may learn wisdom and not fall away. 10 For those who have kept the things that are holy in holiness will be made holy. Those who have been taught them will find what to say in defense. 11 Therefore set your desire on my words. Long for them, and you princes will be instructed. 12 Wisdom is radiant and doesn't fade away;and is easily seen by those

who love her, and found by those who seek her. 13 She anticipates those who desire her, making herself known. 14 He who rises up early to seek her won't have difficulty, for he will find her sitting at his gates. 15 For to think upon her is perfection of understanding, and he who watches for her will quickly be free from care; 16 because she herself goes around, seeking those who are worthy of her, and in their paths she appears to them graciously, and in every purpose she meets them. 17 For her true beginning is desire for instruction; and desire for instruction is love. 18 And love is observance of her laws. To give heed to her laws confirms immortality. 19 Immortality brings closeness to God. 20 So then desire for wisdom promotes to a kingdom. 21 If therefore you delight in thrones and sceptres, you princes of peoples,honor wisdom, that you may reign forever. 22 But what wisdom is, and how she came into being, I will declare. I won't hide mysteries from you; but I will explore from her first beginning, bring the knowledge of her into clear light, and I will not pass by the truth. 23 Indeed, I won't travel with consuming envy, because envy will have no fellowship with wisdom. 24 But a multitude of wise men is salvation to the world, and an understanding king is stability for his people. 25 Therefore be instructed by my words, and you will profit.

7

1 I myself am also mortal, like everyone else, and am a descendant of one formed first and born of the earth. 2 I molded into flesh in the time of ten months in my mother's womb, being compacted in blood from the seed of man and pleasure of marriage. 3 I also, when I was born, drew in the common air, and fell upon the kindred earth, uttering, like all, for my first voice, the same cry. 4 I was nursed with care in swaddling clothes. 5 For no king had a different beginning, 6 but all men have one entrance into life, and a common departure. 7 For this cause I prayed, and understanding was given to me.I asked, and a spirit of wisdom came to me. 8 I preferred her before sceptres and thrones. I considered riches nothing in comparison to her. 9 Neither did I liken to her any priceless gem, because all gold in her presence is a little sand, and silver will be considered as clay before her. 10 I loved her more than health and beauty,and I chose to have her rather than light,because her bright shining is never laid to sleep. 11 All good things came to me with her, and innumerable riches are in her hands. 12 And I rejoiced over them all because wisdom leads them; although I didn't know that she was their mother. 13 As I learned without guile, I impart without grudging. I don't hide her riches. 14 For she is a treasure for men that doesn't fail, and those who use it obtain friendship with God,commended by the gifts which they present through discipline. 15 But may God grant that I may speak

his judgment,and to conceive thoughts worthy of what has been given me; because he is one who guides even wisdom and who corrects the wise. 16 For both we and our words are in his hand, with all understanding and skill in various crafts. 17 For he himself gave me an unerring knowledge of the things that are,to know the structure of the universe and the operation of the elements; 18 the beginning, end, and middle of times; the alternations of the solstices and the changes of seasons; 19 the circuits of years and the positions of stars; 20 the natures of living creatures and the raging of wild beasts; the violence of winds and the thoughts of men; the diversities of plants and the virtues of roots. 21 All things that are either secret or manifest I learned, 22 for wisdom, that is the architect of all things, taught me. For there is in her a spirit that is quick to understand, holy,unique, manifold, subtle, freely moving, clear in utterance, unpolluted, distinct, invulnerable, loving what is good, keen, unhindered, 23 beneficent, loving toward man, steadfast, sure, free from care, all-powerful, all-surveying, and penetrating through all spirits that are quick to understand, pure, most subtle. 24 For wisdom is more mobile than any motion. Yes, she pervades and penetrates all things by reason of her purity. 25 For she is a breath of the power of God,and a pure emanation of the glory of the Almighty. Therefore nothing defiled can find entrance into her. 26 For she is a reflection of everlasting light, an unspotted mirror of the working of God, and an image of his goodness. 27 Although she is one, she has power to do all things. Remaining in herself, she renews all things. From generation to generation passing into holy souls, she makes friends of God and prophets. 28 For God loves nothing as much as one who dwells with wisdom. 29 For she is fairer than the sun, and above all the constellations of the stars. She is better than light. 30 For daylight yields to night, but evil does not prevail against wisdom.

8

1 But she reaches from one end to the other with full strength, and orders all things well. 2 I loved her and sought her from my youth.I sought to take her for my bride. I became enamoured by her beauty. 3 She glorifies her noble birth by living with God. The Sovereign Lord of all loves her. 4 For she is initiated into the knowledge of God, and she chooses his works. 5 But if riches are a desired possession in life, what is richer than wisdom, which makes all things? 6 And if understanding is effective, who more than wisdom is an architect of the things that exist? 7 If a man loves righteousness, the fruits of wisdom's labor are virtues, for she teaches soberness, understanding, righteousness, and courage. There is nothing in life more profitable for people than these. 8 And if anyone longs for wide experience, she knows the things of old, and infers

the things to come. She understands subtleties of speeches and interpretations of dark sayings. She foresees signs and wonders, and the issues of seasons and times. 9 Therefore I determined to take her to live with me,knowing that she is one who would give me good counsel, and encourage me in cares and grief. 10 Because of her, I will have glory among multitudes, and honor in the sight of elders, though I am young. 11 I will be found keen when I give judgment. I will be admired in the presence of rulers. 12 When I am silent, they will wait for me. When I open my lips, they will heed what I say. If I continue speaking, they will put their hands on their mouths. 13 Because of her, I will have immortality, and leave behind an eternal memory to those who come after me. 14 I will govern peoples. Nations will be subjected to me. 15 Dreaded monarchs will fear me when they hear of me. Among the people, I will show myself to be good, and courageous in war. 16 When I come into my house, I will find rest with her. For conversation with her has no bitterness, and living with her has no pain, but gladness and joy. 17 When I considered these things in myself, and thought in my heart how immortality is in kinship to wisdom, 18 and in her friendship is good delight, and in the labors of her hands is wealth that doesn't fail, and understanding is in her companionship, and great renown in having fellowship with her words, I went about seeking how to take her to myself. 19 Now I was a clever child, and received a good soul. 20 Or rather, being good, I came into an undefiled body. 21 But perceiving that I could not otherwise possess wisdom unless God gave her to me— yes, and to know and understand by whom the grace is given— I pleaded with the Lord and implored him, and with my whole heart I said:

9

1 "O God of my ancestors and Lord of mercy, who made all things by your word;2 and by your wisdom you formed man, that he should have dominion over the creatures that were made by you, 3 and rule the world in holiness and righteousness, and execute judgment in uprightness of soul, 4 give me wisdom, her who sits by you on your thrones. Don't reject me from among your servants,5 because I am your servant and the son of your handmaid, a weak and short-lived man, with little power to understand judgment and laws. 6 For even if a man is perfect among the sons of men, if the wisdom that comes from you is not with him, he will count for nothing. 7 You chose me to be king of your people,and a judge for your sons and daughters.8 You gave a command to build a sanctuary on your holy mountain, and an altar in the city where you live, a copy of the holy tent which you prepared from the beginning. 9 Wisdom is with you and knows your works, and was present when you were making the world, and understands what is

pleasing in your eyes, and what is right according to your commandments. 10 Send her from the holy heavens, and ask her to come from the throne of your glory, that being present with me she may work, and I may learn what pleases you well. 11 For she knows all things and understands, and she will guide me prudently in my actions. She will guard me in her glory. 12 So my works will be acceptible. I will judge your people righteously, and I will be worthy of my father's throne. 13 For what man will know the counsel of God? Or who will conceive what the Lord wills? 14 For the thoughts of mortals are unstable,and our plans are prone to fail. 15 For a corruptible body weighs down the soul. The earthy tent burdens a mind that is full of cares. 16 We can hardly guess the things that are on earth, and we find the things that are close at hand with labor; but who has traced out the things that are in the heavens? 17 Who gained knowledge of your counsel, unless you gave wisdom, and sent your holy spirit from on high? 18 It was thus that the ways of those who are on earth were corrected,and men were taught the things that are pleasing to you. They were saved through wisdom."

10

1Wisdom guarded to the end the first formed father of the world, who was created alone, and delivered him out of his own transgression, 2 and gave him strength to rule over all things. 3 But when an unrighteous man fell away from her in his anger, he perished himself in the rage with which he killed his brother. 4 When for his cause the earth was drowning with a flood,wisdom again saved it, guiding the righteous man's course by a paltry piece of wood. 5 Moreover, when nations consenting together in wickedness had been confounded,wisdom knew the righteous man, and preserved him blameless to God,and kept him strong when his heart yearned toward his child. 6 While the ungodly were perishing, wisdom delivered a righteous man,when he fled from the fire that descended out of heaven on the five cities. 7 To whose wickedness a smoking waste still witnesses, and plants bearing fair fruit that doesn't ripen, a disbelieving soul has a memorial: a standing pillar of salt. 8 For having passed wisdom by, not only were they disabled from recognising the things which are good, but they also left behind them for their life a monument of their folly,to the end that where they stumbled, they might fail even to be unseen; 9 but wisdom delivered those who waited on her out of troubles. 10 When a righteous man was a fugitive from a brother's wrath, wisdom guided him in straight paths.She showed him God's kingdom, and gave him knowledge of holy things. She prospered him in his toils, and multiplied the fruits of his labor. 11 When in their covetousness men dealt harshly with him, she stood by him and made him rich. 12 She guarded him from enemies, and she kept him safe from those who lay in wait. Over his severe conflict, she watched as judge, that he might know that godliness is more powerful than every one. 13 When a righteous man was sold, wisdom didn't forsake him, but she delivered him from sin. She went down with him into a dungeon, 14 and in bonds she didn't depart from him, until she brought him the sceptre of a kingdom, and authority over those that dealt like a tyrant with him. She also showed those who had mockingly accused him to be false, and gave him eternal glory. 15Wisdom delivered a holy people and a blameless seed from a nation of oppressors. 16 She entered into the soul of a servant of the Lord, and withstood terrible kings in wonders and signs. 17 She rendered to holy men a reward of their toils. She guided them along a marvelous way, and became to them a covering in the day-time, and a starry flame through the night. 18 She brought them over the Red sea, and led them through much water; 19 but she drowned their enemies, and she cast them up from the bottom of the deep. 20 Therefore the righteous plundered the ungodly, and they sang praise to your holy name, O Lord,and extolled with one accord your hand that fought for them, 21 because wisdom opened the mouth of the mute, and made the tongues of babes to speak clearly.

11

1 Wisdom prospered their works in the hand of a holy prophet. 2 They traveled through a desert without inhabitant,and they pitched their tents in trackless regions. 3 They withstood enemies and repelled foes. 4 They thirsted, and they called upon you, and water was given to them out of the flinty rock, and healing of their thirst out of the hard stone. 5 For by what things their foes were punished, by these they in their need were benefited. 6 When enemies were troubled with clotted blood instead of a river's ever-flowing fountain, 7 to rebuke the decree for the slaying of babies, you gave them abundant water beyond all hope, 8 having shown by the thirst which they had suffered how you punished the adversaries. 9 For when they were tried, although chastened in mercy, they learned how the ungodly were tormented, being judged with wrath. 10 For you tested these as a father admonishing them; but you searched out those as a stern king condemning them. 11 Yes and whether they were far off or near, they were equally distressed; 12 for a double grief seized them,and a groaning at the memory of things past. 13 For when they heard that through their own punishments the others benefited,they recognized the Lord. 14 For him who long before was thrown out and exposed they stopped mocking. In the end of what happened, they marveled, having thirsted in another manner than the righteous. 15 But in return for the senseless imaginings of their unrighteousness,wherein they

were led astray to worship irrational reptiles and wretched vermin, you sent upon them a multitude of irrational creatures to punish them, 16 that they might learn that by what things a man sins, by these he is punished. 17 For your all-powerful hand that created the world out of formless matter didn't lack means to send upon them a multitude of bears, fierce lions, 18 or newly-created and unknown wild beasts, full of rage, either breathing out a blast of fiery breath, or belching out smoke, or flashing dreadful sparks from their eyes; 19 which had power not only to consume them by their violence,but to destroy them even by the terror of their sight. 20 Yes and without these they might have fallen by a single breath, being pursued by Justice, and scattered abroad by the breath of your power; but you arranged all things by measure, number, and weight. 21 For to be greatly strong is yours at all times.Who could withstand the might of your arm? 22 Because the whole world before you is as a grain in a balance, and as a drop of dew that comes down upon the earth in the morning. 23 But you have mercy on all men, because you have power to do all things, and you overlook the sins of men to the end that they may repent. 24 For you love all things that are, and abhor none of the things which you made; For you never would have formed anything if you hated it. 25 How would anything have endured unless you had willed it? Or that which was not called by you, how would it have been preserved? 26 But you spare all things, because they are yours, O Sovereign Lord, you who love the living.

12

1 For your incorruptible spirit is in all things. 2 Therefore you convict little by little those who fall from the right way, and, putting them in remembrance by the things wherein they sin, you admonish them, that escaping from their wickedness they may believe in you, O Lord. 3 For truly the old inhabitants of your holy land,4 hating them because they practiced detestable works of enchantments and unholy rites— 5merciless slaughters of children and sacrificial banquets of men's flesh and of blood 6 allies in an impious fellowship, and murderers of their own helpless babes,it was your counsel to destroy by the hands of our fathers; 7 that the land which in your sight is most precious of all might receive a worthy colony of God's servants. 8 Nevertheless you even spared these as men, and you sent hornets as forerunners of your army, to cause them to perish little by little. 9 Not that you were unable to subdue the ungodly under the hand of the righteous in battle, or by terrible beasts or by a stern word to make away with them at once, 10 but judging them little by little you gave them a chance to repent, not being ignorant that their nature by birth was evil,their wickedness inborn, and that their manner of thought would never be changed. 11 For they were a cursed seed

from the beginning. It wasn't through fear of any that you left them unpunished for their sins. 12 For who will say, "What have you done?"Or "Who will withstand your judgment?" Who will accuse you for the perishing of nations which you caused? Or who will come and stand before you as an avenger for unrighteous men? 13 For there isn't any God beside you that cares for all,that you might show that you didn't judge unrighteously. 14 No king or prince will be able to confront you about those whom you have punished. 15 But being righteous, you rule all things righteously, deeming it a thing alien from your power to condemn one who doesn't deserve to be punished. 16 For your strength is the source of righteousness, and your sovereignty over all makes you to forbear all. 17 For when men don't believe that you are perfect in power, you show your strength, and in dealing with those who think this, you confuse their boldness. 18 But you, being sovereign in strength, judge in gentleness, and with great forbearance you govern us; for the power is yours whenever you desire it. 19 But you taught your people by such works as these,how the righteous must be kind. You made your sons to have good hope, because you give repentance when men have sinned. 20 For if on those who were enemies of your servants and deserving of death, you took vengeance with so great deliberation and indulgence, giving them times and opportunities when they might escape from their wickedness, 21 with how great care you judged your sons, to whose fathers you gave oaths and covenants of good promises! 22 Therefore while you chasten us, you scourge our enemies ten thousand times more, to the intent that we may ponder your goodness when we judge, and when we are judged may look for mercy. 23 Therefore also the unrighteous that lived in a life of folly,you tormented through their own abominations. 24 For truly they went astray very far in the ways of error, Taking as gods those animals which even among their enemies were held in dishonor, deceived like foolish babes. 25 Therefore, as to unreasoning children, you sent your judgment to mock them. 26 But those who would not be admonished by mild correction will experience the deserved judgment of God. 27 For through the sufferings they were indignant of, being punished in these creatures which they supposed to be gods, they saw and recognized as the true God him whom they previously refused to know. Therefore also the result of extreme condemnation came upon them.

13

1 For truly all men who had no perception of God were foolish by nature,and didn't gain power to know him who exists from the good things that are seen. They didn't recognize the architect from his works. 2 But they thought that either fire, or wind, or swift air, or circling stars, or raging water, or

luminaries of heaven were gods that rule the world. 3 If it was through delight in their beauty that they took them to be gods, let them know how much better their Sovereign Lord is than these, for the first author of beauty created them. 4 But if it was through astonishment at their power and influence, then let them understand from them how much more powerful he who formed them is. 5 For from the greatness of the beauty of created things, mankind forms the corresponding perception of their Maker.6 But yet for these men there is but small blame, for they too perhaps go astray while they are seeking God and desiring to find him. 7 For they diligently search while living among his works, and they trust their sight that the things that they look at are beautiful. 8 But again even they are not to be excused. 9 For if they had power to know so much, that they should be able to explore the world, how is it that they didn't find the Sovereign Lord sooner? 10 But they were miserable, and their hopes were in dead things,who called them gods which are works of men's hands, gold and silver, skillfully made, and likenesses of animals,or a useless stone, the work of an ancient hand. 11 Yes and some woodcutter might saw down a tree that is easily moved,skillfully strip away all its bark, and fashion it in attractive form, make a useful vessel to serve his life's needs. 12 Burning the scraps from his handiwork to cook his food, he eats his fill. 13 Taking a discarded scrap which served no purpose,a crooked piece of wood and full of knots, he carves it with the diligence of his idleness, and shapes it by the skill of his idleness. He shapes it in the image of a man,14 or makes it like some worthless animal,smearing it with something red, painting it red, and smearing over every stain in it. 15 Having made a worthy chamber for it,he sets it in a wall, securing it with iron. 16 He plans for it that it may not fall down,knowing that it is unable to help itself (for truly it is an image, and needs help). 17 When he makes his prayer concerning goods and his marriage and children, he is not ashamed to speak to that which has no life. 18 Yes, for health, he calls upon that which is weak. For life, he implores that which is dead. For aid, he supplicates that which has no experience. For a good journey, he asks that which can't so much as move a step. 19 And for profit in business and good success of his hands, he asks ability from that which has hands with no ability.

14

1 Again, one preparing to sail, and about to journey over raging waves, calls upon a piece of wood more fragile than the vessel that carries him. 2 For the hunger for profit planned it, and wisdom was the craftsman who built it. 3 Your providence, O Father, guides it along, because even in the sea you gave a way, and in the waves a sure path,4 showing that you can save out of every danger, that even a man without skill may put to sea. 5

It is your will that the works of your wisdom should not be ineffective. Therefore men also entrust their lives to a little piece of wood, and passing through the surge on a raft come safely to land. 6 For in the old time also, when proud giants were perishing,the hope of the world, taking refuge on a raft, your hand guided the seed of generations of the race of men. 7 For blessed is wood through which comes righteousness; 8 but the idol made with hands is accursed, itself and he that made it;because his was the working, and the corruptible thing was called a god. 9 For both the ungodly and his ungodliness are alike hateful to God; 10 for truly the deed will be punished together with him who committed it. 11 Therefore also there will be a visitation among the idols of the nation,because, though formed of things which God created, they were made an abomination, stumbling blocks to the souls of men, and a snare to the feet of the foolish. 12 For the devising of idols was the beginning of fornication,and the invention of them the corruption of life. 13 For they didn't exist from the beginning, and they won't exist forever. 14 For by the boastfulness of men they entered into the world, and therefore a speedy end was planned for them. 15 For a father worn with untimely grief,making an image of the child quickly taken away, now honored him as a god which was then a dead human being,and delivered to those that were under him mysteries and solemn rites. 16 Afterward the ungodly custom, in process of time grown strong, was kept as a law, and the engraved images received worship by the commandments of princes. 17 And when men could not honor them in presence because they lived far off, imagining the likeness from afar,they made a visible image of the king whom they honored, that by their zeal they might flatter the absent as if present. 18 But worship was raised to a yet higher pitch, even by those who didn't know him,urged forward by the ambition of the architect; 19 for he, wishing perhaps to please his ruler, used his art to force the likeness toward a greater beauty. 20 So the multitude, allured by reason of the grace of his handiwork, now consider an object of devotion him that a little before was honored as a man. 21 And this became an ambush, because men, in bondage either to calamity or to tyranny, invested stones and stocks with the Name that shouldn't be shared. 22 Afterward it was not enough for them to go astray concerning the knowledge of God, but also, while they live in a great war of ignorance, they call a multitude of evils peace. 23 For either slaughtering children in solemn rites, or celebrating secret mysteries,or holding frenzied revels of strange customs, 24 no longer do they guard either life or purity of marriage, but one brings upon another either death by treachery, or anguish by adultery. 25 And all things confusedly are filled with blood and murder, theft and deceit, corruption, faithlessness, tumult, perjury, 26 confusion about what is good, forgetfulness of favors,ingratitude for benefits, defiling of souls, confusion of sex, disorder in marriage, adultery and wantonness. 27 For the worship of idols that may not be named *is a beginning and cause and end of every evil. 28 For their worshipers either make merry to madness, or prophesy lies, or live unrighteously, or lightly commit perjury. 29 For putting their trust in lifeless idols, when they have sworn a wicked oath, they expect not to suffer harm. 30 But on both counts, the just doom will pursue them, because they had evil thoughts of God by giving heed to idols, and swore unrighteously in deceit through contempt for holiness. 31 For it is not the power of things by which men swear, but it is the just penalty for those who sin that always visits the transgression of the unrighteous.

15

1 But you, our God, are gracious and true,patient, and in mercy ordering all things.2 For even if we sin, we are yours, knowing your dominion; but we will not sin, knowing that we have been accounted yours. 3 For to be acquainted with you is perfect righteousness, and to know your dominion is the root of immortality. 4 For we weren't led astray by any evil plan of men's,nor yet by painters' fruitless labor, a form stained with varied colors, 5 the sight of which leads fools into lust. Their desire is for the breathless form of a dead image. 6 Lovers of evil things, and worthy of such hopes, are those who make, desire, and worship them. 7 For a potter, kneading soft earth,laboriously molds each article for our service. He fashions out of the same clay both the vessels that minister to clean uses, and those of a contrary sort, all in like manner. What shall be the use of each article of either sort, the potter is the judge. 8 Also, laboring to an evil end, he molds a vain god out of the same clay, he who, having but a little before been made of earth, after a short space goes his way to the earth out of which he was taken, when he is required to render back the soul which was lent him. 9 However he has anxious care, not because his powers must fail, nor because his span of life is short; But he compares himself with goldsmiths and silversmiths, and he imitates molders in brass, and considers it great that he molds counterfeit gods. 10 His heart is ashes. His hope is of less value than earth. His life is of less honor than clay, 11 because he was ignorant of him who molded him, and of him that inspired into him an active soul, and breathed into him a vital spirit. 12 But he accounted our life to be a game,and our lifetime a festival for profit; for, he says, one must get gain however one can, even if it is by evil 13 For this man, beyond all others, knows that he sins, out of earthy matter making brittle vessels and engraved images. 14 But most foolish and more miserable than a

baby, are the enemies of your people, who oppressed them; 15 because they even considered all the idols of the nations to be gods, which have neither the use of eyes for seeing, nor nostrils for drawing breath, nor ears to hear, nor fingers for handling, and their feet are helpless for walking. 16 For a man made them, and one whose own spirit is borrowed molded them; for no one has power as a man to mold a god like himself. 17 But, being mortal, he makes a dead thing by the work of lawless hands; for he is better than the objects of his worship, since he indeed had life, but they never did. 18 Yes, and they worship the creatures that are most hateful,for, being compared as to lack of sense, these are worse than all others; 19 Neither, as seen beside other creatures, are they beautiful, so that one should desire them, but they have escaped both the praise of God and his blessing.

16

1 For this cause, they were deservedly punished through creatures like those which they worship, and tormented through a multitude of vermin. 2 Instead of this punishment, you, giving benefits to your people, prepared quails for food, a delicacy to satisfy the desire of their appetite, 3 to the end that your enemies, desiring food, might for the hideousness of the creatures sent among them, loathe even the necessary appetite;but these, your people, having for a short time suffered lack, might even partake of delicacies. 4 For it was necessary that inescapable lack should come upon those oppressors, but that to these it should only be showed how their enemies were tormented. 5 For even when terrible raging of wild beasts came upon your people, and they were perishing by the bites of crooked serpents, your wrath didn't continue to the uttermost; 6 but for admonition were they troubled for a short time, having a token of salvation to put them in remembrance of the commandment of your law; 7 for he who turned toward it was not saved because of that which was seen,but because of you, the Savior of all. 8 Yes, and in this you persuaded our enemies that you are he who delivers out of every evil. 9 For the bites of locusts and flies truly killed them. No healing for their life was found, because they were worthy to be punished by such things. 10 But your children weren't overcome by the very fangs of venomous dragons, for your mercy passed by where they were and healed them. 11 For they were bitten to put them in remembrance of your oracles, and were quickly saved, lest, falling into deep forgetfulness, they should become unable to respond to your kindness. 12 For truly it was neither herb nor poultice that cured them,but your word, O Lord, which heals all people. 13 For you have authority over life and death, and you lead down to the gates of Hades, and lead up again. 14 But though a man kills by his wickedness, he can't retrieve the spirit that has departed or release

the imprisoned soul. 15 But it is not possible to escape your hand;16 for ungodly men, refusing to know you, were scourged in the strength of your arm, pursued with strange rains and hails and relentless storms, and utterly consumed with fire. 17 For, what was most marvelous, in the water which quenches all things, the fire burned hotter;for the world fights for the righteous. 18 For at one time the flame was restrained, that it might not burn up the creatures sent against the ungodly, but that these themselves as they looked might see that they were chased by the judgment of God. 19 At another time even in the midst of water it burns more intensely than fire,that it may destroy the produce of an unrighteous land. 20 Instead of these things, you gave your people angels' food to eat,and you provided ready-to-eat bread for them from heaven without toil, having the virtue of every pleasant flavor, and agreeable to every taste.21 For your nature showed your sweetness toward your children, while that bread, serving the desire of the eater, changed itself according to every man's choice. 22 But snow and ice endured fire, and didn't melt,that people might know that fire was destroying the fruits of the enemies, burning in the hail and flashing in the rains; 23 and that this fire, again, in order that righteous people may be nourished, has even forgotten its own power. 24 For the creation, ministering to you, its maker, strains its force against the unrighteous for punishment and in kindness, slackens it on behalf of those who trust in you. 25 Therefore at that time also, converting itself into all forms, it ministered to your all- nourishing bounty, according to the desire of those who had need, 26 that your children, whom you loved, O Lord, might learn that it is not the growth of crops that nourishes a man, but that your word preserves those who trust you. 27 For that which was not destroyed by fire, melted away when it was simply warmed by a faint sunbeam, 28 that it might be known that we must rise before the sun to give you thanks,and must pray to you at the dawning of the light; 29 for the hope of the unthankful will melt as the winter's hoar frost, and will flow away as water that has no use.

17

1 For your judgments are great, and hard to interpret; therefore undisciplined souls went astray. 2 For when lawless men had supposed that they held a holy nation in their power, they, prisoners of darkness, and bound in the fetters of a long night, kept close beneath their roofs, lay exiled from the eternal providence. 3 For while they thought that they were unseen in their secret sins, they were divided from one another by a dark curtain of forgetfulness, stricken with terrible awe, and very troubled by apparitions. 4 For neither did the dark recesses that held them guard them from fears, but terrifying sounds rang around

them, and dismal phantoms appeared with unsmiling faces. 5 And no power of fire prevailed to give light, neither were the brightest flames of the stars strong enough to illuminate that gloomy night; 6 but only the glimmering of a self-kindled fire appeared to them, full of fear. In terror, they considered the things which they saw to be worse than that sight, on which they could not gaze. 7The mockeries of their magic arts were powerless, now, and a shameful rebuke of their boasted understanding: 8 For those who promised to drive away terrors and disorders from a sick soul, these were sick with a ludicrous fearfulness. 9 For even if no troubling thing frighted them, yet, scared with the creeping of vermin and hissing of serpents, 10 they perished trembling in fear, refusing even to look at the air, which could not be escaped on any side. 11For wickedness, condemned by a witness within, is a coward thing, and, being pressed hard by conscience, always has added forecasts of the worst. 12 For fear is nothing else but a surrender of the help which reason offers; 13 and from within, the expectation of being less prefers ignorance of the cause that brings the torment. 14 But they, all through the night which was powerless indeed, and which came upon them out of the recesses of powerless Hades, sleeping the same sleep, 15 now were haunted by monstrous apparitions, and now were paralyzed by their soul's surrendering; for sudden and unexpected fear came upon them. 16 So then whoever it might be, sinking down in his place, was kept captive, shut up in that prison which was not barred with iron; 17 for whether he was a farmer, or a shepherd, or a laborer whose toils were in the wilderness, he was overtaken, and endured that inescapable sentence; for they were all bound with one chain of darkness. 18 Whether there was a whistling wind, or a melodious sound of birds among the spreading branches, or a measured fall of water running violently, 19 or a harsh crashing of rocks hurled down,or the swift course of animals bounding along unseen, or the voice of wild beasts harshly roaring, or an echo rebounding from the hollows of the mountains, all these things paralyzed them with terror. 20 For the whole world was illuminated with clear light, and was occupied with unhindered works, 21 while over them alone was spread a heavy night, an image of the darkness that should afterward receive them; but to themselves, they were heavier than darkness.

18

1 But for your holy ones there was great light. Their enemies, hearing their voice but not seeing their form, counted it a happy thing that they too had suffered, 2 yet for that they do not hurt them, though wronged by them before, they are thankful; and because they had been at variance with them, they begged for pardon.

3 Therefore you provided a burning pillar of fire, to be a guide for your people's unknown journey, and a harmless sun for their glorious exile. 4 For the Egyptians well deserved to be deprived of light and imprisoned by darkness, they who had imprisoned your children, through whom the incorruptible light of the law was to be given to the race of men. 5 After they had taken counsel to kill the babes of the holy ones,and when a single child had been abandoned and saved to convict them of their sin, you took away from them their multitude of children, and destroyed all their army together in a mighty flood. 6 Our fathers were made aware of that night beforehand, that, having sure knowledge, they might be cheered by the oaths which they had trusted. 7 Salvation of the righteous and destruction of the enemies was expected by your people. 8 For as you took vengeance on the adversaries, by the same means, calling us to yourself, you glorified us. 9 For holy children of good men offered sacrifice in secret, and with one consent they agreed to the covenant of the divine law, that they would partake alike in the same good things and the same perils, the fathers already leading the sacred songs of praise. 10 But the discordant cry of the enemies echoed back, and a pitiful voice of lamentation for children was spread abroad. 11 Both servant and master were punished with the same just doom, and the commoner suffering the same as king; 12 Yes, they all together, under one form of death,had corpses without number. For the living were not sufficient even to bury them, Since at a single stroke, their most cherished offspring was consumed. 13 For while they were disbelieving all things by reason of the enchantments, upon the destruction of the firstborn they confessed the people to be God's children. 14 For while peaceful silence wrapped all things, and night in her own swiftness was half spent, 15 your all-powerful word leaped from heaven, from the royal throne, a stern warrior, into the midst of the doomed land, 16 bearing as a sharp sword your authentic commandment,and standing, it filled all things with death,and while it touched the heaven it stood upon the earth. 17 Then immediately apparitions in dreams terribly troubled them, and unexpected fears came upon them. 18 And each, one thrown here half dead, another there, made known why he was dying; 19 for the dreams, disturbing them, forewarned them of this, that they might not perish without knowing why they were afflicted. 20 The experience of death also touched the righteous,and a multitude were destroyed in the wilderness,but the wrath didn't last long. 21 For a blameless man hurried to be their champion, bringing the weapon of his own ministry, prayer, and the atoning sacrifice of incense. He withstood the indignation and set an end to the calamity, showing that he was your servant. 22 And he

overcame the anger, not by strength of body, not by force of weapons, but by his word, he subdued the avenger by bringing to remembrance oaths and covenants made with the fathers. 23 For when the dead had already fallen in heaps one upon another,he intervened and stopped the wrath, and cut off its way to the living. 24 For the whole world was pictured on his long robe, and the glories of the fathers were upon the engraving of the four rows of precious stones, and your majesty was upon the diadem on his head. 25 The destroyer yielded to these, and they feared;for it was enough only to test the wrath.

19

1 But indignation without mercy came upon the ungodly to the end; for God also foreknew their future, 2 how, having changed their minds to let your people go,and having sped them eagerly on their way,they would change their minds and pursue them. 3 For while they were yet in the midst of their mourning, and lamenting at the graves of the dead, they made another foolish decision, and pursued as fugitives those whom they had begged to leave and driven out. 4 For the doom which they deserved was drawing them to this end,and it made them forget the things that had happened to them, hat they might fill up the punishment which was yet lacking from their torments, 5 and that your people might journey on by a marvelous road, but the themselves might find a strange death. 6 For the whole creation, each part in its diverse kind, was made new again,complying with your commandments, that your servants might be kept unharmed. 7 Then the cloud that overshadowed the camp was seen, and dry land rising up out of what had been water,out of the Red sea an unhindered highway,and a grassy plain out of the violent surge,8 by which they passed over with all their army, these who were covered with your hand, having seen strange marvels. 9 For like horses they roamed at large, and they skipped about like lambs, praising you, O Lord, who was their deliverer. 10 For they still remembered the things that happened in the time of their sojourning, how instead of bearing cattle, the land brought forth lice, and instead of fish, the river spewed out a multitude of frogs. 11 But afterwards, they also saw a new kind of birds, when, led on by desire, they asked for luxurious dainties; 12 for, to comfort them, quails came up for them from the sea. 13 Punishments came upon the sinners,not without the signs that were given beforehand by the violence of the thunder, for they justly suffered through their own wickednesses, for the hatred which they practiced toward guests was grievous indeed. 14 For while the others didn’t receive the strangers when they came to them, the Egyptians made slaves of guests who were their benefactors. 15 And not only so, but while punishment of some sort will come upon the

former, since they received as enemies those who were aliens; 16 because these first welcomed with feastings, and then afflicted with dreadful toils, those who had already shared with them in the same rights. 17 And moreover they were stricken with loss of sight (even as were those others at the righteous man's doors), when, being surrounded with yawning darkness, they each looked for the passage through his own door. 18 For as the notes of a lute vary the character of the rhythm,even so the elements, changing their order one with another, continuing always in its sound, as may clearly be conjectured from the sight of the things that have happened. 19 For creatures of the dry land were turned into creatures of the waters, and creatures that swim moved upon the land. 20 Fire kept the mastery of its own power in water, and water forgot its quenching nature. 21 On the contrary, flames didn't consume flesh of perishable creatures that walked among them, neither did they melt the crystalline grains of ambrosial food that were melted easily. 22 For in all things, O Lord, you magnified your people,and you glorified them and didn't lightly regard them, standing by their side in every time and place.

THE BOOK OF SIRACH, or ECCLESIASTICUS

The Prologue.

Whereas many and great things have been delivered to us by the law and the prophets, and by the others that have followed in their steps, for which we must give Israel the praise for instruction and wisdom; and since not only the readers need to become skillful themselves, but also those who love learning must be able to profit those who are outside, both by speaking and writing; my grandfather Jesus, having much given himself to the reading of the law, and the prophets, and the other books of our fathers, and having gained great familiarity with them, was also drawn on himself to write somewhat pertaining to instruction and wisdom, in order that those who love learning, and are devoted to these things, might make progress much more by living according to the law. You are entreated therefore to read with favor and attention, and to pardon us, if in any parts of what we have labored to interpret, we may seem to fail in some of the phrases. For things originally spoken in Hebrew don't have the same force in them when they are translated into another language. Not only these, but the law itself, and the prophecies, and the rest of the books, have no small difference, when they are spoken in their original language. For having come into Egypt in the thirty-eighth year of Energetes the king, and having continued there some time, I found a copy giving no small instruction. I thought it therefore most necessary for me to apply some diligence and travail to translate this book, applying indeed much watchfulness and skill in that space of time to bring the book to an end and publish for them also, who in the land of their travels are desiring to learn, preparing their character in advance, so as to live according to the law.

1

1 All wisdom comes from the Lord, and is with him forever. 2 Who can count the sand of the seas, the drops of rain, and the days of eternity? 3 Who will search out the height of the sky, the breadth of the earth, the deep, and wisdom? 4 Wisdom has been created before all things, and the understanding of prudence from everlasting. 56 To whom has the root of wisdom been revealed? Who has known her shrewd counsels? 78 There is one wise, greatly to be feared, sitting upon his throne: the Lord. 9 He created her. He saw and measured her. He poured her out upon all his works. 10 She is with all flesh according to his gift. He gave her freely to those who love him.11 The fear of the Lord is glory, exultation, gladness, and a crown of rejoicing. 12 The fear of the Lord will delight the heart, and will give gladness, joy, and length of days. 13 Whoever fears the Lord, it will go well with him at the last. He will be blessed in the day of his death.14 To fear the Lord is the beginning of wisdom. It was created together with the faithful in the womb. 15 She laid an eternal foundation with men. She will be trusted among their offspring. 16 To fear the Lord is the fullness of wisdom. She inebriates men with her fruits. 17 She will fill all her house with desirable things, and her storehouses with her produce. 18 The fear of the Lord is the crown of wisdom, making peace and perfect health to flourish.19 He both saw and measured her. He rained down skill and knowledge of understanding, and exalted the honor of those who hold her fast. 20 To fear the Lord is the root of wisdom. Her branches are length of days. 2122 Unjust wrath can never be justified, for his wrath tips the scale to his downfall. 23 A man that is patient will resist for a season, and afterward gladness will spring up to him. 24 He will hide his words until the right moment, and the lips of many will tell of his understanding.25 A wise saying is in the treasures of wisdom; but godliness is an abomination to a sinner. 26 If you desire wisdom, keep the commandments and the Lord will give her to you freely; 27 for the fear of the Lord is wisdom and instruction. Faith and humility are his good pleasure. 28 Don't disobey the fear of the Lord. Don't come to him with a double heart. 29 Don't be a hypocrite in men's sight. Keep watch over your lips. 30 Don't exalt yourself, lest you fall and bring dishonor upon your soul. The Lord will reveal your secrets and will cast you down in the midst of the congregation, because you didn't come to the fear of the Lord and your heart was full of deceit.

2

1 My son, if you come to serve the Lord, prepare your soul for temptation. 2 Set your heart aright, constantly endure, and don't make haste in time of calamity. 3 Cling to him, and don't depart, that you may be increased at your latter end. 4 Accept whatever is brought upon you, and be patient when you suffer humiliation. 5 For gold is tried in the fire, and acceptable men in the furnace of humiliation. 6 Put your trust in him, and he will help you. Make your ways straight, and set your hope on him.7 All you who fear the Lord, wait for his mercy. Don't turn aside, lest you fall. 8 All you who fear the Lord, put your trust in him, and your reward will not fail. 9 All you who fear the Lord, hope for good things, and for eternal gladness and mercy. 10 Look at the generations of old, and see: Who ever put his trust in the Lord, and was ashamed? Or who remained in his fear, and was forsaken? Or who called upon him, and he neglected him? 11 For the Lord is full of compassion and mercy. He forgives sins and saves in time of affliction.12 Woe to fearful hearts, to faint hands, and to the sinner who goes two ways! 13 Woe to the faint heart! For it doesn't believe. Therefore it won't be defended. 14 Woe to you who have lost your patience! And what will you all do when the Lord visits you?15 Those who fear the Lord will not disobey his words. Those who love him will keep his ways. 16 Those who fear the Lord will seek his good pleasure. Those who love him will be filled with the law. 17 Those who fear the Lord will prepare their hearts, and will humble their souls in his sight. 18 We will fall into the hands of the Lord, and not into the hands of men; for as his majesty is, so also is his mercy.

3

1 Hear me, your father, O my children, and do what you hear, that you all may be safe. 2 For the Lord honors the father over the children, and has confirmed the judgment of the mother over her sons. 3 He who honors his father will make atonement for sins. 4 He who gives glory to his mother is as one who lays up treasure. 5 Whoever honors his father will have joy in his own children. He will be heard in the day of his prayer. 6 He who gives glory to his father will have length of days. He who listens to the Lord will bring rest to his mother, 7 and will serve under his parents, as to masters. 8 Honor your father in deed and word, that a blessing may come upon you from him. 9 For the blessing of the father establishes the houses of children, but the curse of the mother roots out the foundations.10 Don't glorify yourself in the dishonor of your father, for your father's dishonor is no glory to you. 11 For the glory of a man is from the honor of his father, and a mother in dishonor is a reproach to her children. 12 My son, help your father in his old age, and don't grieve him as long as he lives. 13 If he fails in understanding, have patience with him. Don't

dishonor him in your full strength. 14 For the kindness to your father will not be forgotten. Instead of sins it will be added to build you up. 15 In the day of your affliction it will be remembered for you, as fair weather upon ice, so your sins will also melt away. 16 He who forsakes his father is as a blasphemer. He who provokes his mother is cursed by the Lord. 17 My son, go on with your business in humility; so you will be loved by an acceptable man. 18 The greater you are, humble yourself the more, and you will find favor before the Lord. 1920 For the power of the Lord is great, and he is glorified by those who are lowly. 21 Don't seek things that are too hard for you, and don't search out things that are above your strength. 22 Think about the things that have been commanded you, for you have no need of the things that are secret. 23 Don't be overly busy in tasks that are beyond you, for more things are shown to you than men can understand. 24 For the conceit of many has led them astray. Evil opinion has caused their judgment to slip. 25There is no light without eyes. There is no wisdom without knowledge.26 A stubborn heart will do badly at the end. He who loves danger will perish in it. 27 A stubborn heart will be burdened with troubles. The sinner will heap sin upon sins. 28 The calamity of the proud has no healing, for a weed of wickedness has taken root in him. 29 The heart of the prudent will understand a proverb. A wise man desires the ear of a listener.30 Water will quench a flaming fire; almsgiving will make atonement for sins. 31 He who repays good turns is mindful of that which comes afterward. In the time of his falling he will find a support.

4

1 My son, don't deprive the poor of his living. Don't make the needy eyes wait long. 2 Don't make a hungry soul sorrowful, or provoke a man in his distress. 3 Don't add more trouble to a heart that is provoked. Don't put off giving to him who is in need. 4 Don't reject a suppliant in his affliction. Don't turn your face away from a poor man. 5 Don't turn your eye away from one who asks. Give no occasion to a man to curse you. 6 For if he curses you in the bitterness of his soul, he who made him will hear his supplication.7 Endear yourself to the assembly. Bow your head to a great man. 8 Incline your ear to a poor man. Answer him with peaceful words in humility. 9 Deliver him who is wronged from the hand of him who wrongs him; Don't be hesitant in giving judgment. 10 Be as a father to the fatherless, and like a husband to their mother. So you will be as a son of the Most High, and he will love you more than your mother does.11 Wisdom exalts her sons, and takes hold of those who seek her. 12 He who loves her loves life. Those who seek her early will be filled with gladness. 13 He who holds her fast will inherit glory. Where he enters, the Lord will bless. 14 Those who serve her minister to the Holy One. The Lord loves those who love her.

15 He who listens to her will judge the nations. He who heeds her will dwell securely. 16 If he trusts her, he will inherit her, and his generations will possess her. 17 For at the first she will walk with him in crooked ways, and will bring fear and dread upon him, and torment him with her discipline, until she may trust his soul, and try him by her judgments. 18 Then she will return him again to the straight way, and will gladden him, and reveal to him her secrets. 19 If he goes astray, she will forsake him, and hand him over to his fall.20 Watch for the opportunity, and beware of evil. Don't be ashamed of your soul. 21 For there is a shame that brings sin, and there is a shame that is glory and grace. 22 Don't show partiality, discrediting your soul. Don't revere any man to your falling. 23 Don't refrain from speaking when it is for safety. Don't hide your wisdom for the sake of seeming fair. 24 For wisdom will be known by speech, and instruction by the word of the tongue. 25 Don't speak against the truth and be shamed for your ignorance. 26 Don't be ashamed to confess your sins. Don't fight the river's current. 27 Don't lay yourself down for a fool to tread upon. Don't be partial to one who is mighty. 28 Strive for the truth to death, and the Lord God will fight for you.29 Don't be hasty with your tongue, or slack and negligent in your deeds. 30 Don't be like a lion in your house, or suspicious of your servants. 31 Don't let your hand be stretched out to receive, and closed when you should repay.

5

1 Don't set your heart upon your goods. Don't say, "They are sufficient for me." 2 Don't follow your own mind and your strength to walk in the desires of your heart. 3 Don't say, "Who will have dominion over me?" for the Lord will surely take vengeance on you.4 Don't say, "I sinned, and what happened to me?" for the Lord is patient. 5 Don't be so confident of atonement that you add sin upon sins. 6 Don't say, "His compassion is great. He will be pacified for the multitude of my sins," for mercy and wrath are with him, and his indignation will rest on sinners. 7 Don't wait to turn to the Lord. Don't put off from day to day; for suddenly the wrath of the Lord will come on you, and you will perish in the time of vengeance.8 Don't set your heart upon unrighteous gains, for you will profit nothing in the day of calamity. 9 Don't winnow with every wind. Don't walk in every path. This is what the sinner who has a double tongue does. 10 Be steadfast in your understanding. Let your speech be consistent.11 Be swift to hear and answer with patience. 12 If you have understanding, answer your neighbor; but if not, put your hand over your mouth. 13 Glory and dishonor is in talk. A man's tongue may be his downfall. 14 Don't be called a whisperer. Don't lie in wait with your tongue; for shame is on the thief, and an evil condemnation is on him who has a double tongue. 15 Don't be ignorant in a great or small matter.

6

1 Don't become an enemy instead of a friend; for an evil name will inherit shame and reproach. So it is with the sinner who has a double tongue.2 Don't exalt yourself in the counsel of your soul, that your soul not be torn in pieces like a bull. 3 You will eat up your leaves, destroy your fruit, and leave yourself like a dry tree. 4 A wicked soul will destroy him who has it, and will make him a laughing stock to his enemies.5 Sweet words will multiply a man's friends. A gracious tongue will multiply courtesies. 6 Let those that are at peace with you be many, but your advisers one of a thousand. 7 If you want to gain a friend, get him in a time of testing, and don't be in a hurry to trust him. 8 For there is a friend just for an occasion. He won't continue in the day of your affliction. 9 And there is a friend who turns into an enemy. He will discover strife to your reproach. 10 And there is a friend who is a companion at the table, but he won't continue in the day of your affliction. 11 In your prosperity he will be as yourself, and will be bold over your servants. 12 If you are brought low, he will be against you, and will hide himself from your face. 13 Separate yourself from your enemies, and beware of your friends.14 A faithful friend is a strong defense. He who has found him has found a treasure. 15 There is nothing that can be taken in exchange for a faithful friend. His excellency is beyond price. 16 A faithful friend is a life-saving medicine. Those who fear the Lord will find him. 17 He who fears the Lord directs his friendship properly; for as he is, so is his neighbor also.18 My son, gather instruction from your youth up. Even when you have gray hair you will find wisdom. 19 Come to her as one who plows and sows and wait for her good fruit; for your toil will be little in her cultivation, and you will soon eat of her fruit. 20 How exceedingly harsh she is to the unlearned! He who is without understanding will not remain in her. 21 She will rest upon him as a mighty stone of trial. He won't hesitate to cast her from him. 22 For wisdom is according to her name. She isn't manifest to many.23 Give ear, my son, and accept my judgment. Don't refuse my counsel. 24 Bring your feet into her fetters, and your neck into her chain. 25 Put your shoulder under her and bear her. Don't be grieved with her bonds. 26 Come to her with all your soul. Keep her ways with your whole power. 27 Search and seek, and she will be made known to you. When you get hold of her, don't let her go. 28 For at the last

you will find her rest; and she will be turned for you into gladness. 29 Her fetters will be to you for a covering of strength, and her chains for a robe of glory. 30 For there is a golden ornament upon her, and her bands are * a purple cord. 31 You shall put her on as a robe of glory, and shall put her on as a crown of rejoicing.32 My son, if you are willing, you will be instructed. If you will yield your soul, you will be prudent. 33 If you love to hear, you will receive. If you incline your ear, you will be wise. 34 Stand in the multitude of the elders. Attach yourself to whomever is wise. 35 Be willing to listen to every godly discourse. Don't let the proverbs of understanding escape you. 36 If you see a man of understanding, get to him early. Let your foot wear out the steps of his doors. 37 Let your mind dwell on the ordinances of the Lord and meditate continually on his commandments. He will establish your heart and your desire for wisdom will be given to you.

7

1 Do no evil, so no evil will overtake you. 2 Depart from wrong, and it will turn away from you. 3 My son, don't sow upon the furrows of unrighteousness, and you won't reap them sevenfold.4 Don't seek preeminence from the Lord, nor the seat of honor from the king. 5 Don't justify yourself in the presence of the Lord, and don't display your wisdom before the king. 6 Don't seek to be a judge, lest you not be able to take away iniquities, lest perhaps you fear the person of a mighty man, and lay a stumbling block in the way of your uprightness.7 Don't sin against the multitude of the city. Don't disgrace yourself in the crowd.8 Don't commit a sin twice, for even in one you will not be unpunished. 9 Don't say, "He will look upon the multitude of my gifts. When I make an offering to the Most High God, he will accept it." 10 Don't be faint-hearted in your prayer. Don't neglect to give alms.11 Don't laugh a man to scorn when he is in the bitterness of his soul, for there is one who humbles and exalts. 12Don't devise a lie against your brother, or do the same to a friend. 13 Refuse to utter a lie, for that habit results in no good. 14 Don't babble in the assembly of elders. Don't repeat your words in your prayer.15 Don't hate hard labor or farm work, which the Most High has created. 16 Don't number yourself among the multitude of sinners. Remember that wrath will not wait. 17 Humble your soul greatly, for the punishment of the ungodly man is fire and the worm.18 Don't exchange a friend for something, neither a true brother for the gold of Ophir. 19 Don't deprive yourself of a wise and good wife, for her grace is worth more than gold. 20 Don't abuse a servant who works faithfully, or a hireling who gives you his life. 21 Let your soul love a wise servant. Don't defraud him of liberty.22 Do you have cattle? Look after them. If they are profitable to you, let them stay by you. 23 Do you have children? Correct them, and make them obedient from their youth. 24 Do you have daughters? Take care of their bodies, and don't be overly indulgent toward them. 25 Give your daughter in marriage, and you will have accomplished a great matter. Give her to a man of understanding.26 Do you have a wife who pleases you? Don't cast her out. But don't trust yourself to one who is hateful.27 Honor your father with your whole heart, and don't forget the birth pangs of your

mother. 28 Remember that you were born of them. What will you repay them for the things that they have done for you?29 Fear the Lord with all your soul; and revere his priests. 30 With all your strength love him who made you. Don't forsake his ministers. 31 Fear the Lord and honor the priest. Give him his portion, even as it is commanded you: the first fruits, the trespass offering, the gift of the shoulders, the sacrifice of sanctification, and the first fruits of holy things.32 Also stretch out your hand to the poor man, that your blessing may be complete. 33 A gift has grace in the sight of every living man. Don't withhold grace for a dead man. 34 Don't avoid those who weep, and mourn with those who mourn. 35 Don't be slow to visit a sick man, for by such things you will gain love. 36 In all your words, remember eternity, and you will never sin.

8

1 Don't contend with a mighty man, lest perhaps you fall into his hands. 2 Don't strive with a rich man, lest perhaps he overpower you; for gold has destroyed many, and turned away the hearts of kings. 3 Don't argue with a loudmouthed man. Don't heap wood upon his fire.4 Don't make fun of a rude man, lest your ancestors be dishonored. 5 Don't reproach a man when he turns from sin. Remember that we are all worthy of punishment. 6 Don't dishonor a man in his old age, for some of us are also growing old. 7 Don't rejoice over anyone's death. Remember that we all die.8 Don't neglect the discourse of the wise. Be conversant with their proverbs; for from them you will learn discipline and how to serve great men. 9 Don't miss the discourse of the aged, for they also learned from their parents, because from them you will learn understanding, and to give an answer in time of need.10 Don't kindle the coals of a sinner, lest you be burned with the flame of his fire. 11 Don't rise up from the presence of an insolent man, lest he lie in wait as an ambush for your mouth. 12 Don't lend to a man who is stronger than you; and if you lend, count it as a loss. 13 Don't be surety beyond your means. If you give surety, think as one who will have to pay.14 Don't go to law with a judge; for according to his honor they will give judgment for him. 15 Don't travel with a reckless man, lest he be burdensome to you; for he will do as he pleases, and you will perish with his folly. 16 Don't fight with a wrathful man. Don't travel with him through the desert, for blood is as nothing in his sight. Where there is no help, he will overthrow you. 17 Don't consult with a fool, for he will not be able to keep a secret. 18 Do no secret thing before a stranger, for you don't know what it will cause. 19 Don't open your heart to every man. Don't let him return you a favor.

9

1 Don't be jealous over the wife of your bosom, and don't teach her an evil lesson against yourself. 2 Don't

give your soul to a woman and let her trample down your strength. 3 Don't go to meet a woman who plays the prostitute, lest perhaps you fall into her snares. 4 Don't associate with a woman who is a singer, lest perhaps you be caught by her tricks. 5 Don't gaze at a virgin, lest perhaps you stumble and incur penalties for her. 6 Don't give your soul to prostitutes, that you not lose your inheritance. 7 Don't look around in the streets of the city. Don't wander in its deserted places. 8 Turn your eye away from a beautiful woman, and don't gaze at another's beauty. Many have been led astray by the beauty of a woman; and with this, passion is kindled like a fire. 9 Don't dine at all with a woman who has a husband, or revel with her at wine, lest perhaps your soul turn away to her, and with your spirit you slide into destruction.10 Don't forsake an old friend; for a new one is not comparable to him. A new friend is like new wine: if it becomes old, you will drink it with gladness.11 Don't envy the success of a sinner; for you don't know what his end will be. 12 Don't delight in the delights of the ungodly. Remember they will not go unpunished to the grave.13 Keep yourself far from the man who has power to kill, and you will not be troubled by the fear of death. If you come to him, commit no fault, lest he take away your life. Know surely that you go about in the midst of snares, and walk upon the battlements of a city.14 As well as you can, aim to know your neighbors, and take counsel with the wise. 15 Let your conversation be with men of understanding. Let all your discourse be in the law of the Most High. 16 Let righteous people be companions at your table. Let your glorying be in the fear of the Lord.17 A work is commended because of the skill of the artisan; so he who rules the people will be considered wise for his speech. 18 A loudmouthed man is dangerous in his city. He who is reckless in his speech will be hated.

10

1 A wise judge will instruct his people. The government of a man of understanding will be well ordered. 2 As is the judge of his people, so are his officials. As the city's ruler is, so are all those who dwell in it. 3 An undisciplined king will destroy his people. A city will be established through the understanding of the powerful. 4 The government of the earth is in the Lord's hand. In due time, he will raise up over it the right person at the right time. 5 A man's prosperity is in the Lord's hand. He will lay his honor upon the person of the scribe.6 Don't be angry with your neighbor for every wrong. Do nothing by works of violence. 7 Pride is hateful before the Lord and men. Arrogance is abhorrent in the judgment of both. 8 Sovereignty is transferred from nation to nation because of injustice, violence, and greed for money. 9Why are dirt and ashes proud? Because in life, my body decays. 10A long disease mocks the physician. The king of today will die tomorrow. 11 For

when a man is dead, he will inherit maggots, vermin, and worms. 12It is the beginning of pride when a man departs from the Lord. His heart has departed from him who made him. 13 For the beginning of pride is sin. He who keeps it will pour out abomination. For this cause the Lord brought upon them strange calamities and utterly overthrew them. 14 The Lord cast down the thrones of rulers and set the lowly in their place. 15 The Lord plucked up the roots of nations and planted the lowly in their place. 16 The Lord overthrew the lands of nations and destroyed them to the foundations of the earth. 17 He took some of them away and destroyed them, and made their memory to cease from the earth. 18 Pride has not been created for men, nor wrathful anger for the offspring of women.19Whose offspring has honor? Human offspring who fear the Lord. Whose offspring has no honor? Human offspring who break the commandments. 20 In the midst of kindred he who rules them has honor. Those who fear the Lord have honor in his eyes. 2122 The rich man, the honorable, and the poor all glory in the fear of the Lord. 23 It is not right to dishonor a poor man who has understanding. It is not fitting to glorify a man who is a sinner. 24 The prince, the judge, and the mighty man will be honored. There is not one of them greater than he who fears the Lord. 25 Free men will minister to a wise servant. A man who has knowledge will not complain.26 Don't flaunt your wisdom in doing your work. Don't boast in the time of your distress. 27Better is he who labors and abounds in all things, than he who boasts and lacks bread. 28 My son, glorify your soul in humility, and ascribe to yourself honor according to your worthiness. 29 Who will justify him who sins against his own soul? Who will honor him who dishonors his own life?30 A poor man is honored for his knowledge. A rich man is honored for his riches. 31 But he who is honored in poverty, how much more in riches? He who is dishonored in riches, how much more in poverty?

11

1 The wisdom of the lowly will lift up his head, and make him sit in the midst of great men.2 Don't commend a man for his good looks. Don't abhor a man for his outward appearance. 3 The bee is little among flying creatures, but what it produces is the best of confections. 4 Don't boast about the clothes you wear, and don't exalt yourself in the day of honor; for the Lord's works are wonderful, and his works are hidden among men. 5 Many kings have sat down upon the ground, but one who was never thought of has worn a crown. 6 Many mighty men have been greatly disgraced. Men of renown have been delivered into other men's hands.7 Don't blame before you investigate. Understand first, and then rebuke. 8 Don't answer before you have heard. Don't interrupt while someone else is speaking. 9 Don't argue about a matter that doesn't concern you.

Don't sit with sinners when they judge.10 My son, don't be busy about many matters; for if you meddle much, you will not be unpunished. If you pursue, you will not overtake, and you will not escape by fleeing. 11 There is one who toils, labors, and hurries, and is even more behind. 12 There is one who is sluggish, and needs help, lacking in strength, and who abounds in poverty, but the Lord's eyes looked upon him for good, and he raised him up from his low condition, 13 and lifted up his head so that many marveled at him.14 Good things and bad, life and death, poverty and riches, are from the Lord. 15-1617 The Lord's gift remains with the godly. His good pleasure will prosper forever. 18 One grows rich by his diligence and self-denial, and this is the portion of his reward: 19 when he says, "I have found rest, and now I will eat of my goods!" he doesn't know how much time will pass until he leaves them to others and dies. 20 Be steadfast in your covenant and be doing it, and grow old in your work.21 Don't marvel at the works of a sinner, but trust the Lord and stay in your labor; for it is an easy thing in the sight of the Lord to swiftly and suddenly make a poor man rich. 22 The Lord's blessing is in the reward of the godly. He makes his blessing flourish in an hour that comes swiftly. 23 Don't say, "What use is there of me? What further good things can be mine?" 24 Don't say, "I have enough. What harm could happen to me now?" 25 In the day of good things, bad things are forgotten. In the day of bad things, a man will not remember things that are good. 26 For it is an easy thing in the sight of the Lord to reward a man in the day of death according to his ways. 27 The affliction of an hour causes delights to be forgotten. In the end, a man's deeds are revealed. 28 Call no man happy before his death. A man will be known in his children.29 Don't bring every man into your house, for many are the tricks of a deceitful man. 30 Like a decoy partridge in a cage, so is the heart of a proud man. Like a spy, he looks for your weakness. 31 For he lies in wait to turn things that are good into evil, and assigns blame in things that are praiseworthy. 32 From a spark of fire, a heap of many coals is kindled, and a sinful man lies in wait to shed blood. 33 Take heed of an evil-doer, for he plans wicked things, lest perhaps he ruin your reputation forever. 34 Receive a stranger into your house, and he will distract you with arguments and estrange you from your own family.

12

1 If you do good, know to whom you do it, and your good deeds will have thanks. 2 Do good to a godly man, and you will find a reward— if not from him, then from the Most High. 3 No good will come to him who continues to do evil, nor to him who gives no alms. 4 Give to the godly man, and don't help the sinner. 5 Do good to one who is lowly. Don't give to an ungodly man. Keep back his bread, and don't give it to him, lest he subdue you with it; for you

would receive twice as much evil for all the good you would have done to him. 6 For the Most High also hates sinners, and will repay vengeance to the ungodly.7 Give to the good man, and don't help the sinner.8 A man's friend won't be fully tried in prosperity. His enemy won't be hidden in adversity. 9 In a man's prosperity, his enemies are grieved. In his adversity, even his friend leaves. 10 Never trust your enemy, for his wickedness is like corrosion in copper. 11 Though he humbles himself and walks bowed down, still be careful and beware of him. You will be to him as one who has wiped a mirror, to be sure it doesn't completely tarnish. 12 Don't set him next to you, lest he overthrow you and stand in your place. Don't let him sit on your right hand, lest he seek to take your seat, and at the last you acknowledge my words, and be pricked with my sayings.13 Who will pity a charmer that is bitten by a snake, or any who come near wild beasts? 14 Even so, who will pity him who goes to a sinner, and is associated with him in his sins? 15 For a while he will stay with you, and if you falter, he will not stay. 16 The enemy will speak sweetly with his lips, and in his heart plan to throw you into a pit. The enemy may weep with his eyes, but if he finds opportunity, he will want more blood. 17 If adversity meets you, you will find him there before you. Pretending to help you, he will trip you. 18 He will shake his head, clap his hands, whisper much, and change his countenance.

13

1 He who touches pitch will be defiled. He who has fellowship with a proud man will become like him. 2 Don't take up a burden above your strength. Have no fellowship with one who is mightier and richer than yourself. What fellowship would the earthen pot have with the kettle? The kettle will strike, and the pot will be dashed in pieces. 3 The rich man does a wrong and threatens. The poor is wronged and apologizes. 4 If you are profitable, he will exploit you. If you are in need, he will forsake you. 5 If you own something, he will live with you. He will drain your resources and will not be sorry. 6 Does he need you? Then he will deceive you, smile at you, and give you hope. He will speak kindly to you and say, "What do you need?" 7 He will shame you by his delicacies until he has made you bare twice or thrice, and in the end he will laugh you to scorn. Afterward he will see you, will forsake you, and shake his head at you.8 Beware that you are not deceived and brought low in your enjoyment. 9 If a mighty man invites you, be reserved, and he will invite you more. 10 Don't press him, lest you be thrust back. Don't stand far off, lest you be forgotten. 11 Don't try to speak with him as an equal, and don't believe his many words; for he will test you with much talk, and will examine you in a smiling manner. 12 He who doesn't keep secrets to himself is unmerciful. He won't hesitate to harm and to bind. 13 Keep them to

yourself and be careful, for you walk in danger of falling. 1415 Every living creature loves its own kind, and every man loves his neighbor. 16 All flesh associates with their own kind. A man will stick to people like himself. 17 What fellowship would the wolf have with the lamb? So is the sinner to the godly. 18 What peace is there between a hyena and a dog? What peace is there between a rich man and the poor? 19 Wild donkeys are the prey of lions in the wilderness; likewise poor men are feeding grounds for the rich. 20 Lowliness is an abomination to a proud man; likewise a poor man is an abomination to the rich.21 When a rich man is shaken, he is supported by his friends, but when the humble is down, he is pushed away even by his friends. 22 When a rich man falls, there are many helpers. He speaks things not to be spoken, and men justify him. A humble man falls, and men rebuke him. He utters wisdom, and is not listened to. 23 A rich man speaks, and all keep silence. They extol what he says to the clouds. A poor man speaks, and they say, "Who is this?" If he stumbles, they will help to overthrow him.24 Riches are good if they have no sin. Poverty is evil only in the opinion of the ungodly.25 The heart of a man changes his countenance, whether it is for good or for evil.26 A cheerful countenance is a sign of a prosperous heart. Devising proverbs takes strenuous thinking.

14

1 Blessed is the man who has not slipped with his mouth, and doesn't suffer from sorrow for sins. 2 Blessed is he whose soul does not condemn him, and who has not given up hope.3 Riches are not appropriate for a stingy person. What would a miser do with money? 4 He who gathers by denying himself gathers for others. Others will revel in his goods. 5 If one is mean to himself, to whom will he be good? He won't enjoy his possessions. 6 There is none more evil than he who is grudging to himself. This is a punishment for his wickedness. 7 Even if he does good, he does it in forgetfulness. In the end, he reveals his wickedness. 8 A miser is evil. He turns away and disregards souls. 9 A covetous man's eye is not satisfied with his portion. Wicked injustice dries up his soul. 10 A miser begrudges bread, and it is lacking at his table.11 My son, according to what you have, treat yourself well, and bring worthy offerings to the Lord. 12 Remember that death will not wait, and that the covenant of Hades hasn't been shown to you. 13 Do good to your friends before you die. According to your ability, reach out and give to them. 14 Don't deprive yourself of a good day. Don't let your share of a desired good pass you by. 15 Won't you leave your labors to another, and your toils be divided by lot? 16 Give, take, and treat yourself well, because there is no seeking of luxury in Hades. 17 All flesh grows old like a garment, for the covenant from the beginning is, "You must

die!" 18 Like the leaves flourishing on a thick tree, some it sheds, and some grow, so also are the generations of flesh and blood: one comes to an end and another is born. 19 Every work rots and falls away, and its builder will depart with it.20 Blessed is the man who meditates on wisdom, and who reasons by his understanding. 21 He who considers her ways in his heart will also have knowledge of her secrets. 22 Go after her like a hunter, and lie in wait in her paths. 23 He who peers in at her windows will also listen at her doors. 24 He who lodges close to her house will also fasten a nail in her walls. 25 He will pitch his tent near at hand to her, and will lodge in a lodging where good things are. 26 He will set his children under her shelter, and will rest under her branches. 27 By her he will be covered from heat, and will lodge in her glory.

15

1 He who fears the Lord will do this. He who has possession of the law will obtain her. 2 She will meet him like a mother, and receive him like a wife married in her virginity. 3 She will feed him with bread of understanding and give him water of wisdom to drink. 4 He will be stayed upon her, and will not be moved. He will rely upon her, and will not be confounded. 5 She will exalt him above his neighbors. She will open his mouth in the midst of the congregation. 6 He will inherit joy, a crown of gladness, and an everlasting name. 7 Foolish men will not obtain her. Sinners will not see her. 8 She is far from pride. Liars will not remember her. 9 Praise is not attractive in the mouth of a sinner; for it was not sent to him from the Lord. 10 For praise will be spoken in wisdom; The Lord will prosper it.11 Don't say, "It is through the Lord that I fell away;" for you shall not do the things that he hates. 12 Don't say, "It is he that caused me to err;" for he has no need of a sinful man. 13 The Lord hates every abomination; and those who fear him don't love them. 14 He himself made man from the beginning and left him in the hand of his own counsel. 15 If you choose, you can keep the commandments. To be faithful is a matter of your choice. 16 He has set fire and water before you. You will stretch forth your hand to whichever you desire. 17 Before man is life and death. Whichever he likes, it will be given to him. 18 For the wisdom of the Lord is great. He is mighty in power, and sees all things. 19 His eyes are upon those who fear him. He knows every act of man. 20 He has not commanded any man to be ungodly. He has not given any man license to sin.

16

1 Don't desire a multitude of unprofitable children, neither delight in ungodly sons. 2 If they multiply, don't delight in them unless the fear of the Lord is in them. 3 Don't trust in their life. Don't rely on their numbers; for one can be better than a thousand, and to die childless than to have ungodly children. 4 For from one who has

understanding, a city will be populated, but a race of wicked men will be made desolate. 5 I have seen many such things with my eyes. My ear has heard mightier things than these.6 In a congregation of sinners, a fire will be kindled. In a disobedient nation, wrath is kindled. 7 He was not pacified toward the giants of old time, who revolted in their strength. 8 He didn't spare Lot's neighbors, whom he abhorred for their pride. 9 He didn't pity the people of perdition who were taken away in their sins, 10 or in like manner, the six hundred thousand footmen who were gathered together in the hardness of their hearts. 11 Even if there is one stiff-necked person, it is a marvel if he will be unpunished; for mercy and wrath are both with him who is mighty to forgive, and he pours out wrath. 12 As his mercy is great, so is his correction also. He judges a man according to his works. 13 The sinner will not escape with plunder. The perseverance of the godly will not be frustrated. 14 He will make room for every work of mercy. Each man will receive according to his works. 15-1617 Don't say, "I will be hidden from the Lord," and "Who will remember me from on high?" I will not be known among so many people, for what is my soul in a boundless creation? 18 Behold, the heaven, the heaven of heavens, the deep, and the earth, will be moved when he visits. 19 The mountains and the foundations of the earth together are shaken with trembling when he looks at them. 20 No heart will think about these things. Who could comprehend his ways? 21 Like a tempest which no man can see, so, the majority of his works are hidden. 22 Who will declare his works of righteousness? Who will wait for them? For his covenant is afar off.23 He who is lacking in understanding thinks about these things. An unwise and erring man thinks foolishly.24 My son, listen to me, learn knowledge, and heed my words with your heart. 25 I will impart instruction with precision, and declare knowledge exactly.26 In the judgment of the Lord are his works from the beginning. From the making of them he determined their boundaries. 27 He arranged his works for all time, and their beginnings to their generations. They aren't hungry or weary, and they don't cease from their works. 28 No one pushes aside his neighbor. They will never disobey his word. 29 After this also the Lord looked at the earth and filled it with his blessings. 30 All manner of living things covered its surface, and they return into it.

17

1 The Lord created mankind out of earth, and turned them back to it again. 2 He gave them days by number, and a set time, and gave them authority over the things that are on it. 3 He endowed them with strength proper to them, and made them according to his own image. 4 He put the fear of man upon all flesh, and gave him dominion over beasts and birds. 56 He gave them counsel, tongue, eyes, ears, and

heart to have understanding. 7 He filled them with the knowledge of wisdom, and showed them good and evil. 8 He set his eye upon their hearts, to show them the majesty of his works. 910 And they will praise his holy name, that they may declare the majesty of his works. 11 He added to them knowledge, and gave them a law of life for a heritage. 12 He made an everlasting covenant with them, and showed them his decrees. 13 Their eyes saw the majesty of his glory. Their ears heard the glory of his voice. 14 He said to them, "Beware of all unrighteousness." So he gave them commandment, each man concerning his neighbor.15 Their ways are ever before him. They will not be hidden from his eyes. 1617For every nation he appointed a ruler, but Israel is the Lord's portion. 1819 All their works are as clear as the sun before him. His eyes are continually upon their ways. 20 Their iniquities are not hidden from him. All their sins are before the Lord. 2122 With him the alms of a man is as a signet. He will keep a man's kindness as the pupil of the eye.23 Afterwards he will rise up and repay them, and render their repayment upon their head. 24 However to those who repent he grants a return. He comforts those who are losing hope.25 Return to the Lord, and forsake sins. Make your prayer before his face offend less. 26 Turn again to the Most High, and turn away from iniquity. Greatly hate the abominable thing. 27 Who will give praise to the Most High in Hades, in place of the living who return thanks? 28 Thanksgiving perishes from the dead, as from one who doesn't exist. He who is in life and health will praise the Lord. 29 How great is the mercy of the Lord, and his forgiveness to those who turn to him! 30 For humans are not capable of everything, because the son of man is not immortal. 31 What is brighter than the sun? Yet even this can be eclipsed. So flesh and blood devise evil. 32 He looks upon the power of the height of heaven, while all men are earth and ashes.

18

1 He who lives forever created the whole universe. 2 The Lord alone is just. 34 He has given power to declare his works to no one. Who could trace out his mighty deeds? 5 Who could measure the strength of his majesty? Who could also proclaim his mercies? 6 As for the wondrous works of the Lord, it is not possible to take from them nor add to them, neither is it possible to explore them. 7 When a man has finished, then he is just at the beginning. When he stops, then he will be perplexed. 8 What is mankind, and what purpose do they serve? What is their good, and what is their evil? 9 The number of man's days at the most are a hundred years. 10 As a drop of water from the sea, and a pebble from the sand, so are a few years in the day of eternity. 11 For this cause the Lord was patient over them, and poured out his mercy upon them. 12 He saw and perceived their end, that it is evil. Therefore he

multiplied his forgiveness. 13 The mercy of a man is on his neighbor; but the mercy of the Lord is on all flesh: reproving, chastening, teaching, and bringing back, as a shepherd does his flock. 14 He has mercy on those who accept chastening, and that diligently seek after his judgments.15 My son, don't add reproach to your good deeds, and no harsh words in any of your giving. 16 Doesn't the dew relieve the scorching heat? So a word is better than a gift. 17 Behold, isn't a word better than a gift? Both are with a gracious person. 18 A fool is ungracious and abusive. The gift of an grudging person consumes the eyes.19 Learn before you speak. Take care of your health before you get sick. 20 Before judgment, examine yourself, and in the hour of scrutiny you will find forgiveness. 21 Humble yourself before you get sick. In the time of sins, repent. 22 Let nothing hinder you to pay your vow in due time. Don't wait until death to be released. 23 Before you make a vow, prepare yourself. Don't be like a man who tests the Lord. 24 Think about the wrath coming in the days of the end, and the time of vengeance, when he turns away his face. 25 In the days of fullness remember the time of hunger. Remember poverty and lack in the days of wealth. 26 From morning until evening, the time changes. All things are speedy before the Lord. 27 A wise man is cautious in everything. In days of sinning, he will beware of offense.28 Every man of understanding knows wisdom. He will give thanks to him who found her. 29 They who were of understanding in sayings also became wise themselves, and poured out apt proverbs.30 Don't go after your lusts. Restrain your appetites. 31 If you give fully to your soul the delight of her desire, she will make you the laughing stock of your enemies. 32 Don't make merry in much luxury, and don't be tied to its expense. 33 Don't be made a beggar by banqueting with borrowed money when you have nothing in your purse.

19

1 A worker who is a drunkard will not become rich. He who despises small things will fall little by little. 2 Wine and women will make men of understanding go astray. He who joins with prostitutes is reckless. 3 Decay and worms will have him as their heritage. A reckless soul will be taken away.4 He who is hasty to trust is shallow-hearted. He who sins offends against his own soul. 5 He who rejoices in wickedness will be condemned.6 He who hates gossip has less wickedness. 7 Never repeat what is told you, and you won't lose anything. 8 Whether it is of friend or foe, don't tell it. Unless it is a sin to you, don't reveal it. 9 For if he has heard you and observed you, when the time comes, he will hate you. 10 Have you heard something? Let it die with you. Be brave: it will not make you burst! 11 A fool will travail in pain with a word, as a woman in labor with a child. 12 As an arrow that sticks in the flesh of the thigh,

so is gossip in a fool.13 Question a friend; it may be he didn't do it. If he did something, it may be that he may do it no more. 14 Question your neighbor; it may be he didn't say it. If he has said it, it may be that he may not say it again. 15 Question a friend; for many times there is slander. Don't trust every word. 16 There is one who slips, and not from the heart. Who is he who hasn't sinned with his tongue? 17 Reprove your neighbor before you threaten him; and give place to the law of the Most High. 18-1920 All wisdom is the fear of the Lord. In all wisdom is the doing of the law. 2122 The knowledge of wickedness is not wisdom. The prudence of sinners is not counsel. 23 There is a wickedness, and it is an abomination. There is a fool lacking in wisdom. 24 Better is one who has little understanding, and fears God, than one who has much intelligence and transgresses the law. 25 There is an exquisite subtlety, and it is unjust. And there is one who perverts favor to gain a judgment.26 There is one who does wickedly, who hangs down his head with mourning; but inwardly he is full of deceit, 27 bowing down his face, and pretending to be deaf in one ear. Where he isn't known, he will take advantage of you. 28 And if for lack of power he is hindered from sinning, if he finds opportunity, he will do mischief. 29 A man will be known by his appearance. One who has understanding will be known by his face when you meet him. 30 A man's attire, grinning laughter, and the way he walks show what he is.

20

1 There is a reproof that is not timely; and there is a person who is wise enough to keep silent. 2 How good is it to reprove, rather than to be angry. He who confesses will be kept back from harm. 34 As is the lust of a eunuch to deflower a virgin, so is he who executes judgments with violence. 5 There is one who keeps silent and is found wise; and there is one who is hated for his much talk. 6 There is one who keeps silent, for he has no answer to make; And there is one who keeps silent, knowing when to speak. 7 A wise man will be silent until his time has come, but the braggart and fool will miss his time. 8 He who uses many words will be abhorred. He who takes authority for himself will be hated in it.9 There is a prosperity that a man finds in misfortunes; and there is a gain that turns to loss. 10 There is a gift that will

not profit you; and there is a gift that pays back double. 11 There are losses because of glory; and there is one who has lifted up his head from a low estate. 12 There is one who buys much for a little, and pays for it again sevenfold. 13 He who is wise in words will make himself beloved; but the pleasantries of fools will be wasted. 14 The gift of a fool will not profit you, for he looks for repayment many times instead of one. 15 He will give little and insult much. He will open his mouth like a crier. Today he will lend, and tomorrow he will ask for it back. Such a one is a hateful man. 16 The fool will say, "I have no friend, and I have no thanks for my good deeds. Those who eat my bread have an evil tongue." 17 How often, and of how many, will he be laughed to scorn!18 A slip on a pavement is better than a slip with the tongue. So the fall of the wicked will come speedily. 19 A man without grace is a tale out of season. It will be continually in the mouth of the ignorant. 20 A parable from a fool's mouth will be rejected; for he won't tell it at the proper time.21 There is one who is hindered from sinning through lack. When he rests, he will not be troubled. 22 There is one who destroys his soul through bashfulness. By a foolish countenance, he will destroy it. 23 There is one who for bashfulness makes promises to his friend; and he makes him his enemy for nothing.24 A lie is an ugly blot on a person. It will be continually in the mouth of the ignorant. 25 A thief is better than a man who is continually lying, but they both will inherit destruction. 26 The destination of a liar is dishonor. His shame is with him continually.27 He who is wise in words will advance himself. And one who is prudent will please great men. 28 He who tills his land will raise his harvest high. He who pleases great men will get pardon for iniquity. 29 Favors and gifts blind the eyes of the wise, and as a muzzle on the mouth, turn away reproofs. 30 Wisdom that is hidden, and treasure that is out of sight—what profit is in either of them? 31 Better is a man who hides his folly than a man who hides his wisdom. 32

21

1 My son, have you sinned? Do it no more; and ask forgiveness for your past sins. 2 Flee from sin as from the face of a snake; for if you go near, it will bite you. Its teeth are like lion's teeth, slaying people's souls. 3 All iniquity is as a two-edged sword. Its stroke has no healing.4 Terror and violence will waste away riches. So the house of an arrogant man will be laid waste. 5 Supplication from a poor man's mouth reaches to the ears of God, and his judgment comes speedily. 6 One who hates reproof is in the path of the sinner. He who fears the Lord will repent in his heart. 7 He who is mighty in tongue is known far away; but the man of understanding knows when he slips.8 He who builds his house with other men's money is like one who gathers stones for his own tomb. 9 The congregation of wicked men is as a bundle of tow with a flame of fire at the end of them. 10 The way of sinners is paved with stones; and at the end of it is the pit of Hades.11 He who keeps the law becomes master of its intent. The fulfilment of the fear of the Lord is wisdom. 12 He who is not clever will not be instructed. There is a cleverness which makes bitterness abound. 13 The knowledge of a wise man will be made to abound as a flood, and his counsel as a fountain of life. 14 The inward parts of a fool are like a broken vessel.

He will hold no knowledge.15 If a man of knowledge hears a wise word, he will commend it and add to it. The wanton man hears it, and it displeases him, so he throws it away behind his back. 16 The chatter of a fool is like a burden in the way, but grace will be found on the lips of the wise. 17 The utterance of the prudent man will be sought for in the congregation. They will ponder his words in their heart.18 As a house that is destroyed, so is wisdom to a fool. The knowledge of an unwise man is talk without sense.19 Instruction is as fetters on the feet of an unwise man, and as manacles on the right hand. 20 A fool lifts up his voice with laughter, but a clever man smiles quietly. 21 Instruction is to a prudent man as an ornament of gold, and as a bracelet upon his right arm.22 The foot of a fool rushes into a house, but a man of experience will be ashamed of entering. 23 A foolish man peers into the door of a house, but a man who is instructed will stand outside. 24 It is rude for someone to listen at a door, but a prudent person will be grieved with the disgrace. 25The lips of strangers will be grieved at these things, but the words of prudent men will be weighed in the balance.26 The heart of fools is in their mouth, but the mouth of wise men is their heart. 27 When the ungodly curses an adversary, he curses his own soul. 28 A whisperer defiles his own soul, and will be hated wherever he travels.

22

1 A slothful man is compared to a stone that is defiled. Everyone will at hiss at him in his disgrace. 2 A slothful man is compared to the filth of a dunghill. Anyone who picks it up will shake it out of his hand.3 An undisciplined child is a disgrace to his father, and a foolish daughter is born to his loss. 4 A prudent daughter will inherit a husband of her own. She who brings shame is the grief of her father. 5 She who is arrogant brings shame on father and husband. She will be despised by both of them. 6 Ill-timed conversation is like music in mourning, but stripes and correction are wisdom in every season.7 He who teaches a fool is like one who glues potsherds together, even like one who wakes a sleeper out of a deep sleep. 8 He who teaches a fool is as one who teaches a man who slumbers. In the end he will say, “What is it?” 9-1011 Weep for the dead, for he lacks light. Weep for a fool, for he lacks understanding. Weep more sweetly for the dead, because he has found rest, but the life of the fool is worse than death. 12 Mourning for the dead lasts seven days, but for a fool and an ungodly man, it lasts all the days of his life.13 Don’t talk much with a foolish man, and don’t go to one who has no understanding. Beware of him, lest you have trouble and be defiled in his onslaught. Turn away from him, and you will find rest, and you won’t be wearied in his madness. 14 What would be heavier than lead? What is its name, but “Fool”? 15 Sand, salt, and a mass of iron is

easier to bear than a man without understanding.16 Timber girded and bound into a building will not be released with shaking. So a heart established in due season on well advised counsel will not be afraid. 17 A heart settled upon a thoughtful understanding is as an ornament of plaster on a polished wall. 18 Fences set on a high place will not stand against the wind; so a fearful heart in the imagination of a fool will not stand against any fear.19 He who pricks the eye will make tears fall. He who pricks the heart makes it show feeling. 20 Whoever casts a stone at birds scares them away. He who insults a friend will dissolve friendship. 21 If you have drawn a sword against a friend, don't despair, for there may be a way back. 22 If you have opened your mouth against a friend, don't be afraid, for there may be reconciliation, unless it is for insulting, arrogance, disclosing of a secret, or a treacherous blow— for these things any friend will flee.23 Gain trust with your neighbor in his poverty, that in his prosperity you may have gladness. Stay steadfast to him in the time of his affliction, that you may be heir with him in his inheritance.24 Before fire is the vapor and smoke of a furnace, so insults precede bloodshed. 25 I won't be ashamed to shelter a friend. I won't hide myself from his face. 26 If any evil happens to me because of him, everyone who hears it will beware of him.27 Who will set a watch over my mouth, and a seal of shrewdness upon my lips, that I may not fall from it, and that my tongue may not destroy me?

23

1 O Lord, Father and Master of my life, don't abandon me to their counsel. Don't let me fall because of them. 2 Who will set scourges over my thought, and a discipline of wisdom over my heart, that they spare me not for my errors, and not overlook their sins? 3 Otherwise my errors might be multiplied, and my sins abound, I fall before my adversaries, and my enemy rejoice over me.4 O Lord, Father and God of my life, don't give me a haughty eyes,5 and turn away evil desire from me.6 Let neither gluttony nor lust overtake me. Don't give me over to a shameless mind.7 Listen, my children, to the discipline of the mouth. He who keeps it will not be caught. 8 The sinner will be overpowered through his lips. By them, the insulter and the arrogant will stumble. 9 Don't accustom your mouth to an oath, and don't be accustomed to naming the Holy One, 10 for as a servant who is continually scourged will not lack bruises, so he also who swears and continually utters the Name will not be cleansed from sin. 11 A man of many oaths will be filled with iniquity. The scourge will not depart from his house. If he offends, his sin will be upon him. If he disregards it, he has sinned doubly. If he has sworn falsely, he will not be justified, for his house will be filled with calamities.12 There is a manner of speech that is clothed with death. Let it not be found in the

heritage of Jacob, for all these things will be far from the godly, and they will not wallow in sins. 13 Don't accustom your mouth to gross rudeness, for it involves sinful speech. 14 Remember your father and your mother, for you sit in the midst of great men, that you be not forgetful before them, and become a fool by your bad habit; so you may wish that you had not been born, and curse the day of your birth. 15 A man who is accustomed to abusive language won't be corrected all the days of his life.16 Two sorts of people multiply sins, and the third will bring wrath: a hot passion, like a burning fire, will not be quenched until it is consumed; a fornicator in the body of his flesh will never cease until he has burned out the fire. 17 All bread is sweet to a fornicator. He will not cease until he dies. 18 A man who goes astray from his own marriage bed says in his heart, "Who sees me? Darkness is around me, and the walls hide me. No one sees me. Of whom am I afraid? The Most High will not remember my sins." 19 The eyes of men are his terror. He doesn't know that the eyes of the Lord are ten thousand times brighter than the sun, seeing all the ways of men, and looking into secret places. 20 All things were known to him before they were created, and also after they were completed. 21 This man will be punished in the streets of the city. He will be seized where he least expects it.22 So also is a wife who leaves her husband, and produces an heir by another man. 23 For first, she was disobedient in the law of the Most High. Second, she trespassed against her own husband. Third, she played the adulteress in fornication, and had children by another man. 24 She shall be brought out into the congregation. Her punishment will extend to her children. 25 Her children will not take root. Her branches will bear no fruit. 26 She will leave her memory for a curse. Her reproach won't be blotted out. 27 And those who are left behind will know that there is nothing better than the fear of the Lord, and nothing sweeter than to heed the commandments of the Lord. 28

24

1 Wisdom will praise her own soul, and will proclaim her glory in the midst of her people. 2 She will open her mouth in the congregation of the Most High, and proclaim her glory in the presence of his power. 3 "I came out of the mouth of the Most High, and covered the earth as a mist. 4 I lived in high places, and my throne is in the pillar of the cloud. 5 Alone I surrounded the circuit of heaven, and walked in the depth of the abyss. 6 In the waves of the sea, and in all the earth, and in every people and nation, I obtained a possession. 7 With all these I sought rest. In whose inheritance shall I lodge? 8 Then the Creator of all things gave me a command. He who created me made my tent to rest, and said, 'Let your dwelling be in Jacob, and your inheritance in Israel.' 9 He created me from the beginning, before the ages. For all ages, I will not cease

to exist. 10 In the holy tabernacle, I ministered before him. So I was established in Zion. 11 In the beloved city, likewise he gave me rest. In Jerusalem was my domain. 12 I took root in a people that was honored, even in the portion of the Lord's own inheritance.13 I was exalted like a cedar in Lebanon, And like a cypress tree on the mountains of Hermon. 14 I was exalted like a palm tree on the sea shore, like rose bushes in Jericho, and like a fair olive tree in the plain. I was exalted like a plane tree. 15 Like cinnamon and aspalathus, I have given a scent to perfumes. Like choice myrrh, I spread abroad a pleasant fragrance, like galbanum, onycha, stacte, and as the smell of frankincense in the tabernacle. 16 Like the terebinth, I stretched out my branches. My branches are glorious and graceful. 17 Like the vine, I put forth grace. My flowers are the fruit of glory and riches. 1819 "Come to me, all you who desire me, and be filled with my fruits. 20 For my memory is sweeter than honey, and my inheritance than the honeycomb. 21 Those who eat me will be hungry for more. Those who drink me will be thirsty for more. 22 He who obeys me will not be ashamed. Those who work with me will not sin."23 All these things are the book of the covenant of the Most High God, the law which Moses commanded us for an inheritance for the assemblies of Jacob. 2425 It is he who makes wisdom abundant, as Pishon, and as Tigris in the days of first fruits. 26 He makes understanding full as the Euphrates, and as the Jordan in the days of harvest, 27 who makes instruction shine forth as the light, as Gihon in the days of vintage. 28 The first man didn't know her perfectly. In like manner, the last has not explored her. 29 For her thoughts are filled from the sea, and her counsels from the great deep.30 I came out as a canal stream from a river, and as an irrigation ditch into a garden. 31 I said, "I will water my garden, and will drench my garden bed." Behold, my stream became a river, and my river became a sea. 32 I will yet bring instruction to light as the morning, and will make these things clear from far away. 33 I will continue to pour out teaching like prophecy, and leave it to all generations. 34 See that I have not labored for myself only, but for all those who diligently seek wisdom.

25

1 I enjoy three things, and they are beautiful before the Lord and men: the agreement of kindred, the friendship of neighbors, and a woman and her husband who walk together in agreement. 2 But my soul hates three sorts of people, and I am greatly offended at their life: a poor man who is arrogant, a rich man who is a liar, and an old fool who is an adulterer.3 If you gathered nothing in your youth, how could you find anything in your old age? 4 How beautiful a thing is judgment in the gray-haired, and for elders to know good counsel! 5 How beautiful is the wisdom of old

men, and understanding and counsel to men who are in honor! 6 Much experience is the crown of the aged. Their glory is the fear of the Lord.7 There are nine things that I have thought of, and in my heart counted happy, and the tenth I will utter with my tongue: a man who has joy with his children, and a man who lives and sees the fall of his enemies. 8 Happy is he who dwells with a wife of understanding, he who has not slipped with his tongue, and he who has not served a man who is unworthy of him. 9 Happy is he who has found prudence, and he who speaks in the ears of those who listen. 10 How great is he who has found wisdom! Yet is there none above him who fears the Lord. 11 The fear of the Lord surpasses all things. To whom shall he who holds it be likened? 1213Any wound but a wound of the heart! Any wickedness but the wickedness of a woman! 14 Any calamity but a calamity from those who hate me! Any vengeance but the vengeance of enemies! 15 There is no venom worse than a snake's venom. There is no wrath worse than an enemy's wrath.16 I would rather dwell with a lion and a dragon than keep house with a wicked woman. 17 The wickedness of a woman changes her appearance, and darkens her countenance like that of a bear. 18 Her husband will sit among his neighbors, and when he hears it, he sighs bitterly. 19 All malice is small compared to the malice of a woman. Let the portion of a sinner fall on her. 20As walking up a sandy hill is to the feet of the aged, so is a wife full of words to a quiet man. 21 Don't be ensnared by a woman's beauty. Don't desire a woman for her beauty. 22 There is anger, impudence, and great reproach if a woman supports her husband. 23 A wicked woman is abasement of heart, sadness of countenance, and a wounded heart. A woman who won't make her husband happy is like hands that hang down, and weak knees. 24 The beginning of sin came from a woman. Because of her, we all die. 25 Don't give water an outlet, and don't give a wicked woman freedom of speech. 26 If she doesn't go as you direct, cut her away from your flesh.

26

1 Happy is the husband of a good wife. The number of his days will be doubled. 2 A faithful wife gives joy to her husband. He will fulfill his years in peace. 3 A good wife is a great gift. She will be given to those who fear the Lord. 4 Whether a man is rich or poor, a good heart makes a cheerful face at all times.5 Of three things my heart was afraid, and concerning the fourth kind I made supplication: The slander of a city, the assembly of a mob, and a false accusation. All these are more grievous than death. 6 A grief of heart and sorrow is a woman who is jealous of another woman. Her tongue-lashing makes it known to all. 7 A wicked woman is like a chafing yoke. He who takes hold of her is like one who grasps a scorpion. 8 A drunken woman causes great wrath. She will not

cover her own shame. 9 The fornication of a woman is in the lifting up of her eyes; it will be known by her eyelids. 10 Keep strict watch on a headstrong daughter, lest she find liberty for herself, and use it. 11 Watch out for an impudent eye, and don't be surprised if it sins against you. 12 She will open her mouth like a thirsty traveller, and drink from every water that is near. She will sit down at every post, and open her quiver to any arrow.13 The grace of a wife will delight her husband. Her knowledge will strengthen his bones. 14 A silent woman is a gift of the Lord. There is nothing worth so much as a well-instructed soul. 15 A modest woman is grace upon grace. There are no scales that can weigh the value of a self-controlled soul. 16 As the sun when it arises in the highest places of the Lord, so is the beauty of a good wife in her well-organized home. 17 As the lamp that shines upon the holy lampstand, so is the beauty of the face on a well-proportioned body. 18 As the golden pillars are upon a base of silver, so are beautiful feet with the breasts of one who is steadfast. 19-2728 For two things my heart is grieved, and for the third anger comes upon me: a warrior who suffers for poverty, men of understanding who are counted as garbage, and one who turns back from righteousness to sin— the Lord will prepare him for the sword!29 It is difficult for a merchant to keep himself from wrong doing, and for a retailer to be acquitted of sin.

27

1 Many have sinned for profit. He who seeks to multiply wealth will turn his eye away. 2 As a nail will stick fast between the joinings of stones, so sin will thrust itself in between buying and selling. 3 Unless a person holds on diligently to the fear of the Lord, his house will be overthrown quickly.4 In the shaking of a sieve, the refuse remains, so does the filth of man in his thoughts. 5 The furnace tests the potter's vessels; so the test of a person is in his thoughts. 6 The fruit of a tree discloses its cultivation, so is the utterance of the thought of a person's heart. 7 Praise no man before you hear his thoughts, for this is how people are tested.8 If you follow righteousness, you will obtain it, and put it on like a long robe of glory. 9 Birds will return to their own kind, so truth will return to those who practice it. 10 The lion lies in wait for prey. So does sin for those who do evil.11 The discourse of a godly man is always wise, but the fool changes like the moon. 12 Limit your time among people void of understanding, but persevere among the thoughtful. 13 The talk of fools is offensive. Their laughter is wantonly sinful. 14 Their talk with much swearing makes hair stand upright. Their strife makes others plug their ears. 15 The strife of the proud leads to bloodshed. Their abuse of each other is a grievous thing to hear.16 He who reveals secrets destroys trust, and will not find a close friend. 17 Love a friend, and keep faith with him; but if you

reveal his secrets, you shall not follow him; 18 for as a man has destroyed his enemy, so you have destroyed the friendship of your neighbor. 19 As a bird which you have released out of your hand, so you have let your neighbor go, and you will not catch him again. 20 Don't pursue him, for he has gone far away, and has escaped like a gazelle out of the snare. 21 For a wound may be bound up, and after abuse there may be reconciliation; but he who reveals secrets is without hope.22 One who winks the eye contrives evil things; and those who know him will keep their distance. 23 When you are present, he will speak sweetly, and will admire your words; but afterward he will twist his speech and set a trap in your words. 24 I have hated many things, but nothing like him. The Lord will hate him.25 One who casts a stone straight up casts it on his own head. A deceitful blow opens wounds. 26 He who digs a pit will fall into it. He who sets a snare will be caught in it. 27 He who does evil things, they will roll back upon him, and he will not know where they came from. 28 Mockery and reproach are from the arrogant. Vengeance lies in wait for them like a lion. 29 Those who rejoice at the fall of the godly will be caught in a snare. Anguish will consume them before they die.30 Wrath and anger, these also are abominations. A sinner will possess them.

28

1 He who takes vengeance will find vengeance from the Lord, and he will surely make his sins firm. 2 Forgive your neighbor the hurt that he has done, and then your sins will be pardoned when you pray. 3 Does anyone harbor anger against another and expect healing from the Lord? 4 Upon a man like himself he has no mercy, and does he make supplication for his own sins? 5 He himself, being flesh, nourishes wrath. Who will make atonement for his sins? 6 Remember your last end, and stop enmity. Remember corruption and death, and be true to the commandments. 7 Remember the commandments, and don't be angry with your neighbor. Remember the covenant of the Highest, and overlook ignorance.8 Abstain from strife, and you will diminish your sins, for a passionate man will kindle strife. 9 A man who is a sinner will trouble friends and sow discord among those who are at peace. 10 As is the fuel of the fire, so it will burn; and as the stoutness of the strife is, so it will burn. As is the strength of the man, so will be his wrath; and as is his wealth, so he will exalt his anger. 11 A contention begun in haste kindles a fire; and hasty fighting sheds blood.12 If you blow on a spark, it will burn; and if you spit upon it, it will be quenched. Both of these come out of your mouth.13 Curse the whisperer and double-tongued, for he has destroyed many who were at peace. 14 A slanderer has shaken many, and dispersed them from nation to nation. It has pulled down strong cities and overthrown the houses of great men. 15 A slanderer has cast out brave

women and deprived them of their labors. 16 He who listens to it will not find rest, nor will he live quietly. 17 The stroke of a whip makes a mark in the flesh, but the stroke of a tongue will break bones. 18 Many have fallen by the edge of the sword, yet not so many as those who have fallen because of the tongue. 19 Happy is he who is sheltered from it, who has not passed through its wrath, who has not drawn its yoke, and has not been bound with its bands. 20 For its yoke is a yoke of iron, and its bands are bands of brass. 21 Its death is an evil death, and Hades is better than it. 22 It will not have rule over godly men. They will not be burned in its flame. 23 Those who forsake the Lord will fall into it. It will burn among them, and won't be quenched. It will be sent against them like a lion. It will destroy them like a leopard. 24 As you hedge your possession about with thorns, and secure your silver and your gold, 25 so make a balance and a weight for your words, and make a door and a bar for your mouth. 26 Take heed lest you slip with it, lest you fall before one who lies in wait.

29

1 He who shows mercy will lend to his neighbor. He who strengthens him with his hand keeps the commandments. 2 Lend to your neighbor in time of his need. Repay your neighbor on time. 3 Confirm your word, and keep faith with him; and at all seasons you will find what you need. 4 Many have considered a loan to be a windfall, and have given trouble to those who helped them. 5 Until he has received, he will kiss a man's hands. For his neighbor's money he will speak submissively. Then when payment is due, he will prolong the time, return excuses, and complain about the season. 6 If he prevails, the creditor will hardly receive half; and he will count it as a windfall. If not, he has deprived him of his money, and he has gotten him for an enemy without cause. He will pay him with cursing and railing. Instead of honor, he will pay him disgrace. 7 Many on account of fraud have turned away. They are afraid of being defrauded for nothing. 8 However be patient with a man in poor estate. Don't keep him waiting for your alms. 9 Help a poor man for the commandment's sake. According to his need don't send him empty away. 10 Lose your money for a brother and a friend. Don't let it rust under a stone and be lost. 11 Allocate your treasure according to the commandments of the Most High and it will profit you more than gold. 12 Store up almsgiving in your store-chambers and it will deliver you out of all affliction. 13 It will fight for you against your enemy better than a mighty shield and a ponderous spear.14 A good man will be surety for his neighbor. He who has lost shame will fail him. 15 Don't forget the kindness of your guarantor, for he has given his life for you. 16 A sinner will waste the property of his guarantor. 17 He who is thankless will fail him who delivered him. 18 Being surety has undone many who

were prospering and shaken them as a wave of the sea. It has driven mighty men from their homes. They wandered among foreign nations. 19 A sinner who falls into suretiship and undertakes contracts for work will fall into lawsuits. 20 Help your neighbor according to your power, and be careful not to fall yourself.21 The essentials of life are water, bread, a garment, and a house for privacy. 22 Better is the life of a poor man under a shelter of logs than sumptuous fare in another man's house. 23 With little or with much, be well satisfied.24 It is a miserable life to go from house to house. Where you are a guest, you dare not open your mouth. 25 You will entertain, serve drinks, and have no thanks. In addition to this, you will hear bitter words. 26 "Come here, you sojourner, set a table, and if you have anything in your hand, feed me with it." 27 "Leave, you sojourner, for an honored guest is here. My brother has come to be my guest. I need my house." 28 These things are grievous to a man of understanding: The scolding about lodging and the insults of creditors.

30

1 He who loves his son will continue to lay stripes upon him, that he may have joy from him in the end. 2 He who chastises his son will have profit from him, and will brag about him among his acquaintances. 3 He who teaches his son will provoke his enemy to jealousy. Before friends, he will rejoice in him. 4 His father dies, and is as though he had not died; for he has left one behind him like himself. 5 In his life, he saw his son and rejoiced. When he died, it was without regret. 6 He left behind him an avenger against his enemies, and one to repay kindness to his friends.7 He who makes too much of his son will bind up his wounds. His heart will be troubled at every cry. 8 An unbroken horse becomes stubborn. An unrestrained son becomes headstrong. 9 Pamper your child, and he will make you afraid. Play with him, and he will grieve you. 10 Don't laugh with him, lest you have sorrow with him, and you gnash your teeth in the end. 11 Give him no liberty in his youth, and don't ignore his follies.12Bow down his neck in his youth, and beat him on the sides while he is a child, lest he become stubborn, and be disobedient to you, and there be sorrow to your soul.13 Chastise your son, and give him work, lest his shameless behavior be an offense to you.14 Better is a poor man who is healthy and fit, than a rich man who is afflicted in his body. 15 Health and fitness are better than all gold, and a strong body better than wealth without measure. 16 There is no wealth better than health of body. There is no gladness above the joy of the heart. 17 Death is better than a bitter life, and eternal rest than a continual sickness.18 Good things poured out upon a mouth that is closed are like food offerings laid upon a grave. 19 What does an offering profit an idol? For it can't eat or smell. So is he who is punished by

the Lord, 20 seeing with his eyes and groaning, like a eunuch embracing a virgin and groaning.21 Don't give your soul to sorrow. Don't afflict yourself deliberately. 22 Gladness of heart is the life of a man. Cheerfulness of a man lengthens his days. 23 Love your own soul, and comfort your heart. Remove sorrow far from you, for sorrow has destroyed many, and there is no profit in it. 24 Envy and wrath shorten life. Anxiety brings old age before its time. 25 Those who are cheerful and merry will benefit from their food.

31

1 Wakefulness that comes from riches consumes the flesh, and anxiety about it takes away sleep. 2 Wakeful anxiety will crave slumber. In a severe disease, sleep will be broken.3 A rich man toils in gathering money together. When he rests, he is filled with his good things. 4 A poor man toils in lack of substance. When he rests, he becomes needy. 5 He who loves gold won't be justified. He who follows destruction will himself have his fill of it. 6 Many have been given over to ruin for the sake of gold. Their destruction meets them face to face. 7 It is a stumbling block to those who sacrifice to it. Every fool will be taken by it. 8 Blessed is the rich person who is found blameless, and who doesn't go after gold. 9 Who is he, that we may call him blessed? For he has done wonderful things among his people. 10 Who has been tried by it, and found perfect? Then let him boast. Who has had the power to transgress, and has not transgressed? And to do evil, and has not done it? 11 His prosperity will be made sure. The congregation will proclaim his alms.12 Do you sit at a great table? Don't be greedy there. Don't say, "There is a lot of food on it!" 13 Remember that a greedy eye is a wicked thing. What has been created more greedy than an eye? Therefore it sheds tears from every face. 14 Don't stretch your hand wherever it looks. Don't thrust yourself with it into the dish. 15 Consider your neighbor's feelings by your own. Be discreet in every point. 16 Eat like a human being those things which are set before you. Don't eat greedily, lest you be hated. 17 Be first to stop for manners' sake. Don't be insatiable, lest you offend. 18 And if you sit among many, Don'treach out your hand before them.19 How sufficient to a well-mannered man is a very little. He doesn't breathe heavily in his bed. 20 Healthy sleep comes from moderate eating. He rises early, and his wits are with him. The pain of wakefulness, colic, and griping are with an insatiable man. 21 And if you have been forced to eat, rise up in the middle of it, and you shall have rest. 22 Hear me, my son, and don't despise me, and in the end you will appreciate my words. In all your works be skillful, and no disease will come to you.23 People bless him who is liberal with his food. The testimony of his excellence will be believed. 24 The city will murmur at him who is a

stingy with his food. The testimony of his stinginess will be accurate.25 Don't show yourself valiant in wine, for wine has destroyed many. 26 The furnace tests the temper of steel by dipping; so does wine test hearts in the quarreling of the proud. 27 Wine is as good as life to men, if you drink it in moderation. What life is there to a man who is without wine? It has been created to make men glad. 28 Wine drunk in season and in moderation is joy of heart and gladness of soul: 29 Wine drunk excessively is bitterness of soul, with provocation and conflict. 30 Drunkenness increases the rage of a fool to his hurt. It diminishes strength and adds wounds.31 Don't rebuke your neighbor at a banquet of wine. Don't despise him in his mirth. Don't speak a word of reproach to him. Don't distress him by making demands of him.

32

1 Have they made you ruler of a feast? Don't be lifted up. Be among them as one of them. Take care of them first, and then sit down. 2 And when you have done all your duties, take your place, that you may be gladdened on their account, and receive a wreath for your good service.3 Speak, you who are older, for it's your right, but with sound knowledge; and don't interrupt the music. 4 Don't pour out talk where there is a performance of music. Don't display your wisdom at the wrong time. 5As a ruby signet in a setting of gold, so is a music concert at a wine banquet. 6 As an emerald signet in a work of gold, so is musical melody with pleasant wine.7 Speak, young man, if you are obliged to, but no more than twice, and only if asked. 8 Sum up your speech, many things in few words. Be as one who knows and yet holds his tongue. 9When among great men, don't behave as their equal. When another is speaking, don't babble.10 Lightning speeds before thunder. Approval goes before one who is modest. 11 Rise up in good time, and don't be last. Go home quickly and don't loiter 12 Amuse yourself there and do what is in your heart. Don't sin by proud speech. 13 For these things bless your Maker, who gives you to drink freely of his good things.14 He who fears the Lord will receive discipline. Those who seek him early will find favor. 15 He who seeks the law shall be filled with it, but the hypocrite will stumble at it. 16 Those who fear the Lord will find true judgment, and will kindle righteous acts like a light. 17 A sinful man shuns reproof, and will find a judgment according to his will.18 A sensible person won't neglect a thought. An insolent and proud man won't crouch in fear, even after he has done a thing by himself without counsel. 19 Do nothing without counsel, but when you have acted, don't regret it. 20 Don't go in a way of conflict. Don't stumble in stony places. 21 Don't be overconfident on a smooth road. 22 Beware of your own children. 23 In every work guard your own soul, for this is the keeping of the commandments.24 He who

believes the law gives heed to the commandment. He who trusts in the Lord will suffer no loss.

33

1 No evil will happen to him who fears the Lord, but in trials once and again he will deliver him. 2 A wise man will not hate the law, but he who is a hypocrite about it is like a boat in a storm. 3 A man of understanding will put his trust in the law. And the law is faithful to him, as when one asks a divine oracle.4 Prepare your speech, and so you will be heard. Bind up instruction, and make your answer. 5 The heart of a fool is like a cartwheel. His thoughts are like a rolling axle. 6 A stallion horse is like a mocking friend. He neighs under every one who sits upon him.7 Why does one day excel another, when all the light of every day in the year is from the sun? 8 They were distinguished by the Lord's knowledge, and he varied seasons and feasts. 9 Some of them he exalted and hallowed, and some of them he has made ordinary days. 10 And all men are from the ground. Adam was created from dust. 11 In the abundance of his knowledge the Lord distinguished them, and made their ways different. 12 Some of them he blessed and exalted, and some of them he made holy and brought near to himself. Some of them he cursed and brought low, and overthrew them from their place. 13 As the clay of the potter in his hand, all his ways are according to his good pleasure, so men are in the hand of him who made them, to render to them according to his judgment.14 Good is the opposite of evil, and life is the opposite of death; so the sinner is the opposite of the godly. 15 Look upon all the works of the Most High like this, they come in pairs, one against another.16 I was the last on watch, like one who gleans after the grape gatherers. 17 By the Lord's blessing I arrived before them, and filled my winepress like one who gathers grapes. 18 Consider that I labored not for myself alone, but for all those who seek instruction. 19 Hear me, you great men of the people, and listen with your ears, you rulers of the congregation.20 To son and wife, to brother and friend, don't give power over yourself while you live, and don't give your goods to another, lest you regret it and must ask for them. 21 While you still live and breath is in you, don't give yourself over to anybody. 22 For it is better that your children should ask from you than that you should look to the hand of your children. 23 Excel in all your works. Don't bring a stain on your honor. 24 In the day that you end the days of your life, in the time of death, distribute your inheritance.25 Fodder, a stick, and burdens are for a donkey. Bread, discipline, and work are for a servant. 26 Set your slave to work, and you will find rest. Leave his hands idle, and he will seek liberty. 27 Yoke and thong will bow the neck. For an evil slave there are racks and tortures. 28 Send him to labor, that he not be idle, for idleness teaches much mischief. 29

Set him to work, as is fit for him. If he doesn't obey, make his fetters heavy. 30 Don't be excessive toward any. Do nothing unjust.31 If you have a slave, treat him like yourself, because you have bought him with blood. 32 If you have a slave, treat him like yourself. For like your own soul, you will need him. If you treat him ill, and he departs and runs away, 33 which way will you go to seek him?

34

1 Vain and false hopes are for a man void of understanding. Dreams give wings to fools. 2 As one who grasps at a shadow and follows after the wind, so is he who sets his mind on dreams. 3 The vision of dreams is a reflection, the likeness of a face near a face. 4 From an unclean thing what can be

cleansed? From that which is false what can be true? 5 Divinations, and soothsayings, and dreams, are vain. The heart has fantasies like a woman in labor. 6 If they are not sent in a visitation from the Most High, don't give your heart to them. 7 For dreams have led many astray. They have failed by putting their hope in them. 8 Without lying the law will be fulfilled. Wisdom is complete in a faithful mouth.9 A well-instructed man knows many things. He who has much experience will declare understanding. 10 He who has no experience knows few things. But he who has traveled increases cleverness. 11 I have seen many things in my travels. My understanding is more than my words. 12 I was often in danger even to death. I was preserved because of these experiences. 13 The spirit of those who fear the Lord will live, for their hope is in him who saves them. 14 Whoever fears the Lord won't be afraid, and won't be a coward, for he is his hope. 15 Blessed is the soul of him who fears the Lord. To whom does he give heed? Who is his support? 16 The eyes of the Lord are on those who love him, a mighty protection and strong support, a cover from the hot blast, a shade from the noonday sun, a guard from stumbling, and a help from falling. 17 He raises up the soul, and enlightens the eyes. He gives health, life, and blessing.18 He who sacrifices a thing wrongfully gotten, his offering is made in mockery. The mockeries of wicked men are not acceptable. 19 The Most High has no pleasure in the offerings of the ungodly, Neither is he pacified for sins by the multitude of sacrifices. 20 Like one who kills a son before his father's eyes is he who brings a sacrifice from the goods of the poor. 21 The bread of the needy is the life of the poor. He who deprives him of it is a man of blood. 22 Like one who murders his neighbor is he who takes away his living. Like a shedder of blood is he who deprives a hireling of his hire.23 When one builds, and another pulls down, what profit do they have but toil? 24 When one prays, and another curses, whose voice will the Lord listen to? 25 He who washes himself after touching a dead body, and touches it again, what does he gain by his washing? 26 Even so a man fasting for his sins, and going again, and doing the same, who will listen to his prayer? What profit does he have in his humiliation?

35

1 He who keeps the law multiplies offerings. He who heeds the commandments sacrifices a peace offering. 2 He who returns a kindness offers fine flour. He who gives alms sacrifices a thank offering. 3 To depart from wickedness pleases the Lord. To depart from unrighteousness is an atoning sacrifice. 4 See that you don't appear in the presence of the Lord empty. 5 Forall these things are done because of the commandment. 6 The offering of the righteous enriches the altar. The sweet fragrance of it is before the Most High. 7 The sacrifice of a righteous man is acceptable. It won't be forgotten. 8 Glorify the Lord with generosity. Don't reduce the first fruits of your hands. 9 In every gift show a cheerful countenance, And dedicate your tithe with gladness. 10 Give to the Most High according as he has given. As your hand has found, give generously. 11 For the Lord repays, and he will repay you sevenfold.12 Don't plan to bribe him with gifts, for he will not receive them. Don't set your mind on an unrighteous sacrifice, For the Lord is the judge, and with him is no respect of persons. 13 He won't accept any person against a poor man. He will listen to the prayer of him who is wronged. 14 He will in no way despise the supplication of the fatherless or the widow, when she pours out her tale. 15 Don't the tears of the widow run down her cheek? Isn't her cry against him who has caused them to fall? 16 He who serves God according to his good pleasure will be accepted. His supplication will reach to the clouds. 17 The prayer of the humble pierces the clouds. until it comes near, he will not be comforted. He won't depart until the Most High visits and he judges righteously and executes judgment. 18 And the Lord will not be slack, neither will he be patient toward them, until he has crushed the loins of the unmerciful. He will repay vengeance to the heathen until he has taken away the multitude of the arrogant and broken in pieces the sceptres of the unrighteous, 19 until he has rendered to every man according to his deeds, and repaid the works of men according to their plans, until he has judged the cause of his people, and he will make them rejoice in his mercy. 20 Mercy is as welcome in the time of his affliction, as clouds of rain in the time of drought.

36

1 Have mercy upon us, O Lord the God of all, and look at us with favor; 2 and send your fear upon all the nations.3 Lift up your hand against the foreign nations and let them see your mighty power. 4 As you showed your holiness in us before them, so be magnified in them

before us. 5 Let them know you, as we also have known you, that there is no God but only you, O God. 6 Show new signs, and work various wonders. Glorify your hand and your right arm.7 Raise up indignation and pour out wrath. Take away the adversary and destroy the enemy. 8 Hasten the time and remember your oath. Let them declare your mighty works. 9 Let him who escapes be devoured by raging fire. May those who harm your people find destruction. 10 Crush the heads of the rulers of the enemies who say, "There is no one but ourselves." 11 Gather all the tribes of Jacob together, and take them for your inheritance, as from the beginning. 12 O Lord, have mercy upon the people that is called by your name, and upon Israel, whom you likened to a firstborn. 13 Have compassion upon the city of your sanctuary, Jerusalem, the place of your rest. 14 Fill Zion. Exalt your oracles and fill your people with your glory. 15 Give testimony to those who were your creatures in the beginning, and fulfill the prophecies that have been spoken in your name. 16 Reward those who wait for you, and men will put their trust in your prophets. 17 Listen, O Lord, to the prayer of your servants, according to the blessing of Aaron concerning your people; and all those who are on the earth will know that you are the Lord, the eternal God.18 The belly will eat any food, but one food is better than another. 19 The mouth tastes meats taken in hunting, so does an understanding heart detect false speech. 20 A contrary heart will cause heaviness. A man of experience will pay him back. 21 A woman will receive any man, but one daughter is better than another. 22 The beauty of a woman cheers the countenance. A man desires nothing more. 23 If kindness and humility are on her tongue, her husband is not like other sons of men. 24 He who gets a wife gets his richest treasure, a help meet for him and a pillar of support. 25 Where no hedge is, the property will be plundered. He who has no wife will mourn as he wanders. 26 For who would trust a nimble robber who skips from city to city? Even so, who would trust a man who has no nest, and lodges wherever he finds himself at nightfall?

37

1 Every friend will say, "I also am his friend"; but there is a friend which is only a friend in name. 2 Isn't there a grief in it even to death when a companion and friend is turned into an enemy? 3 O wicked imagination, why were you formed to cover the dry land with deceit? 4 There is a companion who rejoices in the gladness of a friend, but in time of affliction will be against him. 5 There is a companion who for the belly's sake labors with his friend, yet in the face of battle will carry his buckler. 6 Don't forget a friend in your soul. Don't be unmindful of him in your riches.7 Every counselor extols counsel, but some give counsel in their own interest. 8 Let your soul beware of a counselor,

and know in advance what is his interest (for he will take counsel for himself), lest he cast the lot against you, 9 and say to you, “Your way is good.” Then he will stand near you, to see what will happen to you. 10 Don’t take counsel with one who looks askance at you. Hide your counsel from those who are jealous of you. 11 Don’t consult with a woman about her rival, with a coward about war, with a merchant about business, with a buyer about selling, with an envious man about thankfulness, with an unmerciful man about kindliness, with a sluggard about any kind of work, with a hireling in your house about finishing his work, or with an idle servant about much business. Pay no attention to these in any matter of counsel. 12 But rather be continually with a godly man, whom you know to be a keeper of the commandments, who in his soul is as your own soul, and who will grieve with you, if you fail. 13 Make the counsel of your heart stand, for there is no one more faithful to you than it. 14 For a man’s soul is sometimes inclined to inform him better than seven watchmen who sit on high on a watch-tower. 15 Above all this ask the Most High that he may direct your way in truth.16 Let reason be the beginning of every work. Let counsel go before every action. 17 As a token of the changing of the heart, 18 four kinds of things rise up: good and evil, life and death. That which rules over them continually is the tongue. 19 There is one who is clever and the instructor of many, and yet is unprofitable to his own soul. 20 There is one who is subtle in words, and is hated. He will be destitute of all food. 21 For grace was not given to him from the Lord, because he is deprived of all wisdom. 22 There is one who is wise to his own soul; and the fruits of his understanding are trustworthy in the mouth. 23 A wise man will instruct his own people. The fruits of his understanding are trustworthy. 24 A wise man will be filled with blessing. All those who see him will call him happy. 25 The life of a man is counted by days. The days of Israel are innumerable. 26 The wise man will inherit confidence among his people. His name will live forever.27 My son, test your soul in your life. See what is evil for it, and don’t give in to it. 28 For not all things are profitable for all men. Not every soul has pleasure in everything. 29 Don’t be insatiable in any luxury. Don’t be greedy in the things that you eat. 30 For overeating brings disease, and gluttony causes nausea. 31 Because of gluttony, many have perished, but he who takes heed shall prolong his life.

38

1 Honor a physician according to your need with the honors due to him, for truly the Lord has created him. 2 For healing comes from the Most High, and he shall receive a gift from the king. 3 The skill of the physician will lift up his head. He will be admired in the sight of great men. 4 The Lord created medicines

out of the earth. A prudent man will not despise them. 5 Wasn't water made sweet with wood, that its power might be known? 6 He gave men skill that he might be glorified in his marvelous works. 7 With them he heals and takes away pain. 8 With these, the pharmacist makes a mixture. God's works won't be brought to an end. From him, peace is upon the face of the earth.9 My son, in your sickness don't be negligent, but pray to the Lord, and he will heal you. 10 Put away wrong doing, and direct your hands in righteousness. Cleanse your heart from all sin. 11 Give a sweet savor and a memorial of fine flour, and pour oil on your offering, according to your means. 12 Then give place to the physician, for truly the Lord has created him. Don't let him leave you, for you need him. 13 There is a time when in recovery is in their hands. 14 For they also shall ask the Lord to prosper them in diagnosis and in healing for the maintenance of life. 15 He who sins before his Maker, let him fall into the hands of the physician.16 My son, let your tears fall over the dead, and as one who suffers grievously, begin lamentation. Wind up his body with due honor. Don't neglect his burial. 17 Make bitter weeping and make passionate wailing. Let your mourning be according to his merit, for one day or two, lest you be spoken evil of; and so be comforted for your sorrow. 18 For from sorrow comes death. Sorrow of heart saps one's strength. 19 In calamity, sorrow also remains. A poor man's life is grievous to the heart. 20 Don't give your heart to sorrow. Put it away, remembering the end. 21 Don't forget it, for there is no returning again. You do him no good, and you would harm yourself. 22 Remember his end, for so also will yours be: yesterday for me, and today for you. 23 When the dead is at rest, let his remembrance rest. Be comforted for him when his spirit departs from him.24 The wisdom of the scribe comes by the opportunity of leisure. He who has little business can become wise. 25 How could he become wise who holds the plow, who glories in the shaft of the goad, who drives oxen and is occupied in their labors, and who mostly talks about bulls? 26 He will set his heart upon turning his furrows. His lack of sleep is to give his heifers their fodder. 27 So is every craftsman and master artisan who passes his time by night as by day, those who cut engravings of signets. His diligence is to make great variety. He sets his heart to preserve likeness in his portraiture, and is careful to finish his work. 28 So too is the smith sitting by the anvil and considering the unwrought iron. The smoke of the fire will waste his flesh. He toils in the heat of the furnace. The noise of the hammer deafens his ear. His eyes are upon the pattern of the object. He will set his heart upon perfecting his works. He will be careful to adorn them perfectly. 29 So is the potter sitting at his work and turning the wheel around with his feet, who is always anxiously set at his work. He produces his handiwork in quantity. 30 He will fashion the clay with his arm and will bend its strength in front of his feet. He will apply his heart to finish the glazing. He will be careful to clean the kiln.31 All these put their trust in their hands. Each becomes skillful in his own work. 32 Without these no city would be inhabited. Men wouldn't reside as foreigners or walk up and down there. 33 They won't be sought for in the council of the people. They won't mount on high in the assembly. They won't sit on the seat of the judge. They won't understand the covenant of judgment. Neither will they declare instruction and judgment. They won't be found where parables are. 34 But they will maintain the fabric of the age. Their prayer is in the handiwork of their craft.

39

1 Not so he who has applied his soul and meditates in the law of the Most High. He will seek out the wisdom of all the ancients and will be occupied with prophecies. 2 He will keep the sayings of the men of renown and will enter in amidst the subtleties of parables. 3 He will seek out the hidden meaning of proverbs and be conversant in the dark sayings of parables. 4 He will serve among great men and appear before him who rules. He will travel through the land of foreign nations, for he has learned what is good and evil among men. 5 He will apply his heart to return early to the Lord who made him, and will make supplication before the Most High, and will open his mouth in prayer, and will ask for pardon for his sins.6 If the great Lord wills, he will be filled with the spirit of understanding; he will pour forth the words of his wisdom and in prayer give thanks to the Lord. 7 He will direct his counsel and knowledge, and he will meditate in his secrets. 8 He will show the instruction which he has been taught and will glory in the law of the covenant of the Lord. 9 Many will commend his understanding. So long as the world endures, it won't be blotted out. His memory won't depart. His name will live from generation to generation. 10 Nations will declare his wisdom. The congregation will proclaim his praise. 11 If he continues, he will leave a greater name than a thousand. If he finally rests, it is enough for him.12 Yet more I will utter, which I have thought about. I am filled like the full moon. 13 Listen to me, you holy children, and bud forth like a rose growing by a brook of water. 14 Give a sweet fragrance like frankincense. Put forth flowers like a lily. Scatter a sweet smell and sing a song of praise. Bless the Lord for all his works! 15 Magnify his name and give utterance to his praise with the songs on your lips and with harps! Say this when you utter his praise:16 All the works of the Lord are exceedingly good, and every command will be done in its time. 17 No one can say, "What is this?" "Why is that?" for at the proper time they will all be sought out. At his word, the waters stood as a heap, as did the reservoirs of water at the word of his mouth. 18 At his command all his good pleasure is

fulfilled. There is no one who can hinder his salvation. 19 The works of all flesh are before him. It's impossible to be hidden from his eyes. 20 He sees from everlasting to everlasting. There is nothing too wonderful for him. 21 No one can say, "What is this?" "Why is that?" for all things are created for their own uses.22 His blessing covered the dry land as a river and saturated it as a flood. 23 As he has made the waters salty, so the heathen will inherit his wrath. 24 His ways are plain to the holy. They are stumbling blocks to the wicked. 25 Good things are created from the beginning for the good. So are evil things for sinners. 26 The main things necessary for the life of man are water, fire, iron, salt, wheat flour, and honey, milk, the blood of the grape, oil, and clothing. 27 All these things are for good to the godly, but for sinners, they will be turned into evils.28 There are winds that are created for vengeance, and in their fury they lay on their scourges heavily. In the time of reckoning, they pour out their strength, and will appease the wrath of him who made them. 29 Fire, hail, famine, and death— all these are created for vengeance— 30 wild beasts' teeth, scorpions, adders, and a sword punishing the ungodly to destruction. 31 They will rejoice in his commandment, and will be made ready upon earth when needed. In their seasons, they won't disobey his command.32 Therefore from the beginning I was convinced, and I thought it through and left it in writing: 33 All the works of the Lord are good. He will supply every need in its time. 34 No one can say, "This is worse than that," for they will all be well approved in their time. 35 Now with all your hearts and voices, sing praises and bless the Lord's name!

40

1 Great travail is created for every man. A heavy yoke is upon the sons of Adam, from the day of their coming forth from their mother's womb, until the day for their burial in the mother of all things. 2 The expectation of things to come, and the day of death, trouble their thoughts, and cause fear in their hearts. 3 From him who sits on a throne of glory, even to him who is humbled in earth and ashes, 4 from him who wears purple and a crown, even to him who is clothed in burlap, 5there is wrath, jealousy, trouble, unrest, fear of death, anger, and strife. In the time of rest upon his bed, his night sleep changes his knowledge. 6 He gets little or no rest, and afterward in his sleep, as in a day of keeping watch, he is troubled in the vision of his heart, as one who has escaped from the front of battle. 7 In the very time of his deliverance, he awakens, and marvels that the fear is nothing.8To all creatures, human and animal, and upon sinners sevenfold more, 9 come death, bloodshed, strife, sword, calamities, famine, suffering, and plague. 10 All these things were created for the wicked, and because of them the flood came. 11 All things that are of the earth turn to the earth again. All

things that are of the waters return into the sea.12 All bribery and injustice will be blotted out. Good faith will stand forever. 13 The goods of the unjust will be dried up like a river, and like a great thunder in rain will go off in noise. 14 In opening his hands, a man will be made glad; so lawbreakers will utterly fail. 15 The children of the ungodly won't grow many branches, and are as unhealthy roots on a sheer rock. 16 The reeds by every water or river bank will be plucked up before all grass. 17 Kindness is like a garden of blessings. Almsgiving endures forever.18 The life of one who labors and is content will be made sweet. He who finds a treasure is better than both. 19 Children and the building of a city establish a name. A blameless wife is better than both. 20 Wine and music rejoice the heart. The love of wisdom is better than both. 21 The pipe and the lute make pleasant melody. A pleasant tongue is better than both. 22 Your eye desires grace and beauty, but the green shoots of grain more than both. 23 A friend and a companion is always welcome, and a wife with her husband is better than both. 24 Relatives and helpers are for a time of affliction, but almsgiving rescues better than both. 25 Gold and silver will make the foot stand sure, and counsel is esteemed better than both. 26 Riches and strength will lift up the heart. The fear of the Lord is better than both. There is nothing lacking in the fear of the Lord. In it, there is no need to seek help. 27 The fear of the Lord is like a garden of blessing and covers a man more than any glory.28 My son, don't lead a beggar's life. It is better to die than to beg. 29 A man who looks to the table of another, his life is not to be considered a life. He will pollute his soul with another person's food, but a wise and well-instructed person will beware of that. 30 Begging will be sweet in the mouth of the shameless, but it kindles a fire in his belly.

41

1 O death, how bitter is the memory of you to a man who is at peace in his possessions, to the man who has nothing to distract him and has prosperity in all things, and who still has strength to enjoy food! 2 O death, your sentence is acceptable to a man who is needy and who fails in strength, who is in extreme old age, is distracted about all things, is perverse, and has lost patience! 3 Don't be afraid of the sentence of death. Remember those who have been before you and who come after. This is the sentence from the Lord over all flesh. 4 And why do you refuse when it is the good pleasure of the Most High? Whether life lasts ten, or a hundred, or a thousand years, there is no inquiry about life in Hades.5 The children of sinners are abominable children and they frequent the dwellings of the ungodly. 6 The inheritance of sinners' children will perish and with their posterity will be a perpetual disgrace. 7 Children will complain of an ungodly father, because they suffer disgrace

because of him. 8 Woe to you, ungodly men, who have forsaken the law of the Most High God!9 If you are born, you will be born to a curse. If you die, a curse will be your portion. 10 All things that are of the earth will go back to the earth; so the ungodly will go from a curse to perdition.11 The mourning of men is about their bodies; but the evil name of sinners will be blotted out. 12 Have regard for your name, for it continues with you longer than a thousand great treasures of gold. 13 A good life has its number of days, but a good name continues forever.14 My children, follow instruction in peace. But wisdom that is hidden and a treasure that is not seen, what benefit is in them both? 15 Better is a man who hides his foolishness than a man who hides his wisdom. 16 Therefore show respect for my words; for it is not good to retain every kind of shame. Not everything is approved by all in good faith.17 Be ashamed of sexual immorality before father and mother, of a lie before a prince and a mighty man, 18 of an offense before a judge and ruler, of iniquity before the congregation and the people, of unjust dealing before a partner and friend, 19 and of theft in the place where you sojourn. Be ashamed in regard of the truth of God and his covenant, of leaning on your elbow at dinner, of contemptuous behavior in the matter of giving and taking, 20 of silence before those who greet you, of looking at a woman who is a prostitute, 21 of turning away your face from a kinsman, of taking away a portion or a gift, of gazing at a woman who has a husband, 22 of meddling with his maid—and don't come near her bed, of abusive speech to friends— and after you have given, don't insult, 23 of repeating and speaking what you have heard, and of revealing of secrets. 24 So you will be ashamed of the right things and find favor in the sight of every man.

42

1 Don't be ashamed of these things, and don't sin to save face: 2 of the law of the Most High and his covenant, of judgment to do justice to the ungodly, 3 of reckoning with a partner and with travellers, of a gift from the inheritance of friends, 4 of exactness of scales and weights, of getting much or little, 5 of bargaining dealing with merchants, of frequent correction of children, and of making the back of an evil slave to bleed. 6A seal is good where an evil wife is. Where there are many hands, lock things up. 7 Whatever you hand over, let it be by number and weight. In giving and receiving, let all be in writing. 8Don't be ashamed to instruct the unwise and foolish, and one of extreme old age who contends with those who are young. So you will be well instructed indeed and approved in the sight of every living man.9 A daughter is a secret cause of wakefulness to a father. Care for her takes away sleep— in her youth, lest she pass the flower of her age; when she is married, lest she should be hated; 10 in her virginity, lest she should be defiled

and be with child in her father's house; when she has a husband, lest she should transgress; and when she is married, lest she should be barren. 11 Keep a strict watch over a headstrong daughter, lest she make you a laughingstock to your enemies, a byword in the city and notorious among the people, and shame you in public.12 Don't gaze at every beautiful body. Don't sit in the midst of women. 13 For from garments comes a moth, and from a woman comes a woman's wickedness. 14 Better is the wickedness of a man than a pleasant woman, a woman who puts you to shame and disgrace.15 I will make mention now of the works of the Lord, and will declare the things that I have seen. The Lord's works are in his words. 16 The sun that gives light looks at all things. The Lord's work is full of his glory. 17 The Lord has not given power to the saints to declare all his marvelous works, which the Almighty Lord firmly settled, that the universe might be established in his glory. 18 He searches out the deep and the heart. He has understanding of their secrets. For the Most High knows all knowledge. He sees the signs of the world. 19 He declares the things that are past and the things that shall be, and reveals the traces of hidden things. 20 No thought escapes him. There is not a word hidden from him. 21 He has ordered the mighty works of his wisdom. He is from everlasting to everlasting. Nothing has been added to them, nor diminished from them. He had no need of any counselor. 22 How desirable are all his works! One may see this even in a spark. 23 All these things live and remain forever in all manner of uses. They are all obedient. 24 All things are in pairs, one opposite the other. He has made nothing imperfect. 25 One thing establishes the good things of another. Who could ever see enough of his glory?

43

1 The pride of the heavenly heights is the clear sky, the appearance of heaven, in the spectacle of its glory. 2 The sun, when it appears, bringing tidings as it rises, is a marvelous instrument, the work of the Most High. 3 At noon, it dries up the land. Who can stand against its burning heat? 4 A man tending a furnace is in burning heat, but the sun three times more, burning up the mountains, breathing out fiery vapors, and sending out bright beams, it blinds the eyes. 5 Great is the Lord who made it. At his word, he hastens on its course.6 The moon marks the changing seasons, declares times, and is a sign for the world. 7 From the moon is the sign of feast days, a light that wanes when it completes its course. 8 The month is called after its name, increasing wonderfully in its changing— an instrument of the army on high, shining in the structure of heaven, 9 the beauty of heaven, the glory of the stars, an ornament giving light in the highest places of the Lord. 10 At the word of the Holy One, they will stand in due order. They won't faint in their watches. 11 Look at the rainbow,

and praise him who made it. It is exceedingly beautiful in its brightness. 12 It encircles the sky with its glorious circle. The hands of the Most High have stretched it out.13 By his commandment, he makes the snow fall and swiftly sends the lightnings of his judgment. 14 Therefore the storehouses are opened, and clouds fly out like birds. 15 By his mighty power, he makes the clouds strong and the hailstones are broken in pieces. 16 At his appearing, the mountains will be shaken. At his will, the south wind will blow. 17 The voice of his thunder rebukes the earth. So does the northern storm and the whirlwind. Like birds flying down, he sprinkles the snow. It falls down like the lighting of locusts. 18 The eye is dazzled at the beauty of its whiteness. The heart is amazed as it falls. 19 He also pours out frost on the earth like salt. When it is freezes, it has points like thorns.20 The cold north wind blows and ice freezes on the water. It settles on every pool of water. The water puts it on like it was a breastplate. 21 It will devour the mountains, burn up the wilderness, and consume the green grass like fire. 22 A mist coming speedily heals all things. A dew coming after heat brings cheerfulness.23 By his counsel, he has calmed the deep and planted islands in it. 24 Those who sail on the sea tell of its dangers. We marvel when we hear it with our ears. 25 There are also those strange and wondrous works in it— variety of all that has life and the huge creatures of the sea. 26 Because of him, his messengers succeed. By his word, all things hold together.27 We may say many things, but couldn't say enough. The summary of our words is, "He is everything!" 28 How could we have strength to glorify him? For he is himself the greater than all his works. 29 The Lord is awesome and exceedingly great! His power is marvelous! 30 Glorify the Lord and exalt him as much as you can! For even yet, he will surpass that. When you exalt him, summon your full strength. Don't be weary, because you can't praise him enough. 31 Who has seen him, that he may describe him? Who can magnify him as he is? 32 Many things greater than these are hidden, for we have seen just a few of his works. 33 For the Lord made all things. He gave wisdom to the godly.

44

1 Let us now praise famous men, our ancestors in their generations. 2 The Lord created great glory in them— his mighty power from the beginning. 3 Some ruled in their kingdoms and were men renowned for their power, giving counsel by their understanding. Some have spoken in prophecies, 4 leaders of the people by their counsels, and by their understanding, giving instruction for the people. Their words in their instruction were wise. 5 Some composed musical tunes, and set forth verses in writing, 6 rich men endowed with ability, living peaceably in their homes. 7 All

these were honored in their generations, and were outstanding in their days. 8 Some of them have left a name behind them, so that others declare their praises. 9 But of others, there is no memory. They perished as though they had not been. They become as though they had not been born, they and their children after them. 10 But these were men of mercy, whose righteous deeds have not been forgotten. 11 A good inheritance remains with their offspring. Their children are within the covenant. 12 Their offspring stand fast, with their children, for their sakes. 13 Their offspring will remain forever. Their glory won't be blotted out. 14 Their bodies were buried in peace. Their name lives to all generations. 15 People will declare their wisdom. The congregation proclaims their praise.16 Enoch pleased the Lord, and was taken up, an example of repentance to all generations.17 Noah was found perfect and righteous. In the season of wrath, he kept the race alive. Therefore a remnant was left on the earth when the flood came. 18 Everlasting covenants were made with him, that all flesh should no more be blotted out by a flood.19 Abraham was a great father of a multitude of nations. There was none found like him in glory, 20 who kept the law of the Most High, and was taken into covenant with him. In his flesh he established the covenant. When he was tested, he was found faithful. 21 Therefore he assured him by an oath that the nations would be blessed through his offspring, that he would multiply him like the dust of the earth, exalt his offspring like the stars, and cause them to inherit from sea to sea, and from the Euphrates River to the utmost parts of the earth.22 In Isaac also, he established the same assurance for Abraham his father's sake, the blessing of all men, and the covenant. 23 He made it rest upon the head of Jacob. He acknowledged him in his blessings, gave to him by inheritance, and divided his portions. He distributed them among twelve tribes.

45

1 He brought out of him a man of mercy, who found favor in the sight of all people, a man loved by God and men, even Moses, whose memory is blessed. 2 He made him equal to the glory of the saints, and magnified him in the fears of his enemies. 3 By his words he caused the wonders to cease. God glorified him in the sight of kings. He gave him commandments for his people and showed him part of his glory. 4 He sanctified him in his faithfulness and meekness. He chose him out of all people. 5 He made him to hear his voice, led him into the thick darkness, and gave him commandments face to face, even the law of life and knowledge, that he might teach Jacob the covenant, and Israel his judgments.6 He exalted Aaron, a holy man like Moses, even his brother, of the tribe of Levi. 7 He established an everlasting covenant with him, and gave him the priesthood of the people. He blessed him with

stateliness, and dressed him in a glorious robe. 8 He clothed him in perfect splendor, and strengthened him with symbols of authority: the linen trousers, the long robe, and the ephod. 9 He encircled him with pomegranates; with many golden bells around him, to make a sound as he went, to make a sound that might be heard in the temple, for a reminder for the children of his people; 10 with a holy garment, with gold, blue, and purple, the work of the embroiderer; with an oracle of judgment—Urim and Thummim; 11 with twisted scarlet, the work of the craftsman; with precious stones engraved like a signet, in a setting of gold, the work of the jeweller, for a reminder engraved in writing, after the number of the tribes of Israel; 12 with a crown of gold upon the mitre, having engraved on it, as on a signet, "HOLINESS", an ornament of honor, the work of an expert, the desires of the eyes, goodly and beautiful. 13 Before him there never have been anything like it. No stranger put them on, but only his sons and his offspring perpetually. 14 His sacrifices shall be wholly burned, twice every day continually. 15 Moses consecrated him, and anointed him with holy oil. It was an everlasting covenant with him and to his offspring, all the days of heaven, to minister to the Lord, to serve as a priest, and to bless his people in his name. 16 He chose him out of all living to offer sacrifice to the Lord— incense, and a sweet fragrance, for a memorial, to make atonement for your people. 17 He gave to him in his commandments, authority in the covenants of judgments, to teach Jacob the testimonies, and to enlighten Israel in his law. 18 Strangers conspired against him and envied him in the wilderness: Dathan and Abiram with their company, and the congregation of Korah, with wrath and anger. 19 The Lord saw it, and it displeased him. In the wrath of his anger, they were destroyed. He did wonders upon them, to consume them with flaming fire. 20 He added glory to Aaron, and gave him a heritage. He divided to him the first fruits of the increase, and prepared bread of first fruits in abundance. 21 For they eat the sacrifices of the Lord, which he gave to him and to his offspring. 22 However, in the land of the people, he has no inheritance, and he has no portion among the people, for the Lord himself is your portion and inheritance.23 Phinehas the son of Eleazar is the third in glory, in that he was zealous in the fear of the Lord, and stood fast when the people turned away, and he made atonement for Israel. 24 Therefore, a covenant of peace was established for him, that he should be leader of the sanctuary and of his people, that he and his offspring should have the dignity of the priesthood forever. 25 Also he made a covenant with David the son of Jesse, of the tribe of Judah. The inheritance of the king is his alone from son to son. So the inheritance of Aaron is also to his seed.26May God give you wisdom in your heart to judge his people in righteousness, that their good things may not be abolished, and that their glory may endure for all their generations.

46

1 Joshua the son of Nun was valiant in war, and was the successor of Moses in prophecies. He was made great according to his name for the saving of God's elect, to take vengeance on the enemies that rose up against them, that he might give Israel their inheritance. 2 How was he glorified in the lifting up his hands, and in stretching out his sword against the cities! 3 Who before him stood so firm? For the Lord himself brought his enemies to him. 4 Didn't the sun go back by his hand? Didn't one day become as two? 5 He called upon the Most High, the Mighty One, when his foes pressed in all around him, and the great Lord heard him. 6 With hailstones of mighty power, he caused war to break violently upon the nation, and on the slope he destroyed those who resisted, so that the nations might know his armor, how he fought in the sight of the Lord; for he followed the Mighty One. 7 Also in the time of Moses, he did a work of mercy— he and Caleb the son of Jephunneh— in that they withstood the adversary, hindered the people from sin, and stilled their wicked complaining. 8 And of six hundred thousand people on foot, they two alone were preserved to bring them into their inheritance, into a land flowing with milk and honey. 9 The Lord gave strength to Caleb, and it remained with him to his old age, so that he entered the hill country, and his offspring obtained it for an inheritance, 10 that all the children of Israel might see that it is good to follow the Lord.11 Also the judges, every one by his name, all whose hearts didn't engage in immorality, and who didn't turn away from the Lord— may their memory be blessed! 12 May their bones flourish again out of their place. May the name of those who have been honored be renewed in their children.13 Samuel, the prophet of the Lord, loved by his Lord, established a kingdom and anointed princes over his people. 14 By the law of the Lord he judged the congregation, and the Lord watched over Jacob. 15 By his faithfulness he was proved to be a prophet. By his words he was known to be faithful in vision. 16 When his enemies pressed on him on every side, he called upon the Lord, the Mighty One, with the offering of the suckling lamb. 17 Then the Lord thundered from heaven. He made his voice heard with a mighty sound. 18 He utterly destroyed the rulers of the Tyrians and all the princes of the Philistines. 19 Before the time of his age-long sleep, he testified in the sight of the lord and his anointed, "I have not taken any man's goods, so much as a sandal;" and no one accused him. 20 Even after he fell asleep, he prophesied, and showed the king his end, and lifted up his voice from the earth in prophecy, to blot out the wickedness of the people.

47

1 After him, Nathan rose up to prophesy in the days of David. 2 As is the fat when it is separated from the peace offering, so was David separated from the children of Israel. 3 He played with lions as with kids, and with bears as with lambs of the flock. 4 In his youth didn't he kill a giant, and take away reproach from the people when he lifted up his hand with a sling stone, and beat down the boasting Goliath? 5 For he called upon the Most High Lord, and he gave him strength in his right hand to kill a man mighty in war, to exalt the horn of his people. 6 So they glorified him for his tens of thousands, and praised him for the blessings of the Lord, in that a glorious diadem was given to him. 7 For he destroyed the enemies on every side, and defeated the Philistines his adversaries. He broke their horn in pieces to this day. 8 In every work of his he gave thanks to the Holy One Most High with words of glory. He sang praise with his whole heart, and loved him who made him. 9 He set singers before the altar, to make sweet melody by their music.10 He gave beauty to the feasts, and set in order the seasons to completion while they praised his holy name, and the sanctuary resounded from early morning. 11 The Lord took away his sins, and exalted his horn forever. He gave him a covenant of kings, and a glorious throne in Israel.12 After him a wise son rose up, who because of him lived in security. 13 Solomon reigned in days of peace. God gave him rest all around, that he might set up a house for his name, and prepare a sanctuary forever. 14 How wise you were made in your youth, and filled as a river with understanding! 15 Your influence covered the earth, and you filled it with parables and riddles. 16 Your name reached to the far away islands, and you were loved for your peace. 17 For your songs, proverbs, parables, and interpretations, the countries marveled at you. 18 By the name of the Lord God, who is called the God of Israel, you gathered gold like tin, and multiplied silver like lead. 19 You bowed your loins to women, and in your body you were brought into subjection. 20 You blemished your honor, and defiled your offspring, to bring wrath upon your children. I was grieved for your folly, 21 because the sovereignty was divided, and a disobedient kingdom ruled out of Ephraim. 22 But the Lord will never forsake his mercy. He won't destroy any of his works, nor blot out the posterity of his elect. He won't take away the offspring him who loved him. He gave a remnant to Jacob, and to David a root from his own family.23 So Solomon rested with his fathers. Of his offspring, he left behind him Rehoboam, the foolishness of the people, and one who lacked understanding, who made the people revolt by his counsel. Also Jeroboam the son of Nebat, who made Israel to sin, and gave a way of sin to Ephraim. 24 Their sins were multiplied exceedingly, until they were removed from their land. 25 For they sought out all manner

of wickedness, until vengeance came upon them.

48

1 Then Elijah arose, the prophet like fire. His word burned like a torch. 2 He brought a famine upon them, and by his zeal made them few in number. 3 By the word of the Lord he shut up the heavens. He brought down fire three times. 4 How you were glorified, O Elijah, in your wondrous deeds! Whose glory is like yours? 5 You raised up a dead man from death, from Hades, by the word of the Most High. 6 You brought down kings to destruction, and honorable men from their sickbeds. 7 You heard rebuke in Sinai, and judgments of vengeance in Horeb. 8 You anointed kings for retribution, and prophets to succeed after you. 9 You were taken up in a tempest of fire, in a chariot of fiery horses. 10 You were recorded for reproofs in their seasons, to pacify anger, before it broke out into wrath, to turn the heart of the father to the son, and to restore the tribes of Jacob. 11 Blessed are those who saw you, and those who have been beautified with love; for we also shall surely live.12 Elijah was wrapped in a whirlwind. Elisha was filled with his spirit. In his days he was not moved by the fear of any ruler, and no one brought him into subjection. 13 Nothing was too hard for him. When he was buried, his body prophesied. 14 As in his life he did wonders, so his works were also marvelous in death. 15 For all this the people didn't repent. They didn't depart from their sins, until they were carried away as a plunder from their land, and were scattered through all the earth. The people were left very few in number, but with a ruler from the house of David. 16 Some of them did that which was right, but some multiplied sins.17 Hezekiah fortified his city, and brought water into its midst. He tunneled through rock with iron, and built cisterns for water. 18 In his days Sennacherib invaded, and sent Rabshakeh, and departed. He lifted up his hand against Zion, and boasted great things in his arrogance. 19 Then their hearts and their hands were shaken, and they were in pain, as women in labor. 20 But they called upon the Lord who is merciful, spreading out their hands to him. The Holy One quickly heard them out of Heaven, and delivered them by the hand of Isaiah. 21 He struck the camp of the Assyrians, and his angel utterly destroyed them. 22 For Hezekiah did that which was pleasing to the Lord, and was strong in the ways of his ancestor David, which Isaiah the prophet commanded, who was great and faithful in his vision.23 In his days the sun went backward. He prolonged the life of the king. 24 He saw by an excellent spirit what would come to pass in the future; and he comforted those who mourned in Zion. 25 He showed the things that would happen through the end of time, and the hidden things before they came.

49

1 The memory of Josiah is like the composition of incense prepared by the work of the perfumer. It will be sweet as honey in every mouth, and like music at a banquet of wine. 2 He did what was right in the reforming of the people, and took away the abominations of iniquity. 3 He set his heart right toward the Lord. In lawless days, he made godliness prevail.4 Except David, Hezekiah, and Josiah, all were wicked, because they abandoned the law of the Most High. The kings of Judah came to an end. 5 They gave their power to others, and their glory to a foreign nation. 6 They set the chosen city of the sanctuary on fire and made her streets desolate, as it was written by the hand of Jeremiah. 7 For they mistreated him; yet he was sanctified in the womb to be a prophet, to root out, to afflict, to destroy and likewise to build and to plant.8 Ezekiel saw the vision of glory, which God showed him on the chariot of the cherubim. 9 For truly he remembered the enemies in rainstorm, and to do good to those who directed their ways aright. 10 Also of the twelve prophets, may their bones flourish again out of their place. He comforted the people of Jacob, and delivered them by confident hope.11 How shall we magnify Zerubbabel? He was like a signet ring on the right hand. 12 So was Jesus the son of Josedek, who in their days built the house, and exalted a people holy to the Lord, prepared for everlasting glory. 13 Also of Nehemiah the memory is great. He raised up for us fallen walls, set up the gates and bars, and rebuilt our houses.14 No man was created upon the earth like Enoch, for he was taken up from the earth. 15 Nor was there a man born like Joseph, a leader of his kindred, a supporter of the people. Even his bones were cared for. 16 Shem and Seth were honored among men, but above every living thing in the creation was Adam.

50

1It was Simon, the son of Onias, the high priest, who in his life repaired the house, and in his days strengthened the temple. 2 The foundation was built by him to the height of the double walls, the lofty retaining walls of the temple enclosure. 3 In his days, a water cistern was dug, the brazen vessel like the sea in circumference. 4He planned to save his people from ruin, and fortified the city against siege. 5 How glorious he was when the people gathered around him as he came out of the house of the veil! 6 He was like the morning star among clouds, like the full moon, 7 like the sun shining on the temple of the Most High, like the rainbow shining in clouds of glory, 8 like roses in the days of first fruits, like lilies by a water spring, like the shoot of the frankincense tree in summer time, 9 like fire and incense in the censer, like a vessel of beaten gold adorned with all kinds of precious stones, 10 like an olive tree loaded with fruit, and like a cypress growing high among the clouds. 11 When he put on his glorious robe, and clothed himself in perfect splendor, ascending to the holy altar, he made the court of the sanctuary glorious.12 When he received the portions out of the priests' hands, as he stood by the hearth of the altar, with his kindred like a garland around him, he was like a young cedar in Lebanon surrounded by the trunks of palm trees. 13 All the sons of Aaron in their glory, held the Lord's offering in their hands before all the congregation of Israel. 14 Finishing the service at the altars, that he might arrange the offering of the Most High, the Almighty, 15 he stretched out his hand to the cup of libation, and poured out the cup of the grape. He poured it out at the foot of the altar, a sweet smelling fragrance to the Most High, the King of all. 16 Then the sons of Aaron shouted. They sounded the trumpets of beaten work. They made a great fanfare to be heard, for a reminder before the Most High. 17 Then all the people together hurried, and fell down to the ground on their faces to worship their Lord, the Almighty, God Most High.18 The singers also praised him with their voices. There was a sweet melody in the whole house. 19 And the people implored the Lord Most High, in prayer before him who is merciful, until the worship of the Lord was finished, and so they accomplished his service. 20 Then he went down, and lifted up his hands over the whole congregation of the children of Israel, to give blessing to the Lord with his lips, and to glory in his name. 21 He bowed himself down in worship the second time, to declare the blessing from the Most High.22 Now bless the God of all, who everywhere does great things, who exalts our days from the womb, and deals with us according to his mercy. 23 May he grant us joyfulness of heart, and that peace may be in our days in Israel for the days of eternity, 24 to entrust his mercy with us, and let him deliver us in his time!25 With two nations my soul is vexed, and the third is no nation: 26 Those who sit on the mountain of Samaria, the Philistines, and the foolish people who live in Shechem.27 I have written in this book the instruction of understanding and knowledge, I Jesus, the son of Sirach Eleazar, of Jerusalem, who out of his heart poured forth wisdom. 28 Blessed is he who will exercise these things. He who lays them up in his heart will become wise. 29 For if he does them, he will be strong in all things, for the light of the Lord is his guide.

51

A Prayer of Jesus the son of Sirach. 1 I will give thanks to you, O Lord, O King, and will praise you, O God my Savior. I give thanks to your name, 2 for you have been my protector and helper, and delivered my body out of destruction, and out of the snare of a slanderous tongue, from lips that fabricate lies. You were my helper before those who stood by, 3 and delivered me, according to the abundance of your mercy and of your name, from the gnashings of teeth ready to devour, out of the hand of those seeking my life, out of the many afflictions I endured, 4 from the choking of a fire on every side, and out of the midst of fire that I hadn't kindled, 5 out of the depth of the belly of Hades, from an unclean tongue, and from lying words— 6 the slander of an unrighteous tongue to the king. My soul drew near to death. My life was near to Hades. 7 They surrounded me on every side. There was no one to help me. I was looking for human help, and there was none. 8 Then I remembered your mercy, O Lord, and your working which has been from everlasting, how you deliver those who wait for you, and save them out of the hand of their enemies. 9 I lifted up my prayer from the earth, and prayed for deliverance from death. 10 I called upon the Lord, the Father of my Lord, that he would not forsake me in the days of affliction, in the time when there was no help against the proud. 11 I will praise your name continually. I will sing praise with thanksgiving. My prayer was heard. 12 You saved me from destruction and delivered me from the evil time. Therefore I will give thanks and praise to you, and bless the name of the Lord.13 When I was yet young, before I went abroad, I sought wisdom openly in my prayer. 14 Before the temple I asked for her. I will seek her out even to the end. 15 From the first flower to the ripening grape my heart delighted in her. My foot walked in uprightness. From my youth I followed her steps. 16 I inclined my ear a little, and received her, and found for myself much instruction. 17 I profited in her. I will give glory to him who gives me wisdom. 18 For I determined to practice her. I was zealous for that which is good. I will never be put to shame. 19 My soul has wrestled with her. In my conduct I was exact. I spread out my hands to the heaven above, and bewailed my ignorances of her. 20 I directed my soul to her. In purity I found her. I got myself a heart joined with her from the beginning. Therefore I won't be forsaken. 21 My belly also was troubled to seek her. Therefore I have gained a good possession. 22 The Lord gave me a tongue for my reward. I will praise him with it.23 Draw near to me, all you who are uneducated, and live in the house of instruction. 24 Why therefore are you all lacking in these things, and your souls are very thirsty? 25 I opened my mouth and spoke, "Get her for yourselves without money." 26 Put your neck under the yoke, and let your soul receive instruction. She is near to find.27 See with your eyes how that I labored just a little and found for myself much rest. 28 Get instruction with a great sum of silver, and gain much gold by her. 29 May your soul rejoice in his mercy, and may you all not be put to shame in praising him. 30 Work your work before the time comes, and in his time he will give you your reward.

THE BOOK OF BARUCH

1

1 These are the words of the book which Baruch the son of Nerias, the son of Maaseas, the son of Sedekias, the son of Asadias, the son of Helkias, wrote in Babylon, 2 in the fifth year, in the seventh day of the month, at the time when the Chaldeans took Jerusalem and burned it with fire. 3 Baruch read the words of this book in the hearing of Jechonias the son of Joakim king of Judah, and in the hearing of all the people who came to hear the book, 4 and in the hearing of the mighty men, and of the kings' sons, and in the hearing of the elders, and in the hearing of all the people, from the least to the greatest, even of all those who lived at Babylon by the river Sud. 5 Then they wept, fasted, and prayed before the Lord. 6 They also made a collection of money according to every man's ability; 7 and they sent it to Jerusalem to Joakim the high priest, the son of Helkias, the son of Salom, and to the priests and to all the people who were found with him at Jerusalem, 8 at the same time when he took the vessels of the house of the Lord, that had been carried out of the temple, to return them into the land of Judah, the tenth day of Sivan silver vessels which Sedekias the son of Josias king of Judah had made, 9 after Nabuchodonosor king of Babylon had carried away Jechonias, the princes, the captives, the mighty men, and the people of the land from Jerusalem, and brought them to Babylon. 10 And they said: Behold, we have sent you money; therefore buy with the money burnt offerings, sin offerings, and incense, and prepare an oblation, and offer upon the altar of the Lord our God; 11 and pray for the life of Nabuchodonosor king of Babylon, and for the life of Baltasar his son, that their days may be as the days of heaven above the earth. 12 The Lord will give us strength and light to our eyes. We will live under the shadow of Nabuchodonosor king of Babylon and under the shadow of Baltasar his son, and we shall serve them many days, and find favor in their sight. 13 Pray for us also to the Lord our God, for we have sinned against the Lord our God. To this day the wrath of the Lord and his indignation is not turned from us. 14 You shall read this book which we have sent to you, to make confession in the house of the Lord upon the day of the feast and on the days of the solemn assembly. 15 You shall say: To the Lord our God belongs righteousness, but to us confusion of face, as at this day—to the men of Judah, to the inhabitants of Jerusalem, 16 to our kings, to our princes, to our priests, to our prophets, and to our fathers, 17 because we have sinned before the Lord. 18 We have disobeyed him and have not listened to the voice of the Lord our God, to walk in the commandments of the Lord that he has set before us. 19 Since the day

that the Lord brought our fathers out of the land of Egypt to this present day, we have been disobedient to the Lord our God, and we have been negligent in not listening to his voice. 20 Therefore the plagues have clung to us, along with the curse which the Lord declared through Moses his servant in the day that he brought our fathers out of the land of Egypt to give us a land that flows with milk and honey, as at this day. 21 Nevertheless we didn't listen to the voice of the Lord our God, according to all the words of the prophets whom he sent to us, 22 but we each walked in the imagination of his own wicked heart, to serve strange gods and to do what is evil in the sight of the Lord our God.

2

1 Therefore the Lord has made good his word which he pronounced against us, and against our judges who judged Israel, and against our kings, and against our princes, and against the men of Israel and Judah, 2 to bring upon us great plagues such as never happened before under the whole heaven, as it came to pass in Jerusalem, according to the things that are written in the law of Moses, 3 that we should each eat the flesh of our own son, and each eat the flesh of our own daughter. 4 Moreover he has given them to be in subjection to all the kingdoms that are around us, to be a reproach and a desolation among all the people around us, where the Lord has scattered them. 5 Thus they were cast down and not exalted, because we sinned against the Lord our God in not listening to his voice. 6 To the Lord our God belongs righteousness, but to us and to our fathers confusion of face, as at this day. 7All these plagues have come upon us which the Lord has pronounced against us. 8 Yet have we not entreated the favor of the Lord by everyone turning from the thoughts of his wicked heart. 9 Therefore the Lord has kept watch over the plagues. The Lord has brought them upon us, for the Lord is righteous in all his works which he has commanded us. 10 Yet we have not listened to his voice, to walk in the commandments of the Lord that he has set before us. 11 And now, O Lord, you God of Israel who have brought your people out of the land of Egypt with a mighty hand, with signs, with wonders, with great power, and with a high arm, and have gotten yourself a name, as at this day: 12 O Lord our God, we have sinned. We have been ungodly. We have done wrong in all your ordinances. 13 Let your wrath turn from us, for we are but a few left among the heathen where you have scattered us. 14 Hear our prayer, O Lord, and our petition, and deliver us for your own sake. Give us favor in the sight of those who have led us away captive, 15 that all the earth may know that you are the Lord our God, because Israel and his posterity is called by your name. 16 O Lord, look down from your holy house and consider us. Incline your ear, O Lord, and

hear. 17 Open your eyes, and see; for the dead that are in Hades, whose breath is taken from their bodies, will give to the Lord neither glory nor righteousness; 18 but the soul who is greatly vexed, who goes stooping and feeble, and the eyes that fail, and the hungry soul, will declare your glory and righteousness, O Lord. 19 For we do not present our supplication before you, O Lord our God, for the righteousness of our fathers and of our kings. 20 For you have sent your wrath and your indignation upon us, as you have spoken by your servants the prophets, saying, 21 "The Lord says, 'Bow your shoulders to serve the king of Babylon, and remain in the land that I gave to your fathers. 22 But if you won't hear the voice of the Lord to serve the king of Babylon, 23 I will cause to cease out of the cities of Judah and from the region near Jerusalem the voice of mirth, the voice of gladness, voice of the bridegroom, and the voice of the bride. The whole land will be desolate without inhabitant.' " 24 But we wouldn't listen to your voice, to serve the king of Babylon. Therefore you have made good your words that you spoke by your servants the prophets, that the bones of our kings and the bones of our fathers would be taken out of their places. 25 Behold, they are cast out to the heat by day and to the frost by night. They died in great miseries by famine, by sword, and by pestilence. 26 You have made the house that is called by your name as it is today because of the wickedness of the house of Israel and the house of Judah. 27 Yet, O Lord our God, you have dealt with us after all your kindness and according to all your great mercy, 28 as you spoke by your servant Moses in the day when you commanded him to write your law in the presence of the children of Israel, saying, 29 "If you won't hear my voice, surely this very great multitude will be turned into a small number among the nations where I will scatter them. 30 For I know that they will not hear me, because they are a stiff-necked people; but in the land of their captivity they will take it to heart, 31 and will know that I am the Lord their God. I will give them a heart and ears to hear. 32 Then they will praise me in the land of their captivity, and think about my name, 33 and will return from their stiff neck and from their wicked deeds; for they will remember the way of their fathers who sinned before the Lord. 34 I will bring them again into the land which I promised to their fathers, to Abraham, to Isaac, and to Jacob, and they will rule over it. I will increase them, and they won't be diminished. 35 And I will make an everlasting covenant with them to be their God, and they will be my people. I will no more remove my people Israel out of the land that I have given them."

3

1 O Lord Almighty, you God of Israel, the soul in anguish and the troubled spirit cries to you. 2 Hear, O Lord, and have mercy; for you are a merciful God. Yes, have

mercy upon us, because we have sinned before you. 3 For you are enthroned forever, and we keep perishing. 4 O Lord Almighty, you God of Israel, hear now the prayer of the dead Israelites, and of the children of those who were sinners before you, who didn't listen to the voice of you their God; because of this, these plagues cling to us. 5 Don't remember the iniquities of our fathers, but remember your power and your name at this time. 6 For you are the Lord our God, and we will praise you, O Lord. 7 For this cause, you have put your fear in our hearts, to the intent that we should call upon your name. We will praise you in our captivity, for we have called to mind all the iniquity of our fathers who sinned before you. 8 Behold, we are yet this day in our captivity where you have scattered us, for a reproach and a curse, and to be subject to penalty according to all the iniquities of our fathers who departed from the Lord our God. 9 Hear, O Israel, the commandments of life! Give ear to understand wisdom! 10 How is it, O Israel, that you are in your enemies' land, that you have become old in a strange country, that you are defiled with the dead, 11 that you are counted with those who are in Hades? 12 You have forsaken the fountain of wisdom. 13If you had walked in the way of God, you would have dwelled in peace forever. 14 Learn where there is wisdom, where there is strength, and where there is understanding, that you may also know where there is length of days and life, where there is the light of the eyes and peace. 15 Who has found out her place? Who has come into her treasuries? 16 Where are the princes of the heathen, and those who ruled the beasts that are on the earth, 17 those who had their pastime with the fowls of the air, and those who hoarded up silver and gold, in which people trust, and of their getting there is no end? 18 For those who diligently sought silver, and were so anxious, and whose works are past finding out, 19 they have vanished and gone down to Hades, and others have come up in their place. 20 Younger men have seen the light and lived upon the earth, but they haven't known the way of knowledge, 21 nor understood its paths. Their children haven't embraced it. They are far off from their way. 22 It has not been heard of in Canaan, neither has it been seen in Teman. 23 The sons also of Agar who seek understanding, which are in the land, the merchants of Merran and Teman, and the authors of fables, and the searchers out of understanding—none of these have known the way of wisdom or remembered her paths. 24 O Israel, how great is the house of God! How large is the place of his possession! 25 It is great and has no end. It is high and unmeasurable. 26 Giants were born that were famous of old, great of stature, and expert in war. 27 God didn't choose these, nor did he give the way of knowledge to them, 28 so they perished, because they had no wisdom. They perished through their own foolishness. 29 Who has gone up into heaven, taken her, and brought her down from the clouds? 30 Who has gone over the sea, found her, and will bring her for choice gold? 31 There is no one who knows her way, nor any who comprehend her path. 32 But he that knows all things knows her, he found her out with his understanding. He who prepared the earth for all time has filled it with four-footed beasts. 33 It is he who sends forth the light, and it goes. He called it, and it obeyed him with fear. 34 The stars shone in their watches, and were glad. When he called them, they said, “Here we are.” They shone with gladness to him who made them. 35 This is our God. No other can be compared to him. 36 He has found out all the way of knowledge, and has given it to Jacob his servant and to Israel who is loved by him. 37 Afterward she appeared upon earth, and lived with men.

4

1 This is the book of God’s commandments and the law that endures forever. All those who hold it fast will live, but those who leave it will die. 2 Turn, O Jacob, and take hold of it. Walk toward the shining of its light. 3 Don’t give your glory to another, nor the things that are to your advantage to a foreign nation. 4 O Israel, we are happy; for the things that are pleasing to God are made known to us. 5 Be of good cheer, my people, the memorial of Israel. 6 You were not sold to the nations for destruction, but because you moved God to wrath, you were delivered to your adversaries. 7 For you provoked him who made you by sacrificing to demons and not to God. 8 You forgot the everlasting God who brought you up. You also grieved Jerusalem, who nursed you. 9 For she saw the wrath that came upon you from God, and said, “Listen, you who dwell near Zion; for God has brought upon me great mourning. 10 For I have seen the captivity of my sons and daughters, which the Everlasting has brought upon them. 11 For with joy I nourished them, but sent them away with weeping and mourning. 12 Let no man rejoice over me, a widow and forsaken by many. For the sins of my children, I am left desolate, because they turned away from the law of God 13 and had no regard for his statutes. They didn’t walk in the ways of God’s commandments or tread in the paths of discipline in his righteousness. 14 Let those who dwell near Zion come and remember the captivity of my sons and daughters, which the Everlasting has brought upon them. 15 For he has brought a nation upon them from afar, a shameless nation with a strange language, who didn’t respect old men or pity children. 16 They have carried away the dear beloved sons of the widow, and left her who was alone desolate of her daughters.” 17 But I—how can I help you? 18 For he who brought these calamities upon you will deliver you from the hand of your enemies. 19 Go your way, O my children. Go your way, for I am

left desolate. 20 I have put off the garment of peace, and put on the sackcloth of my petition. I will cry to the Everlasting as long as I live. 21 Take courage, my children. Cry to God, and he will deliver you from the power and hand of the enemies. 22 For I have trusted in the Everlasting, that he will save you; and joy has come to me from the Holy One, because of the mercy that will soon come to you from your Everlasting Savior. 23 For I sent you out with mourning and weeping, but God will give you to me again with joy and gladness forever. 24 For as now those who dwell near Zion have seen your captivity, so they will shortly see your salvation from our God which will come upon you with great glory and brightness of the Everlasting. 25 My children, suffer patiently the wrath that has come upon you from God, for your enemy has persecuted you; but shortly you will see his destruction and will tread upon their necks. 26 My delicate ones have traveled rough roads. They were taken away like a flock carried off by enemies. 27 Take courage, my children, and cry to God; for you will be remembered by him who has brought this upon you. 28 For as it was your decision to go astray from God, return and seek him ten times more. 29 For he who brought these calamities upon you will bring you everlasting joy again with your salvation. 30 Take courage, O Jerusalem, for he who called you by name will comfort you. 31 Miserable are those who afflicted you and rejoiced at your fall. 32 Miserable are the cities which your children served. Miserable is she who received your sons. 33 For as she rejoiced at your fall and was glad of your ruin, so she will be grieved at her own desolation. 34 And I will take away her pride in her great multitude and her boasting will be turned into mourning. 35 For fire will come upon her from the Everlasting for many days; and she will be inhabited by demons for a long time. 36 O Jerusalem, look around you toward the east, and behold the joy that comes to you from God. 37 Behold, your sons come, whom you sent away. They come gathered together from the east to the west at the word of the Holy One, rejoicing in the glory of God.

5

1 Take off the garment of your mourning and affliction, O Jerusalem, and put on forever the beauty of the glory from God. 2 Put on the robe of the righteousness from God. Set on your head a diadem of the glory of the Everlasting. 3 For God will show your splendor everywhere under heaven. 4 For your name will be called by God forever “Righteous Peace, Godly Glory”. 5 Arise, O Jerusalem, and stand upon the height. Look around you toward the east and see your children gathered from the going down of the sun to its rising at the word of the Holy One, rejoicing that God has remembered them. 6 For they went from you on foot, being led away by their enemies, but God

brings them in to you carried on high with glory, on a royal throne. 7 For God has appointed that every high mountain and the everlasting hills should be made low, and the valleys filled up to make the ground level, that Israel may go safely in the glory of God. 8 Moreover the woods and every sweet smelling tree have shaded Israel by the commandment of God. 9 For God will lead Israel with joy in the light of his glory with the mercy and righteousness that come from him.

THE LETTER OF JEREMIAH

A copy of a letter that Jeremiah sent to those who were to be taken to Babylon as exiles by the king of the Babylonians, to give them the message that God had commanded him. 1 Because of the sins which you have committed before God, you will be led away captives to Babylon by Nabuchodonosor king of the Babylonians. 2 So when you come to Babylon, you will remain there many years, and for a long season, even for seven generations. After that, I will bring you out peacefully from there. 3 But now you will see in Babylon gods of silver, gold, wood carried on shoulders, which cause the nations to fear. 4 Beware therefore that you in no way become like these foreigners. Don't let fear take hold of you because of them when you see the multitude before them and behind them, worshiping them. 5 But say in your hearts, "O Lord, we must worship you." 6 For my angel is with you, and I myself care for your souls. 7 For their tongue is polished by the workman, and they themselves are overlaid with gold and with silver; yet they are only fake, and can't speak. 8 And taking gold, as if it were for a virgin who loves to be happy, they make crowns for the heads of their gods. 9 Sometimes also the priests take gold and silver from their gods, and spend it on themselves. 10 They will even give some of it to the common prostitutes. They dress them like men with garments, even the gods of silver, gods of gold, and gods of wood. 11 Yet these gods can't save themselves from rust and moths, even though they are covered with purple garments. 12 They wipe their faces because of the dust of the temple, which is thick upon them. 13 And he who can't put to death one who offends against him holds a sceptre, as though he were judge of a country. 14 He has also a dagger in his right hand, and an axe, but can't deliver himself from war and robbers. 15 By this they are known not to be gods. Therefore don't fear them. 16 For like a vessel that a man uses is worth nothing when it is broken, even so it is with their gods. When they are set up in the temples, their eyes are full of dust through the feet of those who come in. 17 As the courts are secured on every side upon him who offends the king, as being committed to suffer death, even so the priests secure their temples with doors, with locks, and bars, lest they be carried off by robbers. 18 They light candles for them, yes, more than for themselves, even though they can't see one. 19 They are like one of the beams of the temple. Men say their hearts are eaten out when things creeping out of the earth devour both them and their clothing. They don't feel it 20 when their faces are blackened through the smoke that comes out of the temple. 21 Bats, swallows, and birds land on their bodies and heads. So do the cats. 22 By this you may know that they are no gods. Therefore don't fear them. 23 Notwithstanding the gold with which they are covered to make them beautiful, unless someone wipes off the tarnish, they won't shine; for they didn't even feel it when they were molten. 24 Things in which there is no breath are bought at any cost. 25 Having no feet, they are carried upon shoulders. By this, they declare to men that they are worth nothing. 26 Those who serve them are also ashamed, for if they fall to the ground at any time, they can't rise up again by themselves. If they are bowed down, they can't make themselves straight; but the offerings are set before them, as if they were dead men. 27 And the things that are sacrificed to them, their priests sell and spend. In like manner, their wives also lay up part of it in salt; but to the poor and to the impotent they give none of it. 28 The menstruous woman and the woman in childbed touch their sacrifices, knowing therefore by these things that they are no gods. Don't fear them. 29 For how can they be called gods? Because women set food before the gods of silver, gold, and wood. 30 And in their temples the priests sit on seats, having their clothes torn and their heads and beards shaven, and nothing on their heads. 31 They roar and cry before their gods, as men do at the feast when one is dead. 32 The priests also take off garments from them and clothe their wives and children with them. 33 Whether it is evil or good what one does to them, they are not able to repay it. They can't set up a king or put him down. 34 In like manner, they can neither give riches nor money. Though a man make a vow to them and doesn't keep it, they will never exact it. 35 They can save no man from death. They can't deliver the weak from the mighty. 36 They can't restore a blind man to his sight, or deliver anyone who is in distress. 37 They can show no mercy to the widow, or do good to the fatherless. 38 They are like the stones that are cut out of the mountain, these gods of wood that are overlaid with gold and with silver. Those who minister to them will be confounded. 39 How could a man then think or say that they are gods, when even the Chaldeans themselves dishonor them? 40 If they shall see one mute who can't speak, they bring him and ask him to call upon Bel, as though he were able to understand. 41 Yet they can't perceive this themselves, and forsake them; for they have no understanding. 42 The women also with cords around them sit in the ways, burning bran for incense; but if any of them, drawn by someone who passes by, lies with him, she reproaches her fellow, that she was not thought as worthy as herself and her cord wasn't broken. 43 Whatever is done among them is false. How could a man then think or say that they are gods? 44 They are fashioned by carpenters and goldsmiths. They can be nothing else than what the workmen make them to be. 45 And they themselves who fashioned them can never continue long. How then should the things that are fashioned by them? 46 For they have left lies and reproaches to those who come after. 47 For when there comes any war or plague upon them, the priests consult with themselves, where they may be hidden with them. 48 How then can't men understand that they are no gods, which can't save themselves from war or from plague? 49 For seeing they are only wood and overlaid with gold and silver, it will be known hereafter that they are false. 50 It will be manifest to all nations and kings that they are no gods, but the works of men's hands, and that there is no work of God in them. 51 Who then may not know that they are not gods?52 For they can't set up a king in a land or give rain to men. 53 They can't judge their own cause, or redress a wrong, being unable; for they are like crows between heaven and earth. 54 For even when fire falls upon the house of gods of wood overlaid with gold or with silver, their priests will flee away, and escape, but they themselves will be burned apart like beams. 55 Moreover they can't withstand any king or enemies. How could a man then admit or think that they are gods? 56 Those gods of wood overlaid with silver or with gold aren't able to escape from thieves or robbers. 57 The gold, silver, and garments with which they are clothed those who are strong will take from them, and go away with them. They won't be able to help themselves. 58 Therefore it is better to be a king who shows his manhood, or else a vessel in a house profitable for whatever the owner needs, than such false gods or even a door in a house, to keep the things safe that are in it, than such false gods; or better to be a pillar of wood in a palace than such false gods.59 For sun, moon, and stars, being bright and sent to do their jobs, are obedient. 60 Likewise also the lightning when it flashes is beautiful to see. In the same way, the wind also blows in every country. 61 And when God commands the clouds to go over the whole world, they do as they are told. 62 And the fire sent from above to consume mountains and woods does as it is commanded; but these are to be compared to them neither in show nor power. 63 Therefore a man shouldn't think or say that they are gods, seeing they aren't able to judge causes or to do good to men. 64 Knowing therefore that they are no gods, don't fear them. 65 For they can neither curse nor bless kings. 66 They can't show signs in the heavens among the nations, or shine as the sun, or give light as the moon. 67 The beasts are better than they; for they can get under a covert, and help themselves. 68 In no way then is it manifest to us that they are gods. Therefore don't fear them. 69 For as a scarecrow in a garden of cucumbers that keeps nothing, so are their gods of wood overlaid with gold and silver. 70 Likewise also their gods of wood overlaid with gold and with silver, are like a white thorn in an orchard that every bird sits upon. They are also like a dead body that is thrown out into the dark. 71 You will know them to be no gods by the bright purple that rots upon them. They themselves will be consumed afterwards, and will be a reproach in the country. 72 Better therefore is the just man who has no idols; for he will be far from reproach.

THE PRAYER OF MANASSES

1

O Lord Almighty in heaven, God of our fathers Abraham, Isaac, and Jacob, and of their righteous offspring, 2 you who have made heaven and earth, with all their order, 3 who have bound the sea by the word of your commandment, who have shut up the deep, and sealed it by your terrible and glorious name, 4 whom all things fear, yes, tremble before your power, 5 for the majesty of your glory can't be borne, and the anger of your threatening toward sinners is unbearable. 6 Your merciful promise is unmeasurable and unsearchable, 7 for you are the Lord Most High, of great compassion, patient and abundant in mercy, and relent at human suffering. 8You, O Lord, according to your great goodness have promised repentance and forgiveness to those who have sinned against you. Of your infinite mercies, you have appointed repentance to sinners, that they may be saved. You therefore, O Lord, who are the God of the just, have not appointed repentance to the just, to Abraham, Isaac, and Jacob, which have not sinned against you, but you have appointed repentance to me who am a sinner. 9 For I have sinned more than the number of the sands of the sea. My transgressions are multiplied, O Lord, my transgressions are multiplied, and I am not worthy to behold and see the height of heaven for the multitude of my iniquities. 10 I am bowed down with many iron bands, so that I can't lift up my head by reason of my sins, neither have I any relief; for I have provoked your wrath, and done that which is evil before you: I didn't do your will, neither did I keep your commandments. I have set up abominations, and have multiplied detestable things. 11 Now therefore I bow the knee of my heart, asking you for grace. 12 I have sinned, O Lord, I have sinned, and I acknowledge my iniquities; 13 but, I humbly ask you, forgive me, O Lord, forgive me, and please don't destroy me with my iniquities. Don't be angry with me forever, by reserving evil for me. Don't condemn me into the lower parts of the earth. For you, O Lord, are the God of those who repent. 14 In me you will show all your goodness, for you will save me, who am unworthy, according to your great mercy. 15 Then I will praise you forever all the days of my life; for all the army of heaven sings your praise, and yours is the glory forever and ever. Amen.

PSALM 151

1 I was small among my brothers, and youngest in my father's house.I tended my father's sheep. 2 My hands formed a musical instrument, and my fingers tuned a lyre. 3 Who shall tell my Lord? The Lord himself, he himself hears. 4 He sent forth his angel and took me from my father's sheep, and he anointed me with his anointing oil. 5 My brothers were handsome and tall; but the Lord didn't take pleasure in them. 6 I went out to meet the Philistine, and he cursed me by his idols. 7 But I drew his own sword and beheaded him, and removed reproach from the children of Israel.

THE BOOK OF 1 ESDRAS

1

1*Josias held the Passover in Jerusalem to his Lord, and offered the Passover the fourteenth day of the first month, 2 having set the priests according to their daily courses, being arrayed in their vestments, in the Lord's temple. 3 He spoke to the Levites, *the temple servants of Israel, that they should make themselves holy to the Lord, to set the holy ark of the Lord in the house that King Solomon the son of David had built. 4 He said, "You no longer need to carry it on your shoulders. Now therefore serve the Lord your God, and minister to his people Israel, and prepare yourselves by your fathers' houses and kindred, 5 according to the writing of King David of Israel, and according to the magnificence of Solomon his son. Stand in the holy place according to the divisions of your Levite families who minister in the presence of your kindred the descendants of Israel. 6 Offer the Passover in order, prepare the sacrifices for your kindred, and keep the Passover according to the Lord's commandment, which was given to Moses. 7 To the people which were present, Josias gave thirty thousand lambs and kids, and three thousand calves. These things were given from the king's possessions, as he promised, to the people and to the priests and Levites.8 Helkias, Zacharias, and Esyelus, the rulers of the temple, gave to the priests for the Passover two thousand six hundred sheep, and three hundred calves. 9 Jeconias, Samaias, Nathanael his brother, Sabias, Ochielus, and Joram, captains over thousands, gave to the Levites for the Passover five thousand sheep and seven hundred calves. 10 When these things were done, the priests and Levites, having the unleavened bread, stood in proper order according to the kindred, 11 and according to the several divisions by fathers' houses, before the people, to offer to the Lord as it is written in the book of Moses. They did this in the morning. 12 They roasted the Passover lamb with fire, as required. They boiled the sacrifices in the brazen vessels and caldrons with a pleasing smell, 13 and set them before all the people. Afterward they prepared for themselves and for their kindred the priests, the sons of Aaron. 14 For the priests offered the fat until night. The Levites prepared for themselves and for their kindred the priests, the sons of Aaron. 15 The holy singers also, the sons of Asaph, were in their order, according to the appointment of David: Asaph, Zacharias, and Eddinus, who represented the king. 16 Moreover the gatekeepers were at every gate. No one needed to depart from his daily duties, for their kindred the Levites prepared for them. 17 So the things that belonged to the Lord's sacrifices were accomplished in that day, in holding the Passover, 18 and offering sacrifices on the altar of the Lord, according to the commandment of King Josias. 19 So the children of Israel which were present at that time held the Passover and the feast of unleavened bread seven days. 20 Such a Passover had not been held in Israel since the time of the prophet Samuel. 21 Indeed, none of the kings of Israel held such a Passover as Josias with the priests, the Levites, and the Jews, held with all Israel that were present in their dwelling place at Jerusalem. 22 This Passover was held in the eighteenth year of the reign of Josias. 23 The works of Josias were upright before his Lord with a heart full of godliness. 24 Moreover the things that came to pass in his days have been written in times past, concerning those who sinned and did wickedly against the Lord more than any other people or kingdom, and how they grieved him exceedingly, so that the Lord's words were confirmed against Israel.25*Now after all these acts of Josias, it came to pass that Pharaoh the king of Egypt came to make war at Carchemish on the Euphrates; and Josias went out against him. 26 But the king of Egypt sent to him, saying, "What do I have to do with you, O king of Judea? 27 I wasn't sent out from the Lord God against you, for my war is against the Euphrates. Now the Lord is with me, yes, the Lord is with me hastening me forward. Depart from me, and don't be against the Lord."28 However, Josias didn't turn back to his chariot, but tried to fight with him, not regarding the words of the prophet Jeremiah from the Lord's mouth, 29 but joined battle with him in the plain of Megiddo, and the commanders came down against King Josias. 30 Then the king said to his servants, "Carry me away out of the battle, for I am very weak!" Immediately his servants carried him away out of the army. 31 Then he got into his second chariot. After he was brought back to Jerusalem he died, and was buried in the tomb of his ancestors. 32 All Judea mourned for Josias. Jeremiah the prophet lamented for Josias, and the chief men with the women made lamentation for him to this day. This was given out for an ordinance to be done continually in all the nation of Israel. 33 These things are written in the book of the histories of the kings of Judea, and every one of the acts that Josias did, and his glory, and his understanding in the law of the Lord, and the things that he had done before, and the things now told, are reported in the book of the kings of Israel and Judah.34* The people took Joachaz the son of Josias, and made him king instead of Josias his father, when he was twenty-three years old. 35 He reigned in Judah and Jerusalem for three months. Then the king of Egypt deposed him from reigning in Jerusalem. 36 He set a tax upon the people of one hundred talents of silver and one talent of gold. 37 The king of Egypt also made King Joakim his brother king of Judea and Jerusalem. 38 And Joakim imprisoned the nobles and apprehended his brother Zarakes, and brought him up out of Egypt.39*Joakim was twenty-five years old when he began to reign in Judea and Jerusalem. He did that which was evil in the sight of the Lord. 40 King Nabuchodonosor of Babylon came up against him, bound him with a chain of brass, and carried him to Babylon. 41 Nabuchodonosor also took some of the Lord's holy vessels, carried them away, and stored them in his own temple at Babylon. 42 But those things that are reported of him, and of his uncleanness and impiety, are written in the chronicles of the kings. 43 Then Joakim his son reigned in his place. When he was made king, he was eighteen years old. 44 He reigned three months and ten days in Jerusalem. He did that which was evil before the Lord.45 So after a year Nabuchodonosor sent and caused him to be brought to Babylon with the holy vessels of the Lord, 46 and made Sedekias king of Judea and Jerusalem when he was twenty-one years old. He reigned eleven years. 47 He also did that which was evil in the sight of the Lord, and didn't heed the words that were spoken by Jeremiah the prophet from the Lord's mouth. 48 After King Nabuchodonosor had made him to swear by the name of the Lord, he broke his oath and rebelled. Hardening his neck and his heart, he transgressed the laws of the Lord, the God of Israel. 49 Moreover the governors of the people and of the priests did many things wickedly, exceeding all the defilements of all nations, and defiled the temple of the Lord, which was sanctified in Jerusalem. 50 The God of their ancestors sent by his messenger to call them back, because he had compassion on them and on his dwelling place. 51 But they mocked his messengers. In the day when the Lord spoke, they scoffed at his prophets 52 until he, being angry with his people for their great ungodliness, commanded to bring up the kings of the Chaldeans against them. 53 They killed their young men with the sword around their holy temple, and spared neither young man or young woman, old man or child; but he delivered all of them into their hands. 54 They took all the holy vessels of the Lord, both great and small, with the treasure chests of the Lord's ark and the king's treasures, and carried them away to Babylon. 55 They burned the Lord's house, broke down Jerusalem's walls, and burned its towers with fire. 56 As for her glorious things, they didn't stop until they had brought them all to nothing. He carried the people who weren't slain with the sword to Babylon. 57 They were servants to him and to his children until the Persians reigned, to fulfill the word of the Lord by the mouth of Jeremiah: 58 "Until the land has enjoyed its Sabbaths, the hole time of her desolation shall she keep Sabbath, to fulfill seventy years.

2

1 In the *first year of King Cyrus of the Persians, that the word of the Lord by the mouth of Jeremiah might be accomplished, 2 the Lord stirred up the spirit of King Cyrus of the Persians, and he made a proclamation throughout all his kingdom, and also by writing, 3 saying, "Cyrus king of the Persians says: The Lord of Israel, the Most High Lord, has made me king of the whole world, 4 and commanded me to build him a house at Jerusalem that is in Judea. 5 If therefore there are any of you that are of his people, let the Lord, even his Lord, be with him, and let him go up to Jerusalem that is in Judea, and build the house of the Lord of Israel. He is the Lord who dwells in Jerusalem. 6 Therefore, of those who dwell in various places, let those who are in his own place help each one with gold, with silver, 7 with gifts, with horses, and cattle, beside the other things which have been added by vow for the temple of the Lord which is in Jerusalem.8 Then the chief of the families of Judah and of the tribe of Benjamin stood up, with the priests, the Levites, and all whose spirit the Lord had stirred to go up, to build the house for the Lord which is in Jerusalem. 9 Those who lived around them helped them in all things with silver and gold, with horses and cattle, and with very many gifts that were vowed by a great number whose minds were so

moved.10 King Cyrus also brought out the holy vessels of the Lord, which Nabuchodonosor had carried away from Jerusalem and had stored in his temple of idols. 11 Now when King Cyrus of the Persians had brought them out, he delivered them to Mithradates his treasurer, 12 and by him they were delivered to Sanabassar the governor of Judea. 13 This was the number of them: one thousand gold cups, one thousand silver cups, twenty-nine silver censers, thirty gold bowls, two thousand four hundred ten silver bowls, and one thousand other vessels. 14 So all the vessels of gold and of silver were brought up, even five thousand four hundred seventy-nine, 15 and were carried back by Sanabassar, together with the returning exiles, from Babylon to Jerusalem.16*In the time of King Artaxerxes of the Persians, Belemus, Mithradates, Tabellius, Rathumus, Beeltethmus, and Samellius the scribe, with their other associates, dwelling in Samaria and other places, wrote to him against those who lived in Judea and Jerusalem the following letter: 17 "To King Artaxerxes our Lord, from your servants, Rathumus the recorder, Samellius the scribe, and the rest of their council, and the judges who are in Coelesyria and Phoenicia: 18 Let it now be known to our lord the king, that the Jews that have come up from you to us, having come to Jerusalem, are building that rebellious and wicked city, and are repairing its marketplaces and walls, and are laying the foundation of a temple. 19 Now if this city is built and its walls are finished, they will not only refuse to give tribute, but will even stand up against kings. 20 Since the things pertaining to the temple are now in hand, we think it appropriate not to neglect such a matter, 21 but to speak to our lord the king, to the intent that, if it is your pleasure, search may be made in the books of your ancestors. 22 You will find in the chronicles what is written concerning these things, and will understand that that city was rebellious, troubling both kings and cities, 23 and that the Jews were rebellious, and kept starting wars there in the past. For this cause, this city was laid waste. 24 Therefore now we do declare to you, O lord the king, that if this city is built again, and its walls set up again, you will from then on have no passage into Coelesyria and Phoenicia."25 Then the king wrote back again to Rathumus the recorder, Beeltethmus, Samellius the scribe, and to the rest that of their associates who lived in Samaria, Syria, and Phoenicia, as follows: 26 "I have read the letter which you have sent to me. Therefore I commanded to make search, and it has been found that that city of old time has fought against kings, 27 and the men were given to rebellion and war in it, and that mighty and fierce kings were in Jerusalem, who reigned and exacted tribute in Coelesyria and Phoenicia. 28 Now therefore I have commanded to prevent those men from building the city, and heed to be taken that there be nothing done contrary to this order, 29 and that those wicked doings proceed no further to the annoyance of kings." 30 Then King Artaxerxes, his letters being read, Rathumus, and Samellius the scribe, and the rest of their associates, went in haste to Jerusalem with cavalry and a multitude of people in battle array, and began to hinder the builders. So the building of the temple in Jerusalem ceased until the second year of the reign of King Darius of the Persians.

3

1 Now King Darius made a great feast for all his subjects, for all who were born in his house, for all the princes of Media and of Persia, 2 and for all the local governors and captains and governors who were under him, from India to Ethiopia, in the one hundred twenty seven provinces. 3 They ate and drank, and when they were satisfied went home. Then King Darius went into his bedchamber slept, but awakened out of his sleep.4 Then the three young men of the bodyguard, who guarded the king, spoke one to another: 5 "Let every one of us state what one thing is strongest. King Darius will give he whose statement seems wiser than the others great gifts and great honors in token of victory. 6 He shall be clothed in purple, drink from gold cups, sleep on a gold bed, and have a chariot with bridles of gold, a fine linen turban, and a chain around his neck. 7 He shall sit next to Darius because of his wisdom, and shall be called cousin of Darius."8 Then they each wrote his sentence, sealed them, and laid them under King Darius' pillow, 9 and said, "When the king wakes up, someone will give him the writing. Whoever the king and the three princes of Persia judge that his sentence is the wisest, to him shall the victory be given, as it is written." 10 The first wrote, "Wine is the strongest." 11 The second wrote, "The king is strongest." 12 The third wrote, "Women are strongest, but above all things Truth is the victor."13 Now when the king woke up, they took the writing and gave it to him, so he read it. 14 Sending out, he called all the princes of Persia and of Media, the local governors, the captains, the governors, and the chief officers 15 and sat himself down in the royal seat of judgment; and the writing was read before them. 16 He said, "Call the young men, and they shall explain their own sentences. So they were called and came in. 17 They said to them, "Explain what you have written."Then the first, who had spoken of the strength of wine, began 18 and said this: "O sirs, how exceedingly strong wine is! It causes all men who drink it to go astray. 19 It makes the mind of the king and of the fatherless child to be the same, likewise of the bondman and of the freeman, of the poor man and of the rich. 20 It also turns every thought into cheer and mirth, so that a man remembers neither sorrow nor debt. 21 It makes every heart rich, so that a man remembers neither king nor

local governor. It makes people say things in large amounts. 22 When they are in their cups, they forget their love both to friends and kindred, and before long draw their swords. 23 But when they awake from their wine, they don't remember what they have done. 24 O sirs, isn't wine the strongest, seeing that it forces people to do this?" And when he had said this, he stopped speaking.

4

1 Then the second, who had spoken of the strength of the king, began to say, 2 "O sirs, don't men excel in strength who rule over the sea and land, and all things in them? 3 But yet the king is stronger. He is their lord and has dominion over them. In whatever he commands them, they obey him. 4 If he tells them to make war the one against the other, they do it. If he sends them out against the enemies, they go, and conquer mountains, walls, and towers. 5 They kill and are killed, and don't disobey the king's commandment. If they win the victory, they bring everything to the king—all the plunder and everything else. 6 Likewise for those who are not soldiers, and don't have anything to do with wars, but farm, when they have reaped again that which they had sown, they bring some to the king and compel one another to pay tribute to the king. 7 He is just one man! If he commands people to kill, they kill. If he commands them to spare, they spare. 8 If he commands them to strike, they strike. If he commands them to make desolate, they make desolate. If he commands to build, they build. 9 If he commands them to cut down, they cut down. If he commands them to plant, they plant. 10 So all his people and his armies obey him. Furthermore, he lies down, he eats and drinks, and takes his rest; 11 and these keep watch around him. None of them may depart and do his own business. They don't disobey him in anything. 12 O sirs, how could the king not be the strongest, seeing that he is obeyed like this?" Then he stopped talking.13 Then the third, who had spoken of women, and of truth, (this was Zorobabel) began to speak: 14 "O sirs, isn't the king great, and men are many, and isn't wine strong? Who is it then who rules them, or has the lordship over them? Aren't they women? 15 Women have given birth to the king and all the people who rule over sea and land. 16 They came from women. Women nourished up those who planted the vineyards, from where the wine comes. 17 Women also make garments for men. These bring glory to men. Without women, men can't exist. 18 Yes, and if men have gathered together gold and silver and any other beautiful thing, and see a woman who is lovely in appearance and beauty, 19 they let all those things go and gape at her, and with open mouth stare at her. They all have more desire for her than for gold, or silver, or any other beautiful thing. 20 A man leaves his own father who brought him up, leaves

his own country, and joins with his wife. 21 With his wife he ends his days, with no thought for his father, mother, or country. 22 By this also you must know that women have dominion over you. Don't you labor and toil, and bring it all to give to women? 23 Yes, a man takes his sword and goes out to travel, to rob, to steal, and to sail on the sea and on rivers. 24 He sees a lion and walks in the darkness. When he has stolen, plundered, and robbed, he brings it to the woman he loves. 25 Therefore a man loves his wife better than father or mother. 26 Yes, there are many who have lost their minds for women, and become slaves for their sakes. 27 Many also have perished, have stumbled, and sinned, for women. 28 Now don't you believe me? Isn't the king great in his power? Don't all regions fear to touch him? 29 Yet I saw him and Apame the king's concubine, the daughter of the illustrious Barticus, sitting at the right hand of the king, 30 and taking the crown from the king's head, and setting it upon her own head. Yes, she struck the king with her left hand. 31 At this, the king gaped and gazed at her with open mouth. If she smiles at him, he laughs. But if she takes any displeasure at him, he flatters her, that she might be reconciled to him again. 32 O sirs, how can it not be that women are strong, seeing they do this?"33 Then the king and the nobles looked at one another. So he began to speak concerning truth. 34 "O sirs, aren't women strong? The earth is great. The sky is high. The sun is swift in its course, for it circles around the sky, and returns on its course again in one day. 35 Isn't he who makes these things great? Therefore the truth is great, and stronger than all things. 36 All the earth calls upon truth, and the sky blesses truth. All works shake and tremble, but with truth there is no unrighteous thing. 37 Wine is unrighteous. The king is unrighteous. Women are unrighteous. All the children of men are unrighteous, and all their works are unrighteous. There is no truth in them. They shall also perish in their unrighteousness. 38 But truth remains, and is strong forever. Truth lives and conquers forevermore. 39 With truth there is no partiality toward persons or rewards, but truth does the things that are just, instead of any unrighteous or wicked things. All men approve truth's works. 40 In truth's judgment is not any unrighteousness. Truth is the strength, the kingdom, the power, and the majesty of all ages. Blessed be the God of truth!"41 With that, he stopped speaking. Then all the people shouted and said, "Great is truth, and strong above all things!" 42 Then the king said to him, "Ask what you wish, even more than is appointed in writing, and we will give it to you, because you are found wisest. You shall sit next me, and shall be called my cousin."43 Then he said to the king, "Remember your vow, which you vowed to build Jerusalem, in the day when you came to your kingdom, 44 and to send back all the vessels that were taken out of

Jerusalem, which Cyrus set apart when he vowed to destroy Babylon, and vowed to send them back there. 45 You also vowed to build the temple which the Edomites burned when Judea was made desolate by the Chaldeans. 46 Now, O lord the king, this is what I request, and what I desire of you, and this is the princely generosity that may proceed from you: I ask therefore that you make good the vow, the performance of which you have vowed to the King of Heaven with your own mouth." 47 Then King Darius stood up, kissed him, and wrote letters for him to all the treasurers and governors and captains and local governors, that they should safely bring on their way both him, and all those who would go up with him to build Jerusalem. 48 He wrote letters also to all the governors who were in Coelesyria and Phoenicia, and to them in Libanus, that they should bring cedar wood from Libanus to Jerusalem, and that they should help him build the city. 49 Moreover he wrote for all the Jews who would go out of his realm up into Judea concerning their freedom, that no officer, no governor, no local governor, nor treasurer, should forcibly enter into their doors, 50 and that all the country which they occupied should be free to them without tribute, and that the Edomites should give up the villages of the Jews which they held at that time, 51 and that there should be given twenty talents yearly toward the building of the temple, until the time that it was built, 52 and another ten talents yearly for burnt offerings to be presented upon the altar every day, as they had a commandment to make seventeen offerings, 53 and that all those who would come from Babylonia to build the city should have their freedom they and their descendants, and all the priests that came. 54 He wrote also to give them their support and the priests' vestments in which they minister. 55 For the Levites he wrote that their support should be given them until the day that the house was finished and Jerusalem built up. 56 He commanded that land and wages should be given to all who guarded the city. 57 He also sent away all the vessels from Babylon that Cyrus had set apart, and all that Cyrus had given in commandment, he commanded also to be done and to be sent to Jerusalem.58 Now when this young man had gone out, he lifted up his face to heaven toward Jerusalem, and praised the King of heaven, 59 and said, "From you comes victory. From you comes wisdom. Yours is the glory, and I am your servant. 60 Blessed are you, who have given me wisdom. I give thanks to you, O Lord of our fathers. 61 So he took the letters, went out, came to Babylon, and told it all his kindred. 62 They praised the God of their ancestors, because he had given them freedom and liberty 63 to go up and to build Jerusalem and the temple which is called by his name. They feasted with instruments of music and gladness seven days.

5

1 After this, the chiefs of fathers' houses were chosen to go up according to their tribes, with their wives, sons, and daughters, with their menservants and maidservants, and their livestock. 2 Darius sent with them one thousand cavalry to bring them back to Jerusalem with peace, with musical instruments, drums, and flutes. 3 All their kindred were making merry, and he made them go up together with them.4 These are the names of the men who went up, according to their families among their tribes, after their several divisions. 5 The priests, the sons of Phinees, the sons of Aaron: Jesus the son of Josedek, the son of Saraias, and Joakim the son of Zorobabel, the son of Salathiel, of the house of David, of the lineage of Phares, of the tribe of Judah, 6 who spoke wise words before Darius the king of Persia in the second year of his reign, in the month Nisan, which is the first month.7*These are the of Judeans who came up from the captivity, where they lived as foreigners, whom Nabuchodonosor the king of Babylon had carried away to Babylon. 8 They returned to Jerusalem and to the other parts of Judea, every man to his own city, who came with Zorobabel, with Jesus, Nehemias, Zaraias, Resaias, Eneneus, Mardocheus, Beelsarus, Aspharsus, Reelias, Roimus, and Baana, their leaders.9 The number of them of the nation and their leaders: the sons of Phoros, two thousand one hundred seventy two; the sons of Saphat, four hundred seventy two; 10 the sons of Ares, seven hundred fifty six; 11 the sons of Phaath Moab, of the sons of Jesus and Joab, two thousand eight hundred twelve; 12 the sons of Elam, one thousand two hundred fifty four; the sons of Zathui, nine hundred forty five; the sons of Chorbe, seven hundred five; the sons of Bani, six hundred forty eight; 13 the sons of Bebai, six hundred twenty three; the sons of Astad, one thousand three hundred twenty two; 14 the sons of Adonikam, six hundred sixty seven; the sons of Bagoi, two thousand sixty six; the sons of Adinu, four hundred fifty four; 15 the sons of Ater, of Ezekias, ninety two; the sons of Kilan and Azetas, sixty seven; the sons of Azaru, four hundred thirty two; 16 the sons of Annis, one hundred one; the sons of Arom, the sons of Bassai, three hundred twenty three; the sons of Arsiphurith, one hundred twelve; 17 the sons of Baiterus, three thousand five; the sons of Bethlomon, one hundred twenty three; 18 those from Netophas, fifty five; those from Anathoth, one hundred fifty eight; those from Bethasmoth, forty two; 19 those from Kariathiarius, twenty five: those from Caphira and Beroth, seven hundred forty three; 20 the Chadiasai and Ammidioi, four hundred twenty two; those from Kirama and Gabbe, six hundred twenty one; 21 those from Macalon, one hundred twenty two; those from Betolion, fifty two; the sons of

Niphis, one hundred fifty six; 22 the sons of Calamolalus and Onus, seven hundred twenty five; the sons of Jerechu, three hundred forty five; 23 and the sons of Sanaas, three thousand three hundred thirty.24 The priests: the sons of Jeddu, the son of Jesus, among the sons of Sanasib, nine hundred seventy two; the sons of Emmeruth, one thousand fifty two; 25 the sons of Phassurus, one thousand two hundred forty seven; and the sons of Charme, one thousand seventeen. 26 The Levites: the sons of Jesus, Kadmiel, Bannas, and Sudias, seventy four. 27 The holy singers: the sons of Asaph, one hundred twenty eight. 28 The gatekeepers: the sons of Salum, the sons of Atar, the sons of Tolman, the sons of Dacubi, the sons of Ateta, the sons of Sabi, in all one hundred thirty nine.29 The temple servants: the sons of Esau, the sons of Asipha, the sons of Tabaoth, the sons of Keras, the sons of Sua, the sons of Phaleas, the sons of Labana, the sons of Aggaba. 30 the sons of Acud, the sons of Uta, the sons of Ketab, the sons of Accaba, the sons of Subai, the sons of Anan, the sons of Cathua, the sons of Geddur, 31 the sons of Jairus, the sons of Daisan, the sons of Noeba, the sons of Chaseba, the sons of Gazera, the sons of Ozias, the sons of Phinoe, the sons of Asara, the sons of Basthai, the sons of Asana, the sons of Maani, the sons of Naphisi, the sons of Acub, the sons of Achipha, the sons of Asur, the sons of Pharakim, the sons of Basaloth, 32 the sons of Meedda, the sons of Cutha, the sons of Charea, the sons of Barchus, the sons of Serar, the sons of Thomei, the sons of Nasi, the sons of Atipha.33 The sons of the servants of Solomon: the sons of Assaphioth, the sons of Pharida, the sons of Jeeli, the sons of Lozon, the sons of Isdael, the sons of Saphuthi, 34 the sons of Agia, the sons of Phacareth, the sons of Sabie, the sons of Sarothie, the sons of Masias, the sons of Gas, the sons of Addus, the sons of Subas, the sons of Apherra, the sons of Barodis, the sons of Saphat, the sons of Allon.35 All the temple- servants and the sons of the servants of Solomon were three hundred seventy two. 36 These came up from Thermeleth, and Thelersas, Charaathalan leading them, and Allar; 37 and they could not show their families, nor their stock, how they were of Israel: the sons of Dalan the son of Ban, the sons of Nekodan, six hundred fifty two.38 Of the priests, those who usurped the office of the priesthood and were not found: the sons of Obdia, the sons of Akkos, the sons of Jaddus, who married Augia one of the daughters of Zorzelleus, and was called after his name. 39 When the description of the kindred of these men was sought in the register and was not found, they were removed from executing the office of the priesthood; 40 for Nehemias and Attharias told them that they should not be partakers of the holy things until a high priest wearing Urim and Thummim should arise.41 So all those of Israel, from twelve years old and upward, beside menservants and women servants, were in number forty two thousand three hundred sixty. 42 Their menservants and handmaids were seven thousand three hundred thirty and seven; the minstrels and singers, two hundred forty five; 43 four hundred thirty and five camels, seven thousand thirty six horses, two hundred forty five mules, and five thousand five hundred twenty five beasts of burden.44 And some of the chief men of their families, when they came to the temple of God that is in Jerusalem, vowed to set up the house again in its own place according to their ability, 45 and to give into the holy treasury of the works one thousand minas of gold, five thousand minas of silver, and one hundred priestly vestments. 46 The priests and the Levites and some of the people lived in Jerusalem and the country. The holy singers also and the gatekeepers and all Israel lived in their villages.47 But when the seventh month was at hand, and when the children of Israel were each in their own place, they all came together with one purpose into the broad place before the first porch which is toward the east. 48 Then Jesus the son of Josedek, his kindred the priests, Zorobabel the son of Salathiel, and his kindred stood up and made the altar of the God of Israel ready 49 to offer burned sacrifices upon it, in accordance with the express commands in the book of Moses the man of God. 50 Some people joined them out of the other nations of the land, and they erected the altar upon its own place, because all the nations of the land were hostile to them and oppressed them; and they offered sacrifices at the proper times and burnt offerings to the Lord both morning and evening. 51 They also held the feast of tabernacles, as it is commanded in the law, and offered sacrifices daily, as appropriate. 52 After that, they offered the continual oblations and the sacrifices of the Sabbaths, of the new moons, and of all the consecrated feasts. 53 All those who had made any vow to God began to offer sacrifices to God from the new moon of the seventh month, although the temple of God was not yet built. 54 They gave money, food, and drink to the masons and carpenters. 55 They also gave carts to the people of Sidon and Tyre, that they should bring cedar trees from Libanus, and convey them in rafts to the harbor of Joppa, according to the commandment which was written for them by Cyrus king of the Persians.56 In the second year after his coming to the temple of God at Jerusalem, in the second month, Zorobabel the son of Salathiel, Jesus the son of Josedek, their kindred, the Levitical priests, and all those who had come to Jerusalem out of the captivity began work. 57 They laid the foundation of God's temple on the new moon of the second month, in the second year after they had come to Judea and Jerusalem.

58*They appointed the Levites who were at least twenty years old over the Lord's works. Then Jesus, with his sons and kindred, Kadmiel his brother, the sons of Jesus, Emadabun, and the sons of Joda the son of Iliadun, and their sons and kindred, all the Levites, with one accord stood up and started the business, laboring to advance the works in the house of God. So the builders built the Lord's temple.59 The priests stood arrayed in their vestments with musical instruments and trumpets, and the Levites the sons of Asaph with their cymbals, 60 singing songs of thanksgiving and praising the Lord, according to the directions of King David of Israel. 61 They sang aloud, praising the Lord in songs of thanksgiving, because his goodness and his glory are forever in all Israel. 62 All the people sounded trumpets and shouted with a loud voice, singing songs of thanksgiving to the Lord for the raising up of the Lord's house. 63*Some of the Levitical priests and of the heads of their families, the elderly who had seen the former house came to the building of this one with lamentation and great weeping. 64 But many with trumpets and joy shouted with a loud voice, 65 so that the people couldn't hear the trumpets for the weeping of the people, for the multitude sounded loudly, so that it was heard far away.66 * Therefore when the enemies of the tribe of Judah and Benjamin heard it, they came to know what that noise of trumpets meant. 67 They learned that those who returned from captivity built the temple for the Lord, the God of Israel. 68 So they went to Zorobabel and Jesus, and to the chief men of the families, and said to them, "We will build together with you. 69 For we, just like you, obey your Lord, and sacrifice to him from the days of King Asbasareth of the Assyrians, who brought us here."70 Then Zorobabel, Jesus and the chief men of the families of Israel said to them, "It is not for you to build the house for the Lord our God. 71 We ourselves alone will build for the Lord of Israel, as King Cyrus of the Persians has commanded us." 72 But the heathen of the land pressed hard upon the inhabitants of Judea, cut off their supplies, and hindered their building. 73 By their secret plots, and popular persuasions and commotions, they hindered the finishing of the building all the time that King Cyrus lived. So they were hindered from building for two years, until the reign of Darius.

6

1 Now *in the second year of the reign of Darius, Aggaeus and Zacharius the son of Addo, the prophets, prophesied to the Jews in Judea and Jerusalem in the name of the Lord, the God of Israel. 2 Then Zorobabel the son of Salathiel and Jesus the son of Josedek stood up and began to build the house of the Lord at Jerusalem, the prophets of the Lord being with them and helping them. 3At the same time Sisinnes the governor of Syria and Phoenicia came to them, with

Sathrabuzanes and his companions, and said to them, 4 "By whose authority do you build this house and this roof, and perform all the other things? Who are the builders who do these things?" 5 Nevertheless, the elders of the Jews obtained favor, because the Lord had visited the captives; 6 and they were not hindered from building until such time as communication was made to Darius concerning them, and his answer received.7 A copy of the letter which Sisinnes, governor of Syria and Phoenicia, and Sathrabuzanes, with their companions, the rulers in Syria and Phoenicia, wrote and sent to Darius:8 "To King Darius, greetings. Let it be fully known to our lord the king, that having come into the country of Judea, and entered into the city of Jerusalem, we found in the city of Jerusalem the elders of the Jews that were of the captivity 9 building a great new house for the Lord of hewn and costly stones, with timber laid in the walls. 10 Those works are being done with great speed. The work goes on prosperously in their hands, and it is being accomplished with all glory and diligence. 11 Then asked we these elders, saying, 'By whose authority are you building this house and laying the foundations of these works?' 12 Therefore, to the intent that we might give knowledge to you by writing who were the leaders, we questioned them, and we required of them the names in writing of their principal men. 13 So they gave us this answer, 'We are the servants of the Lord who made heaven and earth. 14 As for this house, it was built many years ago by a great and strong king of Israel, and was finished. 15 But when our fathers sinned against the Lord of Israel who is in heaven, and provoked him to wrath, he gave them over into the hands of King Nabuchodonosor of Babylon, king of the Chaldeans. 16 They pulled down the house, burned it, and carried away the people captive to Babylon. 17 But in the first year that Cyrus reigned over the country of Babylon, King Cyrus wrote that this house should be rebuilt. 18 The holy vessels of gold and of silver that Nabuchodonosor had carried away out of the house at Jerusalem and had set up in his own temple, those King Cyrus brought out of the temple in Babylonia, and they were delivered to Zorobabel and to Sanabassarus the governor, 19 with commandment that he should carry away all these vessels, and put them in the temple at Jerusalem, and that the Lord's temple should be built on its site. 20 Then Sanabassarus, having come here, laid the foundations of the Lord's house which is in Jerusalem. From that time to this we are still building. It is not yet fully completed.' 21 Now therefore, if it seems good, O king, let a search be made among the royal archives of our lord the king that are in Babylon. 22 If it is found that the building of the house of the Lord which is in Jerusalem has been done with the consent of King Cyrus, and it seems good to our lord the king, let him send us directions concerning these things." 23Then King Darius commanded that a search be made among the archives that were laid up at Babylon. So at Ekbatana the palace, which is in the country of Media, a scroll was found where these things were recorded: 24 "In the first year of the reign of Cyrus, King Cyrus commanded to build up the house of the Lord which is in Jerusalem, where they sacrifice with continual fire. 25 Its height shall be sixty cubits, and the breadth sixty cubits, with three rows of hewn stones, and one row of new wood from that country. Its expenses are to be given out of the house of King Cyrus. 26 The holy vessels of the house of the Lord, both gold and silver, that Nabuchodonosor took out of the house at Jerusalem and carried away to Babylon, should be restored to the house at Jerusalem, and be set in the place where they were before." 27 Also he commanded that Sisinnes the governor of Syria and Phoenicia, and Sathrabuzanes, and their companions, and those who were appointed rulers in Syria and Phoenicia, should be careful not to meddle with the place, but allow Zorobabel, the servant of the Lord, and governor of Judea, and the elders of the Jews, to build that house of the Lord in its place. 28 "I also command to have it built up whole again; and that they look diligently to help those who are of the captivity of Judea, until the house of the Lord is finished, 29 and that out of the tribute of Coelesyria and Phoenicia a portion shall be carefully given to these men for the sacrifices of the Lord, that is, to Zorobabel the governor for bulls, rams, and lambs, 30 and also corn, salt, wine and oil, and that continually every year without further question, according as the priests who are in Jerusalem may direct to be daily spent, 31 that drink offerings may be made to the Most High God for the king and for his children, and that they may pray for their lives." 32 He commanded that whoever should transgress, yes, or neglect anything written here, a beam shall be taken out of his own house, and he shall be hanged on it, and all his goods seized for the king. 33 "Therefore may the Lord, whose name is called upon there, utterly destroy every king and nation that stretches out his hand to hinder or damage that house of the Lord in Jerusalem. 34 I, King Darius have ordained that these things be done with diligence."

7

1 Then * Sisinnes the governor of Coelesyria and Phoenicia, and Sathrabuzanes, with their companions, following the commandments of King Darius, 2 very carefully supervised the holy work, assisting the elders of the Jews and rulers of the temple. 3 So the holy work prospered, while Aggaeus and Zacharias the prophets prophesied. 4 They finished these things by the commandment of the Lord, the God

of Israel, and with the consent of Cyrus, Darius, and Artaxerxes, kings of the Persians. 5 So the holy house was finished by the twenty-third day of the month Adar, in the sixth year of King Darius. 6 The children of Israel, the priests, the Levites, and the others who returned from captivity who joined them did what was written in the book of Moses. 7 For the dedication of the Lord's temple, they offered one hundred bulls, two hundred rams, four hundred lambs, 8and twelve male goats for the sin of all Israel, according to the number of the twelve princes of the tribes of Israel. 9 The priests and the Levites stood arrayed in their vestments, according to their kindred, for the services of the Lord, the God of Israel, according to the book of Moses. The gatekeepers were at every gate. 10 The children of Israel who came out of captivity held the Passover the fourteenth day of the first month, when the priests and the Levites were sanctified together, 11 with all those who returned from captivity; for they were sanctified. For the Levites were all sanctified together, 12 and they offered the Passover for all who returned from captivity, for their kindred the priests, and for themselves. 13 The children of Israel who came out of the captivity ate, even all those who had separated themselves from the abominations of the heathen of the land, and sought the Lord. 14 They kept the feast of unleavened bread seven days, rejoicing before the Lord, 15 because he had turned the counsel of the king of Assyria toward them, to strengthen their hands in the works of the Lord, the God of Israel.

8

1After these things, when Artaxerxes the king of the Persians reigned, Esdras came, who was the son of Azaraias, the son of Zechrias, the son of Helkias, the son of Salem, 2 the son of Sadduk, the son of Ahitob, the son of Amarias, the son of Ozias, the son of Memeroth, the son of Zaraias, the son of Savias, the son of Boccas, the son of Abisne, the son of Phinees, the son of Eleazar, the son of Aaron, the chief priest. 3 This Esdras went up from Babylon as a skilled scribe in the law of Moses, which was given by the God of Israel. 4 The king honored him, for he found favor in his sight in all his requests. 5 There went up with him also some of the children of Israel, and of the priests, Levites, holy singers, gatekeepers, and temple servants to Jerusalem 6 in the seventh year of the reign of Artaxerxes, in the fifth month (this was the king's seventh year); for they left Babylon on the new moon of the first month and came to Jerusalem, by the prosperous journey which the Lord gave them for his sake. 7 For Esdras had very great skill, so that he omitted nothing of the law and commandments of the Lord, but taught all Israel the ordinances and judgments.8 Now the commission, which was written from King Artaxerxes, came to Esdras the priest and reader of the law of the Lord, was as follows:9 "King Artaxerxes to Esdras the priest and reader of the law of the Lord, greetings. 10 Having determined to deal graciously, I have given orders that those of the nation of the Jews, and of the priests and Levites, and of those within our realm who are willing and freely choose to, should go with you to Jerusalem. 11 As many therefore as are so disposed, let them depart with you, as it has seemed good both to me and my seven friends the counselors, 12 that they may look to the affairs of Judea and Jerusalem, in accordance with what is in the Lord's law, 13 and carry the gifts to the Lord of Israel to Jerusalem, which I and my friends have vowed, and that all the gold and silver that can be found in the country of Babylonia for the Lord in Jerusalem, 14 with that also which is given of the people for the temple of the Lord their God that is at Jerusalem, be collected: even the gold and silver for bulls, rams, and lambs, and what goes with them, 15 to the end that they may offer sacrifices to the Lord upon the altar of the Lord their God, which is in Jerusalem. 16 Whatever you and your kindred decide to do with gold and silver, do that according to the will of your God. 17 The holy vessels of the Lord, which are given you for the use of the temple of your God, which is in Jerusalem, 18 and whatever else you shall remember for the use of the temple of your God, you shall give it out of the king's treasury. 19 I, King Artaxerxes, have also commanded the keepers of the treasures in Syria and Phoenicia, that whatever Esdras the priest and reader of the law of the Most High God shall send for, they should give it to him with all diligence, 20 to the sum of one hundred talents of silver, likewise also of wheat even to one hundred cors, and one hundred firkins of wine, and salt in abundance. 21 Let all things be performed after God's law diligently to the most high God, that wrath come not upon the kingdom of the king and his sons. 22 I command you also that no tax, nor any other imposition, be laid upon any of the priests, or Levites, or holy singers, or gatekeepers, or temple servants, or any that have employment in this temple, and that no man has authority to impose any tax on them. 23 You, Esdras, according to the wisdom of God, ordain judges and justices that they may judge in all Syria and Phoenicia all those who know the law of your God; and those who don't know it, you shall teach. 24 Whoever transgresses the law of your God and of the king shall be punished diligently, whether it be by death, or other punishment, by penalty of money, or by imprisonment."25 Then Esdras the scribe said, "Blessed be the only Lord, the God of my fathers, who has put these things into the heart of the king, to glorify his house that is in Jerusalem, 26 and has honored me in the sight of the king, his counselors, and all his friends and nobles. 27 Therefore I was encouraged by the help of the Lord my God, and gathered together out of Israel men to go up with me. 28 These are the chief according to their families and their several divisions, who went up with me from Babylon in the reign of King Artaxerxes: 29 of the sons of Phinees, Gerson; of the sons of Ithamar, Gamael; of the sons of David, Attus the son of Sechenias; 30 of the sons of Phoros, Zacharais; and with him were counted one hundred fifty men; 31 of the sons of Phaath Moab, Eliaonias the son of Zaraias, and with him two hundred men; 32of the sons of Zathoes, Sechenias the son of Jezelus, and with him three hundred men; of the sons of Adin, Obeth the son of Jonathan, and with him two hundred fifty men; 33 of the sons of Elam, Jesias son of Gotholias, and with him seventy men; 34 of the sons of Saphatias, Zaraias son of Michael, and with him seventy men; 35 of the sons of Joab, Abadias son of Jehiel. Jezelus, and with him two hundred twelve men; 36 of the sons of Banias, Salimoth son of Josaphias, and with him one hundred sixty men; 37 of the sons of Babi, Zacharias son of Bebai, and with him twenty-eight men; 38 of the sons of Azgad: Astath, Joannes son of Hakkatan Akatan, and with him one hundred ten men; 39 of the sons of Adonikam, the last, and these are the names of them, Eliphalat, Jeuel, and Samaias, and with them seventy men; 40 of the sons of Bago, Uthi the son of Istalcurus, and with him seventy men.41 I gathered them together to the river called Theras. There we pitched our tents three days, and I inspected them. 42 When I had found there none of the priests and Levites, 43 then sent I to Eleazar, Iduel, Maasmas, 44 Elnathan, Samaias, Joribus, Nathan, Ennatan, Zacharias, and Mosollamus, principal men and men of understanding. 45 I asked them to go to Loddeus the captain, who was in the place of the treasury, 46 and commanded them that they should speak to Loddeus, to his kindred, and to the treasurers in that place, to send us such men as might execute the priests' office in our Lord's house. 47 By the mighty hand of our Lord, they brought to us men of understanding of the sons of Mooli the son of Levi, the son of Israel, Asebebias, and his sons, and his kindred, who were eighteen, 48 and Asebias, Annuus, and Osaias his brother, of the sons of Chanuneus, and their sons were twenty men; 49 and of the temple servants whom David and the principal men had appointed for the servants of the Levites, two hundred twenty temple servants. The list of all their names was reported.50 There I vowed a fast for the young men before our Lord, to seek from him a prosperous journey both for us and for our children and livestock that were with us; 51 for I was ashamed to ask of the king infantry, cavalry, and an escort for protection against our adversaries. 52 For we had said to the king that the power of our Lord would be with those who seek him, to support them in all ways. 53

Again we prayed to our lord about these things, and found him to be merciful.54 Then I set apart twelve men of the chiefs of the priests, Eserebias, Assamias, and ten men of their kindred with them. 55 I weighed out to them the silver, the gold, and the holy vessels of the house of our Lord, which the king, his counselors, the nobles, and all Israel had given. 56 When I had weighed it, I delivered to them six hundred fifty talents of silver, silver vessels weighing one hundred talents, one hundred talents of gold, 57 twenty golden vessels, and twelve vessels of brass, even of fine brass, glittering like gold. 58 I said to them, "You are holy to the Lord, the vessels are holy, and the gold and the silver are a vow to the Lord, the Lord of our fathers. 59 Watch and keep them until you deliver them to the chiefs of the priests and Levites, and to the principal men of the families of Israel in Jerusalem, in the chambers of our Lord's house. 60 So the priests and the Levites who received the silver, the gold, and the vessels which were in Jerusalem, brought them into the temple of the Lord.61 We left the river Theras on the twelfth day of the first month. We came to Jerusalem by the mighty hand of our Lord which was upon us. The Lord delivered us from from every enemy on the way, and so we came to Jerusalem. 62 When we had been there three days, the silver and gold was weighed and delivered in our Lord's house on the fourth day to Marmoth the priest the son of Urias. 63 With him was Eleazar the son of Phinees, and with them were Josabdus the son of Jesus and Moeth the son of Sabannus, the Levites. All was delivered to them by number and weight. 64 All the weight of them was recorded at the same hour. 65 Moreover those who had come out of captivity offered sacrifices to the Lord, the God of Israel, even twelve bulls for all Israel, ninety-six rams, 66 seventy-two lambs, and twelve goats for a peace offering—all of them a sacrifice to the Lord. 67 They delivered the king's commandments to the king's stewards and to the governors of Coelesyria and Phoenicia; and they honored the people and the temple of the Lord.68 Now when these things were done, the principal men came to me and said, 69 "The nation of Israel, the princes, the priests, and the Levites haven't put away from themselves the foreign people of the land nor the uncleannesses of the Gentiles the Canaanites, Hittites, Pherezites, Jebusites, Moabites, Egyptians, and Edomites. 70 For both they and their sons have married with their daughters, and the holy seed is mixed with the foreign people of the land. From the beginning of this matter the rulers and the nobles have been partakers of this iniquity."71 And as soon as I had heard these things, I tore my clothes and my holy garment, and plucked the hair from off my head and beard, and sat down sad and full of heaviness. 72 So all those who were moved at the word of the

Lord, the God of Israel, assembled to me while I mourned for the iniquity, but I sat still full of heaviness until the evening sacrifice. 73 Then rising up from the fast with my clothes and my holy garment torn, and bowing my knees and stretching out my hands to the Lord, 74 I said, "O Lord, I am ashamed and confounded before your face, 75 for our sins are multiplied above our heads, and our errors have reached up to heaven 76 ever since the time of our fathers. We are in great sin, even to this day. 77 For our sins and our fathers' we with our kindred, our kings, and our priests were given up to the kings of the earth, to the sword, and to captivity, and for a prey with shame, to this day. 78 Now in some measure mercy has been shown to us from you, O Lord, that there should be left us a root and a name in the place of your sanctuary, 79 and to uncover a light in the house of the Lord our God, and to give us food in the time of our servitude. 80 Yes, when we were in bondage, we were not forsaken by our Lord, but he gave us favor before the kings of Persia, so that they gave us food, 81 glorified the temple of our Lord, and raised up the desolate Zion, to give us a sure dwelling in Judea and Jerusalem.82 "Now, O Lord, what shall we say, having these things? For we have transgressed your commandments which you gave by the hand of your servants the prophets, saying, 83 'The land, which you enter into to possess as an inheritance, is a land polluted with the pollutions of the foreigners of the land, and they have filled it with their uncleanness. 84 Therefore now you shall not join your daughters to their sons, neither shall you take their daughters for your sons. 85 You shall never seek to have peace with them, that you may be strong, and eat the good things of the land, and that you may leave it for an inheritance to your children for evermore.' 86 All that has happened is done to us for our wicked works and great sins, for you, O Lord, made our sins light, 87 and gave to us such a root; but we have turned back again to transgress your law in mingling ourselves with the uncleanness of the heathen of the land. 88 You weren't angry with us to destroy us until you had left us neither root, seed, nor name. 89 O Lord of Israel, you are true, for we are left a root this day. 90 Behold, now we are before you in our iniquities, for we can't stand any longer before you because of these things." 91As Esdras in his prayer made his confession, weeping, and lying flat on the ground before the temple, a very great throng of men, women, and children gathered to him from Jerusalem; for there was great weeping among the multitude. 92 Then Jechonias the son of Jeelus, one of the sons of Israel, called out, and said, "O Esdras, we have sinned against the Lord God, we have married foreign women of the heathen of the land, but there is still hope for Israel. 93 Let's make an oath to the Lord about this, that we will put away all our foreign wives with their children, 94 as seems good to you, and to as many as obey the Lord's Law. 95 Arise, and take action, for this is your task, and we will be with you to do valiantly." 96 So Esdras arose, and took an oath from the chief of the priests and Levites of all Israel to do these things; and they swore to it.

9

1 Then Esdras rose up from the court of the temple and went to the chamber of Jonas the son of Eliasib, 2 and lodged there, and ate no bread and drank no water, mourning for the great iniquities of the multitude. 3 A proclamation was made in all Judea and Jerusalem to all those who returned from captivity, that they should be gathered together at Jerusalem, 4 and that whoever didn't meet there within two or three days, in accordance with the ruling of the elders, that their livestock would be seized for the use of the temple, and they would be expelled from the multitude of those who returned from captivity.5 Within three days, all those of the tribe of Judah and Benjamin gathered together at Jerusalem. This was the ninth month, on the twentieth day of the month. 6 All the multitude sat together shivering in the broad place before the temple because of the present foul weather. 7 So Esdras arose up and said to them, "You have transgressed the law and married foreign wives, increasing the sins of Israel. 8 Now make confession and give glory to the Lord, the God of our fathers, 9 and do his will, and separate yourselves from the heathen of the land, and from the foreign women."10 Then the whole multitude cried out, and said with a loud voice, "Just as you have spoken, so we will do. 11 But because the multitude is great, and it is foul weather, so that we can't stand outside, and this is not a work of one day or two, seeing our sin in these things has spread far, 12 therefore let the rulers of the multitude stay, and let all those of our settlements that have foreign wives come at the time appointed, 13 and with them the rulers and judges of every place, until we turn away the wrath of the Lord from us for this matter."14So Jonathan the son of Azael and Ezekias the son of Thocanus took the matter on themselves. Mosollamus and Levis and Sabbateus were judges with them. 15 Those who returned from captivity did according to all these things.16 Esdras the priest chose for himself principal men of their families, all by name. On the new moon of the tenth month they met together to examine the matter. 17 So their cases of men who had foreign wives was brought to an end by the new moon of the first month. 18 Of the priests who had come together and had foreign wives, there were found 19 of the sons of Jesus the son of Josedek, and his kindred, Mathelas, Eleazar, and Joribus, and Joadanus. 20 They gave their hands to put away their wives, and to offer rams to make reconciliation for their error. 21 Of the sons of Emmer: Ananias,

Zabdeus, Manes, Sameus, Hiereel, and Azarias. 22 Of the sons of Phaisur: Elionas, Massias, Ishmael, Nathanael, Ocidelus, and Saloas.23 Of the Levites: Jozabdus, Semeis, Colius who was called Calitas, Patheus, Judas, and Jonas. 24 Of the holy singers: Eliasibus and Bacchurus. 25 Of the gatekeepers: Sallumus and Tolbanes.26 Of Israel, of the sons of Phoros: Hiermas, Ieddias, Melchias, Maelus, Eleazar, Asibas, and Banneas. 27 Of the sons of Ela: Matthanias, Zacharias, Jezrielus, Oabdius, Hieremoth, and Aedias. 28 Of the sons of Zamoth: Eliadas, Eliasimus, Othonias, Jarimoth, Sabathus, and Zardeus. 29 Of the sons of Bebai: Joannes, Ananias, Jozabdus, and Ematheis. 30 Of the sons of Mani: Olamus, Mamuchus, Jedeus, Jasubas, Jasaelus, and Hieremoth. 31 Of the sons of Addi: Naathus, Moossias, Laccunus, Naidus, Matthanias, Sesthel, Balnuus, and Manasseas. 32 Of the sons of Annas: Elionas, Aseas, Melchias, Sabbeus, and Simon Chosameus. 33 Of the sons of Asom: Maltanneus, Mattathias, Sabanneus, Eliphalat, Manasses, and Semei. 34 Of the sons of Baani: Jeremias, Momdis, Ismaerus, Juel, Mamdai, Pedias, Anos, Carabasion, Enasibus, Mamnitamenus, Eliasis, Bannus, Eliali, Someis, Selemias, and Nathanias. Of the sons of Ezora: Sesis, Ezril, Azaelus, Samatus, Zambri, and Josephus. 35 Of the sons of Nooma: Mazitias, Zabadeas, Edos, Juel, and Banaias. 36 All these had taken foreign wives, and they put them away with their children.37 The priests and Levites, and those who were of Israel, lived in Jerusalem and in the country, on the new moon of the seventh month, and the children of Israel in their ettlements.38*The whole multitude gathered together with one accord into the broad place before the porch of the temple toward the east. 39 They said to Esdras the priest and reader, "Bring the law of Moses that was given by the Lord, the God of Israel."40 So Esdras the chief priest brought the law to the whole multitude both of men and women, and to all the priests, to hear the law on the new moon of the seventh month. 41 He read in the broad place before the porch of the temple from morning until midday, before both men and women; and all the multitude gave attention to the law. 42 Esdras the priest and reader of the law stood up upon the pulpit of wood which had been prepared. 43 Beside him stood Mattathias, Sammus, Ananias, Azarias, Urias, Ezekias, and Baalsamus on the right hand, 44 and on his left hand, Phaldeus, Misael, Melchias, Lothasubus, Nabarias, and Zacharias. 45 Then Esdras took the book of the law before the multitude, and sat honorably in the first place before all. 46 When he opened the law, they all stood straight up. So Esdras blessed the Lord God Most High, the God of armies, the Almighty. 47 All the people answered, "Amen." Lifting up their hands, they fell to the ground and worshiped the Lord. 48 Also Jesus, Annus, Sarabias, Iadinus, Jacubus, Sabateus, Auteas, Maiannas, Calitas, Azarias, Jozabdus, Ananias, and Phalias, the Levites, taught the law of the Lord, and read to the multitude the law of the Lord, explaining what was read. 49 Then Attharates said to Esdras the chief priest and reader, and to the Levites who taught the multitude, even to all, 50 "This day is holy to the Lord now they all wept when they heard the law 51 go then, eat the fat, drink the sweet, and send portions to those who have nothing; 52 for the day is holy to the Lord. Don't be sorrowful, for the Lord will bring you to honor." 53 So the Levites commanded all things to the people, saying, "This day is holy. Don't be sorrowful." 54 Then they went their way, every one to eat, drink, enjoy themselves, to give portions to those who had nothing, and to rejoice greatly, 55 because they understood the words they were instructed with, and for which they had been assembled.

THE BOOK OF 2 ESDRAS

1

1 The second book of the prophet Esdras, the son of Saraias, the son of Azaraias, the son of Helkias, the son of Salemas, the son of Sadoc, the son of Ahitob, 2 the son of Achias, the son of Phinees, the son of Heli, the son of Amarias, the son of Aziei, the son of Marimoth, the son of Arna, the son of Ozias, the son of Borith, the son of Abissei, the son of Phinees, the son of Eleazar, 3 the son of Aaron, of the tribe of Levi, who was captive in the land of the Medes, in the reign of Artaxerxes king of the Persians. 4 The Lord's word came to me, saying, 5 "Go your way and show my people their sinful deeds, and their children their wickedness which they have done against me, that they may tell their children's children, 6 because the sins of their fathers have increased in them, for they have forgotten me, and have offered sacrifices to foreign gods. 7 Didn't I bring them out of the land of Egypt, out of the house of bondage? But they have provoked me to wrath and have despised my counsels. 8 So pull out the hair of your head and cast all evils upon them, for they have not been obedient to my law, but they are a rebellious people. 9 How long shall I endure them, to whom I have done so much good? 10 I have overthrown many kings for their sakes. I have struck down Pharoah with his servants and all his army. 11 I have destroyed all the nations before them. In the east, I have scattered the people of two provinces, even of Tyre and Sidon, and have slain all their adversaries. 12 Speak therefore to them, saying: 13 "The Lord says, truly I brought you through the sea, and where there was no path I made highways for you. I gave you Moses for a leader and Aaron for a priest. 14 I

gave you light in a pillar of fire. I have done great wonders among you, yet you have forgotten me, says the Lord. 15 "The Lord Almighty says: The quails were for a token to you. I gave you a camp for your protection, but you complained there. 16 You didn't celebrate in my name for the destruction of your enemies, but even to this day you still complain. 17 Where are the benefits that I have given you? When you were hungry and thirsty in the wilderness, didn't you cry to me, 18 saying, 'Why have you brought us into this wilderness to kill us? It would have been better for us to have served the Egyptians than to die in this wilderness.' 19 I had pity on your mourning and gave you manna for food. You ate angels' bread. 20 When you were thirsty, didn't I split the rock, and water flowed out in abundance? Because of the heat, I covered you with the leaves of the trees. 21 I divided fruitful lands among you. I drove out the Canaanites, the Pherezites, and the Philistines before you. What more shall I do for you?" says the Lord. 22 The Lord Almighty says, "When you were in the wilderness, at the bitter stream, being thirsty and blaspheming my name, 23 I gave you not fire for your blasphemies, but threw a tree in the water, and made the river sweet. 24 What shall I do to you, O Jacob? You, Judah, would not obey me. I will turn myself to other nations, and I will give my name to them, that they may keep my statutes. 25 Since you have forsaken me, I also will forsake you. When you ask me to be merciful to you, I will have no mercy upon you. 26 Whenever you call upon me, I will not hear you, for you have defiled your hands with blood, and your feet are swift to commit murder. 27 It is not as though you have forsaken me, but your own selves," says the Lord. 28 The Lord Almighty says, "Haven't I asked you as a father his sons, as a mother her daughters, and a nurse her young babies, 29 that you would be my people, and I would be your God, that you would be my children, and I would be your father? 30 I gathered you together, as a hen gathers her chicks under her wings. But now, what should I do to you? I will cast you out from my presence. 31 When you offer burnt sacrifices to me, I will turn my face from you, for I have rejected your solemn feast days, your new moons, and your circumcisions of the flesh. 32 I sent to you my servants the prophets, whom you have taken and slain, and torn their bodies in pieces, whose blood I will require from you," says the Lord. 33 The Lord Almighty says, "Your house is desolate. I will cast you out as the wind blows stubble. 34 Your children won't be fruitful, for they have neglected my commandment to you, and done that which is evil before me. 35 I will give your houses to a people that will come, which not having heard of me yet believe me. Those to whom I have shown no signs will do what I have commanded. 36 They have seen no prophets, yet they will remember their former condition. 37 I call to witness the gratitude of the people who will come, whose little ones rejoice with gladness. Although they see me not with bodily eyes, yet in spirit they will believe what I say." 38 And now, father, behold with glory, and see the people that come from the east: 39 to whom I will give for leaders, Abraham, Isaac, and Jacob, Oseas, Amos, and Micheas, Joel, Abdias, and Jonas, 40 Nahum, and Abacuc, Sophonias, Aggaeus, Zachary, and Malachy, who is also called the Lord's messenger.

2

1 The Lord says, "I brought this people out of bondage. I gave them my commandments by my servants the prophets, whom they would not listen to, but made my counsels void. 2 The mother who bore them says to them, 'Go your way, my children, for I am a widow and forsaken. 3 I brought you up with gladness, and I have lost you with sorrow and heaviness, for you have sinned before the Lord God, and done that which is evil before me. 4 But now what can I do for you? For I am a widow and forsaken. Go your way, my children, and ask for mercy from the Lord.' 5 As for me, O father, I call upon you for a witness in addition to the mother of these children, because they would not keep my covenant, 6 that you may bring them to confusion, and their mother to ruin, that they may have no offspring. 7 Let them be scattered abroad among the heathen. Let their names be blotted out of the earth, for they have despised my covenant. 8 Woe to you, Assur, you who hide the unrighteous with you! You wicked nation, remember what I did to Sodom and Gomorrah, 9 whose land lies in lumps of pitch and heaps of ashes. That is what I will also do to those who have not listened to me," says the Lord Almighty. 10 The Lord says to Esdras, "Tell my people that I will give them the kingdom of Jerusalem, which I would have given to Israel. 11 I will also take their glory back to myself, and give these the everlasting tabernacles which I had prepared for them. 12 They will have the tree of life for fragrant perfume. They will neither labor nor be weary. 13 Ask, and you will receive. Pray that your days may be few, that they may be shortened. The kingdom is already prepared for you. Watch! 14 Call heaven and earth to witness. Call them to witness, for I have left out evil, and created the good, for I live, says the Lord. 15 "Mother, embrace your children. I will bring them out with gladness like a dove does. Establish their feet, for I have chosen you, says the Lord. 16 I will raise those who are dead up again from their places, and bring them out from their tombs, for I recognize my name in them. 17 Don't be afraid, you mother of children, for I have chosen you, says the Lord. 18 For your help, I will send my servants Esaias and Jeremiah, after whose counsel I have sanctified and prepared for you twelve trees laden with various fruits, 19 and as many springs

flowing with milk and honey, and seven mighty mountains, on which roses and lilies grow, with which I will fill your children with joy. 20 Do right to the widow. Secure justice for the fatherless. Give to the poor. Defend the orphan. Clothe the naked. 21 Heal the broken and the weak. Don't laugh a lame man to scorn. Defend the maimed. Let the blind man have a vision of my glory. 22 Protect the old and young within your walls. 23 Wherever you find the dead, set a sign upon them and commit them to the grave, and I will give you the first place in my resurrection. 24 Stay still, my people, and take your rest, for your rest will come. 25 Nourish your children, good nurse, and establish their feet. 26 As for the servants whom I have given you, not one of them will perish, for I will require them from among your number. 27 Don't be anxious, for when the day of suffering and anguish comes, others will weep and be sorrowful, but you will rejoice and have abundance. 28 The nations will envy you, but they will be able to do nothing against you, says the Lord. 29 My hands will cover you, so that your children don't see Gehenna. 30 Be joyful, mother, with your children, for I will deliver you, says the Lord. 31 Remember your children who sleep, for I will bring them out of the secret places of the earth and show mercy to them, for I am merciful, says the Lord Almighty. 32 Embrace your children until I come, and proclaim mercy to them, for my wells run over, and my grace won't fail." 33 I, Esdras, received a command from the Lord on Mount Horeb to go to Israel, but when I came to them, they rejected me and rejected the Lord's commandment. 34 Therefore I say to you, O nations that hear and understand, "Look for your shepherd. He will give you everlasting rest, for he is near at hand who will come at the end of the age. 35 Be ready for the rewards of the kingdom, for the everlasting light will shine on you forevermore. 36 Flee the shadow of this world, receive the joy of your glory. I call to witness my savior openly. 37 Receive that which is given to you by the Lord, and be joyful, giving thanks to him who has called you to heavenly kingdoms. 38 Arise and stand up, and see the number of those who have been sealed at the Lord's feast. 39 Those who withdrew themselves from the shadow of the world have received glorious garments from the Lord. 40 Take again your full number, O Zion, and make up the reckoning of those of yours who are clothed in white, which have fulfilled the law of the Lord. 41 The number of your children, whom you long for, is fulfilled. Ask the power of the Lord, that your people, which have been called from the beginning, may be made holy." 42 I, Esdras, saw upon Mount Zion a great multitude, whom I could not number, and they all praised the Lord with songs. 43 In the midst of them, there was a young man of a high stature, taller than all the rest, and upon every one of their heads he set crowns, and he was more exalted than they were. I marveled greatly at this. 44 So I asked the angel, and said, "What are these, my Lord?" 45 He answered and said to me, "These are those who have put off the mortal clothing, and put on the immortal, and have confessed the name of God. Now are they crowned, and receive palms." 46 Then said I to the angel, "Who is the young man who sets crowns on them, and gives them palms in their hands?" 47 So he answered and said to me, "He is the Son of God, whom they have confessed in the world." Then I began to praise those who stood so valiantly for the name of the Lord. 48 Then the angel said to me, "Go your way, and tell my people what kind of things, and how great wonders of the Lord God you have seen."

3

1 In the thirtieth year after the ruin of the city, I Salathiel, also called Esdras, was in Babylon, and lay troubled upon my bed, and my thoughts came up over my heart, 2 for I saw the desolation of Zion and the wealth of those who lived at Babylon. 3 My spirit was very agitated, so that I began to speak words full of fear to the Most High, and said, 4 "O sovereign Lord, didn't you speak at the beginning when you formed the earth—and that yourself alone—and commanded the dust 5 and it gave you Adam, a body without a soul? Yet it was the workmanship of your hands, and you breathed into him the breath of life, and he was made alive in your presence. 6 You led him into the garden which your right hand planted before the earth appeared. 7 You gave him your one commandment, which he transgressed, and immediately you appointed death for him and his descendants. From him were born nations, tribes, peoples, and kindred without number. 8 Every nation walked after their own will, did ungodly things in your sight, and despised your commandments, and you didn't hinder them. 9 Nevertheless, again in process of time, you brought the flood on those who lived in the world and destroyed them. 10 It came to pass that the same thing happened to them. Just as death came to Adam, so was the flood to these. 11 Nevertheless, you left one of them, Noah with his household, and all the righteous men who descended from him. 12 "It came to pass that when those who lived upon the earth began to multiply, they also multiplied children, peoples, and many nations, and began again to be more ungodly than their ancestors. 13 It came to pass, when they did wickedly before you, you chose one from among them, whose name was Abraham. 14 You loved, and to him only you showed the end of the times secretly by night, 15 and made an everlasting covenant with him, promising him that you would never forsake his descendants. To him, you gave Isaac, and to Isaac you gave Jacob and Esau. 16 You set apart Jacob for yourself, but rejected Esau. Jacob became a great multitude. 17

It came to pass that when you led his descendants out of Egypt, you brought them up to Mount Sinai. 18 You bowed the heavens also, shook the earth, moved the whole world, made the depths tremble, and troubled the age. 19 Your glory went through four gates, of fire, of earthquake, of wind, and of ice, that you might give the law to the descendants of Jacob, and the commandment to the descendants of Israel. 20 "Yet you didn't take away from them their wicked heart, that your law might produce fruit in them. 21 For the first Adam, burdened with a wicked heart transgressed and was overcome, as were all who are descended from him. 22 Thus disease was made permanent. The law was in the heart of the people along with the wickedness of the root. So the good departed away and that which was wicked remained. 23 So the times passed away, and the years were brought to an end. Then you raised up a servant, called David, 24 whom you commanded to build a city to your name, and to offer burnt offerings to you in it from what is yours. 25 When this was done many years, then those who inhabited the city did evil, 26 in all things doing as Adam and all his generations had done, for they also had a wicked heart. 27 So you gave your city over into the hands of your enemies.

28 "Then I said in my heart, 'Are their deeds of those who inhabit Babylon any better? Is that why it gained dominion over Zion?' 29 For it came to pass when I came here, that I also saw impieties without number, and my soul saw many sinners in this thirtieth year, so that my heart failed me. 30 For I have seen how you endure them sinning, and have spared those who act ungodly, and have destroyed your people, and have preserved your enemies; 31 and you have not shown how your way may be comprehended. Are the deeds of Babylon better than those of Zion? 32 Or is there any other nation that knows you beside Israel? Or what tribes have so believed your covenants as these tribes of Jacob? 33 Yet their reward doesn't appear, and their labor has no fruit, for I have gone here and there through the nations, and I see that they abound in wealth, and don't think about your commandments. 34 Weigh therefore our iniquities now in the balance, and theirs also who dwell in the world, and so will it be found which way the scale inclines. 35 Or when was it that they who dwell on the earth have not sinned in your sight? Or what nation has kept your commandments so well? 36 You will find some men by name who have kept your precepts, but you won't find nations."

4

1 The angel who was sent to me, whose name was Uriel, gave me an answer, 2 and said to me, "Your understanding has utterly failed you regarding this world. Do you think you can comprehend the way of the Most High?" 3 Then I said, "Yes, my Lord."He answered me, "I have

been sent to show you three ways, and to set before you three problems. 4 If you can solve one for me, I also will show you the way that you desire to see, and I will teach you why the heart is wicked." 5 I said, "Say on, my Lord."Then said he to me, "Go, weigh for me the weight of fire, or measure for me blast of wind, or call back for me the day that is past." 6 Then answered I and said, "Who of the sons of men is able to do this, that you should ask me about such things?" 7 He said to me, "If I had asked you, 'How many dwellings are there in the heart of the sea? Or how many springs are there at the fountain head of the deep? Or how many streams are above the firmament? Or which are the exits of hell? Or which are the entrances of paradise?' 8 perhaps you would say to me, 'I never went down into the deep, or as yet into hell, neither did I ever climb up into heaven.' 9 Nevertheless now I have only asked you about the fire, wind, and the day, things which you have experienced, and from which you can't be separated, and yet have you given me no answer about them." 10 He said moreover to me, "You can't understand your own things that you grew up with. 11 How then can your mind comprehend the way of the Most High? How can he who is already worn out with the corrupted world understand incorruption?" When I heard these things, I fell on my face 12 and said to him, "It would have been better if we weren't here at all, than that we should come here and live in the midst of ungodliness, and suffer, and not know why." 13 He answered me, and said, "A forest of the trees of the field went out, and took counsel together, 14 and said, 'Come! Let's go and make war against the sea, that it may depart away before us, and that we may make ourselves more forests.' 15 The waves of the sea also in like manner took counsel together, and said, 'Come! Let's go up and subdue the forest of the plain, that there also we may gain more territory.' 16 The counsel of the wood was in vain, for the fire came and consumed it. 17 Likewise also the counsel of the waves of the sea, for the sand stood up and stopped them. 18 If you were judge now between these two, which would you justify, or which would you condemn?" 19 I answered and said, "It is a foolish counsel that they both have taken, for the ground is given to the wood, and the place of the sea is given to bear its waves." 20 Then answered he me, and said, "You have given a right judgment. Why don't you judge your own case? 21 For just as the ground is given to the wood, and the sea to its waves, even so those who dwell upon the earth may understand nothing but what is upon the earth. Only he who dwells above the heavens understands the things that are above the height of the heavens." 22 Then answered I and said, "I beg you, O Lord, why has the power of understanding been given to me? 23 For it was not in my mind to be curious of the ways above, but of such things as pass by us daily, because Israel is given up as a reproach to the heathen. The people whom you have loved have been given over to ungodly nations. The law of our forefathers is made of no effect, and the written covenants are nowhere regarded. 24 We pass away out of the world like locusts. Our life is like a vapor, and we aren't worthy to obtain mercy. 25 What will he then do for his name by which we are called? I have asked about these things. " 26 Then he answered me, and said, "If you are alive you will see, and if you live long, you will marvel, for the world hastens quickly to pass away. 27 For it is not able to bear the things that are promised to the righteous in the times to come; for this world is full of sadness and infirmities. 28 For the evil about which you asked me has been sown, but its harvest hasn't yet come. 29 If therefore that which is sown isn't reaped, and if the place where the evil is sown doesn't pass away, the field where the good is sown won't come. 30 For a grain of evil seed was sown in the heart of Adam from the beginning, and how much wickedness it has produced to this time! How much more it will yet produce until the time of threshing comes! 31 Ponder now by yourself, how much fruit of wickedness a grain of evil seed has produced. 32 When the grains which are without number are sown, how great a threshing floor they will fill!" 33 Then I answered and said, "How long? When will these things come to pass? Why are our years few and evil?" 34 He answered me, and said, "Don't hurry faster than the Most High; for your haste is for your own self, but he who is above hurries on behalf of many. 35 Didn't the souls of the righteous ask question of these things in their chambers, saying, 'How long will we be here? When does the fruit of the threshing floor come?' 36 To them, Jeremiel the archangel answered, 'When the number is fulfilled of those who are like you. For he has weighed the world in the balance. 37 By measure, he has measured the times. By number, he has counted the seasons. He won't move or stir them until that measure is fulfilled.' " 38 Then I answered, "O sovereign Lord, all of us are full of ungodliness. 39 Perhaps it is for our sakes that the threshing time of the righteous is kept back—because of the sins of those who dwell on the earth." 40 So he answered me, "Go your way to a woman with child, and ask of her when she has fulfilled her nine months, if her womb may keep the baby any longer within her." 41 Then I said, "No, Lord, that can it not." He said to me, "In Hades, the chambers of souls are like the womb. 42 For just like a woman in labor hurries to escape the anguish of the labor pains, even so these places hurry to deliver those things that are committed to them from the beginning. 43 Then you will be shown those things which you desire to see." 44 Then I answered, "If I have found favor in your sight, and if it is possible, and if I am worthy, 45 show me this also, whether there is more to come than is past, or whether the greater part has gone over us. 46 For what is gone I know, but I don't know what is to come." 47 He said to me, "Stand up on my right side, and I will explain the parable to you." 48 So I stood, looked, and saw a hot burning oven passed by before me. It happened that when the flame had gone by I looked, and saw that the smoke remained. 49 After this, a watery cloud passed in front of me, and sent down much rain with a storm. When the stormy rain was past, the drops still remained in it." 50 Then said he to me, "Consider with yourself; as the rain is more than the drops, and the fire is greater than the smoke, so the quantity which is past was far greater; but the drops and the smoke still remained." 51 Then I prayed, and said, "Do you think that I will live until that time? Or who will be alive in those days?" 52 He answered me, "As for the signs you asked me about, I may tell you of them in part; but I wasn't sent to tell you about your life, for I don't know.

5

1 "Nevertheless, concerning the signs, behold, the days will come when those who dwell on earth will be taken with great amazement, and the way of truth will be hidden, and the land will be barren of faith. 2 Iniquity will be increased above what now you see, and beyond what you have heard long ago. 3 The land that you now see ruling will be a trackless waste, and men will see it desolate. 4 But if the Most High grants you to live, you will see what is after the third period will be troubled. The sun will suddenly shine in the night, and the moon in the day. 5 Blood will drop out of wood, and the stone will utter its voice. The peoples will be troubled, and the stars will fall. 6 He will rule whom those who dwell on the earth don't expect, and the birds will fly away together. 7 The Sodomite sea will cast out fish, and make a noise in the night, which many have not known; but all will hear its voice. 8 There will also be chaos in many places. Fires will break out often, and the wild animals will change their places, and women will bring forth monsters. 9 Salt waters will be found in the sweet, and all friends will destroy one another. Then reason will hide itself, and understanding withdraw itself into its chamber. 10 It will be sought by many, and won't be found. Unrighteousness and lack of restraint will be multiplied on earth. 11 One country will ask another, 'Has righteousness, or a man that does righteousness, gone through you?' And it will say, 'No.' 12 It will come to pass at that time that men will hope, but won't obtain. They will labor, but their ways won't prosper. 13 I am permitted to show you such signs. If you will pray again, and weep as now, and fast seven days, you will hear yet greater things than these." 14 Then I woke up, and an extreme trembling went through my body, and my mind was so troubled that it fainted. 15 So the angel who had come to talk with me held me, comforted me, and set me on my

feet. 16 In the second night, it came to pass that Phaltiel the captain of the people came to me, saying, "Where have you been? Why is your face sad? 17 Or don't you know that Israel is committed to you in the land of their captivity? 18 Get up then, and eat some bread, and don't forsake us, like a shepherd who leaves the flock in the power of cruel wolves." 19 Then said I to him, "Go away from me and don't come near me for seven days, and then you shall come to me." He heard what I said and left me. 20 So I fasted seven days, mourning and weeping, like Uriel the angel had commanded me. 21 After seven days, the thoughts of my heart were very grievous to me again, 22 and my soul recovered the spirit of understanding, and I began to speak words before the Most High again. 23 I said, "O sovereign Lord of all the woods of the earth, and of all the trees thereof, you have chosen one vine for yourself. 24 Of all the lands of the world you have chosen one country for yourself. Of all the flowers of the world, you have chosen one lily for yourself. 25 Of all the depths of the sea, you have filled one river for yourself. Of all built cities, you have consecrated Zion for yourself. 26 Of all the birds that are created you have named for yourself one dove. Of all the livestock that have been made, you have provided for yourself one sheep. 27 Among all the multitudes of peoples you have gotten yourself one people. To this people, whom you loved, you gave a law that is approved by all. 28 Now, O Lord, why have you given this one people over to many, and have dishonored the one root above others, and have scattered your only one among many? 29 Those who opposed your promises have trampled down those who believed your covenants. 30 If you really do hate your people so much, they should be punished with your own hands." 31 Now when I had spoken these words, the angel that came to me the night before was sent to me, 32 and said to me, "Hear me, and I will instruct you. Listen to me, and I will tell you more." 33 I said, "Speak on, my Lord." Then said he to me, "You are very troubled in mind for Israel's sake. Do you love that people more than he who made them?" 34 I said, "No, Lord; but I have spoken out of grief; for my heart is in agony every hour while I labor to comprehend the way of the Most High, and to seek out part of his judgment." 35 He said to me, "You can't." And I said, "Why, Lord? Why was I born? Why wasn't my mother's womb my grave, that I might not have seen the travail of Jacob, and the wearisome toil of the people of Israel?" 36 He said to me, "Count for me those who haven't yet come. Gather together for me the drops that are scattered abroad, and make the withered flowers green again for me. 37 Open for me the chambers that are closed, and bring out the winds for me that are shut up in them. Or show me the image of a voice. Then I will declare to you the travail that you asked to see." 38 And I said, "O sovereign Lord, who may know these things except he who doesn't have his dwelling with men? 39 As for me, I lack wisdom. How can I then speak of these things you asked me about?" 40 Then said he to me, "Just as you can do none of these things that I have spoken of, even so you can't find out my judgment, or the end of the love that I have promised to my people." 41 I said, "But, behold, O Lord, you have made the promise to those who are alive at the end. What should they do who have been before us, or we ourselves, or those who will come after us?" 42 He said to me, "I will compare my judgment to a ring. Just as there is no slowness of those who are last, even so there is no swiftness of those who be first." 43 So I answered, "Couldn't you make them all at once that have been made, and that are now, and that are yet to come, that you might show your judgment sooner?" 44 Then he answered me, "The creature may not move faster than the creator, nor can the world hold them at once who will be created in it." 45 And I said, "How have you said to your servant, that you will surely make alive at once the creature that you have created? If therefore they will be alive at once, and the creation will sustain them, even so it might now also support them to be present at once." 46 And he said to me, "Ask the womb of a woman, and say to her, 'If you bear ten children, why do you it at different times? Ask her therefore to give birth to ten children at once." 47 I said, "She can't, but must do it each in their own time." 48 Then said he to me, "Even so, I have given the womb of the earth to those who are sown in it in their own times. 49 For just as a young child may not give birth, neither she who has grown old any more, even so have I organized the world which I created." 50 I asked, "Seeing that you have now shown me the way, I will speak before you. Is our mother, of whom you have told me, still young? Or does she now draw near to old age?" 51 He answered me, "Ask a woman who bears children, and she will tell you. 52 Say to her, 'Why aren't they whom you have now brought forth like those who were before, but smaller in stature?' 53 She also will answer you, 'Those who are born in the strength of youth are different from those who are born in the time of old age, when the womb fails.' 54 Consider therefore you also, how you are shorter than those who were before you. 55 So are those who come after you smaller than you, as born of the creature which now begins to be old, and is past the strength of youth." 56 Then I said, "Lord, I implore you, if I have found favor in your sight, show your servant by whom you visit your creation."

6

1 He said to me, "In the beginning, when the earth was made, before the portals of the world were fixed and before the gatherings of the winds blew, 2 before the voices of the thunder sounded and before the

flashes of the lightning shone, before the foundations of paradise were laid, 3 before the fair flowers were seen, before the powers of the earthquake were established, before the innumerable army of angels were gathered together, 4 before the heights of the air were lifted up, before the measures of the firmament were named, before the footstool of Zion was established, 5 before the present years were reckoned, before the imaginations of those who now sin were estranged, and before they were sealed who have gathered faith for a treasure— 6 then I considered these things, and they all were made through me alone, and not through another; just as by me also they will be ended, and not by another." 7 Then I answered, "What will be the dividing of the times? Or when will be the end of the first and the beginning of the age that follows?" 8 He said to me, "From Abraham to Isaac, because Jacob and Esau were born to him, for Jacob's hand held Esau's heel from the beginning. 9 For Esau is the end of this age, and Jacob is the beginning of the one that follows. 10The beginning of a man is his hand, and the end of a man is his heel. Seek nothing else between the heel and the hand, Esdras!" 11 Then I answered, "O sovereign Lord, if I have found favor in your sight, 12 I beg you, show your servant the end of your signs which you showed me part on a previous night." 13 So he answered, "Stand up upon your feet, and you will hear a mighty sounding voice. 14 If the place you stand on is greatly moved 15 when it speaks don't be afraid, for the word is of the end, and the foundations of the earth will understand 16 that the speech is about them. They will tremble and be moved, for they know that their end must be changed." 17 It happened that when I had heard it, I stood up on my feet, and listened, and, behold, there was a voice that spoke, and its sound was like the sound of many waters. 18 It said, "Behold, the days come when I draw near to visit those who dwell upon the earth, 19 and when I investigate those who have caused harm unjustly with their unrighteousness, and when the affliction of Zion is complete, 20 and when the seal will be set on the age that is to pass away, then I will show these signs: the books will be opened before the firmament, and all will see together. 21 The children a year old will speak with their voices. The women with child will deliver premature children at three or four months, and they will live and dance. 22 Suddenly the sown places will appear unsown. The full storehouses will suddenly be found empty. 23 The trumpet will give a sound which when every man hears, they will suddenly be afraid. 24 At that time friends will make war against one another like enemies. The earth will stand in fear with those who dwell in it. The springs of the fountains will stand still, so that for three hours they won't flow. 25 "It will be that whoever remains after all these things that I have told you of, he will be saved and will see my salvation, and the end of my world. 26 They will see the men who have been taken up, who have not tasted death from their birth. The heart of the inhabitants will be changed and turned into a different spirit. 27 For evil will be blotted out and deceit will be quenched. 28 Faith will flourish. Corruption will be overcome, and the truth, which has been so long without fruit, will be declared." 29 When he talked with me, behold, little by little, the place I stood on rocked back and forth. 30 He said to me, "I came to show you these things tonight. 31 If therefore you will pray yet again, and fast seven more days, I will again tell you greater things than these. 32 For your voice has surely been heard before the Most High. For the Mighty has seen your righteousness. He has also seen your purity, which you have maintained ever since your youth. 33 Therefore he has sent me to show you all these things, and to say to you, 'Believe, and don't be afraid! 34 Don't be hasty to think vain things about the former times, that you may not hasten in the latter times.' "35 It came to pass after this, that I wept again, and fasted seven days in like manner, that I might fulfill the three weeks which he told me. 36 On the eighth night, my heart was troubled within me again, and I began to speak in the presence of the Most High. 37 For my spirit was greatly aroused, and my soul was in distress. 38 I said, "O Lord, truly you spoke at the beginning of the creation, on the first day, and said this: 'Let heaven and earth be made,' and your word perfected the work. 39 Then the spirit was hovering, and darkness and silence were on every side. The sound of man's voice was not yet there. 40 Then you commanded a ray of light to be brought out of your treasuries, that your works might then appear. 41 "On the second day, again you made the spirit of the firmament and commanded it to divide and to separate the waters, that the one part might go up, and the other remain beneath. 42 "On the third day, you commanded that the waters should be gathered together in the seventh part of the earth. You dried up six parts and kept them, to the intent that of these some being both planted and tilled might serve before you. 43 For as soon as your word went out, the work was done. 44 Immediately, great and innumerable fruit grew, with many pleasant tastes, and flowers of inimitable color, and fragrances of most exquisite smell. This was done the third day. 45 "On the fourth day, you commanded that the sun should shine, the moon give its light, and the stars should be in their order; 46 and gave them a command to serve mankind, who was to be made. 47 "On the fifth day, you said to the seventh part, where the water was gathered together, that it should produce living creatures, fowls and fishes; and so it came to pass 48 that the mute and lifeless water produced living things as it was told, that the nations might therefore praise your wondrous works. 49 "Then you preserved two living creatures. The one you called Behemoth, and the other you called Leviathan. 50 You separated the one from the other; for the seventh part, namely, where the water was gathered together, might not hold them both. 51 To Behemoth, you gave one part, which was dried up on the third day, that he should dwell in it, in which are a thousand hills; 52 but to Leviathan you gave the seventh part, namely, the watery part. You have kept them to be devoured by whom you wish, when you wish. 53 "But on the sixth day, you commanded the earth to produce before you cattle, animals, and creeping things. 54 Over these, you ordained Adam as ruler over all the works that you have made. Of him came all of us, the people whom you have chosen. 55 "All this have I spoken before you, O Lord, because you have said that for our sakes you made this world. 56 As for the other nations, which also come from Adam, you have said that they are nothing, and are like spittle. You have likened the abundance of them to a drop that falls from a bucket. 57 Now, O Lord, behold these nations, which are reputed as nothing, being rulers over us and devouring us. 58 But we your people, whom you have called your firstborn, your only children, and your fervent lover, are given into their hands. 59 Now if the world is made for our sakes, why don't we possess our world for an inheritance? How long will this endure?"

7

1 When I had finished speaking these words, the angel which had been sent to me the nights before was sent to me. 2 He said to me, "Rise, Esdras, and hear the words that I have come to tell you." 3 I said, "Speak on, my Lord." Then he said to me, "There is a sea set in a wide place, that it might be broad and vast, 4 but its entrance is set in a narrow place so as to be like a river. 5 Whoever desires to go into the sea to look at it, or to rule it, if he didn't go through the narrow entrance, how could he come into the broad part? 6 Another thing also: There is a city built and set in a plain country, and full of all good things, 7 but its entrance is narrow, and is set in a dangerous place to fall, having fire on the right hand, and deep water on the left. 8 There is one only path between them both, even between the fire and the water, so that only one person can go there at once. 9 If this city is now given to a man for an inheritance, if the heir doesn't pass the danger before him, how will he receive his inheritance?" 10 I said, "That is so, Lord." Then said he to me, "Even so also is Israel's portion. 11 I made the world for their sakes. What is now done was decreed when Adam transgressed my statutes. 12 Then the entrances of this world were made narrow, sorrowful, and toilsome. They are but few and evil, full of perils, and involved in great toils. 13 For the entrances of the greater world are wide and safe, and produce fruit of immortality. 14

So if those who live don't enter these difficult and vain things, they can never receive those that are reserved for them. 15 Now therefore why are you disturbed, seeing you are but a corruptible man? Why are you moved, since you are mortal? 16 Why haven't you considered in your mind that which is to come, rather than that which is present?" 17 Then I answered and said, "O sovereign Lord, behold, you have ordained in your law that the righteous will inherit these things, but that the ungodly will perish. 18 The righteous therefore will suffer difficult things, and hope for easier things, but those who have done wickedly have suffered the difficult things, and yet will not see the easier things." 19 He said to me, "You are not a judge above God, neither do you have more understanding than the Most High. 20 Yes, let many perish who now live, rather than that the law of God which is set before them be despised. 21 For God strictly commanded those who came, even as they came, what they should do to live, and what they should observe to avoid punishment. 22 Nevertheless, they weren't obedient to him, but spoke against him and imagined for themselves vain things. 23 They made cunning plans of wickedness, and said moreover of the Most High that he doesn't exist, and they didn't know his ways. 24 They despised his law and denied his covenants. They haven't been faithful to his statutes, and haven't performed his works. 25 Therefore, Esdras, for the empty are empty things, and for the full are the full things. 26 For behold, the time will come, and it will be, when these signs of which I told you before will come to pass, that the bride will appear, even the city coming forth, and she will be seen who now is withdrawn from the earth. 27 Whoever is delivered from the foretold evils will see my wonders. 28 For my son Jesus will be revealed with those who are with him, and those who remain will rejoice four hundred years. 29 After these years my son Christ will die, along with all of those who have the breath of life. 30 Then the world will be turned into the old silence seven days, like as in the first beginning, so that no human will remain. 31 After seven days the world that is not yet awake will be raised up, and what is corruptible will die. 32 The earth will restore those who are asleep in it, and the dust those who dwell in it in silence, and the secret places will deliver those souls that were committed to them. 33 The Most High will be revealed on the judgment seat, and compassion will pass away, and patience will be withdrawn. 34 Only judgment will remain. Truth will stand. Faith will grow strong. 35 Recompense will follow. The reward will be shown. Good deeds will awake, and wicked deeds won't sleep. 36 The pit of torment will appear, and near it will be the place of rest. The furnace of hell will be shown, and near it the paradise of delight. 37 Then the Most High will say to the nations that are raised from the dead, 'Look and understand whom you have denied, whom you haven't served, whose commandments you have despised. 38 Look on this side and on that. Here is delight and rest, and there fire and torments.' Thus he will speak to them in the day of judgment. 39 This is a day that has neither sun, nor moon, nor stars, 40 neither cloud, nor thunder, nor lightning, neither wind, nor water, nor air, neither darkness, nor evening, nor morning, 41 neither summer, nor spring, nor heat, nor winter, neither frost, nor cold, nor hail, nor rain, nor dew, 42 neither noon, nor night, nor dawn, neither shining, nor brightness, nor light, except only the splendor of the glory of the Most High, by which all will see the things that are set before them. 43 It will endure as though it were a week of years. 44 This is my judgment and its prescribed order; but I have only shown these things to you." 45 I answered, "I said then, O Lord, and I say now: Blessed are those who are now alive and keep your commandments! 46 But what about those for whom I prayed? For who is there of those who are alive who has not sinned, and who of the children of men hasn't transgressed your covenant? 47 Now I see that the world to come will bring delight to few, but torments to many. 48 For an evil heart has grown up in us, which has led us astray from these commandments and has brought us into corruption and into the ways of death. It has shown us the paths of perdition and removed us far from life— and that, not a few only, but nearly all who have been created." 49 He answered me, "Listen to me, and I will instruct you. I will admonish you yet again. 50 For this reason, the Most High has not made one world, but two. 51 For because you have said that the just are not many, but few, and the ungodly abound, hear the explanation. 52 If you have just a few precious stones, will you add them to lead and clay?" 53 I said, "Lord, how could that be?" 54 He said to me, "Not only that, but ask the earth, and she will tell you. Defer to her, and she will declare it to you. 55 Say to her, 'You produce gold, silver, and brass, and also iron, lead, and clay; 56 but silver is more abundant than gold, and brass than silver, and iron than brass, and lead than iron, and clay than lead.' 57 Judge therefore which things are precious and to be desired, what is abundant or what is rare?" 58 I said, "O sovereign Lord, that which is plentiful is of less worth, for that which is more rare is more precious." 59 He answered me, "Weigh within yourself the things that you have thought, for he who has what is hard to get rejoices over him who has what is plentiful. 60 So also is the judgment which I have promised; for I will rejoice over the few that will be saved, because these are those who have made my glory to prevail now, and through them, my name is now honored. 61 I won't grieve over the multitude of those who perish; for these are those who are now like mist, and have become like flame and smoke; they are set on fire and burn hotly, and are extinguished."

62 I answered, "O earth, why have you produced, if the mind is made out of dust, like all other created things? 63 For it would have been better that the dust itself had been unborn, so that the mind might not have been made from it. 64 But now the mind grows with us, and because of this we are tormented, because we perish and we know it. 65 Let the race of men lament and the animals of the field be glad. Let all who are born lament, but let the four- footed animals and the livestock rejoice. 66 For it is far better with them than with us; for they don't look forward to judgment, neither do they know of torments or of salvation promised to them after death. 67 For what does it profit us, that we will be preserved alive, but yet be afflicted with torment? 68 For all who are born are defiled with iniquities, and are full of sins and laden with transgressions. 69 If after death we were not to come into judgment, perhaps it would have been better for us." 70 He answered me, "When the Most High made the world and Adam and all those who came from him, he first prepared the judgment and the things that pertain to the judgment. 71 Now understand from your own words, for you have said that the mind grows with us. 72 They therefore who dwell on the earth will be tormented for this reason, that having understanding they have committed iniquity, and receiving commandments have not kept them, and having obtained a law they dealt unfaithfully with that which they received. 73 What then will they have to say in the judgment, or how will they answer in the last times? 74 For how long a time has the Most High been patient with those who inhabit the world, and not for their sakes, but because of the times which he has foreordained!" 75 I answered, "If I have found grace in your sight, O Lord, show this also to your servant, whether after death, even now when every one of us gives up his soul, we will be kept in rest until those times come, in which you renew the creation, or whether we will be tormented immediately." 76 He answered me, "I will show you this also; but don't join yourself with those who are scorners, nor count yourself with those who are tormented. 77 For you have a treasure of works laid up with the Most High, but it won't be shown you until the last times. 78 For concerning death the teaching is: When the decisive sentence has gone out from the Most High that a man shall die, as the spirit leaves the body to return again to him who gave it, it adores the glory of the Most High first of all. 79 And if it is one of those who have been scorners and have not kept the way of the Most High, and that have despised his law, and who hate those who fear God, 80 these spirits won't enter into habitations, but will wander and be in torments immediately, ever grieving and sad, in seven ways. 81 The first way, because they have despised the

law of the Most High. 82 The second way, because they can't now make a good repentance that they may live. 83 The third way, they will see the reward laid up for those who have believed the covenants of the Most High. 84 The fourth way, they will consider the torment laid up for themselves in the last days. 85 The fifth way, they will see the dwelling places of the others guarded by angels, with great quietness. 86 The sixth way, they will see how immediately some of them will pass into torment. 87 The seventh way, which is more grievous than all the aforesaid ways, because they will pine away in confusion and be consumed with shame, and will be withered up by fears, seeing the glory of the Most High before whom they have sinned while living, and before whom they will be judged in the last times. 88 "Now this is the order of those who have kept the ways of the Most High, when they will be separated from their mortal body. 89 In the time that they lived in it, they painfully served the Most High, and were in jeopardy every hour, that they might keep the law of the lawgiver perfectly. 90 Therefore this is the teaching concerning them: 91 First of all they will see with great joy the glory of him who takes them up, for they will have rest in seven orders. 92 The first order, because they have labored with great effort to overcome the evil thought which was fashioned together with them, that it might not lead them astray from life into death. 93 The second order, because they see the perplexity in which the souls of the ungodly wander, and the punishment that awaits them. 94 The third order, they see the testimony which he who fashioned them gives concerning them, that while they lived they kept the law which was given them in trust. 95 The fourth order, they understand the rest which, being gathered in their chambers, they now enjoy with great quietness, guarded by angels, and the glory that awaits them in the last days. 96 The fifth order, they rejoice that they have now escaped from that which is corruptible, and that they will inherit that which is to come, while they see in addition the difficulty and the pain from which they have been delivered, and the spacious liberty which they will receive with joy and immortality. 97 The sixth order, when it is shown to them how their face will shine like the sun, and how they will be made like the light of the stars, being incorruptible from then on. 98 The seventh order, which is greater than all the previously mentioned orders, because they will rejoice with confidence, and because they will be bold without confusion, and will be glad without fear, for they hurry to see the face of him whom in their lifetime they served, and from whom they will receive their reward in glory. 99 This is the order of the souls of the just, as from henceforth is announced to them. Previously mentioned are the ways of torture which those who would not give heed will suffer from after this." 100 I answered, "Will time therefore be given to the souls after they are separated from the bodies, that they may see what you have described to me? 101 He said, "Their freedom will be for seven days, that for seven days they may see the things you have been told, and afterwards they will be gathered together in their habitations." 102 I answered, "If I have found favor in your sight, show further to me your servant whether in the day of judgment the just will be able to intercede for the ungodly or to entreat the Most High for them, 103 whether fathers for children, or children for parents, or kindred for kindred, or kinsfolk for their next of kin, or friends for those who are most dear." 104 He answered me, "Since you have found favor in my sight, I will show you this also. The day of judgment is a day of decision, and displays to all the seal of truth. Even as now a father doesn't send his son, or a son his father, or a master his slave, or a friend him that is most dear, that in his place he may understand, or sleep, or eat, or be healed, 105 so no one will ever pray for another in that day, neither will one lay a burden on another, for then everyone will each bear his own righteousness or unrighteousness." 106 I answered, "How do we now find that first Abraham prayed for the people of Sodom, and Moses for the ancestors who sinned in the wilderness, 107 and Joshua after him for Israel in the days of *Achan, 108 and Samuel in the days of Saul, and David for the plague, and Solomon for those who would worship in the sanctuary, 109 and Elijah for those that received rain, and for the dead, that he might live, 110 and Hezekiah for the people in the days of Sennacherib, and many others prayed for many? 111 If therefore now, when corruption has grown and unrighteousness increased, the righteous have prayed for the ungodly, why will it not be so then also?" 112 He answered me, "This present world is not the end. The full glory doesn't remain in it. Therefore those who were able prayed for the weak. 113 But the day of judgment will be the end of this age, and the beginning of the immortality to come, in which corruption has passed away, 114 intemperance is at an end, infidelity is cut off, but righteousness has grown, and truth has sprung up. 115 Then no one will be able to have mercy on him who is condemned in judgment, nor to harm someone who is victorious." 116 I answered then, "This is my first and last saying, that it would have been better if the earth had not produced Adam, or else, when it had produced him, to have restrained him from sinning. 117 For what profit is it for all who are in this present time to live in heaviness, and after death to look for punishment? 118 O Adam, what have you done? For though it was you who sinned, the evil hasn't fallen on you alone, but on all of us who come from you. 119 For what profit is it to us, if an immortal time is promised to us, but we have done deeds that bring death? 120 And that there is promised us an everlasting hope, but we have most miserably failed? 121 And that there are reserved habitations of health and safety, but we have lived wickedly? 122 And that the glory of the Most High will defend those who have led a pure life, but we have walked in the most wicked ways of all? 123 And that a paradise will be revealed, whose fruit endures without decay, in which is abundance and healing, but we won't enter into it, 124 for we have lived in perverse ways? 125 And that the faces of those who have practiced self-control will shine more than the stars, but our faces will be blacker than darkness? 126 For while we lived and committed iniquity, we didn't consider what we would have to suffer after death." 127 Then he answered, "This is the significance of the battle which humans born on the earth will fight: 128 if they are overcome, they will suffer as you have said, but if they get the victory, they will receive the thing that I say. 129 For this is the way that Moses spoke to the people while he lived, saying, 'Choose life, that you may live!' 130 Nevertheless they didn't believe him or the prophets after him, not even me, who have spoken to them. 131 Therefore there won't be such heaviness in their destruction, as there will be joy over those who are assured of salvation." 132 Then I answered, "I know, Lord, that the Most High is now called merciful, in that he has mercy upon those who have not yet come into the world; 133 and compassionate, in that he has compassion upon those who turn to his law; 134 and patient, in that he is patient with those who have sinned, since they are his creatures; 135 and bountiful, in that he is ready to give rather than to take away; 136 and very merciful, in that he multiplies more and more mercies to those who are present, and who are past, and also to those who are to come— 137 for if he wasn't merciful, the world wouldn't continue with those who dwell in it 138 and one who forgives, for if he didn't forgive out of his goodness, that those who have committed iniquities might be relieved of them, not even one ten thousandth part of mankind would remain living; 139 and a judge, for if he didn't pardon those who were created by his word, and blot out the multitude of sins, 140 there would perhaps be very few left of an innumerable multitude."

8

1 He answered me, "The Most High has made this world for many, but the world to come for few. 2 Now I will tell you a parable, Esdras. Just as when you ask the earth, it will say to you that it gives very much clay from which earthen vessels are made, but little dust that gold comes from. Even so is the course of the present world. 3 Many have been created, but few will be saved."4 I answered, "Drink your fill of understanding then, O my soul, and let my heart devour wisdom. 5 For you have come here apart from your will, and depart against your

will, for you have only been given a short time to live. 6 O Lord over us, grant to your servant that we may pray before you, and give us seed for our heart and cultivation for our understanding, that fruit may grow from it, by which everyone who is corrupt, who bears the likeness of a man, may live. 7 For you alone exist, and we all one workmanship of your hands, just as you have said. 8 Because you give life to the body that is now fashioned in the womb, and give it members, your creature is preserved in fire and water, and your workmanship endures nine months as your creation which is created in it. 9 But that which keeps and that which is kept will both be kept by your keeping. When the womb gives up again what has grown in it, 10 you have commanded that out of the parts of the body, that is to say, out of the breasts, be given milk, which is the fruit of the breasts, 11 that the body that is fashioned may be nourished for a time, and afterwards you guide it in your mercy. 12 Yes, you have brought it up in your righteousness, nurtured it in your law, and corrected it with your judgment. 13 You put it to death as your creation, and make it live as your work. 14 If therefore you lightly and suddenly destroy him which with so great labor was fashioned by your commandment, to what purpose was he made? 15 Now therefore I will speak. About man in general, you know best, but about your people for whose sake I am sorry, 16 and for your inheritance, for whose cause I mourn, for Israel, for whom I am heavy, and for the seed of Jacob, for whose sake I am troubled, 17 therefore I will begin to pray before you for myself and for them; for I see the failings of us who dwell in the land; 18 but I have heard the swiftness of the judgment which is to come. 19 Therefore hear my voice, and understand my saying, and I will speak before you." The beginning of the words of Esdras, before he was taken up. He said, 20 "O Lord, you who remain forever, whose eyes are exalted, and whose chambers are in the air, 21 whose throne is beyond measure, whose glory is beyond comprehension, before whom the army of angels stand with trembling, 22 at whose bidding they are changed to wind and fire, whose word is sure, and sayings constant, whose ordinance is strong, and commandment fearful, 23 whose look dries up the depths, and whose indignation makes the mountains to melt away, and whose truth bears witness— 24 hear, O Lord, the prayer of your servant, and give ear to the petition of your handiwork. 25 Attend to my words, for as long as I live, I will speak, and as long as I have understanding, I will answer. 26 Don't look at the sins of your people, but on those who have served you in truth. 27 Don't regard the doings of those who act wickedly, but of those who have kept your covenants in affliction. 28 Don't think about those who have lived wickedly before you, but remember those who have willingly known your fear. 29 Let it not be your will to destroy those who have lived like cattle, but look at those who have clearly taught your law. 30 Don't be indignant at those who are deemed worse than animals, but love those who have always put their trust in your glory. 31 For we and our fathers have passed our lives in ways that bring death, but you are called merciful because of us sinners. 32 For if you have a desire to have mercy upon us who have no works of righteousness, then you will be called merciful. 33 For the just, which have many good works laid up with you, will be rewarded for their own deeds. 34 For what is man, that you should take displeasure at him? Or what is a corruptible race, that you should be so bitter toward it? 35 For in truth, there is no man among those who are born who has not done wickedly, and among those who have lived, there is none which have not done wrong. 36 For in this, O Lord, your righteousness and your goodness will be declared, if you are merciful to those who have no store of good works." 37 Then he answered me, "Some things you have spoken rightly, and it will happen according to your words. 38 For indeed I will not think about the fashioning of those who have sinned, or about their death, their judgment, or their destruction; 39 but I will rejoice over the creation of the righteous and their pilgrimage, their salvation, and the reward that they will have. 40 Therefore as I have spoken, so it will be. 41 For as the farmer sows many seeds in the ground, and plants many trees, and yet not all that is sown will come up in due season, neither will all that is planted take root, even so those who are sown in the world will not all be saved." 42 Then I answered, "If I have found favor, let me speak before you. 43 If the farmer's seed doesn't come up because it hasn't received your rain in due season, or if it is ruined by too much rain and perishes, 44 likewise man, who is formed with your hands and is called your own image, because he is made like you, for whose sake you have formed all things, even him have you made like the farmer's seed. 45 Don't be angry with us, but spare your people and have mercy upon your inheritance, for you have mercy upon your own creation." 46 Then he answered me, "Things present are for those who live now, and things to come for those who will live hereafter. 47 For you come far short of being able to love my creature more than I. But you have compared yourself to the unrighteous. Don't do that! 48 Yet in this will you be admirable to the Most High, 49 in that you have humbled yourself, as it becomes you, and have not judged yourself among the righteous, so as to be much glorified. 50 For many grievous miseries will fall on those who dwell in the world in the last times, because they have walked in great pride. 51 But understand for yourself, and for those who inquire concerning the glory of those like you, 52 because paradise is opened to you. The tree of life is planted. The time to come is prepared. Plenteousness is made ready. A city is built. Rest is allowed. Goodness is perfected, and wisdom is perfected beforehand. 53 The root of evil is sealed up from you. Weakness is done away from you, and death is hidden. Hell and corruption have fled into forgetfulness. 54 Sorrows have passed away, and in the end, the treasure of immortality is shown. 55 Therefore ask no more questions concerning the multitude of those who perish. 56 For when they had received liberty, they despised the Most High, scorned his law, and forsook his ways. 57 Moreover they have trodden down his righteous, 58 and said in their heart that there is no God—even knowing that they must die. 59 For as the things I have said will welcome you, so thirst and pain which are prepared for them. For the Most High didn't intend that men should be destroyed, 60 but those who are created have themselves defiled the name of him who made them, and were unthankful to him who prepared life for them. 61 Therefore my judgment is now at hand, 62 which I have not shown to all men, but to you, and a few like you." Then I answered, 63 "Behold, O Lord, now you have shown me the multitude of the wonders which you will do in the last times, but you haven't shown me when."

9

1 He answered me, "Measure diligently within yourself. When you see that a certain part of the signs are past, which have been told you beforehand, 2 then will you understand that it is the very time in which the Most High will visit the world which was made by him. 3 When earthquakes, tumult of peoples, plans of nations, wavering of leaders, and confusion of princes are seen in the world, 4 then will you understand that the Most High spoke of these things from the days that were of old, from the beginning. 5 For just as with everything that is made in the world, the beginning is evident and the end manifest, 6 so also are the times of the Most High: the beginnings are manifest in wonders and mighty works, and the end in effects and signs. 7 Everyone who will be saved, and will be able to escape by his works, or by faith by which they have believed, 8 will be preserved from the said perils, and will see my salvation in my land and within my borders, which I have sanctified for myself from the beginning. 9 Then those who now have abused my ways will be amazed. Those who have cast them away despitefully will live in torments. 10 For as many as in their life have received benefits, and yet have not known me, 11 and as many as have scorned my law, while they still had liberty and when an opportunity to repent was open to them, didn't understand, but despised it, 12 must know it in torment after death. 13 Therefore don't be curious any longer how the ungodly will be punished, but inquire how the righteous will be saved, those who the world belongs to, and for

whom the world was created." 14 I answered, 15 "I have said before, and now speak, and will say it again hereafter, that there are more of those who perish than of those who will be saved, 16 like a wave is greater than a drop." 17 He answered me, "Just as the field is, so also the seed. As the flowers are, so are the colors. As the work is, so also is the judgment on it. As is the farmer, so also is his threshing floor. For there was a time in the world 18 when I was preparing for those who now live, before the world was made for them to dwell in. Then no one spoke against me, 19 for no one existed. But now those who are created in this world that is prepared, both with a table that doesn't fail and a law which is unsearchable, are corrupted in their ways. 20 So I considered my world, and behold, it was destroyed, and my earth, and behold, it was in peril, because of the plans that had come into it. 21 I saw and spared them, but not greatly, and saved myself a grape out of a cluster, and a plant out of a great forest. 22 Let the multitude perish then, which were born in vain. Let my grape be saved, and my plant, for I have made them perfect with great labor. 23 Nevertheless, if you will wait seven more days—however don't fast in them, 24 but go into a field of flowers, where no house is built, and eat only of the flowers of the field, and you shall taste no flesh, and shall drink no wine, but shall eat flowers only 25 and pray to the Most High continually, then I will come and talk with you." 26 So I went my way, just as he commanded me, into the field which is called Ardat. There I sat among the flowers, and ate of the herbs of the field, and this food satisfied me. 27 It came to pass after seven days that I lay on the grass, and my heart was troubled again, like before. 28 My mouth was opened, and I began to speak before the Lord Most High, and said, 29 "O Lord, you showed yourself among us, to our fathers in the wilderness, when they went out of Egypt, and when they came into the wilderness, where no man treads and that bears no fruit. 30 You said, 'Hear me, O Israel. Heed my words, O seed of Jacob. 31 For behold, I sow my law in you, and it will bring forth fruit in you, and you will be glorified in it forever.' 32 But our fathers, who received the law, didn't keep it, and didn't observe the statutes. The fruit of the law didn't perish, for it couldn't, because it was yours. 33 Yet those who received it perished, because they didn't keep the thing that was sown in them. 34 Behold, it is a custom that when the ground has received seed, or the sea a ship, or any vessel food or drink, and when it comes to pass that that which is sown, or that which is launched, 35 or the things which have been received, should come to an end, these come to an end, but the receptacles remain. Yet with us, it doesn't happen that way. 36 For we who have received the law will perish by sin, along with our heart which received it. 37

Notwithstanding the law doesn't perish, but remains in its honor." 38 When I spoke these things in my heart, I looked around me with my eyes, and on my right side I saw a woman, and behold, she mourned and wept with a loud voice, and was much grieved in mind. Her clothes were torn, and she had ashes on her head. 39 Then let I my thoughts go in which I was occupied, and turned myself to her, 40 and said to her, "Why are you weeping? Why are you grieved in your mind?" 41 She said to me, "Leave me alone, my Lord, that I may weep for myself and add to my sorrow, for I am very troubled in my mind, and brought very low." 42 I said to her, "What ails you? Tell me." 43 She said to me, "I, your servant, was barren and had no child, though I had a husband thirty years. 44 Every hour and every day these thirty years I made my prayer to the Most High day and night. 45 It came to pass after thirty years that God heard me, your handmaid, and saw my low estate, and considered my trouble, and gave me a son. I rejoiced in him greatly, I and my husband, and all my neighbors. We gave great honor to the Mighty One. 46 I nourished him with great care. 47 So when he grew up, and I came to take him a wife, I made him a feast day.

10

1 "So it came to pass that when my son was entered into his wedding chamber, he fell down and died. 2 Then we all put out the lamps, and all my neighbors rose up to comfort me. I remained quiet until the second day at night. 3 It came to pass, when they had all stopped consoling me, encouraging me to be quiet, then rose I up by night, and fled, and came here into this field, as you see. 4 Now I don't intend to return into the city, but to stay here, and not eat or drink, but to continually mourn and fast until I die." 5 Then I left the reflections I was engaged in, and answered her in anger, 6 "You most foolish woman, don't you see our mourning, and what has happened to us? 7 For Zion the mother of us all is full of sorrow, and much humbled. 8It is right now to mourn deeply, since we all mourn, and to be sorrowful, since we are all in sorrow, but you are mourning for one son. 9 Ask the earth, and she will tell you that it is she which ought to mourn for so many that grow upon her. 10 For out of her, all had their beginnings, and others will come; and, behold, almost all of them walk into destruction, and the multitude of them is utterly doomed. 11 Who then should mourn more, she who has lost so great a multitude, or you, who are grieved but for one? 12 But if you say to me, 'My lamentation is not like the earth's, for I have lost the fruit of my womb, which I brought forth with pains, and bare with sorrows;' 13 but it is with the earth after the manner of the earth. The multitude present in it has gone as it came. 14 Then say I to you, 'Just as you have brought forth with sorrow, even so the earth also has given her fruit, namely, people, ever since the beginning to him who made her.' 15

Now therefore keep your sorrow to yourself, and bear with a good courage the adversities which have happened to you. 16 For if you will acknowledge the decree of God to be just, you will both receive your son in time, and will be praised among women. 17 Go your way then into the city to your husband." 18 She said to me, "I won't do that. I will not go into the city, but I will die here." 19 So I proceeded to speak further to her, and said, 20 "Don't do so, but allow yourself to be persuaded by reason of the adversities of Zion; and be comforted by reason of the sorrow of Jerusalem. 21 For you see that our sanctuary has been laid waste, our altar broken down, our temple destroyed, 22 our lute has been brought low, our song is put to silence, our rejoicing is at an end, the light of our candlestick is put out, the ark of our covenant is plundered, our holy things are defiled, and the name that we are called is profaned. Our free men are despitefully treated, our priests are burned, our Levites have gone into captivity, our virgins are defiled and our wives ravished, our righteous men carried away, our little ones betrayed, our young men are brought into bondage, and our strong men have become weak. 23 What is more than all, the seal of Zion has now lost the seal of her honor, and is delivered into the hands of those who hate us. 24 Therefore shake off your great heaviness, and put away from yourself the multitude of sorrows, that the Mighty One may be merciful to you again, and the Most High may give you rest, even ease from your troubles." 25 It came to pass while I was talking with her, behold, her face suddenly began to shine exceedingly, and her countenance glistered like lightning, so that I was very afraid of her, and wondered what this meant. 26 Behold, suddenly she made a great and very fearful cry, so that the earth shook at the noise. 27 I looked, and behold, the woman appeared to me no more, but there was a city built, and a place shown itself from large foundations. Then I was afraid, and cried with a loud voice, 28 "Where is Uriel the angel, who came to me at the first? For he has caused me to fall into this great trance, and my end has turned into corruption, and my prayer a reproach!" 29 As I was speaking these words, behold, the angel who had come to me at first came to me, and he looked at me. 30 Behold, I lay as one who had been dead, and my understanding was taken from me. He took me by the right hand, and comforted me, and set me on my feet, and said to me, 31 "What ails you? Why are you so troubled? Why is your understanding and the thoughts of your heart troubled?" 32 I said, "Because you have forsaken me; yet I did according to your words, and went into the field, and, behold, I have seen, and still see, that which I am not able to explain." 33 He said to me, "Stand up like a man, and I will instruct you." 34 Then I said, "Speak on, my Lord; only don't forsake me, lest I die before my time. 35 For I have seen what I didn't know, and hear what I don't know. 36 Or is my sense deceived, or my soul in a dream? 37 Now therefore I beg you to explain to your servant what this vision means." 38 He answered me, "Listen to me, and I will inform you, and tell you about the things you are afraid of, for the Most High has revealed many secret things to you. 39 He has seen that your way is righteous, because you are continually sorry for your people, and make great lamentation for Zion. 40 This therefore is the meaning of the vision. 41 The woman who appeared to you a little while ago, whom you saw mourning, and began to comfort her, 42 but now you no longer see the likeness of the woman, but a city under construction appeared to you, 43 and she told you of the death of her son, this is the interpretation: 44 This woman, whom you saw, is Zion, whom you now see as a city being built. 45 She told you that she had been barren for thirty years because there were three thousand years in the world in which there was no offering as yet offered in her. 46 And it came to pass after three thousand years that Solomon built the city and offered offerings. It was then that the barren bore a son. 47 She told you that she nourished him with great care. That was the dwelling in Jerusalem. 48 When she said to you, 'My son died when he entered into his marriage chamber, and that misfortune befell her,' this was the destruction that came to Jerusalem. 49 Behold, you saw her likeness, how she mourned for her son, and you began to comfort her for what has happened to her. These were the things to be opened to you. 50 For now the Most High, seeing that you are sincerely grieved and suffer from your whole heart for her, has shown you the brightness of her glory and the attractiveness of her beauty. 51 Therefore I asked you to remain in the field where no house was built, 52 for I knew that the Most High would show this to you. 53 Therefore I commanded you to come into the field, where no foundation of any building was. 54 For no human construction could stand in the place in which the city of the Most High was to be shown. 55 Therefore don't be afraid nor let your heart be terrified, but go your way in and see the beauty and greatness of the building, as much as your eyes are able to see. 56 Then will you hear as much as your ears may comprehend. 57 For you are more blessed than many, and are called by name to be with the Most High, like only a few. 58 But tomorrow at night you shall remain here, 59 and so the Most High will show you those visions in dreams of what the Most High will do to those who live on the earth in the last days." So I slept that night and another, as he commanded me.

11

1 It came to pass the second night that I saw a dream, and behold, an eagle which had twelve feathered wings and three heads came up from the sea. 2 I saw, and behold,

she spread her wings over all the earth, and all the winds of heaven blew on her, and the clouds were gathered together against her. 3 I saw, and out of her wings there grew other wings near them; and they became little, tiny wings. 4 But her heads were at rest. The head in the middle was larger than the other heads, yet rested it with them. 5 Moreover I saw, and behold, the eagle flew with her wings to reign over the earth and over those who dwell therein. 6 I saw how all things under heaven were subject to her, and no one spoke against her—no, not one creature on earth. 7 I saw, and behold, the eagle rose on her talons, and uttered her voice to her wings, saying, 8 "Don't all watch at the same time. Let each one sleep in his own place and watch in turn; 9 but let the heads be preserved for the last." 10 I saw, and behold, the voice didn't come out of her heads, but from the midst of her body. 11 I counted her wings that were near the others, and behold, there were eight of them. 12 I saw, and behold, on the right side one wing arose and reigned over all the earth. 13 When it reigned, the end of it came, and it disappeared, so that its place appeared no more. The next wing rose up and reigned, and it ruled a long time. 14 It happened that when it reigned, its end came also, so that it disappeared, like the first. 15 Behold, a voice came to it, and said, 16 "Listen, you who have ruled over the earth all this time! I proclaim this to you, before you disappear, 17 none after you will rule as long as you, not even half as long." 18 Then the third arose, and ruled as the others before, and it also disappeared. 19 So it went with all the wings one after another, as every one ruled, and then disappeared. 20 I saw, and behold, in process of time the wings that followed were set up on the right side, that they might rule also. Some of them ruled, but in a while they disappeared. 21 Some of them also were set up, but didn't rule. 22 After this I saw, and behold, the twelve wings disappeared, along with two of the little wings. 23 There was no more left on the eagle's body, except the three heads that rested, and six little wings. 24 I saw, and behold, two little wings divided themselves from the six and remained under the head that was on the right side; but four remained in their place. 25 I saw, and behold, these under wings planned to set themselves up and to rule. 26 I saw, and behold, there was one set up, but in a while it disappeared. 27 A second also did so, and it disappeared faster than the first. 28 I saw, and behold, the two that remained also planned between themselves to reign. 29 While they thought about it, behold, one of the heads that were at rest awakened, the one that was in the middle, for that was greater than the two other heads. 30 I saw how it joined the two other heads with it. 31 Behold, the head turned with those who were with it, and ate the two under wings that planned to reign. 32 But this head held the whole earth in possession, and ruled over those who dwell in it with much oppression. It had stronger governance over the world than all the wings that had gone before. 33 After this I saw, and behold, the head also that was in the middle suddenly disappeared, like the wings. 34 But the two heads remained, which also reigned the same way over the earth and over those who dwell in it. 35 I saw, and behold, the head on the right side devoured the one that was on the left side. 36 Then I heard a voice, which said to me, "Look in front of you, and consider the thing that you see." 37 I saw, and behold, something like a lion roused out of the woods roaring. I heard how he sent out a man's voice to the eagle, and spoke, saying, 38 "Listen and I will talk with you. The Most High will say to you, 39 'Aren't you the one that remains of the four animals whom I made to reign in my world, that the end of my times might come through them? 40 The fourth came and overcame all the animals that were past, and ruled the world with great trembling, and the whole extent of the earth with grievous oppression. He lived on the earth such a long time with deceit. 41 You have judged the earth, but not with truth. 42 For you have afflicted the meek, you have hurt the peaceful, you have hated those who speak truth, you have loved liars, destroyed the dwellings of those who produced fruit, and threw down the walls of those who did you no harm. 43 Your insolence has come up to the Most High, and your pride to the Mighty. 44 The Most High also has looked at his times, and behold, they are ended, and his ages are fulfilled. 45 Therefore appear no more, you eagle, nor your horrible wings, nor your evil little wings, nor your cruel heads, nor your hurtful talons, nor all your worthless body, 46 that all the earth may be refreshed and relieved, being delivered from your violence, and that she may hope for the judgment and mercy of him who made her.'

12

1 It came to pass, while the lion spoke these words to the eagle, I saw, 2 and behold, the head that remained disappeared, and the two wings which went over to it arose and set themselves up to reign; and their kingdom was brief and full of uproar. 3 I saw, and behold, they disappeared, and the whole body of the eagle was burned, so that the earth was in great fear. Then I woke up because of great perplexity of mind and great fear, and said to my spirit, 4 "Behold, you have done this to me, because you search out the ways of the Most High. 5 Behold, I am still weary in my mind, and very weak in my spirit. There isn't even a little strength in me, because of the great fear with which I was frightened tonight. 6 Therefore I will now ask the Most High that he would strengthen me to the end." 7 Then I said, "O sovereign Lord, if I have found favor in your sight, and if I am justified with you more than many others, and if my prayer has indeed come up before your face, 8 strengthen me then, and show me, your servant, the interpretation and

plain meaning of this fearful vision, that you may fully comfort my soul. 9 For you have judged me worthy to show me the end of time and the last events of the times." 10 He said to me, "This is the interpretation of this vision which you saw: 11 The eagle, whom you saw come up from the sea, is the fourth kingdom which appeared in a vision to your brother Daniel. 12 But it was not explained to him, as I now explain it to you or have explained it. 13 Behold, the days come that a kingdom will rise up on earth, and it will be feared more than all the kingdoms that were before it. 14 Twelve kings will reign in it, one after another. 15 Of those, the second will begin to reign, and will reign a longer time than others of the twelve. 16 This is the interpretation of the twelve wings which you saw. 17 As for when you heard a voice which spoke, not going out from the heads, but from the midst of its body, this is the interpretation: 18 That after the time of that kingdom, there will arise no small contentions, and it will stand in peril of falling. Nevertheless, it won't fall then, but will be restored again to its former power. 19 You saw the eight under wings sticking to her wings. This is the interpretation: 20 That in it eight kings will arise, whose times will be short and their years swift. 21 Two of them will perish when the middle time approaches. Four will be kept for a while until the time of the ending of it will approach; but two will be kept to the end. 22 You saw three heads resting. This is the interpretation: 23 In its last days, the Most High will raise up three kingdoms and renew many things in them. They will rule over the earth, 24 and over those who dwell in it, with much oppression, more than all those who were before them. Therefore they are called the heads of the eagle. 25 For these are those who will accomplish her wickedness, and who will finish her last actions. 26 You saw that the great head disappeared. It signifies that one of them will die on his bed, and yet with pain. 27 But for the two that remained, the sword will devour them. 28 For the sword of the one will devour him that was with him, but he will also fall by the sword in the last days. 29 You saw two under wings passing over to the head that is on the right side. 30 This is the interpretation: These are they whom the Most High has kept to his end. This is the brief reign that was full of trouble, as you saw. 31 "The lion, whom you saw rising up out of the forest, roaring, speaking to the eagle, and rebuking her for her unrighteousness, and all her words which you have heard, 32 this is the anointed one, whom the Most High has kept to the end [of days, who will spring up out of the seed of David, and he will come and speak] to them and reprove them for their wickedness and unrighteousness, and will heap up before them their contemptuous dealings. 33 For at first he will set them alive in his judgment, and when he has reproved them, he will destroy them. 34 For he will deliver the rest of my people with mercy, those who have been preserved throughout my borders, and he will make them joyful until the coming of the end, even the day of judgment, about which I have spoken to you from the beginning. 35 This is the dream that you saw, and this is its interpretation. 36 Only you have been worthy to know the secret of the Most High. 37 Therefore write all these things that you have seen in a book, and put it in a secret place. 38 You shall teach them to the wise of your people, whose hearts you know are able to comprehend and keep these secrets. 39 But wait here yourself seven more days, that you may be shown whatever it pleases the Most High to show you." Then he departed from me. 40 It came to pass, when all the people saw that the seven days were past, and I had not come again into the city, they all gathered together, from the least to the greatest, and came to me, and spoke to me, saying, 41 "How have we offended you? What evil have we done against you, that you have utterly forsaken us, and sit in this place? 42 For of all the prophets, only you are left to us, like a cluster of the vintage, and like a lamp in a dark place, and like a harbor for a ship saved from the tempest. 43 Aren't the evils which have come to us sufficient? 44 If you will forsake us, how much better had it been for us if we also had been consumed in the burning of Zion! 45 For we are not better than those who died there." Then they wept with a loud voice. I answered them, 46 "Take courage, O Israel! Don't be sorrowful, you house of Jacob; 47 for the Most High remembers you. The Mighty has not forgotten you forever. 48 As for me, I have not forsaken you. I haven't departed from you; but I have come into this place to pray for the desolation of Zion, and that I might seek mercy for the humiliation of your sanctuary. 49 Now go your way, every man to his own house, and after these days I will come to you." 50 So the people went their way into the city, as I told them to do. 51 But I sat in the field seven days, as the angel commanded me. In those days, I ate only of the flowers of the field, and my food was from plants.

13

1 It came to pass after seven days, I dreamed a dream by night. 2 Behold, a wind arose from the sea that moved all its waves. 3 I saw, and behold, [this wind caused to come up from the midst of the sea something like the appearance of a man. I saw, and behold,] that man flew with the clouds of heaven. When he turned his face to look, everything that he saw trembled. 4 Whenever the voice went out of his mouth, all who heard his voice melted, like the wax melts when it feels the fire. 5 After this I saw, and behold, an innumerable multitude of people was gathered together from the four winds of heaven to make war against the man who came out of the sea. 6 I saw, and behold, he carved himself a great mountain, and flew up onto it. 7 I tried to see the region or place from

which the mountain was carved, and I couldn't. 8 After this I saw, and behold, all those who were gathered together to fight against him were very afraid, and yet they dared to fight. 9 Behold, as he saw the assault of the multitude that came, he didn't lift up his hand, or hold a spear or any weapon of war; 10 but I saw only how he sent out of his mouth something like a flood of fire, and out of his lips a flaming breath, and out of his tongue he shot out a storm of sparks. 11 These were all mixed together: the flood of fire, the flaming breath, and the great storm, and fell upon the assault of the multitude which was prepared to fight, and burned up every one of them, so that all of a sudden an innumerable multitude was seen to be nothing but dust of ashes and smell of smoke. When I saw this, I was amazed. 12 Afterward, I saw the same man come down from the mountain, and call to himself another multitude which was peaceful. 13 Many people came to him. Some of them were glad. Some were sorry. Some of them were bound, and some others brought some of those as offerings. Then through great fear I woke up and prayed to the Most High, and said, 14 "You have shown your servant these wonders from the beginning, and have counted me worthy that you should receive my prayer. 15 Now show me also the interpretation of this dream. 16 For as I conceive in my understanding, woe to those who will be left in those days! Much more woe to those who are not left! 17 For those who were not left will be in heaviness, 18 understanding the things that are laid up in the latter days, but not attaining to them. 19 But woe to them also who are left, because they will see great perils and much distress, like these dreams declare. 20 Yet is it better for one to be in peril and to come into these things, than to pass away as a cloud out of the world, and not to see the things that will happen in the last days." He answered me, 21 "I will tell you the interpretation of the vision, and I will also open to you the things about which you mentioned. 22 You have spoken of those who are left behind. This is the interpretation: 23 He that will endure the peril in that time will protect those who fall into danger, even those who have works and faith toward the Almighty. 24 Know therefore that those who are left behind are more blessed than those who are dead. 25 These are the interpretations of the vision: Whereas you saw a man coming up from the midst of the sea, 26 this is he whom the Most High has been keeping for many ages, who by his own self will deliver his creation. He will direct those who are left behind. 27 Whereas you saw that out of his mouth came wind, fire, and storm, 28 and whereas he held neither spear, nor any weapon of war, but destroyed the assault of that multitude which came to fight against him, this is the interpretation: 29 Behold, the days come when the Most High will begin to deliver those who are on the earth. 30 Astonishment of mind will come upon those who dwell on the earth. 31 One will plan to make war against another, city against city, place against place, people against people, and kingdom against kingdom. 32 It will be, when these things come to pass, and the signs happen which I showed you before, then my Son will be revealed, whom you saw as a man ascending. 33 It will be, when all the nations hear his voice, every man will leave his own land and the battle they have against one another. 34 An innumerable multitude will be gathered together, as you saw, desiring to come and to fight against him. 35 But he will stand on the top of Mount Zion. 36 Zion will come, and will be shown to all men, being prepared and built, like you saw the mountain carved without hands. 37 My Son will rebuke the nations which have come for their wickedness, with plagues that are like a storm, 38 and will rebuke them to their face with their evil thoughts, and the torments with which they will be tormented, which are like a flame. He will destroy them without labor by the law, which is like fire. 39 Whereas you saw that he gathered to himself another multitude that was peaceful, 40 these are the ten tribes which were led away out of their own land in the time of Osea the king, whom Salmananser the king of the Assyrians led away captive, and he carried them beyond the River, and they were taken into another land. 41 But they made this plan among themselves, that they would leave the multitude of the heathen, and go out into a more distant region, where mankind had never lived, 42 that there they might keep their statutes which they had not kept in their own land. 43 They entered by the narrow passages of the river Euphrates. 44 For the Most High then did signs for them, and stopped the springs of the River until they had passed over. 45 For through that country there was a long way to go, namely, of a year and a half. The same region is called Arzareth. 46 Then they lived there until the latter time. Now when they begin to come again, 47 the Most High stops the springs of the River again, that they may go through. Therefore you saw the multitude gathered together with peace. 48 But those who are left behind of your people are those who are found within my holy border. 49 It will be therefore when he will destroy the multitude of the nations that are gathered together, he will defend the people who remain. 50 Then will he show them very many wonders." 51 Then I said, "O sovereign Lord, explain this to me: Why have I seen the man coming up from the midst of the sea?" 52 He said to me, as no one can explore or know what is in the depths of the sea, even so no man on earth can see my Son, or those who are with him, except in the time of his day. 53 This is the interpretation of the dream which you saw, and for this only you are enlightened about this, 54 for you have forsaken your own ways, and applied your diligence to mine, and have searched out my law. 55 You have ordered your life in wisdom, and have called understanding your mother. 56 Therefore I have shown you this, for there is a reward laid up with the Most High. It will be, after another three days I will speak other things to you, and declare to you mighty and wondrous things." 57 Then I went out and passed into the field, giving praise and thanks greatly to the Most High because of his wonders, which he did from time to time, 58 and because he governs the time, and such things as happen in their seasons. So I sat there three days.

14

1 It came to pass upon the third day, I sat under an oak, and, behold, a voice came out of a bush near me, and said, "Esdras, Esdras!" 2 I said, "Here I am, Lord," and I stood up on my feet. 3 Then he said to me, "I revealed myself in a bush and talked with Moses when my people were in bondage in Egypt. 4 I sent him, and he led my people out of Egypt. I brought him up to Mount Sinai, where I kept him with me for many days. 5 I told him many wondrous things, and showed him the secrets of the times and the end of the seasons. I commanded him, saying, 6 'You shall publish these openly, and these you shall hide.' 7 Now I say to you: 8 Lay up in your heart the signs that I have shown, the dreams that you have seen, and the interpretations which you have heard; 9 for you will be taken away from men, and from now on you will live with my Son and with those who are like you, until the times have ended. 10 For the world has lost its youth, and the times begin to grow old. 11For the age is divided into twelve parts, and ten parts of it are already gone, even the half of the tenth part. 12 There remain of it two parts after the middle of the tenth part. 13 Now therefore set your house in order, reprove your people, comfort the lowly among them, and instruct those of them who are wise, and now renounce the life that is corruptible, 14 and let go of the mortal thoughts, cast away from you the burdens of man, put off now your weak nature, 15 lay aside the thoughts that are most grievous to you, and hurry to escape from these times. 16 For worse evils than those which you have seen happen will be done after this. 17 For look how much the world will be weaker through age, so much that more evils will increase on those who dwell in it. 18 For the truth will withdraw itself further off, and falsehood will be near. For now the eagle which you saw in vision hurries to come." 19 Then I answered and said, "Let me speak in your presence, O Lord. 20 Behold, I will go, as you have commanded me, and reprove the people who now live, but who will warn those who will be born afterward? For the world is set in darkness, and those who dwell in it are without light. 21 For your law has been burned, therefore no one knows the things that are done by you, or the works that will be done. 22 But if I have found favor before you, send the Holy Spirit to me, and

I will write all that has been done in the world since the beginning, even the things that were written in your law, that men may be able to find the path, and that those who would live in the latter days may live." 23 He answered me and said, "Go your way, gather the people together, and tell them not to seek you for forty days. 24 But prepare for yourself many tablets, and take with you Sarea, Dabria, Selemia, Ethanus, and Asiel, these five, which are ready to write swiftly; 25 and come here, and I will light a lamp of understanding in your heart which will not be put out until the things have ended about which you will write. 26 When you are done, some things you shall publish openly, and some things you shall deliver in secret to the wise. Tomorrow at this hour you will begin to write." 27 Then went I out, as he commanded me, and gathered all the people together, and said, 28 "Hear these words, O Israel! 29 Our fathers at the beginning were foreigners in Egypt, and they were delivered from there, 30 and received the law of life, which they didn't keep, which you also have transgressed after them. 31 Then the land of Zion was given to you for a possession; but you yourselves and your ancestors have done unrighteousness, and have not kept the ways which the Most High commanded you. 32 Because he is a righteous judge, in due time, he took from you what he had given you. 33 Now you are here, and your kindred are among you. 34 Therefore if you will rule over your own understanding and instruct your hearts, you will be kept alive, and after death you will obtain mercy. 35 For after death the judgment will come, when we will live again. Then the names of the righteous will become manifest, and the works of the ungodly will be declared. 36 Let no one therefore come to me now, nor seek me for forty days." 37 So I took the five men, as he commanded me, and we went out into the field, and remained there. 38 It came to pass on the next day that, behold, a voice called me, saying, "Esdras, open your mouth, and drink what I give you to drink." 39 Then opened I my mouth, and behold, a full cup was handed to me. It was full of something like water, but its color was like fire. 40 I took it, and drank. When I had drunk it, my heart uttered understanding, and wisdom grew in my breast, for my spirit retained its memory. 41 My mouth was opened, and shut no more. 42 The Most High gave understanding to the five men, and they wrote by course the things that were told them, in characters which they didn't know, and they sat forty days. Now they wrote in the day-time, and at night they ate bread. 43 As for me, I spoke in the day, and by night I didn't hold my tongue. 44 So in forty days, ninety-four books were written. 45 It came to pass, when the forty days were fulfilled, that the Most High spoke to me, saying, "The first books that you have written, publish openly, and let the worthy and unworthy read them; 46 but keep the last seventy, that you may deliver them to those who are wise among your people; 47 for in them is the spring of understanding, the fountain of wisdom, and the stream of knowledge." 48 I did so.

15

1 "Behold, speak in the ears of my people the words of prophecy which I will put in your mouth," says the Lord. 2 "Cause them to be written on paper, for they are faithful and true. 3 Don't be afraid of their plots against you. Don't let the unbelief of those who speak against you trouble you. 4 For all the unbelievers will die in their unbelief. 5 "Behold," says the Lord, "I bring evils on the whole earth: sword, famine, death, and destruction. 6 For wickedness has prevailed over every land, and their hurtful works have reached their limit. 7 Therefore," says the Lord, 8 "I will hold my peace no more concerning their wickedness which they profanely commit, neither will I tolerate them in these things, which they wickedly practice. Behold, the innocent and righteous blood cries to me, and the souls of the righteous cry out continually. 9 I will surely avenge them," says the Lord, "and will receive to me all the innocent blood from among them. 10 Behold, my people is led like a flock to the slaughter. I will not allow them now to dwell in the land of Egypt, 11 but I will bring them out with a mighty hand and with a high arm, and will strike Egypt with plagues, as before, and will destroy all its land." 12 Let Egypt and its foundations mourn, for the plague of the chastisement and the punishment that God will bring upon it. 13 Let the farmers that till the ground mourn, for their seeds will fail and their trees will be ruined through the blight and hail, and a terrible tempest. 14 Woe to the world and those who dwell in it! 15 For the sword and their destruction draws near, and nation will rise up against nation to battle with weapons in their hands. 16 For there will be sedition among men, and growing strong against one another. In their might, they won't respect their king or the chief of their great ones. 17 For a man will desire to go into a city, and will not be able. 18 For because of their pride the cities will be troubled, the houses will be destroyed, and men will be afraid. 19 A man will have no pity on his neighbors, but will assault their houses with the sword and plunder their goods, because of the lack of bread, and for great suffering. 20 "Behold," says God, "I call together all the kings of the earth to stir up those who are from the rising of the sun, from the south, from the east, and Libanus, to turn themselves one against another, and repay the things that they have done to them. 21 Just as they do yet this day to my chosen, so I will do also, and repay into their bosom." The Lord God says: 22 "My right hand won't spare the sinners, and my sword won't cease over those who shed innocent blood on the earth. 23 A fire has gone out from his wrath and has consumed the foundations of the earth and the sinners, like burnt straw. 24 Woe

to those who sin and don't keep my commandments!" says the Lord. 25 "I will not spare them. Go your way, you rebellious children! Don't defile my sanctuary!" 26 For the Lord knows all those who trespass against him, therefore he will deliver them to death and destruction. 27 For now evils have come upon the whole earth, and you will remain in them; for God will not deliver you, because you have sinned against him. 28 Behold, a horrible sight appearing from the east! 29 The nations of the dragons of Arabia will come out with many chariots. From the day that they set out, their hissing is carried over the earth, so that all those who will hear them may also fear and tremble. 30 Also the Carmonians, raging in wrath, will go out like the wild boars of the forest. They will come with great power and join battle with them, and will devastate a portion of the land of the Assyrians with their teeth. 31 Then the dragons will have the upper hand, remembering their nature. If they will turn themselves, conspiring together in great power to persecute them, 32 then these will be troubled, and keep silence through their power, and will turn and flee. 33 From the land of the Assyrians, an enemy in ambush will attack them and destroy one of them. Upon their army will be fear and trembling, and indecision upon their kings. 34 Behold, clouds from the east, and from the north to the south! They are very horrible to look at, full of wrath and storm. 35 They will clash against one another. They will pour out a heavy storm on the earth, even their own storm. There will be blood from the sword to the horse's belly, 36 and to the thigh of man, and to the camel's hock. 37 There will be fearfulness and great trembling upon earth. They who see that wrath will be afraid, and trembling will seize them. 38 After this, great storms will be stirred up from the south, from the north, and another part from the west. 39 Strong winds will arise from the east, and will shut it up, even the cloud which he raised up in wrath; and the storm that was to cause destruction by the east wind will be violently driven toward the south and west. 40 Great and mighty clouds, full of wrath, will be lifted up with the storm, that they may destroy all the earth and those who dwell in it. They will pour out over every high and lofty one a terrible storm, 41 fire, hail, flying swords, and many waters, that all plains may be full, and all rivers, with the abundance of those waters. 42 They will break down the cities and walls, mountains and hills, trees of the forest, and grass of the meadows, and their grain. 43 They will go on steadily to Babylon and destroy her. 44 They will come to it and surround it. They will pour out the storm and all wrath on her. Then the dust and smoke will go up to the sky, and all those who are around it will mourn for it. 45 Those who remain will serve those who have destroyed it. 46 You, Asia, who are partaker in the beauty of Babylon, and in the glory of her person— 47 woe to you, you wretch, because you have made yourself like her. You have decked out your daughters for prostitution, that they might please and glory in your lovers, which have always lusted after you! 48 You have followed her who is hateful in all her works and inventions. Therefore God says, 49 "I will send evils on you: widowhood, poverty, famine, sword, and pestilence, to lay waste your houses and bring you to destruction and death. 50 The glory of your power will be dried up like a flower when the heat rises that is sent over you. 51 You will be weakened like a poor woman who is beaten and wounded, so that you won't be able to receive your mighty ones and your lovers. 52 Would I have dealt with you with such jealousy," says the Lord, 53 "if you had not always slain my chosen, exalting and clapping of your hands, and saying over their dead, when you were drunk? 54 "Beautify your face! 55 The reward of a prostitute will be in your bosom,therefore you will be repaid. 56 Just as you will do to my chosen," says the Lord, "even so God will do to you, and will deliver you to your adversaries. 57 Your children will die of hunger. You will fall by the sword. Your cities will be broken down, and all your people in the field will perish by the sword. 58 Those who are in the mountains will die of hunger, eat their own flesh, and drink their own blood, because of hunger for bread and thirst for water. 59 You, unhappy above all others, will come and will again receive evils. 60 In the passage, they will rush on the hateful city and will destroy some portion of your land, and mar part of your glory, and will return again to Babylon that was destroyed. 61 You will be cast down by them as stubble, and they will be to you as fire. 62 They will devour you, your cities, your land, and your mountains. They will burn all your forests and your fruitful trees with fire. 63 They will carry your children away captive, and will plunder your wealth, and mar the glory of your face."

16

1 Woe to you, Babylon, and Asia! Woe to you, Egypt and Syria! 2 Put on sackcloth and garments of goats' hair, wail for your children and lament; for your destruction is at hand. 3 A sword has been sent upon you, and who is there to turn it back? 4 A fire has been sent upon you, and who is there to quench it? 5 Calamities are sent upon you, and who is there to drive them away? 6 Can one drive away a hungry lion in the forest? Can one quench a fire in stubble, once it has begun to burn? 7 Can one turn back an arrow that is shot by a strong archer? 8 The Lord God sends the calamities, and who will drive them away? 9 A fire will go out from his wrath, and who may quench it? 10 He will flash lightning, and who will not fear? He will thunder, and who wouldn't tremble? 11 The Lord will threaten, and who will not be utterly broken in pieces at his presence? 12 The earth and its foundations quake. The sea rises up with waves from the deep, and its waves will be

troubled, along with the fish in them, at the presence of the Lord, and before the glory of his power. 13 For his right hand that bends the bow is strong, his arrows that he shoots are sharp, and will not miss when they begin to be shot into the ends of the world. 14 Behold, the calamities are sent out, and will not return again until they come upon the earth. 15 The fire is kindled and will not be put out until it consumes the foundations of the earth. 16 Just as an arrow which is shot by a mighty archer doesn't return backward, even so the calamities that are sent out upon earth won't return again. 17 Woe is me! Woe is me! Who will deliver me in those days? 18 The beginning of sorrows, when there will be great mourning; the beginning of famine, and many will perish; the beginning of wars, and the powers will stand in fear; the beginning of calamities, and all will tremble! What will they do when the calamities come? 19 Behold, famine and plague, suffering and anguish! They are sent as scourges for correction. 20 But for all these things they will not turn them from their wickedness, nor be always mindful of the scourges. 21 Behold, food will be so cheap on earth that they will think themselves to be in good condition, and even then calamities will grow on earth: sword, famine, and great confusion. 22 For many of those who dwell on earth will perish of famine; and others who escape the famine, the sword will destroy. 23 The dead will be cast out like dung, and there will be no one to comfort them; for the earth will be left desolate, and its cities will be cast down. 24 There will be no farmer left to cultivate the earth or to sow it. 25 The trees will give fruit, but who will gather it? 26 The grapes will ripen, but who will tread them? For in all places there will be a great solitude; 27 for one man will desire to see another, or to hear his voice. 28 For of a city there will be ten left, and two of the field, who have hidden themselves in the thick groves, and in the clefts of the rocks. 29 As in an orchard of olives upon every tree there may be left three or four olives, 30 or as when a vineyard is gathered, there are some clusters left by those who diligently search through the vineyard, 31 even so in those days, there will be three or four left by those who search their houses with the sword. 32 The earth will be left desolate, and its fields will be for briers, and its roads and all her paths will grow thorns, because no sheep will pass along them. 33 The virgins will mourn, having no bridegrooms. The women will mourn, having no husbands. Their daughters will mourn, having no helpers. 34 Their bridegrooms will be destroyed in the wars, and their husbands will perish of famine. 35 Hear now these things, and understand them, you servants of the Lord. 36 Behold, the Lord's word: receive it. Don't doubt the things about which the Lord speaks. 37 Behold, the calamities draw near, and are not delayed. 38 Just as a woman with child in the ninth month, when the hour of her delivery draws near, within two or three hours great pains surround her womb, and when the child comes out from the womb, there will be no waiting for a moment, 39 even so the calamities won't delay coming upon the earth. The world will groan, and sorrows will seize it on every side. 40 "O my people, hear my word: prepare for battle, and in those calamities be like strangers on the earth. 41 He who sells, let him be as he who flees away, and he who buys, as one who will lose. 42 Let he who does business be as he who has no profit by it, and he who builds, as he who won't dwell in it, 43 and he who sows, as if he wouldn't reap, so also he who prunes the vines, as he who won't gather the grapes, 44 those who marry, as those who will have no children, and those who don't marry, as the widowed. 45 Because of this, those who labor, labor in vain; 46 for foreigners will reap their fruits, plunder their goods, overthrow their houses, and take their children captive, for in captivity and famine they will conceive their children. 47 Those who conduct business, do so only to be plundered. The more they adorn their cities, their houses, their possessions, and their own persons, 48 the more I will hate them for their sins," says the Lord. 49 Just as a respectable and virtuous woman hates a prostitute, 50 so will righteousness hate iniquity, when she adorns herself, and will accuse her to her face, when he comes who will defend him who diligently searches out every sin on earth. 51 Therefore don't be like her or her works. 52 For yet a little while, and iniquity will be taken away out of the earth, and righteousness will reign over us. 53 Don't let the sinner say that he has not sinned; for God will burn coals of fire on the head of one who says "I haven't sinned before God and his glory." 54 Behold, the Lord knows all the works of men, their imaginations, their thoughts, and their hearts. 55 He said, "Let the earth be made," and it was made, "Let the sky be made," and it was made. 56 At his word, the stars were established, and he knows the number of the stars. 57 He searches the deep and its treasures. He has measured the sea and what it contains. 58 He has shut the sea in the midst of the waters, and with his word, he hung the earth over the waters. 59 He has spread out the sky like a vault. He has founded it over the waters. 60 He has made springs of water in the desert and pools on the tops of the mountains to send out rivers from the heights to water the earth. 61 He formed man, and put a heart in the midst of the body, and gave him breath, life, and understanding, 62 yes, the spirit of God Almighty. He who made all things and searches out hidden things in hidden places, 63 surely he knows your imagination, and what you think in your hearts. Woe to those who sin, and try to hide their sin! 64 Because the Lord will exactly investigate all your works, and he will put you all to shame. 65 When your sins are brought out before men, you will be ashamed, and your own iniquities will stand as your accusers in that day. 66 What will you do? Or how will you hide your sins before God and his angels? 67 Behold, God is the judge. Fear him! Stop sinning, and forget your iniquities, to never again commit them. So will God lead you out, and deliver you from all suffering.

68 For, behold, the burning wrath of a great multitude is kindled over you, and they will take away some of you, and feed you with that which is sacrificed to idols. 69 Those who consent to them will be held in derision and in contempt, and be trodden under foot. 70 For there will be in various places, and in the next cities, a great insurrection against those who fear the Lord. 71 They will be like mad men, sparing none, but spoiling and destroying those who still fear the Lord. 72 For they will destroy and plunder their goods, and throw them out of their houses. 73 Then the trial of my elect will be made known, even as the gold that is tried in the fire. 74 Hear, my elect ones, says the Lord: "Behold, the days of suffering are at hand, and I will deliver you from them. 75 Don't be afraid, and don't doubt, for God is your guide. 76 You who keep my commandments and precepts," says the Lord God, "don't let your sins weigh you down, and don't let your iniquities lift themselves up." 77 Woe to those who are choked with their sins and covered with their iniquities, like a field is choked with bushes, and its path covered with thorns, that no one may travel through! 78 It is shut off and given up to be consumed by fire.

BOOK OF MEQABYAN I

1

1 In the land there lived a man named Tseerutsaydan, a lover of sin, who took pride in the multitude of his horses and the strength of his soldiers under his command. 2 This man had numerous priests who ministered to the idols he adored, offering sacrifices to them both day and night, bowing before them in reverence. 3 In the dimness of his understanding, he believed these idols granted him stability and might. 4 In his heart, he was convinced that these idols bestowed upon him dominion over his entire kingdom. 5 Similarly, in times of war, he felt assured that these idols endowed him with all the necessary power and authority. 6 Day and night, he devotedly offered sacrifices to these idols. 7 He assigned priests specifically for the service of his idols. 8 As these priests consumed the defiled offerings, they deceitfully assured him that the idols, too, partook in these meals continuously. 9 Furthermore, they trained others to be as zealous as themselves in offering sacrifices and partaking in the feasts. They also encouraged more individuals to be diligent in their sacrificial offerings. 10 Yet, Tseerutsaydan placed his faith in

these idols, which provided neither gain nor aid. 11 Blinded by his limited understanding and the dullness of his heart, he imagined that these idols had created him, sustained him, and bestowed kingship upon him. Such was the deception of Satan upon his reasoning, preventing him from recognizing his true Creator, who brought him from nonexistence into being. This ignorance led him and his kin towards the eternal damnation of Gehenna's Fire, condemned along with him who falsely proclaimed these lifeless idols as gods. 12 It was only fitting to deem these idols as lifeless, for they never exhibited any signs of vitality. 13 Under the guise of Satan's influence, which deceives many, the spirit of deceit would inhabit these idol images. This spirit would echo their thoughts and desires, presenting revelations as they wished. Thus, it led the believers of these idols, whose understanding was as futile as ashes, into deeper delusion. 14 They would be astounded when their desires were seemingly fulfilled by these idols, compelling them to act according to Satan's will, even to the extent of sacrificing their own children, spilling the innocent blood of their daughters and sons. 15 Such heinous acts did not grieve them, for Satan relished these offerings, furthering their malevolent intentions. This path led them to Gehenna, a place of no return, eternal in its torment, where they would suffer alongside the deceiver. 16 Tseerutsaydan, in his pride, possessed seventy idols, fifty fashioned in the likeness of men and twenty in the likeness of women. 17 He glorified these powerless idols, extolling them lavishly while presenting his offerings at dawn and dusk. 18 He ordered others to make sacrifices to these idols, partaking in the tainted offerings himself and commanding others to do the same, thus fostering wickedness. 19 Tseerutsaydan had five temples constructed for these idols made of iron, brass, and lead. 20 Adorned in silver and gold, these temples were enclosed with veils and tents, enhancing their splendor. 21 He assigned guardians for these temples and consistently offered an abundance of sacrifices to his idols: ten fattened oxen, ten lean cows, ten plump sheep, and ten lean goats, along with various birds. 22 He believed that these idols partook in these offerings, presenting them with lavish quantities of grapes and wheat kneaded with oil. 23 He instructed his priests, "Take and offer these to my creators. Let them feast on what I have slaughtered and drink the grapes I have presented. Should it not suffice, I will provide more." 24 He commanded everyone to partake in these tainted feasts. 25 Driven by his malicious intent, Tseerutsaydan sent his enforcers throughout his kingdom. They were to find and bring forth anyone who neither sacrificed nor bowed to the idols, subjecting such individuals to execution by fire and sword. Their possessions would be seized, their homes burnt, and their wealth annihilated. 26 "For these idols are deemed noble and exalted, believed to have created us out of their benevolence; and I shall bring punishment and suffering upon anyone who fails to worship my creators, or to offer sacrifices to them. 27 And they shall face my wrath and affliction, for these idols are thought to have formed the Earth and the Heavens, the vast seas, the moon and sun, the stars, the rains and winds, and all living beings in this world, providing sustenance and

satisfaction for us." 28Yet, those who venerate these idols shall endure stern tribulations, receiving no kindness from them.

2

1In the tribe of Benjamin, there was a man named Maccabeus; 2 a father of three valiant and handsome sons, beloved by all in the lands of Midian and Media under Tseerutsaydan's rule. 3 When the king's command reached them, they were asked, "Will you not bow to Tseerutsaydan's idols? Will you not offer sacrifices to them? 4 Should you resist, we will capture you and bring you before the king, destroying your wealth as he has decreed." 5 These striking young men responded, "We worship only the True Creator, our Father in Heaven, who made the Earth, the heavens, and all within them, the seas, the moon, the sun, the clouds, and the stars." 6 The king's men, four in number, accompanied by a hundred shield and spear bearers, sought to apprehend these devout men. 7 However, these holy men eluded capture, untouched by their pursuers, displaying their formidable warrior strength in seizing shields and spears. 8 One among them was renowned for overpowering panthers, effortlessly subduing them as one might a chicken. 9 Another was famed for slaying lions with a single stone or a swift strike with a stick. 10 A third was celebrated for defeating a hundred foes single-handedly in battle with his sword. Their prowess and deeds were renowned across Babylon and Moab. 11 They were mighty warriors, not only in strength but also in their noble character and striking appearance. 12 Their physical beauty was remarkable, yet it was their unwavering devotion to the Lord and fearless acceptance of death that truly set them apart. 13 When they confronted enemy troops, no one could capture them. These warrior brothers found refuge in a high mountain. 14 The enemy soldiers returned to their city, fortifying it with fear, threatening the people to surrender the Meqabyans or face the city's destruction by fire. 15 The inhabitants, rich and poor, men and women, orphans and widows, cried out in unison, pleading with the warriors from the mountains not to bring ruin upon them. 16 United in their fear and faith in the Lord, they turned eastward, raising their hands in prayer, begging for mercy: "Lord, should we betray these men who defy Your Commandments and Your Law? 17They trust in material wealth and the work of human hands, but we refuse to heed the words of this transgressor who denies Your Law," they proclaimed. 18 "He likens himself to a creator, yet You are the true Creator who gives life and death. He spills blood and consumes flesh. 19 We do not wish to face this wicked man or hear his blasphemous words. 20 Yet, if it is Your will, we will confront him. Trusting in You, we are prepared to offer our lives in sacrifice, rejecting his demands to worship his idols. 21 We trust in You, Lord, the discerner of hearts and minds, the God of our ancestors Abraham, Isaac, and Jacob, who followed Your Will and lived faithfully according to Your Law. 22 You understand the thoughts of all, aiding both sinners and the righteous. Nothing is hidden from You, and those who seek refuge find it in Your presence. 23 You alone are our Creator, and in this trial, we seek Your strength and protection, ready to sacrifice our lives for the glory of Your Name. 24 Just as You heard Jacob's plea in Egypt, we now implore Your divine assistance." 25 Suddenly, two men of remarkable beauty appeared before them, and fiery swords, terrifying as lightning, descended, slaying the aggressors, allowing the faithful to rise unharmed and more radiant than before, their beauty enhanced beyond their former glory.

3

1 "As you have witnessed the servants of the Most High, the Lord, Abya, Seela, and Fentos, who died and were resurrected, know that you too shall rise after death, shining as brightly as the sun in the Kingdom of Heaven. 2 Accompanying these men, they embraced martyrdom. 3 In that moment, they prayed, praised, and bowed to the Lord. Neither death nor the king's threats could instill fear in them. 4 Approaching the young men, they were treated like harmless sheep, yet they remained unafraid. When they were captured, they were beaten, bound, whipped, and presented before the king. 5 The king demanded of them, "Why do you stubborn ones not offer sacrifices and bow before my creators?" 6 The brothers, cleansed from sin, honored, chosen, joyful, and shining like precious jewels of immense value - Seela, Abya, and Fentos - spoke in unison. 7 They boldly told the plague-like king, "We will neither bow nor offer sacrifices to your tainted idols, devoid of consciousness or understanding." 8 They further declared, "We refuse to bow to idols crafted from silver and gold, stone and wood, lifeless figures without reasoning, soul, or knowledge, powerless to aid their friends or harm their foes." 9 The king retorted, "Why do you act so? Do you not know they punish those who insult and wrong them? Why do you disrespect my glorified creators?" 10 They replied, "In our eyes, they are nothing but trifles. We will continue to scorn them and refuse to glorify them." 11 The king

threatened, "I will subject you to punishment befitting the evil of your actions. I will mar your beautiful faces with whipping, severe suffering, and fire. 12 Now tell me, will you offer sacrifices to my creators, or face punishment by the sword and whip?" 13 They firmly responded, "We will neither offer sacrifices nor bow to tainted idols." The king then ordered them to be beaten with thick sticks and whipped severely, their bodies mangled to the point of revealing their inner organs. 14 After this brutal treatment, they were thrown into jail to await the king's further decision to punish and execute them. 15 They were confined in harsh imprisonment, suffering in the cell for three days and nights. 16 On the third day, the king commanded a town crier to summon counselors, nobles, community elders, and officials. 17 As King Tseerutsaydan sat in the public square, he ordered the presentation of the honored men - Seela, Abya, and Fentos - who were brought forth, wounded and bound. 18 The king questioned them, "After three days of contemplation, have you changed your minds, or do you persist in your previous defiance?" 19 The noble warriors of the Lord replied, "Disciplined as we are, we shall never consent to worship the sinful and evil idols you revere." 20 Enraged, the king ordered them to be placed in a high location and their wounds to be reopened, their blood spilling onto the ground. 21 He then commanded them to be scorched with torches, charring their flesh, which his servants promptly executed. The honored men proclaimed, "You who have forsaken the Lord's Law, speak! Our reward in Heaven will only increase as you intensify our suffering." 22 Further, he ordered wild beasts - bears, tigers, and lions, starved and ferocious - to be unleashed upon them, intending for the animals to devour them completely. 23 The beast keepers released the animals, binding the feet of the holy martyrs and cruelly beating and restraining them with stakes. 24 As the beasts pounced on them with roaring fury, they halted and bowed before the martyrs, turning back to their keepers and instilling fear in them. The beasts were then led back to the square, presented before the king. 25 In this chaos, seventy-five of the king's soldiers were slain. 26 The crowd was gripped with terror and confusion, prompting the king to flee his throne. The beasts were eventually restrained and returned to their quarters. 27 The two brothers of Seela, Abya, and Fentos came to their rescue, freeing them from their bonds and urging, "Come, let us escape before these doubters and wrongdoers find us." 28 The martyrs replied, "It is not our way to flee after standing as witnesses. If you fear, then go, but we will not run." 29 Their younger siblings declared, "We will stand with you before the king, ready to die alongside you." 30 Observing from his balcony, the king noticed the five brothers standing together. His officials identified them, infuriating the king, who roared with anger like a wild boar. 31 The king, intent on punishing all five, ordered their imprisonment. They were harshly bound and confined, showing no mercy. 32 King Tseerutsaydan lamented, "These defiant youths have exhausted me. Their unyielding spirits match the evil of their deeds. They seem unrepentant, only further corrupting their minds. 33 I will inflict suffering proportional to their wicked actions, burning their flesh to ash, which I will then scatter like dust over the mountains." 34 After declaring this, the king waited three days before summoning the noble men. As they approached, he ordered a large pit oven to be heated with malicious intent, adding substances to intensify the flames: fat, soapberries, sea foam, resin, and sulfur. 35 As the fire blazed, messengers informed the king that his commands had been executed, and he then ordered the men to be thrown into the fiery pit. 36 The youths obeyed, and as the martyrs entered the flames, they entrusted their souls to the Lord. 37 Onlookers saw angels receive their souls, escorting them to the Garden where the patriarchs Abraham, Isaac, and Jacob resided, a place of joy and happiness.

4

1 Witnessing their death, the king ordered their bodies to be burned to ashes and scattered by the wind. However, the fire failed to singe even a hair on their bodies, and they were removed from the pit. 2 Attempts to burn their bodies continued from morning till evening without success. The decision was then made to cast their bodies into the sea. 3 Following the king's command, the bodies were thrown into the sea, weighed down with stones and millstones. Yet, by the Lord's Spirit of Support, they floated, unable to be sunk or destroyed. 4 The king lamented, "Their death has wearied me more than their life. Let us leave their bodies for the beasts, but what can I do?" 5 As he commanded, vultures and beasts did not touch the bodies. Birds shielded them from the sun's heat, and for fourteen days, the martyrs' bodies remained untouched, glowing like the sun. 6 Angels surrounded them, casting a light as if encircling a tent. 7 The king, at a loss for action, eventually decided to bury the bodies of the five martyrs. 8 That night, as the king who had forsaken the Lord's Law lay in bed, he envisioned the five martyrs standing before him, angry, swords in hand. 9 Believing they had come to harm him, he awoke terrified, contemplating fleeing his chamber. His fear was so intense, he thought they sought his life. 10 He pleaded, "My lords, what do you desire? What can I do for you?" 11 They responded, "Are we not the ones you burned and cast into the sea? The Lord preserved our bodies because we believed in Him. You failed to destroy us. Those who believe in Him will never perish.

Offer glory and praise to the Lord, for we who believed in Him were not shamed by our trials. 12 “Unaware such retribution would befall me, what compensation can I offer you for the wrongs I committed?” 13 “Tell us what you will give us, lest you seize our bodies in death and cast us into Sheol while we live. 14 We have suffered at your hands; forgive us our sins, for it is the kindness of the Lord’s Law you have transgressed,” they said. 15 The martyrs replied, “We will not retaliate for the wrongs you’ve done us. The Lord is the one who inflicts hardship on souls. He will be the one to punish you. 16 We appeared to you as a sign of our well- being, for your time is short, and your understanding clouded. You thought you had killed us, but you only secured our salvation. 16 Yet you, along with the priests of your idols, will descend to Gehenna, eternally trapped. 18 Woe to the idols you worship, forsaking the Lord who created you. You are like smoke today, soon to vanish. Do you not realize it is the Lord who created you from nothing?” 19The king, in response, asked, “What shall I do to make amends for my actions against you?” 20 “Seek salvation, lest you fall into the fiery Gehenna. It is not for our benefit, but to teach you. 21 Your idols are mere silver, gold, stone, and wood, crafted by human hands, devoid of reasoning or soul. 22 They have no power to kill or save, to bring fortune to friends or misfortune to foes. They neither degrade nor elevate, enrich nor impoverish. They lead you astray under the sway of demons, who seek not the salvation of anyone. 23 They care not for the salvation of people like you, deluded ones, who think these idols created you, when it is you who fashioned them. 24 As they are imbued with the influence of Satan and demons, they shall fulfill your desires only to plunge you into the abyss of Gehenna. 25 Abandon this folly. Let our martyrdom be our reward, urging you to benefit your soul by worshipping our Creator, the Lord," they advised him. 26 The king was struck with fear and wonder, especially upon seeing all five apparitions draw their swords. In awe, he bowed before them. 27 "Now I understand that those who were once dust and died shall indeed rise again. My own end is near," he realized. 28 Following this revelation, the king ceased desecrating their remains. He began to indulge in his idols and misguided beliefs, leading others astray from the worship of the Lord who created them. But he was not alone in his error. 29 People sacrificed their children to demons, embracing the chaos and deception taught by Satan, displeasing to the Lord. 30 They engaged in unspeakable acts, marrying within their families, defiling their own bodies, and indulging in all manner of abhorrent deeds. Led astray by Satan, they stubbornly refused to repent. 31 Tseerutsaydan, oblivious to his Creator, remained steeped in arrogance, boasting of his idols. 32 "How can the Lord grant His kingdom to those who do not know Him in Law and Worship?" Yet if they repented, they would find their way back to Him. This is His test. 33 If they genuinely repented, the Lord would embrace them, preserving their kingdom. But refusal would lead them to eternal punishment in the fiery Gehenna. 34 It is the duty of a king to revere his Creator as befits his sovereignty, and of a judge to dispense fair judgments in accordance with the stature of his rule. 35 Likewise, elders, chiefs, envoys, and lesser rulers should serve their Creator in proportion to their rank and influence. 36 For He is the Lord of Heaven and Earth, the sole Creator of all existence. None other in Heaven or Earth can bestow riches or poverty, honor or dishonor.

5

1 "Among the sixty warriors, one was filled with pride. The Lord caused his body to swell from his feet to his head with a mere spoon of sulfur, leading to his demise by plague. 2 Another, Hiram, who constructed an iron bed, was consumed by pride due to his strength. The Lord took him away in death. 3 Nebuchadnezzar also succumbed to pride, proclaiming, 'There is no king but me; I am the creator who commands the Sun to rise in this world.' His arrogance knew no bounds. 4 The Lord separated him from the company of men, banishing him to the wilderness for seven years. There, he shared his life with the birds of Heaven and the beasts of the wild, until he recognized that it was the Lord who had created him. 5 When he finally acknowledged and worshipped the Lord, he was restored to his kingdom. Who can stand against the Lord, the Creator, with earthly arrogance? 6 Who has ever defied His Law and Order and not been swallowed by the Earth? 7 Yet you, Tseerutsaydan, indulge in pride against your Creator, risking the Lord's wrath, which might cast you down to the grave, a victim of your own arrogance. 8 After entering Sheol, where there is gnashing of teeth and eternal mourning, you risk being cast into the abyss of Gehenna, from which there is no escape. 9 You, who are mortal and soon to perish, emulate the proud kings who have left this world behind. 10 We declare, 'You are but ruins, not the Lord; for it is the Lord who created the Earth, the Heavens, and you.' 11 He humbles the proud and honors the humble. He strengthens the weary. 12 He brings death to the living and raises the dead from their earthly graves. 13 He frees His servants from the bondage of sin. 14 O King Tseerutsaydan, why do you glory in your worthless idols? 15 The Lord created the Earth and the Heavens, the vast seas, the moon and the Sun, and set the times and seasons. 16 Humans toil in their fields from dawn till dusk, while the stars in the Heavens are steadfast in His command. 17 He oversees all in Heaven, and nothing occurs without His knowledge. 18 He has commanded the Angels of Heaven to serve Him and to glorify His

Name. Angels are sent to all who inherit life. 19 Raphael, a divine servant, was sent to Tobit and saved Tobias from death in Raguel's land. 20 The holy Michael was dispatched to Gideon to guide him to vanquish the Iloflee, and to Moses, helping Israel cross the Red Sea. 21 With the Lord alone guiding them, no false idol accompanied them. 22 He blessed their crops upon the Earth. 23 He nourished them with His grain and cherished them with honey as solid as rock. 24 To govern His people justly and fulfill the will of the Lord who created you, He has granted you authority over four kingdoms. 25 The Lord has elevated you above all, trusting you to love the Lord as He has loved you. 26 It is your duty to love your Creator, the Lord, as He has entrusted you with His people. Do His will, that your days may be long in this world, and His presence be with you in support. 27 Fulfill His will, that He may protect you from your enemies, establish your reign, and shelter you under His wings of support. 28 The Lord chose and crowned you over Israel, just as He chose Saul among the children of Israel, elevating him from tending his father's donkeys to ruling over Israel. 29 He bestowed upon Saul great fortune, setting him apart from his kin. Likewise, the Lord has crowned you over His people. 30 Henceforth, guard His people. As the Lord has placed you over them to decide life and death, treat justly those who do good and those who mix good with evil." 31 "As the Lord has granted you authority over all, to enact His will, whether in punishment or salvation, deal justly with those who do good and those who mingle good and evil in their deeds. 32 Recognize that you are a servant of the Lord, who rules over all in Heaven. Do His will, that He may fulfill your desires and heed your prayers. 33 No one governs Him, for He governs all. 34 No one appoints Him, for He appoints all. 35 No one dismisses Him, for He dismisses all. 36 No one reproaches Him, for He reproaches all. 37 No one can urge Him to action, for He motivates all. As the ruler of Heaven and Earth, none can escape His authority; everything is laid bare before Him, and nothing is hidden from His sight. 38 He sees all, though none can see Him. He hears the prayers of those who cry out for salvation, for He has created humanity in His image and listens to their pleas. 39 As an eternal King, He sustains all from His unchanging nature."

6

1 "In bestowing crowns of truth upon kings who faithfully execute His Will, these monarchs have inscribed upright and just decrees in His honor. 2 For their adherence to the Will of the Lord, He will illuminate, with an inextinguishable light, the abodes of Isaac, Abraham, Jacob, Solomon, David, and Hezekiah, situated in the Garden where reside all the magnificent kings, whose dwellings are bathed in light. 3 The brilliance of Heaven's Hall outshines any earthly hall. Its floor, adorned with

silver, gold, and precious jewels, radiates purity and splendor. 4 These features of Heaven's Hall, glowing resplendently, surpass human comprehension. The hall itself shines as if it were made of the finest jewels. 5 As the Lord, the Knower of all natures, has discerned, the Heaven Hall He created is beyond human understanding and shines in absolute radiance. Its floor, skillfully crafted from silver, gold, jewels, white silk, and blue silk, is immaculate and pure." 6 "This celestial realm is exceedingly beautiful, a true reflection of divine artistry. 7 The righteous, steadfast in their faith and virtues, are destined to inherit this heavenly place, graced by the Lord's love and forgiveness. 8 From this paradise flows a stream of well-being, radiant as the sun, surrounded by a tent of light and enveloped in a delightful fragrance. 9 The garden is adorned with fruits of unique beauty and exquisite taste, amid groves of olives and grapes, each aspect breathtakingly lovely, and the aroma of the fruits enchantingly sweet. 10 In such a place, a mortal's soul would part from the body, overwhelmed by the sheer joy and happiness that permeates the air, all due to the intoxicating scents. 11 The noble kings who lived according to the Lord's Will shall find their joy here. Their honor and their esteemed place are recognized in the eternal Kingdom of Heaven, a haven of well-being. 12 It is revealed that their earthly reign, renowned and honored, will be mirrored in their heavenly rule; they will be exalted in Heaven as they were revered on Earth. Their righteous deeds in this world will bring them happiness. 13 However, those kings who ruled wickedly, whom the Lord had entrusted with kingdoms, failed to judge justly. They ignored the cries of the suffering and the poor, neglecting truth and justice, and failed to provide refuge to the orphaned and the wronged. 14 They did not protect the oppressed from the wealthy who exploited them, nor did they share their abundance with those in need of food or drink; they turned a deaf ear to the pleas of the destitute." 15 "And these rulers shall be led to Gehenna, a place of utter darkness, at the time of the great Day when the Lord comes and His wrath is executed upon them. As David sang in his psalms, 'O Lord, do not rebuke me in Your anger, nor chasten me in Your wrath.' Their tribulations and disgrace will multiply in accordance with the grandeur of their former glory. 16 In this world, there are nobles and kings who govern, yet they fail to adhere to the Lord's law. 17 But the Lord, the Sovereign over all, reigns in Heaven. Every soul and their well-being are under His dominion. He bestows honor upon those who honor Him, for His rule is absolute, and His love extends to those who love Him. 18 As the Lord of both Earth and Heaven, He discerns the innermost thoughts and intentions. To those who approach Him with sincerity and purity of thought, He will grant the fulfillment of their prayers. 19 He will bring low the haughty and the mighty who commit injustices against the orphan, the child bereaved of parents, and the widow, punishing those who exert their power to oppress the vulnerable." 20 "Your ascension to the throne was not by your own strength or ability. The Lord allowed it to test you, as He did with Saul, who reigned over his people in his time. The Lord placed you upon the throne of the kingdom, but it was not by your own might that you attained it. This trial was similar to Saul's, who disregarded the words of the prophet Samuel and the Lord's command, failing to serve his own army or the king of Amalek. Your rule is not a result of your own capability. 21 The Lord commanded the prophet Samuel, saying, 'Go, for they have grieved Me by breaking My Law, by worshipping idols, by bowing down to them, by their shrines, and by all their detestable deeds without merit.' He instructed Saul, 'Go to the land of Amalek and utterly destroy their armies, their kings, every person, and all livestock.' 22 Thus, He sent Saul against those who had saddened the Lord, to annihilate them. 23 But Saul spared the king of Amalek, as well as much livestock, treasures, women, and handsome young men. Because he disdained what belonged to Me and did not heed My command, the Lord instructed Samuel, 'Go and divide his kingdom.' 24 'Instead, anoint the son of Jesse, David, to rule over Israel,' the Lord decreed. 25 But upon Saul, impose a tormenting spirit, for his defiance. 26 Since he rejected My command after I gave him the kingdom to fulfill My Will, I removed him from the kingdom that was rightfully his. Go and tell him, 'Will you thus disregard the Lord, Who crowned you over His people Israel, Who placed you on the throne of His sovereignty?'" 27 "Furthermore, tell Saul, 'You did not recognize the Lord, who bestowed upon you such great honor and renown.' This was the message given to Samuel. 28 The prophet Samuel then went to King Saul, finding him seated at the dining table with the king of Amalek, Agag, at his left side. 29 Samuel confronted Saul, asking, 'Why have you utterly disregarded the Lord's command to annihilate both the people and the livestock of Amalek?' 30 At these words, fear gripped the king, and he rose from his throne. Pleading with Samuel, 'Pray for us,' he grasped Samuel's garment, but Samuel would not relent. In the struggle, Samuel's robe tore. 31 Samuel then declared to Saul, 'The Lord has divided your kingdom.' 32 Saul, in the presence of his people, implored Samuel, 'Honor me and seek atonement for my sin before the Lord, that He might forgive me.' But Samuel, steadfast in his adherence to the Lord's command, refused to yield, fearing the Lord who created him more than the mortal king. 33 As a result, Samuel executed the king of Amalek, Agag, before he could even finish his meal." 34

"Subsequently, a demon overcame Saul, who had violated the Law of the Lord. As the Supreme King who rules over all, the Lord punished him, striking him down for his sins, for he felt no shame in his transgressions. 35 For the Lord is the Sovereign over all creation, He who has the power to strip authority from all nobles and kings who do not revere Him; yet,no one holds dominion over Him. 36 As He declared, the lineage of David shall be celebrated and honored, while that of Saul shall be disgraced. Thus, He extinguished the kingdom from Saul and his descendants. 37 This action was taken because it grieved the Lord, and He sought to avenge the wicked deeds of those who caused Him sorrow. He exacted retribution and eradicated the lineage of Saul's children; for whoever fails to avenge the enemies of the Lord is Himself an enemy of the Lord. 38 When one has the capacity to exact vengeance and wield authority, yet fails to punish the sinner or one who disobeys the Lord's Law, he becomes an adversary of the Lord. In this way, the Lord annihilated the lineage of Saul's children."

7

1"What significance do you hold as a king or ruler before the Lord? 2Is it not the Lord who created you from nothingness, bringing you into existence to fulfill His Will, to live steadfastly by His commandments, and to heed His judgment? Just as you exhibit anger towards your servants and rule over them, so too does the Lord have authority over you and can express His displeasure. 3As you harshly punish those who sin, the Lord, too, has the power to chastise you and cast you into Gehenna, from which there is no escape, for all eternity. 4Just as you punish those who do not obey you or fail to pay tribute, why do you not offer your homage to the Lord? 5He is the one who created you, granting you the authority that others might fear you, and crowned you over all His creation, that you might govern His people with righteousness. Why then do you not fear your Creator, the Lord? 6Render judgment justly and truthfully, as the Lord has appointed you. Show no partiality, whether to the lowly or the great. Whom else should you fear but Him? Uphold His worship and obey the Commandments." 7 "As Moses instructed the children of Israel, 'Before you are set the choices of water and fire. Reach out for what you desire, but stray neither to the right nor to the left. 8Heed the words I convey to you, that you may listen to His Word and follow His Commandments, lest you wonder, 'Is it beyond the sea, or across the depths, or beyond the river? Who will bring it to me, that I may see it, hear His Word, and follow His Commandments?' 9 Do not question, 'Who will ascend to Heaven to bring down the Word of the Lord for me to hear and obey?' for the Word of the Lord is near you, on your lips and in your heart, that you may speak it and act upon it with your deeds. 10 You do not truly hear your Creator, the Lord, unless you heed His Book; nor do you love Him or keep His Commandments unless you adhere to His Law. 11 Your fate is to enter Gehenna eternally unless you embrace His Commandments and do the Will of the Lord, who has set you apart with honor and renown above all your kin, that you might guide them in truth. Fail to do so, and your destiny shall be Gehenna, everlasting." 12 "The Lord has exalted you above all others, crowning you as ruler over all His people, that you might govern them justly, according to what is right. In doing so, you should always bear in mind the name of your Creator, who fashioned you and granted you dominion over a kingdom. 13Among those who transgress against you, there are those you discipline and those you forgive, reflecting upon the deeds of the Lord; and there are those for whom you must judge impartially, aligning your thoughts with righteousness. 14 Do not show favoritism based on appearance when disputes arise before you. Remember that earthly wealth is fleeting; thus, do not be swayed by bribes to excuse the guilty or to harm the innocent. 15 If you follow the Lord's Will, He will extend your days in this world; but if you cause Him sorrow, He will shorten them." 16"Bear in mind that after your demise, you will rise again to stand before the Lord, facing judgment for every deed you have performed, whether it be righteous or wicked. 17If your deeds are virtuous, you will dwell in the Garden within the Kingdom of Heaven, residing in the abodes of venerable kings, bathed in eternal light. The Lord does not belittle the authority of your lordship; however, if your actions are malevolent, your place will be in Sheol Gehenna, where reside the wicked kings. 18When you behold the grandeur of your reign, the honors bestowed upon your warriors, your displayed shields and spears, your horses and legions under your command, the drummers, and the harpists playing before you; 19 And when you see all these glories, should you elevate your mind in arrogance, stiffen your neck in pride, and forget the Lord Who bestowed upon you all this honor, yet when He commands you to relinquish it all, you refuse to obey, 20 You have then utterly disregarded the task He assigned to you, and He will transfer your rulership to another." 21 "As death will inevitably come upon you, and judgment will be passed at the time of Resurrection, where every action of mankind will be scrutinized, the Lord will thoroughly investigate and pass judgment upon you. 22No longer will the kings of this world be honored, for in the time of Judgment, the Lord, as the true Judge of Righteousness, will see the poor and the wealthy stand side by side. The crowns in which the world's nobles take pride will fall way. 23Judgment is set, and souls will tremble. Then, the deeds of both sinners and the righteous will be laid bare for examination. 24Nothing and no one will remain concealed. Just as a woman in labor cannot halt the birth of her child, and just as the earth cannot retain those who dwell upon her, so too will all be revealed. 25And as the clouds cannot hold back the rain but must release it as commanded by the Lord, so has the Word of the Lord created all things, brought them forth from nothingness, and consigned all to the grave. Likewise, when the time of Resurrection comes, it will be impossible for the dead not to rise." 26 "As Moses declared, 'Man does not live by bread alone, but by every word that proceeds from the mouth of the Lord.' Similarly, it will be the Word of the Lord that will awaken all from their graves. 27Behold, it is acknowledged that the dead shall rise again through the Word of the Lord. 28 Furthermore, the Lord proclaimed in Deuteronomy, addressing the nobles and kings who follow His Will: 'When the day appointed for their destruction arrives, I shall exact vengeance and destroy them on the day of Judgment, at the moment when they falter,' He declared. 29 The Lord also spoke to those who understand His Judgment, saying, 'Recognize and understand that I am your Creator, the Lord; it is I who brings death and delivers salvation. 30 I discipline through trials and extend forgiveness. I cast down into Sheol, and likewise, I elevate to the Garden; no one can evade My sovereign power,' He proclaimed to them." 31 "Regarding the nobles and kings who failed to obey His Law, the Lord declared: 'Just as earthly kingdoms are transient, passing from morning to evening, adhere to My statutes and My Law, so that you may enter into the eternal Kingdom of Heaven.' This is His proclamation. 32 The Lord's calling is twofold: for the righteous, it is an invitation to honor; for sinners, it heralds tribulation. He will bring misfortune upon the sinner, but bestow honor upon the righteous. 33 He will cast away those who did not fulfill His Will, but He will exalt those who abided by His commandments and executed His Will faithfully."

8

1 "Listen to my words, and I will explain how the dead shall rise. They shall be like plants that grow and flourish, with grapes that extend their vines. As the Lord produces the fruit known as 'imhibe 'albo,' from it they shall press wine. 2Understand that the plant you have sown, initially small, now stretches out with shoots, bearing fruit and leaves. 3The Lord allows its roots to draw sustenance from both the earth and water. 4He nurtures its wood with the elements of fire and wind. The roots convey water to the leaves, and the earth provides stability to the wood. 5But it is the soul, created by the Lord, that enables these plants to produce fruit; and the resurrection of the dead is akin to this process. 6When a soul departs from the body, He commands, 'Gather the souls from the four elements; from earth, water, wind, and fire, for each

has returned to its own.' 7Thus, the essence of the earth remains firmly in its element, becoming earth again; and the essence of water stays true to its nature, reverting back to water." 8 "Similarly, the essence of the wind remains true to its nature, transforming back into wind; and the essence of fire retains its character, becoming a blazing flame. 9But the soul, once separated from the flesh by the Lord, returns to its Creator. Until the appointed time for resurrection, when it is to be reunited with the body, the Lord keeps it in the Garden, in a place of His choosing. 10The souls of the righteous are placed in a dwelling of light within the Garden, while the souls of sinners are consigned to a dwelling of darkness in Sheol, there to remain until the Lord decides otherwise. 11The Lord instructed the prophet Ezekiel, 'Summon the souls from the four corners of the earth, that they may be gathered and become whole once again.'12When He commanded with a single word, the souls were indeed gathered from the four corners, fulfilling His command." 13 "The essence of water brought forth greenery, while the essence of fire produced flames. 14Similarly, the essence of the earth materialized as soil, and the essence of the wind transformed into a breeze. 15 The Lord retrieved each soul from the place in the Garden where it was kept. United by a single divine command, a resurrection was effected. 16 Let me illustrate with an example you witness daily. As day turns to dusk, you sleep. With the break of dawn, you awaken and rise from your bed. This sleep is akin to death. 17Waking up symbolizes resurrection. The night, when all slumber and their bodies are enshrouded in darkness, is like this world. 18 The morning light, dispelling the darkness and filling the world with brightness, when people wake and go about their day, symbolizes the resurrection of the dead. 19The Kingdom of Heaven, where humanity is rejuvenated, can be compared to this awakening. The resurrection of the dead is similar. Just as this world is fleeting, like the night, so is the promise of a new dawn in the Kingdom of Heaven." 20 "As David declared, 'He has set a tabernacle for the sun,' the way the sun brightens upon rising is a symbol of the Kingdom of Heaven.21Just as the sun illuminates this world, so shall Christ shine like the sun in the new Kingdom of Heaven. As He proclaimed, 'I am a Sun that never sets and a Torch that never fades,' He, the Lord, is its everlasting Light. 22He will swiftly resurrect the dead. Let me present another analogy, this time from the seeds you sow for sustenance, whether it be a grain of wheat, barley, or lentil, or any seed planted in the earth - none can grow unless it first decomposes and decays. 23Similarly, human flesh, when it decays and is consumed by the earth, loses its vigor and its form. 24As the earth consumes its substance, it then begins to grow, sprouting to about a seventh of its original size. The Lord sends clouds bearing rain as He wills, and the roots draw nourishment from the earth, sprouting leaves. 25Without decay and rot, no growth can occur; but once it has grown, it produces numerous shoots." 26"By the will of the Lord, fruit emerges from the buds that have grown, and He wraps their vigor in husks. 27Observe how the seeds you planted have multiplied; yet you cannot count the grains, the leaves, the ears of corn, or the straw. 28Do not be ignorant and fail to understand; look at your seeds and see how they have flourished. In the same way, know that the dead shall be resurrected according to their deeds, each receiving a fate befitting their actions. 29Listen to this: If you plant wheat, it will not grow as barley, nor will barley grow if you plant wheat. Let this be clear to you: what you sow is what you will reap. If you sow wheat, will you harvest barley? If you sow watercress, will you gather linseed? 30Consider the nature of plants: if you plant figs, will they grow as nuts? If you plant almonds, will they yield grapes? 31When you plant something sweet, can it grow bitter? Or if you plant something bitter, can it possibly become sweet? " 32 "Similarly, consider this if a sinner dies, can they possibly rise as a righteous person at the time of Resurrection? And if a righteous person passes away, can they emerge as a sinner in the Resurrection? Each one will face consequences in accordance with their actions, receiving recompense for their sins and the deeds of their hands. Yet no one will be judged for the sins of another. 33A tree on a highland is planted and it extends its long branches. It may completely dry up; and without the rain from heaven, its leaves will not stay green. 34Even a cedar tree, deeply rooted, will be uprooted unless it is nourished by the summer rains. 35In the same way, the dead will not rise unless they are touched by the Dew of Well-being, as ordained by the Lord."

9

1"If the highland mountains and the regions of Gilboa do not receive the Rains of Forgiveness, as decreed by the Lord, they will not produce grass for the beasts and animals. 2Similarly, the mountains of Elam and Gilead will not yield lush leaves for the sheep and goats, nor for the oribi and animals in the wilderness, nor for the ibexes and hartebeest. 3In the same way, if Pardon and Dew, as commanded by the Lord, do not descend upon the skeptics and criminals who have chosen error and crime as their way of life, the dead will not be resurrected. This applies to those like Deemas and Cyprus, who engage in idolatry and sorcery, who delve into root-working and incite conflict, 4 And to those who practice witchcraft, causing strife among people, 5As well as to those who indulge in desires, turning away from the Law; and to the people of Media and Athens, who place their faith in idols, and they who play and sing for them, while they played violins and drums, and strummed harps -

they won't arise, unless Dew of Pardon alights for them, being commanded from THE LORD. 6 These are who will be convicted on the day when dead persons arise, and when Definite Judgement is done; yet persons who save themselves, and who lust in the Work of their hands - they err by their idols. 7 Thou wasteful of heart, dull one, does it seem to thee that dead persons won't arise? 8 At the time a trumpet was blown, by the tongue of the Angels' Chief, Holy Michael - that dead ones arise then - as thou won't remain in a grave without arising, don't think a thing that is thus. 9 Hills and mountains shall be level, and shall be a cleared path. 10And Resurrection shall be done for all fleshly ones.

10

1"Otherwise, why would the ancients have desired to be buried in the tombs of their forefathers, starting from Adam, through Seth and Abel, Shem and Noah, Isaac and Abraham, Joseph and Jacob, Aaron and Moses? Why was it important for them not to be interred elsewhere? 2Was it not so that they might rise together with their kin at the time of Resurrection? Was it not to avoid having their bones intermingled with those of the wicked and the idolaters, that they chose not to be buried in foreign lands? 3 Do not let your reasoning be led astray, questioning, 'How can the dead arise after they have died, those who were buried by the tens of thousands in a single grave, their bodies decayed and decomposed?' 4 When you gaze upon a grave, do not speak such thoughts in the folly of your reasoning, wondering, 'There is barely a fistful of earth remaining, how can the dead possibly arise?' 5Would you doubt that the seed you have sown will not sprout? Just as surely as the seed you plant grows, so will the dead be raised." 6"In the same manner, the souls that the Lord has sown shall swiftly rise again. Just as He fashioned humanity in His truth, bringing them forth from non-existence, so shall He promptly awaken them by His life-giving Word. There will be no delay in their resurrection. 7 And just as He once transitioned them from the realm of the living to the domain of the dead, is it not within His power to reverse this, from death back to life? 8 Indeed, for the Lord, salvation and resurrection are entirely within the realm of possibility."

11

1"Armon was laid to waste, and its fortifications were destroyed. The Lord brought upon them calamities corresponding to their wickedness, the deeds they committed with their own hands. Those in Edom and Zebulon who bowed to idols will be humbled. As the Lord draws near, He will judge those in Sidon and Tyre, who from their youth did not turn away from their idols and their iniquity. 2Because they indulged in sin, seductive fornication, and idol worship, the Lord will exact vengeance and annihilate them for failing to steadfastly follow the commandments of their Creator, the Lord. The daughters of Judah will suffer greatly for these transgressions. 3Jerusalem stood resolute in persecuting prophets, reveling in joy and happiness, yet she faltered in upholding the Nine Laws and in true worship. When the dead are raised, her sins will be laid bare for all to see. 4At that time, the Lord will judge her with the wisdom of His divine nature, repaying and annihilating her for all the sins she committed from her youth until her old age. 5She fell into the grave and turned to dust, like her ancestors who persisted in their transgressions. In the time of Resurrection, the Lord will bring retribution and destruction upon those who violated His Law." 6"Judgment will be passed upon them, as Moses once spoke regarding their state, 'Their abodes of law have become like the dwellings of Sodom.' 7Their lineage is likened to that of Gomorrah, their laws are destructive in nature, and their deeds are steeped in wickedness.8 Their statutes are akin to the venom of serpents, lethal as the poison of vipers, bringing destruction from their very midst."

12

1"O child of Jerusalem, your transgressions are akin to those of Gomorrah and Sodom. Such is the plight of Jerusalem, as foretold by the prophets. 2Your tribulations are comparable to those of Gomorrah and Sodom, where the principles of their law were deeply rooted in adultery and pride. 3They were drenched not with the rains of repentance and humility, but with the downpour of adultery and arrogance, preventing the soil of their legal reasoning from being fertile and leading them away from the shedding of innocent blood, theft, and the forgetfulness of their Creator, the Lord. 4 They became oblivious to their Creator, the Lord, lost in their wicked deeds and idol worship, reveling in the works of their own hands, indulging in unnatural desires towards men and animals. 5Their understanding was veiled, preventing them from discerning hidden truths; their ears were dulled, so they neither heard nor followed the Will of the Lord, which He cherishes. They failed to recognize the Lord in their actions; their rationale was as corrupt as the laws of Sodom, their lineage bearing the tainted fruit of Gomorrah. 6Upon examining their deeds, they reveal nothing but toxicity, entrenched in a curse from the very day of their inception, their foundation laid in an era destined for ruin. 7As their legal thoughts and their reasoning have solidified in sinful acts; as their bodies have been consumed by the fiery deeds of Satan, intent on constructing sin - their principles and reasoning have never yielded any righteous deeds." 8"When one is led to shame and undergoes baptism by one who is enlightened, it is a mark of chastisement and destruction. Such a person solidifies the thoughts of those who have imbibed in iniquity; they become those who reject me, abhorrent beings who have strayed far from the Lord. 9 They are entrenched in their malevolent actions, becoming a dwelling place for the Devil. The practice of consuming food sacrificed to idols has taken root in the House of Israel; they venture to the mountains and the trees, 10Engaging in the idol worship prevalent among the peoples in their vicinity, offering their daughters and sons to demons, entities devoid of the knowledge of good, only familiar with evil. 11They shed innocent blood, reveling in the outpouring of wine from Sodom, offered perpetually to their idols. 12They exalt and venerate Dagon, the deity worshiped by the Philistines, sacrificing their livestock and well-fed cattle to please him, delighting in the slothful ways of demons who have taught them to make such offerings. In their indulgence and spilling of wine, they carry out the desires of these entities." 13"She offers these sacrifices to appease the demons, learning slothfulness from them, rather than recognizing her Creator, the Lord, who sustains her at all times. He who has loved, nurtured, and raised her from her youth, through her days of beauty and into her old age, until her final moments. 14But in the time of Resurrection, I shall exact vengeance and pass judgment on her. Since she has not returned to My Law and has not steadfastly lived by My Commandments, her dwelling in Gehenna will be eternal. 15If her idols were true gods, let them rise with her and descend into Gehenna to save her, when I express my wrath and bring about her destruction, when I cast away all the idol priests who share in her depravity. 16As she has sinned and shown disrespect towards the Holy Objects and My Sanctuary, the Temple, I have brought her low for all these transgressions. 17Even when it was proclaimed, 'Behold, this is the lineage of the Lord, and she is the dwelling of the Creator of Israel, the Lord, the illustrious King's city, Jerusalem, set apart from the ungodly; she is the abode of the Most High Lord's Name,' I have made her desolate, as she brought sorrow to My Name that was called upon in her." 18"She claims allegiance to Me, professing to be My servant and I her Lord. Yet she behaves deceitfully, like a transgressor, not showing the reverence and obedience befitting of one who acknowledges Me as their Lord. 19They have become a stumbling block to her, leading her astray, causing her to stray from Me. She is now devoted to other idols, which neither nourish nor clothe her. 20She offers sacrifices to these idols, consumes the offerings herself, sheds blood in their name, indulges in the pouring and drinking of wine for them. She burns incense, letting its fragrance rise for them. These idols dictate her actions, and she is bound to their commands. 21Furthermore, she sacrifices her own daughters and sons to these false gods, singing praises to them out of misguided love, taking pleasure in the words she speaks and the deeds her hands perform. 22Woe befalls her on the day of Final Judgment, and woe unto the idols she adores and clings to; she will descend with them into the depths of Gehenna beneath Sheol, where the worm never sleeps and the fire is never quenched. 23Woe to you, miserable child of Jerusalem, for you have forsaken Me, your Creator, and turned to worship foreign idols." 24"I will bring upon you a hardship befitting your actions. As you have caused Me grief, disregarded My Word, and failed to perform righteous deeds, I will judge you according to your false pretenses. 25You have brought sorrow upon My Word and have not steadfastly adhered to My Law, which you swore to uphold - that you would keep My Law so that I might support you, save you from your adversaries, and that you might follow My ordinances which I have laid down for you. Therefore, I will forsake you and will not hasten to rescue you from your troubles. 26 You have not abided by these commitments, and thus, I have turned away from you. As I created you, yet you did not heed My Commandments or My Word, I will judge you at the time of Judgment; I had exalted you to be My own people. 27Just as Gomorrah and Sodom were cut off from Me, so have you been estranged from Me. 28I judged and obliterated them; as Sodom and Gomorrah were severed from Me, you too have distanced yourself from Me. Now, as I was angered and annihilated them, so have I been angered and have destroyed you. As you belong to the lineage of Sodom and Gomorrah, which I eradicated, so I have obliterated you. Those whom I created have grieved Me by their transgressions, engaging in illicit relations, pursuing unnatural desires with animals and men as with women. Therefore, I have erased the memory of their names from this world, so they might not revel in their felicity and joy." 29"There is no reverence for the Lord evident in their expressions, from the youngest to the oldest. They abet each other in all their wicked deeds. Yet the Lord does not show His wrath against each individual, that they might cease their wrongdoings. As their actions are inherently evil, they find contentment in sin and iniquity. 30All manner of evil deeds — theft, pride, and avarice — are conceived in their thoughts. 31As a result, the Lord turned away from them and laid waste to their lands. They now await His judgment, to be consumed by fire until their very foundations are eradicated. They have been utterly destroyed, never to return. 32Firmly entrenched in their sinful ways, they will dwell in ruin forever, until the Day of Arrival, when the Final Judgment is passed. Their malevolent deeds have grieved Me deeply, and I will neither pardon nor forgive them. 33I have forsaken them. You will find no excuse when I express My wrath and take action against you, for all your actions are marked by theft, sin, adultery, greed, and falsehood

— all manner of erroneous deeds and transgressions that I abhor. You, wretched child of Jerusalem, will face the same judgment as them when the Day of Judgment arrives." 34"I had destined you for honor, yet you have debased yourself. I once called you My treasure, but you turned away to belong to another. 35I had chosen you for honor, yet you aligned yourself with the Devil. Therefore, I will exact retribution and annihilate you, in accordance with the wickedness of your deeds. 36Because you did not heed My words, and because you failed to observe the commandments I set forth when I loved you, I, the Lord who created you, will amplify my vengeance upon you. I will judge you and all sinners like you; on the day of Judgment, I will inflict suffering upon them commensurate with their evil actions. 37As you have neglected My Word and disregarded My Judgment, I will condemn you alongside them. 38Woe unto you, Gomorrah and Sodom, devoid of reverence for the Lord in your thoughts. 39Similarly, woe befalls your sister, the child of Jerusalem, who will face judgment alongside you in the fires of Gehenna. You both will descend into the Gehenna prepared for you, where there is no escape, forever; and woe unto all sinners who have committed your sins. 40As you have failed to abide by My Commandments and My Word, both you and she who did not adhere to My Commandments and My Word will descend into Sheol together, on the day when Judgment is rendered." 41"Yet those who are virtuous, who have adhered to My Commandments and My Word, shall partake of the wealth accumulated by sinners; as the Lord has decreed, they shall inherit the spoils amassed by the wicked, and the righteous shall rejoice in their abundance. 42In contrast, the evildoers and sinners will lament and be filled with sorrow for all the sins they committed, having strayed from My Commandments. 43He who embraces My Word and steadfastly follows My Commandments is the one who will receive My blessings and be honored in My presence. 44All who observe My Word and remain firm in My Commandments will partake of the bounties of the Earth and shall dwell in the Garden, where reside the just kings known for their upright reasoning."

13

1"As they face ruin and destruction under My wrath when I enact judgment upon them, woe be to the lands of Tyre and Sidon, and to all the region of Judah, which today stands in arrogance. 2The Lord Almighty proclaims: 'Out of their midst shall arise the offspring of the Devil, the very epitome of arrogance – the False Messiah. He is the adversary of truth, filled with self- importance, who boasts and does not recognize his Creator.' The Lord declares, 'Woe unto them. I have allowed him to emerge as a manifestation of My anger, to reveal My power through him.' 3And these regions – Capernaum, Samaria, Galilee, Damascus, Syria, Achaia, Cyprus, and all the Jordan area – are peoples who have stiffened their resolve in sin, enveloped in the shadow of death and darkness. For the Devil has shrouded their judgment in sin, and they are subservient to that arrogant being, having turned away from revering the Lord. 4Woe then, to those who follow demons, offering sacrifices in their name. As they have rejected the Lord, their Creator, they are akin to mindless beasts. The False Messiah, a child of the Devil who has forsaken the Law of the Lord, will erect his image in many places, claiming divinity. He will revel in the whims of his mind, the deeds of his hands, in theft, and all manner of sins, treachery, and iniquities, indulging in theft and every form of adultery committed by man."5For it has been decreed by the Lord that he, the False Messiah, will carry out these deeds in a time marked by rampant sinfulness. 6The sun will darken, and the moon will turn to blood; stars will fall from the sky. All earthly endeavors will fade away in the wake of the wonders the Lord will perform in the Time of Completion, as He brings an end to the earth and all who dwell in sin within it. 7As the Lord takes pride in the creation He has wrought, and as He swiftly brings to pass all His desires in a single moment, even the death of the Lord will vanquish a minor foe like the Devil. 8For the Lord Almighty declares, 'I will pass judgment and bring destruction; but after the Second Coming, the Devil will have no power.' 9And on the day he faces My wrath, he will be cast down into Gehenna, the place for which he has pleaded, a place of intense suffering. As he leads all who are with him to punishment, ruin, and treachery, remember that I am the one who sends forth from Gehenna and consigns to Gehenna; thus, he will be sent down to Gehenna. 10As the Lord imparts strength and might to the weak, and conversely, brings frailty to the strong and mighty, let not the powerful take pride in their strength 11As He is the Supreme Judge, who delivers the oppressed from their oppressors, He will avenge the grievances of the widows and the orphans. 12Woe to you who swell with pride and stiffen in your self-importance, believing that I will neither govern nor pass judgment upon you. In his hubris and arrogance, he has declared, 'I will elevate my throne to the stars and the heavens, and I will be like the Most High Lord.' 13Recall how the Lord spoke of the fall of the Devil from heaven, he who shone like a morning star, created before all else. Woe unto you. 14You dared to utter such words in your arrogance, failing to consider the Lord who created you with His divine authority. Why do you exalt yourself, only to descend into Gehenna, entrenched in your obstinate reasoning? 15You have been cast down, set apart from all angels like yourself, for they humbly extol their Creator, acknowledging He who formed them from fire and wind. They do not deviate from His

Commandments; they guard their thoughts from treachery, ensuring they do not stray from His directives. 16 But you have committed a grave treachery in the arrogance of your reasoning. You have become a wretched being, set apart from your peers, for you have embraced all manner of sin and iniquity, theft and deceit. You live steadfastly in these sins, much like those who have forsaken the Law of the Lord and other sinners like yourself, those of your own kind who perpetrate crimes akin to yours and who live by your commands and desires, through which you propagate sin. 17Woe unto you, for the demons you have led astray with your malevolence; together you will descend into Gehenna. 18O children of the Lord who have been led astray by that deceitful Devil, woe unto you. As you have followed his ways, as he and his legions have instructed you, you too will descend into Gehenna, from which there is no escape, forever.19 Even in the time of Moses, the servant of the Lord, you grieved the Lord at the waters of strife, at Horeb, with Amalek, and on Mount Sinai. 20Furthermore, when you sent scouts into Canaan and they reported back, saying, 'The journey is long, and their walls and fortresses reach to the heavens; mighty warriors dwell there,' you desired to return to Egypt, where you had endured laborious toil; in doing so, you spurned the Word of the Lord. 21You failed to remember the Lord, who delivered you from affliction, performed wondrous deeds in Egypt, and guided you under the protection of His Angel. He covered you with a cloud by day to shield you from the scorching sun, and at night, He illuminated your path with a pillar of fire to prevent you from stumbling in the dark. 22When Pharaoh's army caused fear among you, you cried out to Moses, and Moses in turn cried out to the Lord. The Lord intervened through His Angel to protect you from Pharaoh. 23He led Pharaoh's forces into the Red Sea, bringing them into distress. The Lord guided only Israel, affirming that no other deity accompanied them. He submerged their adversaries in the sea simultaneously, sparing none of those who fled. 24He enabled Israel to walk through the sea on dry land, safeguarding them from any harm from the Egyptians. He led them to Mount Sinai and sustained them with manna for forty years. 25Despite the Lord's benevolence, the children of Israel continually grieved Him. He bestowed numerous blessings upon them, yet they neglected to worship the Lord. 26They harbored evil in their hearts from their youth through to old age. This was stated by the Lord's mouth in the Torah, where the genealogies of the forefathers are recorded. As He declared, 'The thoughts of Adam's descendants are but ashes, their actions geared towards theft, always hastening towards wickedness. None among them seeks to do what is righteous, except for the amassing of wealth through violence, lying under oath, betraying their peers, indulging in theft and robbery.' Thus, they filled their minds with malevolence. 27In their lifetime, they consistently gravitated towards sinful actions. The children of Israel, who utterly disregarded the Law of the Lord, grieved Him deeply, from the earliest times until the Era of Fulfillment.

14

1"When the Lord annihilated the descendants of Cain, the early generations, with the waters of destruction due to their sinfulness, He baptized the Earth in the Waters of Destruction, purifying it from all the transgressions of Cain's offspring. 2Declaring His regret for having created mankind, He eliminated all the wrongdoers, sparing only eight individuals. After this purging, He allowed humanity to proliferate again, and they replenished the Earth, inheriting the legacy of their forefather Adam. 3 Noah and his descendants made a covenant with the Lord, vowing that the Lord would not again devastate the Earth with a deluge, and that they would not consume what was already dead or that which died naturally; they would not turn to idols but would worship only the Lord who created them. The Lord, in turn, promised to be a loving Father to them, not to destroy them all at once for their empty transgressions, to ensure the timely arrival of early and latter rains, and to provide sustenance for both livestock and humans, including grass, grain, fruits, and plants, as long as they performed righteous deeds pleasing to the Lord. 4 Despite these commandments, the children of Israel grieved the Lord with their sins. They failed to steadfastly adhere to His Law as their forefathers Isaac, Abraham, and Jacob had, who did not forsake the Law of their Creator, the Lord. 5 From the youngest to the oldest, those among the children of Israel who did not uphold the Lord's Law strayed in their actions."6 Whether they were priests, leaders, or scribes, everyone among them violated the Law of the Lord.7 They did not steadfastly live by the decrees and laws of the Lord, which Moses imparted to them in Deuteronomy, urging, 'Love your Creator, the Lord, with all your being and all your mind.' 8They failed to adhere to the commandments and laws given by Moses in the book of the Law, which stated, 'Love your neighbor as yourself, do not worship foreign idols, do not covet another man's wife. Do not commit murder. Do not steal. 9Do not bear false witness. Do not covet your neighbor's possessions, whether it be their donkey, their ox, or anything your fellow has acquired.' 10Despite receiving these instructions, the children of Israel, who were wicked, reverted to treachery and sin, engaging in adultery, deceit, theft, and idol worship. 11 They grieved the Lord at Horeb by fashioning a golden calf. They bowed down to it, declaring, 'These are our gods who brought us out of Egypt.' 12 They took pleasure in the creations of their own hands. After eating, drinking, and being filled, they rose to dance and sing. 13 The Lord had spoken to Moses, saying, 'Your people, whom you led out of Egypt, the land of rulership, have strayed from My Law and committed wrong. They have fashioned an image of a cow and bowed down to this idol.' Therefore, Moses was deeply angered and descended from Mount Sinai. 14As Moses came down, filled with wrath against his people, he was accompanied by his close aide, Joshua. Hearing noises, Joshua remarked, 'I hear what sounds like the cry of warriors in the camp of Israel.' 15But Moses corrected him, 'No, that is not the sound of battle; it is the noise of celebration, for they have indulged in undiluted wine.' He descended and saw their idolatry. In his fury, he shattered the idol, grinding it to dust, and mixed it in the water that the Israelites were to drink at the base of the mountain. 16Following this, Moses ordered the priests to execute each other as punishment for the grave sin they had committed in the presence of the Lord. 17 They understood that their defiance of the Lord was a more grievous offense than the act of slaying themselves and their fathers, and so they carried out Moses's command. 18Moses admonished them, saying, 'You have grieved the Lord, who has nurtured and sustained you, who liberated you from a land of tyranny, and who promised to grant you the inheritance He vowed to your forefathers and their descendants. Yet despite these blessings, you have only brought joy to the Lord through your disobedience.' 19For they persistently engaged in sin and wrongdoing, continually causing sorrow to the Lord. 20They are unlike their ancestors, Isaac, Abraham, and Jacob, who delighted the Lord with their righteous deeds. The Lord had promised them the bounties of the Earth and the rewards prepared in Heaven for those who love Him, from their youth to their old age. They do not resemble Abraham, Isaac, and Jacob, who pleased the Lord with their actions, earning a land of inheritance filled with happiness and joy in this world, and a blissful garden in the afterlife, reserved for the righteous. This reward was prepared for Abraham, Isaac, and Jacob, who brought joy to the Lord in their lifetime and loved Him, whom no eye has seen, no ear has heard, and no mind has conceived. 21 Their descendants, however, who have turned away from the Lord and lived in wickedness, committed to their own flawed judgments, have not heeded the commandments of the Lord, who fed, cared for, and protected them since their infancy. 22 They failed to remember the Lord, who led them out of Egypt, saving them from laborious brick-making and oppressive rule. 23Instead, they deeply grieved Him, and as a result, He incited neighboring peoples against them, leading to their adversaries rising in hostility and imposing taxes as they pleased.

15

1In that era, the people of Midian rose against Israel in hostility and mobilized their forces to wage war against them. Their king was named Akrandis, and he swiftly amassed a large army from Cilicia, Syria, and Damascus. 2Setting up camp across the Jordan, he dispatched envoys with a message: 'To avoid my wrath and the seizure of your wealth, pay tribute to Israel on my behalf.' He warned, 'Should you fail to pay this tax, I will come to inflict punishment, seize your livestock, take your mares, and capture your children. 3I will take you as captives to a land unknown to you, where you will serve as water bearers and wood gatherers,' he declared. 4'Do not be arrogant, claiming, "We are the descendants of the Lord, and no harm can befall us." Is it not the Lord who has sent me to annihilate you and plunder your riches? Am I not the one chosen by the Lord to subdue all your tribes? 5Can your foreign gods save you, just as they failed to save the others I vanquished? I seized their horses and mares, slew them, and took their children captive.' 6If you do not deliver the tribute I have demanded, I will obliterate you as I have others," he warned. Crossing the Jordan, he intended to plunder their livestock, wealth, and capture their wives. 7 In response, the children of Israel mourned deeply before the Lord, crying out in utter despair, yet found themselves without a savior. 8The Lord then strengthened three brothers: Judah, Mebikyas, and Maccabeus. Renowned for their handsome appearance, they were formidable warriors. 9The Israelites, deeply affected by their plight, wept profusely. The sorrow pierced their hearts, echoing through the cries of the people. Orphans, widows, officials, priests, and all families of Israel, both men and women, young and old, mourned, covering their heads with ashes, while their nobles donned sackcloth. 10The brave and striking brothers resolved to rescue their people. They agreed, 'Let us sacrifice our lives for our brethren.' 11 Encouraging each other, 'Be strong, be courageous,' they armed themselves, securing swords and spears, ready to face the foe. 12Upon reaching the enemy camp, Mebikyus boldly attacked the king as he dined, swiftly decapitating him in a single stroke while he ate. Maccabeus and Judah fiercely engaged the enemy soldiers positioned to the king's left and right, wielding their swords to lethal effect. 13With their king defeated, panic ensued among his troops. They turned their spears against each other in desperation, leading to a chaotic retreat. Their bows were broken, symbolizing their complete defeat. 14The handsome and brave brothers emerged from the battle unscathed, untouched by harm. The enemy soldiers, in a frenzy of retribution, turned against one another, severely diminishing their numbers. 15In their defeat, they fled across the Jordan, discarding all their wealth in their haste. The spoils of war lay abandoned. Witnessing the enemy's retreat, the children of Israel ventured into the deserted camp, claiming both the abandoned treasures and the spoils of war. 16Through the valor of these brothers and Mebikyu, the Lord delivered Israel from its adversaries. 17For a brief period, Israel rejoiced and celebrated, bringing joy to the Lord. 18However, this period of devotion was short-lived. The children of Israel soon reverted to their sinful ways, neglecting the proper worship and reverence due to the Lord. 19The Lord will once again bring sorrow upon them through foreign peoples, strangers who do not know them. These invaders will harvest their fields, devastate their vineyards, plunder their flocks, and openly slaughter and feast upon their livestock right before their eyes. 20They will seize their wives, daughters, and sons. Since the Israelites have continuously grieved the Lord, as they are a people who have forsaken His Law, their children will be mercilessly struck down before their very eyes, with no hope of rescue.

16

1The perpetrators of these acts are the people of Tyre and Sidon, and those dwelling beyond the Jordan River, along the seashore - including the regions of Haran and Gilead, Jebus and Canaan, Edom and Gergesenes, and the Amalekites. 2All these nations, firmly established in their tribes, lands, and regions, speaking their unique languages, act in this manner, as determined by the Lord's will. 3Among them, there are those who recognize the Lord and engage in commendable deeds. 4Among these peoples, there are those whose deeds are wicked, who do not acknowledge the Lord who created them. For their transgressions, the Lord subjected them to the dominion of Shalmaneser, the king of Syria. 5As Shalmaneser looted and seized the wealth of Damascus, and as he divided the spoils of Samaria before the king of Egypt, they fell under his control. 6The inhabitants of the region of Gilboa, as well as those in Persia and Media, Cappadocia, and Suesia, residing in the western mountains, in the stronghold of Gilead, and in Phasthos, part of the land of Judah, 7these too are peoples who dwell in their respective lands but do not know the Lord or follow His Commandments, their minds stubborn and unyielding. 8The Lord will recompense them according to the wickedness of their actions and the deeds of their hands. 9 The tribes of Gilead, the region of Caesarea, and the Amalekites have united in their efforts to ravage the land of the Lord, a land filled with truth, where the Creator of Israel is exalted - He who is Most Glorious and Victorious. Countless angels in chariots of Cherubim, who stand in His presence, serve Him with fear and trembling. He will inflict upon these people the just consequences of their evil deeds and the actions of their hands.

17

1The people of Amalek and Edom do not worship the Lord, under whose authority the dominions of Earth and Heaven are held. As they are transgressors who do not adhere to the ways of truth, they show no hesitation in desecrating His sanctuary, the Temple. 2 They lack reverence for the Lord, engaging instead in bloodshed, adultery, consuming animals that were beaten or offered to idols, and all manners of death-tainted acts. They are indeed contemptible sinners. 3Devoid of moral virtues and religious principles, they despise righteous deeds. Ignorant of the Lord and unfamiliar with acts of love, they engage only in thievery, sin, causing disturbances, and other abominable acts, including indulging in games and songs as taught by their father, the Devil. They are bereft of virtue and piety. 4Dominated by the Devil and his demonic forces, they are schooled in all manner of malevolence tailored to each individual—encompassing theft, lies, robbery, consumption of forbidden food, adultery, and other immoralities. 5The Devil indoctrinates them in these practices: pursuing illicit relationships, bloodshed, idol worship, consuming animals that died of themselves, murder, envy, deceit, greed, and all manner of wickedness abhorred by the Lord. The Devil, their adversary, imparts this corrupt education, aiming to alienate them from the laws of the Lord who governs the entire world. 6But the Lord's way embraces innocence and humility, shunning harm to a brother and cherishing one's neighbor; it is about fostering harmony and love with all. 7 Shun hypocrisy and favoritism; do not engage in wrongdoing, robbery, or adultery. Do not commit iniquity or evil against your companions, nor deceive to oppress others with violence.8 Avoid mocking gestures and head-shaking that provoke evil. These actions lead others astray, setting them on a path towards eternal judgment.

18

1Consider that you will depart in death to the Lord, in whose hand all resides; you will stand before Him to be judged for all the sins you have committed.2As it was with those arrogant and wicked ones, the offspring of the powerful, who were no mightier than others before them. For they, in their stature and power, did not recognize the Lord before them, nor did they understand that He was their Creator, who brought them into being from nothingness. 3And when their fathers, being like unto 'Angels', praised upon the Holy Mount with Angels - at the time their will misled them, they descended to this world where Definite Judgement shall be done forever. 4As the Lord in the Antiquity had created human flesh for them - that it might mislead them because of the arrogance of their reasonings, and might test them as it were they kept His LAW and His Command - they married wives from Cain's children. 5 But they didn't keep His LAW. He lowered them into Gehenna fire with their father the Devil; for the Lord has been vexed upon the offspring of Seth who wronged like unto persons, and persons' era diminished because of their sin. 6And they took Adam's children toward sin with them. He lowered them into Sheol where they shall receive a verdict. 7As the era of persons has been divided because Seth's children erred by Cain's children - when a person's years were nine hundred in the Antiquity, they returned to living a hundred twenty years. 8And as they are flesh and blood, the Lord said, My Spirit of Support won't live firmed up upon them. 9And consequently our era was divided; for, because of our sin and our iniquity, our era has been divided from our fathers who preceded; and when they are in their infancy again, they are dying. 10But our fathers' era had abounded, because they kept His LAW, and because they didn't sadden the Lord. 11 But our fathers' era had abounded, because they were vexed upon their daughters that they might teach them, and because they were vexed upon their sons lest they demolish the Lord's LAW.12 Because they didn't demolish the Lord's LAW with their daughters and their sons, consequently their era had truly abounded.

19

1"At the time Cain's children abounded, they worked drums and harps, santees and violins; and they made songs and all the games. 2Children who were attractive and comely were birthed for Cain from the wife of the kind man Abel, whom he killed because of her, for she was attractive; and after he killed his brother, he took that and she who was his money. 3And separating from his father, he seized them and went to the region of Qiefaz that is to the West; and that attractive one's children were attractive like unto their mother. 4And consequently Seth's children descended to Cain's children; and after they saw them, they didn't wait one hour; and they made the women whom they chose, wives for themselves. 5As they have taken us into error together with them because of their error, consequently the Lord was vexed upon us and was vexed upon them. 6 And the Devil, deceiving with the promise, 'You will become creators like unto your Creator, the Lord', led our mother Eve and our father Adam into his falsehood. 7Believing this deceit to be truth in their naivety, they transgressed the law of the Lord, He who brought them into being from non-existence, so they might bow and exalt His glorious Name. 8But the Lord, their Creator, humbled these beings, Adam and Eve, who aspired to divinity; and He also humbled the proud deceiver. 9As David said, 'Adam fell due to the sin born of the

Devil's pride' - they were chastised, for our father Adam fell prey to the Devil's arrogance, judged rightly by the Lord. 10And the children of Seth, led astray by those of Cain, drew us into their sin. Thus, the lifespan the Lord granted us was shorter than that of our ancestors. 11They had acted righteously, steadying their minds in the Lord, instructing their daughters and sons not to stray from the teachings of the Lord's law, ensuring no malevolent foe could influence them. 12Yet, if they practiced righteousness without imparting its wisdom to their offspring, their virtuous deeds held no value. 13As David proclaimed, 'They did not withhold from their children, but imparted the praises of the Lord, His marvelous deeds, and His strength' - their efforts are fruitless if they fail to educate their offspring, so they too may understand, adhere to His wishes, and pass on the truth of the Lord's laws, maintaining them as faithfully as their forebears who delighted the Lord with their virtuous deeds. 14Those who conveyed the truth from their ancestors during their youth did not forsake His commandments, as their forefathers learned to worship the Lord and follow the Nine Commandments from their own ancestors. 15Their children, in turn, learned from their parents to perform righteous acts and to offer praises to their Creator, for they have adhered to His laws and loved Him. 16The Lord will heed their prayers and not disregard their supplications; for He is merciful and forgiving. 17Even as His anger multiplies, He will relent in His retribution, refraining from total destruction in His discipline.

20

1Consider, our brethren, and remember the teachings of old—that the Lord cherishes the true deeds of those who perform righteous acts. 2He blesses their offspring in this life, ensuring that their names endure in honor through eternity; their descendants shall not suffer want for bread in this world. 3For He shall advocate on their behalf and will not allow them to fall into the hands of their foes; He will rescue them from the clutches of those who despise them. 4And for those who love His Name, He shall be their support in times of hardship, safeguarding them and forgiving all their transgressions.

21

1David placed his trust in the Lord, who in return believed in him and became his sanctuary from the pursuit of King Saul. 2As he remained faithful and adhered to His laws during the uprisings of his son Absalom, the 'Philistines, the Edomites, the Amalekites, and one of the four giants of Rephaim, the Lord delivered David from all these adversities brought upon him by his adversaries 3Victory comes by the will of the Lord, and those who opposed Him were vanquished by their foes. However, the Lord did not deliver the wicked kings who lacked faith in Him. 4Hezekiah, who trusted in the Lord, was rescued from the clutches of the haughty Sennacherib. 5In contrast, his son Manasseh, who did not place his faith in the Lord and failed to revere the Lord who greatly honored and exalted him, was captured and taken away by his adversaries. These foes who overcame Manasseh were not his equals in status. 6The Lord then withheld the kingdom He had granted to Manasseh, for he had not performed righteous deeds in the sight of his Creator, the Lord, to extend his reign, to have the Lord defend him against his foes, or to gain strength and stability. 7Trust in the Lord is more potent than reliance on numerous armies, horses, bows, and shields. 8Faith in the Lord prevails. Those who trust in Him shall be established, honored, and exalted above all. 9The Lord does not show partiality based on appearance; those who lacked faith in Him, trusting instead in their wealth, ultimately fell from the grace and honor He bestowed upon them. 10He will protect those who believe in Him; however, He will let those who regard Him as irrelevant flounder in their ignorance. As they did not orient their thoughts towards following the Lord or adhering to His laws, He will not hasten to their aid in times of distress or when they face opposition from enemies. 11But for one who is steadfast in worshipping the Lord and observing His laws, He will be a sanctuary during times of hardship. 12He will vanquish their foes, seize their livestock, take captive the people of their enemy's lands, send timely rains, foster the growth of crops, and fill their storehouses with bountiful harvests. 13 By sending the early and latter rains, greening the pastures, and ensuring timely downpours, He will bring joy to the subjects under their rule. 14He will bless them with joy, allowing them to feast on the spoils of others; to be satiated with the plunder taken from their foes; to seize livestock, sheep, and cattle; to dine on their enemies' tables; and to capture their enemies' offspring. 15The Lord will bestow all these blessings upon the one He loves; conversely, He will subject those who despise Him to the ravages of their enemies. 16He will bind their hands and feet, delivering them into the clutches of their foes, subjecting them to ridicule. As they have become perpetrators of violence and violators of the Lord's law, they will not find joy in the prosperity of their lineage. 17They will not stand firm in the time of judgment; the Lord will bring affliction upon those who commit sins, imposing the consequences of their wicked actions upon them. 18It is ordained by the Lord to reward those who perform righteous deeds, preserving them under His dominion. 19For He reigns supreme over all of His creation, bestowing benevolent deeds and eternal wellbeing, so they may exalt the Lord, their Creator. He has decreed adherence to His law;

unlike mankind, no other part of His creation has ever strayed from His command. 20The Lord has directed every being in His creation, each steadfast in their appointed roles, fully aware and obedient to His law. 21However, humans often show defiance against the Lord, who has graced them with dominion over animals, beasts, and birds of the sky. 22Whether in the sea or on land, the Lord has entrusted all of His creation to mankind, granting Adam authority to utilize them as he sees fit, to consume them as food, similar to the grains that grow on Earth, to govern and levy them, ensuring they serve humanity. He ordained them to have dominion over all He created, so that those in authority may serve the Lord, who bestowed upon them honor, and to revere Him. 23Yet, should they stray from His laws, He will strip them of the sovereignty He granted. As the sovereign of both Earth and Heaven, He will bestow it upon those who fulfill His desires. 24 He anoints whom He chooses and deposes whom He wills. He has the power to end life or grant salvation, to inflict suffering or offer pardon. 25 There is no Creator like Him. As the supreme authority over all His creations, with no other beside Him in the heavens above or the earth below, no one can question His judgments. 26 The Lord exercises His authority to appoint and dismiss, to bring life or death, to administer hardship or grant forgiveness, to impoverish or bestow honor. 27He listens to those who earnestly seek Him in their prayers. He regards the supplications of those who align with His will through pure intentions, responding to their prayers and fulfilling their requests. 28He ordains that both the mighty and the meek be subject to His will. All that exists on the hills and mountains, within the roots of trees, in caves and underground wells, across dry land and seas, belongs to them. 29For those who adhere to the Creator's will, all of creation is their inheritance; He will not deprive them of abundance and will reward their devotion. 30He promises to bestow upon them the same honor He reserved in Heaven for their forefathers, Isaac, Abraham, and Jacob. He will grant them what He prepared for Hezekiah, David, and Samuel, who faithfully followed His laws and commands. 31To ensure their joy in His sovereignty, He offers the same honor He designated for their ancestors, Isaac, Abraham, and Jacob, whom He pledged to endow with a rich inheritance, to those who have served Him since ancient times.

22

1Reflect upon those who have performed virtuous deeds, and do not let their achievements fade from 2Strive to emulate them, so that your name may be revered as theirs, and you may share in their joy in the Heavenly Kingdom, a realm of radiance reserved for nobles and kings who lived in accordance with the Lord's wishes and showed kindness. 3Conversely, be aware of the fate that awaits corrupt nobles and kings. After death, they will face condemnation and disgrace among humankind for their failure to align their actions with what they saw and heard. 4Know with certainty that those who failed to follow the Lord's will shall face harsher judgment in the Heavenly Kingdom than even the worst offenders and those who disregarded His laws. 5Embrace kindness, purity, and integrity; avoid the path of those who ignored the Lord's laws and incurred His wrath due to their wickedness. 6Uphold justice and protect the orphaned child and the widow from those who unjustly exploit them. 7Act as a protector to the orphan, defending them from the grasp of the oppressor, and be deeply moved by their tears, lest you find yourself in the fiery abyss reserved for unrepentant sinners. 8Direct your steps towards the way of Love and unity. For the Lord's gaze is upon His friends, and His ears are attuned to their supplications. Strive for Love, and make her your guide. 9 But the Lord's countenance of wrath is set against those who commit wicked deeds, intent on erasing their names from the world; He shall not safeguard anyone who dwells near fortresses or mountains. 10 For I am the Lord, zealous for My divinity; a Creator who exacts vengeance and annihilates those who despise Me and neglect My commandments; My face of mercy shall not shine until I have obliterated those who defy My Word. 11 And I will bestow honor upon those who revere Me and abide by My commandments.

23

1 Do not follow the ways of Cain, who in a misguided belief of love, took the life of his innocent brother. 2 Consumed by jealousy over a woman, Cain's actions embody envy, betrayal, and wickedness. 3 In contrast, Abel's purity mirrors that of an unblemished lamb, his life's offering akin to the sanctity of a sacrifice made to the Lord with a heart unclouded by sin. Unlike those who tread Cain's path, Abel's way remains untrodden. 4 Indeed, all who embrace purity are cherished by the Lord, akin to the benevolent Abel. They, who walk steadfastly in the path of Abel's righteousness, truly embody the love of the Lord. 5 Yet, the Lord turns away from those who embrace malevolence; their ultimate judgment awaits, inscribed in the annals of their conscience. At the time of reckoning, their deeds will be laid bare before humanity, angels, and the entirety of creation. 6 In that moment, the guilty shall face profound disgrace. Those who have strayed from the Lord's commandments, shunning His will, shall bear the weight of their shame. 7 A dire proclamation awaits them, decreeing their banishment to Gehenna, an abyss without escape, where eternity stretches endlessly.

24

1But when Gideon placed his faith in the Lord, he overcame the vast armies of the uncircumcised, a multitude vast as locusts, with merely a handful of tens of thousands. 2 O nobles and kings, know there is no creator but Me. Do not be misled by false deities. 3As I, your Creator, the Lord, brought you into this world from your mothers' wombs, nurtured, clothed, and fed you, why do you turn to others? Why do you honor idols, forsaking Me? 4I have bestowed upon you all; what have you offered in return? Adherence to My laws, orders, and commands is all I seek, that I may grant you wellbeing. What more could I desire from you? 5The Lord of all declares: Avoid idol worship, sorcery, and the spread of despair. 6For the Lord's retribution will befall those who engage in such acts, as well as those who listen, comply, and befriend them. Steer clear of idolatry. 7Be wary, for those who do not know or care for you will rise against you. Unless you, who fear the Lord, follow His Will, they will consume the fruits of your labor. As spoken by His prophets, Enoch, and Asaph, if you fail to follow the Lord's Will, others will reap the benefits of your efforts. 8The Lord has spoken of the evil ones who will appear, adorned in finery, having no law but indulgence in food, drink, and adorning themselves with silver and gold, living entrenched in sin, engaging in all the works abhorred by the Lord. 9These individuals are preoccupied with feasting and revelry. From dawn to dusk, upon awakening from their slumber, they relentlessly pursue wicked deeds. Misery and hardship mark their journey, devoid of any path of love or compassion. 10They are strangers to acts of love and unity, lacking any reverence for the Lord. Corrupted, devoid of faith and virtue, they are consumed by greed, eating and drinking in isolation. Given to drunkenness, their transgressions know no bounds, indulging in seduction, bloodshed, theft, betrayal, and ruthless exploitation of the impoverished. 11Bereft of kindness and law, they show no fear of the Lord who created them. Their faces betray no sign of respect or reverence. 12They hold no regard for anyone they encounter, neither honoring the aged nor respecting the wisdom of elders. Their obsession with wealth is so intense that they claim it as their own even before it is seen. Void of the fear of the Lord, the mere sight of wealth stirs in them a voracious appetite. 13 Their leaders are notorious for consuming funds entrusted to them, always hungry for more. Deceptive and unreliable, they never stand by their words, changing their stance as swiftly as night follows day. 14They turn a deaf ear to the cries of the suffering and the impoverished, and their rulers are quick to embrace wickedness. They create turmoil for those trying to save the oppressed from the clutches of the greedy and powerful. 15 While they should be rescuing the wronged and the displaced, these rulers begrudge dispensing justice. Instead, they burden people with heavy levies and ruthlessly plunder wealth, proving themselves to be nothing but vile offenders. 16 Their greed is boundless; they lack compassion even when they feast on a calf alongside its mother or a bird with its eggs. They claim everything they see and hear as their own, driven by an insatiable urge to accumulate. 17Their love is only for amassing wealth for themselves, showing no kindness towards the ill and the needy. They cruelly exploit those who have little, hoarding wealth to indulge their own gluttony and revel in their ill-gotten gains. 18These individuals will vanish as swiftly as a scarab beetle emerging from its burrow, leaving no trace behind and never returning home. Their failure to perform righteous deeds during their lifetimes will lead to their downfall when the Lord's anger is kindled, and He decides to act. 19When the Lord chooses to ignore them, their end will come abruptly, as if caught in a single act of divine retribution. The Lord's patience, often mistaken for leniency, is merely an opportunity for them to repent. Yet, without repentance, their destruction is inevitable and swift, just like those who preceded them and disregarded the Lord's laws. 20These are the ones who metaphorically consume the flesh and blood of others, always ready to commit acts of violence and sin. Devoid of any fear of the Lord, their every waking moment is dedicated to sinful pursuits. 21Their existence revolves around indulgence in food and drink, leading them towards a path of ruin and sin. Their actions are destructive, not just to themselves but also to many others in this world, corrupting and destroying lives with their heedless actions.

25

1The Lord, sovereign over all, declares a warning to those entrenched in the deceitful works of Satan. He proclaims a dire fate for their physical form when His patience wears thin and His judgment is exacted. 2These individuals remain ignorant of the Lord's true nature and deeds. They have relegated His Law to the background of their lives, neglecting the divine commandments. 3In the final era, the Lord will bring upon them the full weight of their misdeeds. Just as their sins are recorded before Him, so will He exact His vengeance on the day of final judgment. 4The Lord's dominion extends from one horizon to the other, encompassing all creation. No one can elude His authority, whether in the heavens, on the earth, in the depths below, or in the vast seas. 5He commands the creatures of the earth and sea, from the serpents below to the fish in the waters, the birds in the skies, and the wild donkeys in the deserts. All are His possessions, spanning the breadth of the world. 6The Lord, who performs awe-inspiring works and miraculous deeds, holds unquestioned authority over all of creation. There is no one who can question His actions or His paths. 7The Lord, supreme over all, holds command over the chiefs and hosts of angels. Every creation bearing a name, from the beasts roaming the wilderness to the birds soaring in the sky and the livestock on the ground, belongs to His vast treasury. 8He wields power over the winds of the south and the arid climates of the east. In the final era, even the mighty Red Sea will be silenced by the awe and renown of the Lord as He approaches, affecting regions far and wide, from Saba to Nubia, India, and Ethiopia. 9Sovereign over both the living and the dead, the Lord's authority extends over all lands and peoples. His presence will be felt across the globe, commanding respect and reverence. 10His gaze watches over all from a position of lofty righteousness and power, surpassing any earthly dominion. His congregation is held firmly within His control, His kingdom reigning supreme over all others. 11His reign is greater than any other, His kingdom prevailing above all. His capability is limitless, nothing being beyond His reach or ability. 12He controls the clouds in the heavens and causes grass to grow for the livestock on earth. He ensures that every fruit blossoms and ripens. 13The Lord provides for all His creations, from the smallest ant beneath the earth to the grandest of beasts. He responds to the prayers of those who seek Him, never overlooking the needs of orphans and widows. 14In the eyes of the Lord, the rebellious acts of the wicked are as fleeting as a gust of wind, and the schemes of wrongdoers as insignificant as a puddle of murky water. He is more inclined to heed the prayers of the righteous and the pure, those who call out to Him with sincere hearts. 15The earthly beauty and wealth of those who forsake the Lord's laws, adorned in silver and gold, are as transient as a bird in flight. Their riches will not withstand the test of time; moths will consume their fine garments, leaving them with nothing. 16Just as weevils ravage the grain, so too will the possessions of sinners fade away, like a day that has passed or words spoken that cannot be taken back. Their wealth is no more enduring than a fleeting shadow, and in the Lord's eyes, it is as insubstantial as garments woven from falsehoods. 17Yet, those who are kind and just, who aid the poor and uphold the rights of the suffering and the orphaned, are honored by the Lord. He will not overlook them, for in their generosity, they have clothed the naked with the garments provided by the Lord, serving as His instruments of compassion and justice. 18Those who are righteous and just do not distort the judgment of the faithful or withhold the wages of the laborer. The way of the Lord is truth, as unwavering and balanced as a double-edged sword. They refuse to commit injustices, maintaining fairness in all their dealings, regardless of the time or the situation.

26

1On their beds, the impoverished reflect deeply. Without the acceptance of the wealthy, they are akin to barren, dry wood, devoid of greenery; their roots cannot thrive where there is no moisture, and without roots, no leaves can flourish. 2Just as leaves enhance the beauty of a flower and contribute to the fruit's growth, so too is religion essential for a person's complete

development. Without a foundation of faith, one cannot bear the fruits of virtue.3If a person steadfastly upholds their faith, they engage in virtuous deeds, delighting the Lord with their commitment to truth and righteousness. 4The Lord, in His fairness, responds to the sincere prayers of His followers, rewarding the truthfulness of their words and deeds. He does not allow the honest to suffer injustice because of their integrity. 5The Lord, embodying truth and a lover of honesty, will not absolve sinners lacking genuine repentance for their misdeeds. As He holds sovereignty over all souls on Earth and in Heaven, His judgment is impartial, not favoring the rich over the poor, and He requires sincere repentance for redemption.

27

1The world was crafted from nothingness by the Creator, who meticulously formed hills and mountains, stabilizing the Earth upon the waters. To prevent the seas from overflowing, He bordered them with sand. In the beginning, the Lord proclaimed, "Let there be light," and thus, light was brought into existence in a world shrouded in darkness. 2The Lord, in His infinite wisdom, brought forth all creation, meticulously arranging the world with precision and fairness. He ordained the night to be cloaked in darkness. 3And again he commanded, "Let there be light," bringing forth the dawn and dispelling the shadows. 4The upper waters were raised to the heavens as the Lord stretched them out like a canopy, securing them with the winds. He contained the lower waters in the depths, setting boundaries with sands. 5With His commanding authority, He ensured these waters remained within their confines, preventing them from engulfing the land. Within these waters, He placed a multitude of creatures, including the great Leviathan and Behemoth, as well as countless other beings, both visible and hidden from sight. 6On the third day, the Lord brought forth a bounty of vegetation upon the Earth, crafting every variety of root, tree, and fruit-bearing plant, each according to its kind. Among these, He created a special tree, pleasing to the eye and delightful to taste, and abundant grasses, serving as sustenance for birds, livestock, and wild animals. 7This tree, created for both beauty and nourishment, stood alongside a myriad of plants, each with seeds within, to feed the diverse creatures of the earth. 8As evening faded and morning dawned, the fourth day witnessed the Lord's command: "Let there be lights in the heavens." Thus, He set the moon, sun, and stars in the cosmos to illuminate the world, defining day and night, and guiding the rhythm of life. 9Henceforth, the moon, sun, and stars took their turns, ushering in the cycles of day and night. 10On the fifth day, the Lord crafted all aquatic animals and avian species, both those visible and those hidden from sight, populating the waters and the skies. 11The sixth day saw the creation of terrestrial animals and creatures of various kinds. Having shaped and prepared all, the Lord then created Adam in His own image and likeness. 12To Adam, He granted dominion over all animals, beasts, and marine life, including the immense Leviathan and Behemoth, denizens of the deep. 13The Lord granted Adam, formed in His likeness, dominion over all the cattle and sheep of the world, both those visible and those hidden. 14Placed within the Garden, Adam, created in the Lord's image, was tasked to tend and nourish the plants, to cultivate and cherish them, while singing praises to the Lord. 15However, with a stern warning, the Lord cautioned, "Upon eating from the Fig Tree of Knowledge, you shall surely face death." 16Thus, He commanded Adam to abstain from the Fig Tree, the bearer of knowledge of good and evil, the harbinger of death. 17But Eve, beguiled by the serpent's deceit, tasted the forbidden fruit, and shared it with Adam. 18By partaking of the fruit, Adam cast the shadow of death over himself and his descendants. 19Having transgressed the Lord's edict, and consumed the forbidden fruit, the Lord's displeasure fell upon Adam. He was exiled from the Garden to toil upon the earth, cursed with thorns and thistles, reaping the fruits of his labor in hardship. 20Cast into a world of sorrow, Adam began his life of toil and struggle, laboring upon the earth, sustaining himself amidst hardship and strife.

28

1Among Adam's progeny, flourishing in number, emerged those who revered and exalted the Lord, steadfast in upholding His commandments. 2Among them were prophets, visionaries of both past deeds and future happenings; yet, there also existed sinners, fabricators of falsehoods, and perpetrators of injustice. Cain, the eldest, embodied wickedness, culminating in the slaying of his brother Abel. 3The Lord's judgement fell upon Cain for his heinous act of fratricide, and the earth itself faced His wrath for absorbing Abel's innocent blood. 4Confronted by the Lord, "Where is thy brother Abel?" Cain retorted with prideful defiance, "Am I my brother Abel's guardian?" 5While Abel lived a life of purity, Cain's legacy was marred by sin, having extinguished the life of his righteous brother. 6Subsequently, Seth, a son of virtue, was born to Adam, who fathered a total of sixty children, a blend of the righteous and the wicked. 7From his lineage arose the virtuous and the prophetic, as well as traitors and sinners. 8Among them were the blessed, those who emulated the righteousness of their forefather Adam, adhering to his teachings and those of Seth, spanning the generations up to Noah, a man of unwavering devotion to the Lord's Law. 9Noah diligently imparted the Lord's Law to his offspring, urging them to preserve it and pass it down, just as he had received and upheld it. 10They existed in a continuum of teaching and learning, faithfully educating their subsequent generations. 11However, Satan's influence pervaded, manifesting in idols that promised eternal vows but led only to the grave. Many, seduced by these deceptions and heeding Satan's sinful teachings, fell into perdition. 12The era was marked by idol worship, following a misguided tradition, until the emergence of Abraham, a paragon of virtue who wholeheartedly embraced the Lord's Will. 13Abraham, distinct from his kin, was steadfast in adherence to the Law from an early age. The Lord, recognizing his unwavering faith, made a covenant with him, symbolized by the elements of wind and fire. 14This solemn promise from the Lord guaranteed Abraham a land to inherit and descendants to flourish for eternity. 15The Lord similarly pledged to Isaac, promising to bestow upon him the inheritance of his father, Abraham. In the same way, He vowed to Jacob, ensuring the legacy of his father, Isaac, would continue through him. 16From Jacob's lineage, the twelve tribes of Israel emerged, with some appointed as priests and kings. The Lord blessed them, envisioning their abundant growth and widespread proliferation. 17Despite being beneficiaries of their forefathers' legacy and receiving the Lord's sustenance and affection, they persistently grieved Him through their actions. 18In their moments of destruction and despair, they would seek the Lord in worship, turning away from sin and returning to His embrace, for His love for them remains steadfast. In these times of repentance, the Lord would extend His forgiveness. 19His mercy, stemming from His benevolence towards all creation, would lead to their pardon, more a reflection of their ancestors' virtues than their own merits. 20The Lord generously offers His providence, ensuring the satiation of the hungry and the sustenance of those in need. His watchful care extends to all, promising abundance and forgiveness. 21Even the offspring of crows and the beasts that implore Him are not neglected. When the children of Israel call upon Him, especially in times of delay from their foes, the Lord will intervene to rescue them. 22Despite the Lord's forgiveness, they repeatedly fell back into sin, distressing Him. Consequently, He permitted their neighboring peoples to rise against them, leading to their devastation, slaughter, and captivity. 23In their anguish and lamentation, they would call out to the Lord. There were times when He delivered them through prophets, sending them aid in their direst hours. 24At other times, the Lord rescued them through the actions of their rulers. However, when they grieved the Lord, their adversaries imposed taxes and captured them. 25David emerged as a savior, liberating them from the grasp of the Philistines. Yet, they continued to grieve the Lord, prompting Him to stir up other nations as sources of their distress. 26There were moments when the Lord offered salvation through the likes of Jephthah. But time and again, they neglected the Lord, especially during moments of ease, only to face His wrath in the form of malevolent enemies. 27As they grappled with adversity and were overpowered, they would once more turn to the Lord in desperation. He then delivered them through the valor of Gideon. Nevertheless, their actions continued to displease the Lord. 28This cycle of sin, suffering, and supplication persisted, with the Lord repeatedly allowing hostile nations to afflict them. Each time, they would return to Him in tears, seeking His mercy. 29Once more, the Lord intervened and rescued them from their adversaries through the might of Samson, granting them a brief respite from their trials. Yet, they soon relapsed into their previous sinful behaviors, provoking the Lord's displeasure. 30In response to their continuous transgressions, the Lord allowed other nations to torment them. Desperate, they cried out to the Lord for deliverance. Heeding their pleas, He provided salvation through the leadership of Barak and Deborah.31After this deliverance, they briefly returned to worshipping the Lord. However, they soon lapsed back into their old sinful ways, causing grief to the Lord. 32The Lord, in His righteous indignation, permitted other nations to oppress them again. Judith became the instrument of their next deliverance. Yet, following a short period of peace, they fell back into sin. 33Consequently, the Lord let them fall under the dominion of enemy nations. They lamented and prayed to the Lord when Abimelech, a fierce warrior, threatened the land of Judah. The Lord struck Abimelech down. 34Deliverance came through the children in the region and Mattathiah's valor. Upon the death of Abimelech, his forces dispersed in defeat, and the Israelites pursued them up to the Jabbok River, ensuring none of the enemy survived. Following a brief period of calm, the Israelites once again turned away from the Lord, prompting Him to allow foreign nations to dominate them. When they cried out to the Lord, He chose not to heed their pleas this time, as they had repeatedly grieved Him and consistently violated His laws. 35Consequently, they, along with their priests, were captured and exiled to the land of the Babylonians. 36Even in exile, the

Israelites, betraying their faith, continued to displease the Lord by engaging in sinful acts and idol worship. 37The Lord's patience reached its limit, and He contemplated their annihilation. Haman, in a plot to eliminate the Israelites, offered ten thousand gold pieces to King Artaxerxes, convincing him not to allow the survival of the Israelite children in Persia, from India to Ethiopia. This plan was formed when Haman fueled the king's anger against the Israelites. 38Haman executed his plan by drafting a decree under the king's authority, sealing it with the royal seal, and dispatching it throughout the Persian Empire. 39The king provided Haman with his royal seal, empowering him to enact the annihilation of the Israelites on a chosen date as per the king's directive. Furthermore, Haman was instructed to confiscate their wealth, including gold and silver, for the royal treasury. 40When news of this grim decree reached the Israelites, they were engulfed in grief and turned to the Lord in fervent prayer. Mordechai, learning of this peril, relayed the information to Esther. 41Esther urged the Israelites to fast and pray, calling for a collective appeal to the Lord for mercy and deliverance. She instructed all the Israelite communities to engage in fervent prayer. 42Embracing humility, Mordechai donned sackcloth and covered himself in dust, symbolizing repentance and mourning. Similarly, the Israelites across the land fasted, prayed, and sought the Lord's forgiveness. 43Esther, despite being queen, adopted a posture of deep humility and sorrow, wearing sackcloth, forgoing royal adornments, and earnestly praying to the God of her ancestors for intervention. 44Her genuine appeal moved the Lord, who caused her to find favor in the eyes of King Artaxerxes of Persia. She then prepared a thoughtful banquet in honor of the God of her forefathers. 45During the banquet attended by Haman and King Artaxerxes, the tables turned on Haman. The very fate he had planned for Mordechai – death by hanging – became his own, as he was executed on a tall wooden structure. 46In response to the Israelites' fervent prayers, the king issued a decree allowing them to remain as they were, without the burden of taxes, robbery, or injustice. This royal edict protected their wealth and ensured they wouldn't be harmed or exploited. 47The Lord's mercy on Israel, following their repentance and cries for help, was evident. Consequently, they were respected and honored in Persia, their place of residence. This protection extended to their property, safeguarding them from destruction and plunder. 48However, the Israelites' peace was not permanent. When they failed to uphold their devotion to the Lord, He permitted adversarial nations to torment them. These periods of hardship led the Israelites to cry out once more for divine intervention and deliverance from their oppressors.

29

1The Israelites faced harsh enslavement in Egypt, where they were forced to labor intensively, making bricks. They endured the grueling task of collecting mud and forming bricks without the provision of straw, a vital component. 2Egyptian overseers drove them relentlessly, appointing taskmasters to ensure the swift completion of their work. Under these oppressive conditions, the Israelites appealed to the Lord, seeking His aid to free them from the severe burden of constructing Egypt's infrastructure. 3When the Israelites suffered under Pharaoh's tyrannical rule in Egypt, the Lord sent them Moses and Aaron as deliverers. Their mission, divinely ordained, was to liberate the Israelites from Pharaoh's oppressive regime and lead them to a place where they could freely worship the Lord. Despite Pharaoh's stubborn resistance, fueled by arrogance, the Lord ensured the safe exodus of His people from Egypt. 4The Lord's judgment against the arrogant is unyielding. As an example, Pharaoh and his army were submerged in the Red Sea, a direct consequence of his pride and refusal to release the Israelites. Similarly, rulers who fail to perform righteous deeds, especially those appointed and anointed by the Lord, will face divine retribution. Their disregard for the Lord's commands, particularly in their roles as leaders, invites His wrath.5The Lord makes it clear that those who honor Him and His commands will be blessed. Kings and rulers are expected to uphold His word, ensure just treatment of their subjects, especially those serving the greater good, and recognize His supreme authority. 6The Lord declares that if rulers align their kingdoms with His divine principles, He will ensure the stability and prosperity of their realms. 7A reciprocal relationship is emphasized: if people perform virtuous deeds in accordance with the Lord's laws, He will reciprocate with blessings. Obedience to His laws guarantees protection and integrity. 8The Lord assures that love and devotion towards Him will be rewarded with care and healing. This mutual closeness is a testament to the Lord's commitment to those who faithfully follow Him. 9The Lord, the sovereign ruler of all, promises salvation from hardships to those who place their faith in Him. This assurance is a testament to His power and grace. 10The Lord's call is for unity and closeness. He implores sinners and transgressors to purify themselves from sin and turn away from wickedness. In doing so, He promises a reciprocal approach, drawing nearer to those who seek Him earnestly. 11The Lord is willing to set aside His wrath for those who reform. His return in kindness and forgiveness is guaranteed to those who cleanse themselves of their sins and embrace righteousness. 12As the Lord protected David from his numerous adversaries, including the formidable Goliath, the envious Saul, and his own son Absalom, He similarly pledges to safeguard those who adhere to His laws and execute His will. This protection is an assurance of His unwavering support and intervention in times of adversity. 13Those who are faithful in observing the Lord's commandments and fulfilling His desires are promised honor and joy, not just in this life but also in the life to come. The Lord's promise of crowning them above all signifies a reward of great magnitude, highlighting the joy and honor reserved for the righteous. 14Those who have served the Lord with devotion and honor, exemplified by the prophet Samuel, will be esteemed alongside kings. Samuel's life, marked by his commitment to the Lord from a young age, is a model of faithful service. The Lord, embodying the law, selected Samuel for His purposes. 15Samuel's role as a messenger to Eli, the elder servant, when he served in the Lord's Temple, was marked by compassion and favor. His service in the temple was not just a duty but a demonstration of his deep love and mercy. 16As Samuel matured in his service at the Lord's Temple, he was entrusted with greater responsibilities. The Lord appointed and anointed him, enabling him to appoint leaders and anoint kings according to the Lord's will. Samuel's close relationship with the Lord was evident in his chosen role to guide and anoint leaders for the people of Israel. 17During Saul's reign, the Lord instructed His prophet Samuel to anoint David, a descendant of Judah. This command reflects the Lord's approval and affection for David, chosen to be a leader under His divine guidance. This anointing signifies the Lord's direct involvement in the leadership of His people and His careful selection of those who would lead according to His will.

30

1"The Lord abhors the lineage of Saul, for he has grieved Me by violating My command. Saul's neglect of My laws led to My withdrawal of support, and his line will no longer be crowned by Me," declared the Lord. 2The Lord's disapproval was rooted in Saul's failure to honor His laws and decrees. This disobedience led to the removal of the kingdom and divine gifts from Saul's descendants eternally. 3The Lord stated, "Those who, like Saul, have not observed My laws, words, and decrees, will see their kingdoms and blessings stripped away. Their lineage will no longer enjoy My favor." 4"As they did not exalt Me when I exalted them, I shall bring them low," the Lord proclaimed. "Though I granted them honor, they did not honor Me in return, so they shall no longer be magnified or favored." 5The Lord lamented, "They failed to do good unto Me as I did unto them; they did not acknowledge My forgiveness when I forgave them." 6"Though I made them rulers, they did not acknowledge Me as their ruler," the Lord reflected. "As they did not honor Me when I honored them above all, I shall no longer exalt or honor them, for they disregarded My laws."7The Lord declared, "I have rescinded the gifts I bestowed upon them and will not restore the fortunes I have withheld, as per My vow of displeasure. Those who honor and love Me, I will honor and love in return." 8"Those who did not honor Me nor abide by My laws will be stripped of the gifts I granted them," declared the Lord. "I will distance them from the blessings I once bestowed." 9The Lord, Sovereign over all, proclaimed, "My affection is reserved for those who have loved Me. I will exalt those who have esteemed Me." 10"As the Lord of all, none can elude My dominion, whether on Earth or in Heaven. I am the Lord who both takes life and gives it, who brings sorrow and offers forgiveness." 11"Glory and honor are within My realm to bestow. I confer honor upon those I favor. As the judge and avenger, I bring low those I disdain." 12"I am the Lord who responds to those who love Me and invoke My name. I am the provider for all, rich and poor alike, nourishing birds, animals, and sea creatures, not just mankind." 13 "My provision extends to all creatures, from crocodiles to whales, from gophers to hippos. I sustain all life, not solely human life. All creation is under My care." 14 "I nourish every being that seeks Me, providing for each according to My will and love." 15"Those who did not honor Me nor abide by My laws will be stripped of the gifts I granted them," declared the Lord. "I will distance them from the blessings I once bestowed." 16The Lord, Sovereign over all, proclaimed, "My affection is reserved for those who have loved Me. I will exalt those who have esteemed Me." 17"As the Lord of all, none can elude My dominion, whether on Earth or in Heaven. I am the Lord who both takes life and gives it, who brings sorrow and offers forgiveness." 18 "Glory and honor are within My realm to bestow. I confer honor upon those I favor. As the judge and avenger, I bring low those I disdain." 19 "I am the Lord who responds to those who love Me and invoke My name. I am the provider for all, rich and poor alike. 20 “I am the one who nourishes the birds, animals and sea creatures, not just mankind." 21 "My provision extends to all creatures, from crocodiles to whales, from gophers to hippos. I sustain all life, not solely human life. All creation is under My care." 22"I nourish every being that seeks Me, providing for each according to My will and love."

31

1"Kings do not rule without My agreement, and sufferers exist by My decree; they are not impoverished except by My design. The mighty rise by My intention, yet their strength is not theirs alone, but granted by My will." 2 "I bestowed favor upon David and wisdom upon Solomon; I extended Hezekiah's years. Goliath's time I shortened; to Samson, I granted strength, and then I diminished it." 3 "I rescued My servant David from the mighty Goliath, the warrior. Again, I delivered him from the clutches of King Saul and from another formidable adversary, for he had adhered to My commandments. I protected him from those who challenged and opposed him." 4 "My affection was with David, and so is My love for all nobles and kings who uphold My laws. As they have brought Me joy, I shall empower them with victory and strength against their foes." 5 "Furthermore, to ensure they inherit the land of their ancestors, I will grant them a pure and resplendent land of inheritance, as I promised their forefathers."

32

1"The Lord of all declares, 'You, the nobles and kings, listen to My words and obey My commandments. Do not displease Me by following the path of the Israelites who grieved Me with their worship of false idols - those whom I nurtured and saved, for I am their Creator, the Lord of all. Heed My words; all whom I raised with love and nourished from their birth; 2 "Whom I brought forth to the bounty of the earth; who feasted on the richness provided by the land, appropriately allotted; who enjoyed the vineyards and olive trees they did not plant, and the wells of clear water they did not dig; 3"Listen to My words, so you do not distress Me as the children of Israel did, by turning to other gods when I, the Lord, am their Maker," He admonishes. "I who supplied them with sheep's milk, honeycomb, and fine wheat, clothed them in garments adorned with decorations, and granted all their desires - 4 "Without ever denying them anything they asked of Me."

33

1"The Lord of all declares, 'You, the nobles and kings, listen to My words and obey My commandments. Do not displease Me by following the path of the Israelites who grieved Me with their worship of false idols - those whom I nurtured and saved, for I am their Creator, the Lord of all. Heed My words; all whom I raised with love and nourished from their birth; 2 "Whom I brought forth to the bounty of the earth; who feasted on the richness provided by the land, appropriately allotted; who enjoyed the vineyards and olive trees they did not plant, and the wells of clear water they did not dig; 3"Listen to My words, so you do not distress Me as the children of Israel did, by turning to other gods when I, the Lord, am their Maker," He admonishes. "I who supplied them with sheep's milk, honeycomb, and fine wheat, clothed them in garments adorned with decorations, and granted all their desires - 4"Without ever denying them anything they asked of Me." 5"Even if you are a king, are you not still a mortal destined to die and decay, to become worms and dust tomorrow?" 6"Yet now you boast and exude pride as if you were immortal," says the Lord of all. 7"Remember, though you may appear well today, you are mortal and tomorrow you may not be. But if you adhere to My commandments and My teachings, 8 "I will grant you a distinguished land, shared with noble kings who followed My Will - a realm radiant with light, where crowns gleam and thrones of silver and gold are graced by those who wear them," He declares. 9 "There, amidst this splendid domain, those who have performed righteous deeds will find joy. 10"But for those who have sinned, who have not upheld My laws," proclaims the Lord of all, 11"They are not destined to enter this illustrious land reserved for the honored kings."

34

1"The dominion of Media will collapse, while the empire of Rome will solidify its hold over Macedonia's territories," declares the Lord. "Similarly, Nineveh's rule will assert itself over the lands of Persia. 2"In like manner, Ethiopia will establish its power over the realm of Alexandria. With the rise of various peoples, Moab's kingdom will assert itself over the realm of Amalek. 3"Brother will rise against brother, leading to vengeance and destruction by the Lord, as He has foretold the downfall of these nations. 4"Nations will conflict with one another, people will confront their own, and lands will battle against each other," He proclaims. 5 "Disputes will erupt, leading to warfare, famines, pestilence, earthquakes, and droughts. As love fades from this world, the chastisement of the Lord descends upon it. 6 "For the day approaches unexpectedly when the Lord, striking as swiftly as lightning visible from east to west, shall arrive, instilling fear in all." 7"On the day of Judgement, when the Lord delivers His verdict, each person will face the consequences of their actions, measured by the frailty of their deeds and the gravity of their sins," declares the Lord. "For it has been proclaimed that I, the Lord, will exact vengeance on the Day of Judgement, when their paths are obstructed, as the time for their reckoning has arrived. 8 "At that moment, the Lord will consign forever to Gehenna those who refuse to live according to His laws and indulge in sin. 9"Those dwelling in the western isles, Nubia, India, Saba, Ethiopia, and Egypt will come to recognize me as the Lord, the sovereign of Earth and Heaven, the bestower of love and honor, the savior and the taker of life. 10 "I am the one who commands the Sun to rise and set, who orchestrates both calamity and blessing. 11"I am the one who will bring forth unfamiliar peoples to ravage and consume the fruits of your labor – your herds of sheep and cattle. 12 "They will seize your offspring, striking them down before your eyes, and you will be powerless to protect them. This devastation befalls you because you did not heed the Lord's commands, and His spirit of support did not reside within you. 13"Thus, your opulence and your plans will be laid to waste, as you disregarded the Lord's decrees," declares the Lord. 14"Those imbued with the Lord's Spirit of Support will possess comprehensive knowledge, akin to how Nebuchadnezzar recognized the Lord's Spirit dwelling in Daniel," says the Lord. "To them, the veil of secrecy will be lifted, revealing both the seen and the unseen. Indeed, nothing remains concealed from one who is graced by the Lord's Spirit. 15"Such individuals, blessed with the Lord's Spirit, will discern all mysteries, understanding both the overt and the covert aspects of life. Yet, this clarity is only granted to those touched by the Lord's Spirit. 16"As we are mortal beings destined to perish, the sins we have concealed and committed will inevitably come to light. 17 "Like the refining of silver and gold in fire, sinners too will undergo scrutiny on the Day of the Lord's Return, for they have failed to adhere to the Lord's Commandments. 18 "On that decisive day, the deeds of all nations, including every action of the children of Israel, will be subject to a thorough evaluation.

35

1"Woe to you, leaders of Israel, for the Lord is angered by your failure to render just decisions for the orphan," proclaims the Lord. "Your neglect of truth and justice has invoked His wrath. 2 "Woe to those who frequent taverns from dawn till dusk, indulging in drunkenness; who show bias in their judgments and disregard the pleas of widows and orphans, living in sin and corruption. 3 "The Lord has spoken to the nobles of Israel, declaring: 'If you had steadfastly followed My Commandments, upheld My Law, and embraced what I cherish, then perhaps your fate would be different. But woe unto you for your transgressions,' says the Lord. 4 "He warns of impending ruin, punitive trials, and sufferings that will befall you, leading to your demise as surely as moths and weevils consume fabric; your existence and lands will vanish without trace," declares the Lord. 5 "Your lands will become desolate, and all who once admired its abundance will stand aghast, clapping their hands in disbelief, lamenting, 'Was this not the land abounding in riches, beloved by many? It is reduced to this desolation by the sins of its inhabitants.'"6 "Observers will comment, 'Her downfall is due to her pride and self-aggrandizement, her obstinate mindset leading to her desolation by the Lord. Transformed into a barren land by the arrogance of its people, overgrown with thorns and thistles, she is now a tragic sight to behold.' 7"This land, once prosperous, is now overrun with weeds and nettles, devolving into a desolate wilderness, a haven for wild beasts. 8"The Lord's judgement is firmly established upon this place. She will endure the full force of the Lord's wrath, a consequence of her people's vanity and sins. Thus, she stands as a warning, instilling fear in all who venture near her."

36

1 O people of Macedon, raise not your voices in prideful boasting. For the Lord, who watches over all, is poised to bring your downfall, Amalekites, harden not your hearts with stubborn thoughts. 2Though you may rise as high as the heavens, know that you shall descend to the depths of Gehenna. 3 In the times of old, when Israel first journeyed to the land of Egypt, traversing through Moab and Media, it was commanded, "Boast not against the Lord, for it is not for man to challenge the Lord." 4 Ye descendants of Ishmael, born of a bondwoman, why do you stand firm in your conceit with wealth that is not yours? Consider this: will not the Lord judge you when He rises to bring judgment upon the Earth, on the day of your reckoning? 5The Lord, who reigns above all, declared, "In that time, you shall reap the fruits of your own deeds; why then do you elevate your thoughts in arrogance? Why do you stiffen your neck in defiance?" 6 "I shall deal with you as you have dealt with those not of your kin; for you act as you please, giving way to sin; and I shall forsake you in the place to which you were cast." 7The Lord, Sovereign of all, proclaimed, "This shall be your fate; but if you engage in righteous deeds, if you embrace what I hold dear, then I shall listen to your pleas." 8And should you fulfill My Will, I shall in turn fulfill your desires; I shall contend with your adversaries on your behalf, and I shall bless your offspring and your lineage. 9 Your flocks of sheep and herds of cattle shall I increase; if you steadfastly adhere to My Commandments and do that which pleases Me, the Lord over all has spoken, I shall bestow blessings upon all that your hand touches. 10But if you forsake My Will, if you do not remain steadfast in My Law and My Commandments, all the afflictions previously spoken of shall befall you; for you have not endured hardship while remaining true to My Command; you have not lived in accordance with My Law; and you shall not escape My wrath that shall perpetually descend upon you. 11 And as you have not cherished what I cherish, I, who brought you forth from nonexistence into being, 12 all this was within your power - to take life and to heal, to act as you will, to construct and to destroy; to honor and to disgrace; to exalt and to humble; and as you have neglected My Worship and My Praise, I, who granted you dominion and honor among those under your authority; you shall not evade My wrath that is destined to come upon you. 13 And if you do the Will of the Lord and steadfastly follow His Commandments, He shall bestow His love upon you, that you may rejoice in His sovereignty and share in the inheritance of a land held in high esteem by those who are chosen. 14For it has been spoken, "If they are true to Me, I shall endow them with love and honor, and bring them joy in the

house of worship where prayers ascend; for the Lord, who governs all, has declared, they shall be favored and selected, akin to a cherished offering." 15Forsake not the deeds that bring prosperity and righteousness, that you may transition from death unto life eternal. 16And those who engage in virtuous deeds, the Lord shall safeguard in all their righteous endeavors, that they may serve Him, as did Job, whom the Lord shielded from all adversities. 17The Lord shall preserve them in all their noble efforts, that they may be devoted servants unto Him, as was Abraham, whom He rescued when he vanquished the kings; and as Moses, whom He delivered from the clutches of Canaan and Pharaoh - in whose time Abraham sojourned, and who ceaselessly tormented him, night and day, attempting to sway him towards idolatry. 18 Yet, when confronted with the idols that were their treasure, he bore his trials steadfastly, rejecting them. 19For Abraham, from his youth a believer in the Almighty, stood as a faithful friend to the Lord; unwavering in his devotion, he worshiped the Lord who had created him. 20In his profound love for the Lord, Abraham ceased not to worship Him until his dying breath; he strayed not from His Law until the end of his days; and he instructed his children to uphold the Law of the Lord. 21 As their father Abraham adhered to His Law, so too did they not stray from the path of the Lord's commands. As the Lord declared unto the angels, "I have in this world a friend named Abraham," so were Abraham's offspring, Jacob and Isaac, His loyal servants, who never deviated from the Law of the Lord. 22 The Lord, exalted amongst them and ruler over all, proclaimed, "Abraham is My beloved friend; Isaac, My trusted confidant; and Jacob, a friend dear to My heart." 23Yet, even as the Lord cherished the children of Israel, they lived in continual defiance, causing Him grief, even as He bore with them, providing them with manna in the wilderness. 24Their garments did not wear out, for they were sustained by the manna, the bread of understanding; and their feet did not swell. 25 But their thoughts continually strayed from the Lord. As those who indulged in sin from the earliest times, they harbored no hope for salvation. 26 They were akin to a bow that shoots astray; yet, they did not follow the path of their forefathers, Isaac, Abraham, and Jacob, who served the Lord in their righteous ways. They continually grieved Him with their idols upon the mountains and hills. 27They feasted upon the mountains, in the caves and beneath the trees. They would slaughter an ox; they offered sacrifices, and reveled in the works of their hands. They consumed the remnants of their offerings; they drank from their libations, and in their revelry, they cavorted with demons, singing in their company. 28And the demons reveled in their festivities and songs, encouraging their drunkenness and licentiousness without restraint; and they engaged in thievery and avarice, which the Lord abhors. 29 They worshipped the idols of Canaan, Midian, Baal, Apis, Dagon, Serapis, and Artemis, the false gods of 'Eloflee'. 30 Amidst the peoples of their region, to all manner of idols they offered sacrifices; and all Israel bowed to these idols, imitating the peoples in their worship, believing these idols could see and hear. They partook in festivities, songs, and loud celebrations, as was the custom among the idolaters. 31 All the tribes of Israel followed suit, professing, 'We will worship the Lord,' yet failing to adhere to His Commandments and His Law as conveyed by Moses in the Torah. They were called to uphold the Law of the Lord, to shun idol worship. 32 They were warned against deviating to worship foreign idols, forsaking the Creator of their forefathers, who had nourished them with honey from Maga, with grain from their fields, and with manna from the heavens, 33Moses admonished them, saying, 'Do not bow down to these,' for He is their Creator, their Sustainer, loving those who love Him, and never forsaking those who seek Him. 34Yet, they ceased not to grieve the Lord; and in their waywardness, they caused sorrow to the Lord, even in times of divine blessings bestowed upon them. 35And when they were stricken with sorrow, they would cry out to Him, and He would deliver them from their afflictions; and once more, they would be filled with joy, living through many generations. 36 But in time, they would again turn their hearts to sin, grieving the Lord as before; and He would stir up peoples in their midst to chastise them; and they would be oppressed and burdened. 37 Yet again, they would turn back and cry out to their Creator, the Lord. 38And He would forgive them, not for their own sake, but for the sake of their forefathers—Noah, Isaac, Abraham, and Jacob—who served the Lord faithfully from ancient times, to whom He had pledged His covenant. It was not for their own deeds that He granted them pardon. 39He cherished those who adhered to His Law, desiring to increase their progeny like the stars of heaven and the sands of the sea. 40 But when the time comes that their numbers are as countless as the sands, among them will be the souls of sinners, set apart from the children of Israel, destined for Gehenna. 41As the Lord had spoken to Abraham, "Look towards the heavens at night, and try to number the stars if you can;" and as He said, "Your descendants, the righteous, will shine in the heavens like those stars;" they are like the luminaries in the sky, but what they bear are the souls of the virtuous, born of Israel. 42And as the Lord once instructed Abraham, "Look towards the edges of the river and the sea, observe what lies amidst the sands. Attempt to count them, as you might count the grains; and so will be the number of your sinful children, who shall descend into Gehenna when the dead are raised; they are the souls of sinners."43Abraham placed his faith in the Lord, and this faith was accounted to him as righteousness. He found favor in this world, and in his old age, his wife Sarai bore him a son named Isaac. 44For he believed that those who perform righteous deeds shall rise and enter the eternal Kingdom of Heaven; and there, they shall find their everlasting dominion. 45 But he also believed that those who commit sins shall be cast into the everlasting Gehenna when the dead are raised; yet, the righteous, who have done virtuous deeds, shall reign with Him eternally. 46And he held the belief that a true and unerring judgment would be passed upon the sinful; for in the heavenly realm, they shall find the eternal Kingdom of Life. "May glory and praise be given unto the Lord in truth and without deceit; and thus, the first book recounting the tales of the Meqabyans is concluded and fulfilled. SELAH."

BOOK OF MEQABYAN II

1

1 Herein is recounted the tale of Maccabeus, who ventured into Mesopotamia, a land within the bounds of Syria, and wrought destruction upon the people of Israel, slaying them in their own lands, from the Jabbok to the precincts of Jerusalem, laying waste to the land. 2 For the peoples of Syria and Edom, aligned with the Amalekites, joined forces with the man of Moab, Maccabeus, who laid siege to the land of Jerusalem. They encamped from Samaria to the square of Jerusalem, extending to all its territories, and in the throes of war, spared not those who fled, save but a few. 3 And when the children of Israel strayed from righteousness, the Lord stirred the man of Moab, Maccabeus, against them; and by the sword, he smote them. 4 Thus, the enemies of the Lord, those nations, boasted against His hallowed land, taking oaths in their transgressions. 5 The forces of 'Iloflee and Edom made their encampments. Sent by the Lord, for they had spurned His Word, they set forth to exact vengeance and ravage the land of the Lord. 6 The domain of Maccabeus was Ramoth, in the land of Moab; and he rose from his realm in might, his followers swearing allegiance alongside him. 7 And so, they made their encampment in the land of Gilboa, spanning from Mesopotamia to Syria, with the singular intent to devastate the lands blessed by the Lord. There, Maccabeus implored the Amalekites and the 'Philistines for their alliance. He offered them abundant silver and gold, along with chariots and horses, that they might join him in his wrongful deeds. 8 United, they stormed the fortress. Those dwelling within were slaughtered, their blood flowing like water. 9 They reduced Jerusalem to a shadow of itself, akin to a

keeper's hut in a vineyard; within its walls, a cacophony of sin resounded. All manner of wicked acts, abhorred by the Lord, were committed there, defiling the land once filled with praise and honor. 10 The flesh of your allies and the corpses of your servants were left as sustenance for the wild beasts of the desert and the birds of the sky. 11 They plundered the orphans and widows; heedless of the Lord, they acted as instructed by Satan. Their cruelty persisted until the Lord, who scrutinizes the heart and mind, was roused to wrath, as they violently removed the unborn from the wombs of expectant mothers. 12 They returned to their own lands, rejoicing in their malevolent acts against the tribes of the Lord; they carried away the spoils from a land once revered and honored. 13 Upon their return, as they entered their homes, they celebrated with joyous songs and clapping, reveling in their conquest and plunder.

2

1 The prophet, known as Re`ay, spoke unto him, saying, "This day, your joy is but fleeting, for the time of true joy and gladness has passed. The Lord, whom Israel has exalted, is poised to enact His vengeance and bring ruin upon you for the chastisement you never doubted would come. 2 Will you then boast, 'My steeds are fleet; thus, I shall flee and elude capture'? 3 But I say unto you, those who pursue you are swifter than the vultures; you shall not elude the judgment and destruction of the Lord that is destined to befall you. 4 Will you claim, 'I am clad in iron, impervious to the thrust of spears and the sting of arrows'? The Lord, who favors Israel, has declared, 'Not by the spear or arrow shall I exact my vengeance and bring your downfall,'" He proclaimed to him. "I will inflict upon you maladies of the heart, ailments and chronic pains, more grievous and unyielding than any weapon; yet even these shall not be the means of my retribution. 5 You have kindled My wrath. I will visit upon you a sickness of the heart, and there will be none to aid you; you shall not escape My dominion until I have utterly erased the mention of your name from this world." 6 For you have stiffened your neck in arrogance and raised yourself against My land, when I act swiftly, as quick as the blink of an eye, you shall come to recognize Me as your Creator. Before Me, you are as grass consumed by fire in the gusts of wind; you are like dust, dispersed and scattered by the breezes from the earth, such is your stature in My sight. 7 You have incited My wrath, yet you did not acknowledge your Maker; and I shall forsake all your kin; nor shall I spare any who approached your stronghold. 8 Now, turn away from the multitude of your sins. If you repent from your wrongdoing, and earnestly seek atonement in grief and sorrow before the Lord, and if you plead with Him with a pure heart, the Lord will absolve you of all your transgressions committed before Him," he advised him. 9 Thereupon, Maccabeus donned

sackcloth and lamented before the Lord for his sins, for the Lord's anger had been kindled against him. 10 For the eyes of the Lord are ever watchful, for He does not overlook; and His ears are ever attentive, for He does not neglect; He does not render His spoken Word false; and He acts swiftly, at once; for the Lord is mindful not to delay the chastisement He has decreed through the words of His prophet. 11 Maccabeus shed his garments and donned sackcloth, cast dust upon his head, and cried and wept before his Creator, the Lord, for the sins he had committed.

3

1 The prophet journeyed from Ramoth to bring word to him; for Ramoth, situated within Moab, lies close to Syria. 2 He excavated a pit and submerged himself up to his neck, shedding earnest tears; he entered into deep repentance for the sins he had committed before the Lord. 3 And the Lord spoke to the prophet, saying, "Depart from Ramoth in the land of Judah, and go to the ruler of Moab, Maccabeus," He instructed him. "Convey to him these words from the Lord," He said. "Tell him, 'I, the Lord, your Creator, have sent you by My command to lay waste to My land, so that you may not boast, 'I have razed the revered city of Jerusalem by the might of my power and the vastness of my forces;' for it was not you who accomplished this deed." 4 "For she has grieved Me greatly with her avarice, treachery, and lasciviousness. 5 And so, I withdrew My protection and delivered her into your hands; and now, the Lord has pardoned your transgression, not for your sake, who hardened your heart, boasting, 'I have subdued the city of Jerusalem with the strength of my rule,' but for the sake of your offspring whom you have begotten. 6 Be not doubtful, for those who waver in doubt are not suited for the path of repentance; and now, embrace repentance with a fully committed heart." 7 Blessed indeed are those who repent with complete understanding, who do not revert to former vices and sins, alongside all who have turned away from their wrongdoings. 8 Blessed are those who return to their Creator, the Lord, with humility and sorrow, with prostration and fervent supplications. Blessed are those who are disciplined and repent, for He has said to them, "You are My treasures, who have sought forgiveness after leading others astray." 9 To the haughty Maccabeus, who turned back to Him in repentance after leading others astray, He said, "I absolve you of your sin for your fear and your dread; for I am the Lord, your Creator, who visits the iniquity of the fathers upon the children unto the seventh generation, if they continue in their fathers' sins; and who extends mercy unto ten thousand generations to those who love Me and keep My Law." 10 "And now, I shall reaffirm My covenant with you on account of your children whom you have sired; and the Lord,

who reigns over all and has favored Israel, declares, 'I will acknowledge the repentance you have shown for your sins.'" 11 At that moment, he emerged from the pit and prostrated himself before the prophet, swearing, "As I have caused grief to the Lord, do with me as you see fit; yet may the Lord deal with me accordingly, should I ever stray from your guidance. We have strayed from the Law, not steadfast in His Commandments as our forefathers were. You know that our ancestors instructed us, and we have followed idols. 12 For I am a sinner, entrenched in my wrongdoing, obstinate in my pride and arrogance, thus transgressing the Commandments of the Lord. Until this moment, I had not heeded the words of the Lord's servants, the prophets; nor did I adhere to His Law and His Commandments that He enjoined upon me." 13 He said to him, "Since none among your ancestors acknowledged their sin as you have, I perceive that today the prophet has witnessed true repentance." 14 "But now, forsake your idol worship and turn to the knowledge of the Lord, that you might attain genuine repentance," he advised him. Maccabeus fell and bowed at the prophet's feet, who then raised him and instructed him in all the righteous deeds that behooved him. 15 Maccabeus then returned to his home, diligently following the directives of the Lord. 16 He dedicated himself anew to the worship of the Lord, purging his household of idols, enchantments, idolaters, pessimists, and sorcerers. 17 Each morning and evening, emulating the practices of his forefathers, he instructed the children he had taken from Jerusalem in all the Commandments, Ordinances, and Laws of the Lord. 18 Among these captured children, he selected those with knowledge to oversee his household. 19 Moreover, from among the younger ones, he chose astute children to mentor and educate the younger, less knowledgeable ones, creating a chamber for learning where they could be taught the Law of the Lord as practiced by the children of Israel. From these captured children of Israel, he learned about the Ordinances and Laws, and the Nine Laws; realizing that the customs and temples of the people of Moab were devoid of true value. 20 He demolished their temples, idols, and magical practices, along with the sacrifices and offerings made to these idols, both morning and evening, including the offerings of goat kids and herds of fattened sheep. 21 Maccabeus then proceeded to destroy the idols he once revered and supplicated, in which he had placed his faith for all his endeavors, offering sacrifices in the afternoon and at noon, following the counsel of the priests and fulfilling the demands of these idols. 22 He had believed that these idols safeguarded him, following their guidance without question or doubt. 23 But Maccabeus abandoned their practices. 24 After heeding the words of Ra`ay, whom they called a prophet, he committed himself to a path of repentance. As the children of Israel once grieved the Lord, and as He disciplined them with hardships when they acknowledged their faults and cried out to the Lord, all his people began to perform righteous deeds, surpassing even the children of Israel in their devotion during that period. 25 When he learned of their capture and the harsh treatment they endured at the hands of their oppressors, and that they cried out to the Lord for deliverance, he remembered the covenant made with their forefathers. At that moment, he believed that the Lord would forgive them for the sake of their forefathers, Isaac, Abraham, and Jacob 26 Yet, each time the Lord delivered them from their afflictions, they would soon forget the Lord who rescued them, returning to their idol worship. 27 Then, the Lord would raise up nations to oppress them, and under the weight of this new tribulation and sorrow, they would again call out to the Lord. Because of His love for them, as they were the creations of His authority, He would show kindness and grant them forgiveness. 28 However, after being saved, they would once more fall into sin, grieving Him with their persistent misdeeds and their idol worship in their assemblies. 29 So, the Lord would again stir up against them the peoples of Moab, 'Iloflee, Syria, Midian, and Egypt; and when these enemies prevailed over them, they would cry and lament. As these foes dominated and burdened them, the Lord would raise up leaders for them, to deliver them in His time of favor.

4

1 There was a time in the days of Joshua when the Lord delivered them. 2 And in the days of Gideon, the Lord again was their savior. 3 Likewise, in the times of Samson, and Deborah and Barak, and Judith, the Lord provided salvation; whether through male or female leaders, He raised up saviors to rescue them from the hands of their adversaries who oppressed them severely. 4 And as the Lord loved, He would deliver them from those who harshly oppressed them. 5 They would find immense joy in all that He had done for them, rejoicing in the bounty of their land and the increase of their herds in the wilderness, and their livestock. 6 He would bless their crops and their animals, looking upon them with merciful eyes, and He would not let their livestock dwindle, for they are the descendants of the righteous, whom He cherished deeply. 7 Yet, when they turned to evil deeds, He would allow them to fall into the hands of their foes. 8 And as they faced destruction, they would seek Him in worship, turning away from their sinful ways and seeking repentance before the Lord. 9 When they fully returned to Him with genuine understanding, He would forgive their transgressions. He would no longer hold their past sins against them, for He understood their nature as flesh and blood, burdened with the deceptive thoughts of this world

and influenced by demons. 10 When Maccabeus learned of the divine actions taken by the Lord in His holy place, the Temple, he was profoundly moved to repentance. 11 Witnessing and understanding this, he did not hesitate to engage in righteous actions; he emulated the virtuous deeds of the children of Israel, who, when forgiven by the Lord after deviating from His Law, wept and cried out as they were chastised; and when the Lord forgave them again, they steadfastly observed His Law. 12 Maccabeus, in turn, amended his ways and adhered to the Law; he remained resolute in following the Commandments of Israel's Creator, the Lord. 13 Having learned of the proud traditions of the children of Israel, he, too, took pride in upholding the Law of the Lord. 14 He encouraged his family and offspring to steadfastly observe the Commandments of the Lord and all His Laws. 15 He rejected the practices condemned by Israel and embraced and observed the Laws upheld by Israel. Although his lineage was of Moab, he abstained from foods forbidden by Israel. 16 He faithfully offered tithes, consecrating all that was firstborn among his cattle, sheep, and donkeys, and turning his gaze towards Jerusalem, he offered the sacrifices as practiced by the children of Israel. 17 Maccabeus would offer various types of sacrifices: sin offerings and vow offerings, sacrifices for well-being, and fellowship offerings, along with the regular burnt offerings. 18 He would present the firstfruits of his harvest, and he would press and pour out grape offerings just as Israel does. These he would give to the priest he had appointed, and in all things, he would emulate the practices of Israel, even in the preparation of fragrant incense. 19 He constructed a candlestick, a basin, a table, and a tent, along with the four rings of the ark; he prepared refined oil for the lamps in the Holy of Holies and made the curtain as Israel does for the Holy of Holies when serving the Lord. 20 Just as they performed righteous deeds when steadfast in His Ordinances and His Law, and when the Lord did not forsake them to their enemies, Maccabeus also endeavored to do good works in their likeness. 21 He would continually pray to the Creator of Israel, the Lord, asking Him to be his Guide, and praying that he would not be separated from the children of Israel, whom the Lord had chosen and who performed His Will. 22 Furthermore, Maccabeus would implore the Lord to grant him offspring in Zion and a dwelling in Jerusalem; to bestow upon him a Heavenly Seed of Virtue in Zion and a Heavenly House of the Soul in Jerusalem. He prayed for deliverance from the calamities foretold by the prophets, that the Lord might accept his repentance, marked by the many tears shed in sorrow and his earnest turn towards penitence. 23 He sought assurance that his children would not suffer in this world because of his actions, and that he himself would be guided rightly in all his endeavors and journeys. 24 The people of Moab, under Maccabeus' rule, rejoiced in their newfound faith, inspired by their leader's steadfast commitment to righteous deeds. They respected his judgments, adhered to his agreements, and set aside the language and customs of their own land, recognizing the superiority and rectitude of Maccabeus' ways. 25 They would gather to listen to Maccabeus' judgments, which were known for their fairness and truth. 26 Maccabeus possessed great wealth, including female and male servants, camels, donkeys, and five hundred horses clad in armor. He was victorious over the Amalekites, 'Philistines, and Syrians, a stark contrast to the times when he, as an idol worshipper, suffered defeats at their hands. 27 With his newfound devotion to the Lord, Maccabeus became invincible in battle; from the moment he began to worship the Lord, no enemy could triumph over him. 28 His adversaries would approach with the might of their idols, invoking their names and cursing Maccabeus, yet none could overcome him, for he had placed his faith firmly in his Creator, the Lord. 29 As he continued in this manner, vanquishing his foes, he reigned over the peoples under his dominion, establishing his authority through his victories. 30 He avenged and brought ruin upon the enemies of those who were wronged. He rendered fair judgments for orphans, 31 and provided support for widows in their time of need. He shared his food with those who were hungry and clothed the unclothed with garments from his own wardrobe. 32 Maccabeus found joy in the fruits of his labor. Generously, he shared his wealth without reservation, contributing tithes to the Temple. Maccabeus passed away having lived a life of happiness and contentment, fulfilled by his righteous deeds.

5

1 After his passing, Maccabeus left behind young children who matured, adhering to the teachings of their father. They maintained the order of their household and cared for all their kin, ensuring that no poor person, widow, or orphan suffered or grieved alone. 2 Revering the Lord, they used their wealth to aid the poor and faithfully executed the responsibilities entrusted to them by their father. They offered solace to orphans and widows in their distress, becoming as parents to them. They rescued them from those who sought to harm them, providing comfort amidst all turmoil and sorrow that befell them. 3 For five years, they lived in this manner, embodying the virtues taught by their father. 4 However, after this period, the king of the Chaldeans, Tseerutsaydan, invaded. He devastated their lands and captured the children of Maccabeus, annihilating all their settlements. 5 He seized all their wealth. The children, having strayed into various misdeeds and

sins such as adultery, blasphemy, and greed, and having forgotten their Creator, fell into the hands of those who did not adhere to the Law and Commandments of the Lord and who served idols. These captors took them away to their own land. 6 In their captivity, they were forced to consume things abhorrent to the Lord: meat torn by beasts, blood, carcasses, and refuse discarded by scavengers—things explicitly forbidden by the Lord, yet they had strayed from all the true Commandments inscribed in the Torah. 7 They had forgotten that the Lord, their Creator, who brought them forth from their mothers' wombs and nourished them, was their true sustenance and healer. 8 They transgressed further by marrying within forbidden degrees of kinship, such as their aunts and their fathers' wives, their stepmothers. They indulged in robbery, wicked acts, and sins like adultery, without any regard for the Law or the time of Judgment, engaging in all manners of evil deeds, including incestuous marriages, and lived without adherence to any Law. 9 Their paths were darkened and treacherous; their actions were mired in sin and adultery. 10 However, the children of Maccabeus remained steadfast in their observance. They refused to eat what scavengers had touched or what had died of natural causes. They did not partake in the malevolent practices of the Chaldeans, for their actions were wicked, not chronicled in this book of sinners' deeds; they were full of doubt, criminality, betrayal, and filled with robbery and sin, like the offspring of the heathen. 11 The deeds that were pleasing to their Creator, the Lord, were absent among them, lost in their deviation from His path. 12 Further astray they went, turning to the worship of an idol named Be'el Phegor, placing their trust in it as though it were equivalent to their true Creator, the Lord, despite it being deaf and mute. It was merely an idol, a creation of human hands, fashioned by a smith who worked with silver and gold. This idol, devoid of life or understanding, had neither breath nor knowledge; it possessed neither sight nor hearing. 13 It could neither eat nor drink; 14 it was incapable of killing or saving. 15 It could neither sow nor uproot; 16 it could not harm an enemy, nor benefit a friend. 17 It lacked the power to impoverish or to bestow honor. 18 This idol was but an obstacle, leading the Chaldean people astray in their idleness, yet it held no power to chastise or forgive.

6

1 Tseerutsaydan, an adversary of the Lord, full of arrogance, appointed priests and those who would conceal the truth to serve his idols. 2 He offered sacrifices to these idols and poured out libations as if in their honor. 3 In his delusion, he believed these idols could partake of these offerings, as if they could eat and drink. 4 With each new dawn, Tseerutsaydan would

offer cows, donkeys, and heifers in sacrifice, both morning and evening, and he would partake of these defiled offerings himself. 5 Furthermore, he coerced others to join in these sacrificial rituals to his idols, insisting not just on their participation but their active involvement. 6 When the priests of these idols observed the children of Maccabeus, noting their comeliness and their devout worship of the Lord, they desired to lead them astray, to entice them into offering sacrifices and partaking of the abhorred offerings. However, these noble descendants of Maccabeus steadfastly refused. 7 They adhered to their father's teachings, committed to performing righteous deeds and deeply revering the Lord. Thus, they could not be swayed, 8 even when they were bound, insulted, and robbed. 9 Word reached King Tseerutsaydan that they had rejected the idea of sacrificing and bowing to his idols. 10 This news deeply angered and saddened the king. He ordered that the children of Maccabeus be brought before him. When they were presented, the king demanded, on behalf of his idols, "Offer a sacrifice to my idols." 11 In response, they firmly declared, "We will neither engage in this matter nor offer sacrifices to your defiled idols." 12 Though he tried to intimidate them with numerous threats, he could not sway them, for they had fortified their minds, steadfast in their belief in the Lord. 13 He then kindled a fierce fire and cast them into it, but they willingly gave their bodies over for the sake of the Lord. 14 After their martyrdom, they appeared to him at night, swords in hand, as he reclined on his royal throne, filling him with immense fear. 15 Distraught, he pleaded, "My lords, please guide me rightly; what must I do to appease you? Spare me from death, and I will do all that you command." 16 They instructed him on what was proper, saying, "Acknowledge that the Lord is your Creator; understand that the Lord is the one who can remove you from your kingdom where you boast. He can cast you into the fiery Gehenna along with your father, the Devil. We have worshiped our Creator, the Lord, without transgressing against you; and as we revered Him in fear, you condemned us to the flames. Similarly, you will face your tribulations through the same fire." 17 "For He is the Creator of all; the Earth and the heavens, the sea, and everything within them. 18 He fashioned the moon, the sun, and the stars; and the architect of all creation is the Lord. 19 There is no other creator beside Him, neither on Earth nor in the heavens, for He possesses the power over all, and nothing is beyond His reach. As He is the one who takes life and grants salvation, who disciplines with hardship and offers forgiveness, so you, who have burned us in the fire for our reverence of the Lord, will endure your own struggles through the same means," they proclaimed to him. 20 "As He reigns over the Earth and the heavens, no one can escape His dominion. 21 Among all

His creations, none have strayed from His commandments, except for you, who are a sinner, and others like you, misled by your father Satan. You, your priests, and your idols shall all descend into Gehenna, from which there is no escape, for all eternity." 22 "Your mentor is Satan, who instructed you in these wicked deeds, leading you to act maliciously against us. But it is not you alone who have done this; thus, you shall all descend into Gehenna together. 23 You have presumed to liken yourself to your Creator, the Lord; yet you have failed to recognize the Lord who fashioned you. 24 Engulfed in your arrogance, you glorify your idols and the creations of your own hands, but this will continue only until the Lord brings you low. He will judge you for all the sins and wrongdoings you have committed in this world."

7

1 "Alas for you who do not recognize the Lord, your Creator, for you revere idols as if they were your equals, bringing upon yourself a remorse that will offer no comfort when you find yourselves trapped in the anguish of Sheol. Woe to you who have not heeded His Word and His Law. 2 There will be no escape for you, your priests, or those who offer sacrifices to these idols as if they were the Lord. Your idols, lifeless and soulless, cannot exact vengeance or show favor; they neither punish the wicked nor reward the righteous. 3 Woe unto you who offer sacrifices to these idols, for they are merely creations of human hands, where Satan finds a dwelling to deceive the minds of the idle, such as yourself. He leads you towards the fiery Gehenna, along with the priests who serve demons and command you and your idols." 4 "You fail to understand that your actions are futile and lead you astray. 5 Even the animals that the Lord created for your sustenance, along with dogs and wild beasts, are superior to you; for they face only death, without further condemnation. 6 But as for you, after death, you will endure suffering in the fires of Gehenna, from which there is no escape, for all eternity. In this sense, animals are better off than you." 7 Having delivered these words, they departed and vanished from his sight. 8 Tseerutsaydan spent the night in profound terror, trembling uncontrollably. This fear clung to him relentlessly, not subsiding until the break of dawn.

8

1 Tseerutsaydan remained entrenched in malicious thoughts and prideful arrogance. 2 Resolute as iron, as foreseen by Daniel regarding his kingdom, he exerted his influence over the neighboring lands and their peoples. 3 He was steadfast in his wickedness, his idleness, and in causing distress to others. 4 He continued the destruction previously mentioned, consuming the resources of the people. 5 Zealous in his pursuit of evil, akin to his father, the Devil, he hardened his heart and, with his

forces, laid waste to what little was left. 6 He boasts, "My reign is as enduring as the Sun's," yet he fails to acknowledge the Lord, his Creator. 7 In his misguided thoughts, he believes that even the Sun owes its existence to him. 8 He rises to power, establishing his camp in the territory of the Tribe of Zebulon, starts organizing forces in Macedonia, and receives provisions from Samaria, accepting gifts and tributes from the region. 9 He encamps in the lands of nomadic peoples, extending his reach to Sidon, imposing taxes on Achaia, and flaunting his arrogance as far as the flowing sea. Then, he returns and dispatches envoys to the shores of India. 10 In this way, his pride ascends as high as the heavens. 11 He persists in his haughtiness and wickedness, devoid of any humility. 12 His path is one of darkness and peril, marked by crime, arrogance, bloodshed, and affliction. 13 All his actions are detestable to the Lord. He follows the teachings of his mentor in malice and deceit, the Devil, causing suffering to orphans and showing no kindness to the impoverished. 14 By his might, he has overthrown and annihilated the kings of various peoples. 15 He has dominated the leaders of his enemies, ruled over numerous nations, and imposed taxes according to his whims. 16 Relentless in his conquests, there was no one he did not subjugate, from the sea of Tarshish to the sea of Jericho. 17 He worships idols and partakes in forbidden foods: the flesh of animals that died naturally or were torn by beasts, blood, meat from animals slaughtered by the sword, and offerings made to idols. All his actions lack righteousness; he knows no justice. As a tyrant over those under his rule, he imposes heavy taxes as he pleases. 18 Acting according to his desires, he shows no reverence for the Lord, living in wickedness before the Lord who created him. 19 Unlike his Creator, he acts malevolently towards his peers, especially when angered, subduing them. Just as he has inflicted suffering, so too shall the Lord repay him for his hardships. 20 As declared by the Lord, "I shall avenge and annihilate the sinners who do not adhere to My Commandments, so as to erase the memory of their names from this world." Just as He eradicated those who came before, so will He exact vengeance and destruction upon Tseerutsaydan when the time comes. 21 As the wicked have perpetrated evil, so shall they face the consequences of their actions. 22 Conversely, those who perform righteous deeds as ordained by the Lord will be followed by blessings and favorable outcomes. 23 Just as Joshua defeated the five kings of Canaan, trapping them in a cave, and as he prayed for the sun to stand still in Gibeon to vanquish their armies—resulting in the sun halting in the midst of the sky until the destruction of the Hivite, Canaanite, Perizzite, Hittite, and Jebusite forces; and as he slew approximately twenty thousand at once, capturing and humiliating them, and executing them with a spear in a cave and sealing it with a stone—similarly, such affliction will befall all those who distress the Lord through their malevolent deeds.

9

1 "O feeble man, not the Lord, why do you revel in pride? You who are a mere mortal today will tomorrow become nothing but dust and ashes, eventually turning to worms in your grave. 2 Your guide is the Devil, who bears the burden of all human sins, having led our forefather Adam astray. Sheol awaits you, as it does those who follow in your sinful ways. 3 Just as he, in his arrogance, refused to bow before Adam, whom the Creator had fashioned, 4 so too have you failed to bow before your Creator, the Lord, following in the footsteps of the Devil. 5 As your ancestors, who did not recognize or worship the Lord, are destined for Gehenna, so shall you share in their fate. 6 Just as they faced the Lord's vengeance and destruction for their wicked deeds in this world and descended into Gehenna, 7 you too will descend into Gehenna, just like them. 8 You have incited the Lord's wrath and neglected to worship Him, the one who granted you dominion over five kingdoms. Do you really think you can escape the Lord's authority?" 9 You do not act as you should, fulfilling the Lord's commands; thus He has tested you. If you engage in righteous deeds in this world, the Lord will ensure the success of all your endeavors and will bless everything you undertake. He will make your past and present enemies subject to you. 10 You will find joy in your undertakings and accomplishments, in the children born of your lineage, in your herds and their abundance, and in all tasks to which you set your hand and all plans you conceive in your heart. Authority has been granted to you by the Lord to act, to work, to build, and to destroy; all shall be governed by His will for you. 11 However, if you do not heed the word of the Lord or live steadfastly in His Law, as did the sinners before you who failed to honor the Lord appropriately and did not firmly believe in His righteous Law, you will not be able to escape the Lord's dominion, for the judgment of the Lord is just. 12 Everything is laid bare before Him; there is nothing that is hidden from His sight. 13 He is the one who has the power to take away the authority of kings and to topple the thrones of the mighty. 14 He raises up those who were lowly and lifts those who have fallen. 15 He frees those who were bound and revives those who were dead. As the Dew of Mercy emanates from Him, in His time of favor, He will resurrect those whose flesh has decayed and turned to dust. 16 After raising and judging those who committed evil, He will send them to Gehenna, for they have caused Him grief. 17 These are the ones who have violated the Lord's Commandments and His Law, and He will erase their

progeny from the world. 18 The path of the righteous is more challenging than that of sinners, for sinners do not desire to follow the ways of the righteous. 19 Just as the heavens are far from the earth, so too are the deeds of the righteous far removed from the actions of the wicked. 20 The deeds of sinners are characterized by theft and sin, adultery and wrongdoing, greed and treachery. They indulge in iniquity, rob others of their possessions, and live in moral corruption. 21 The path of sinners swiftly leads to the shedding of innocent blood, to acts of destruction that bring no gain, and to causing sorrow to orphans. It includes consuming blood, eating animals that died of themselves, consuming camel and pig meat, and engaging in relations with a woman during her menstrual period or immediately after childbirth. 22 All these actions are characteristic of sinners' behavior. They are snares laid by Satan, forming a broad and easy road leading directly to the everlasting fires of Gehenna and to Sheol. 23 In contrast, the path of the righteous is exceedingly narrow, leading towards welfare, innocence, humility, unity, love, prayer, fasting, and the purity of the flesh. It involves abstaining from harmful practices, not eating animals killed by the sword or that died of themselves, refraining from coveting a young man's wife, and avoiding adultery. 24The righteous avoid actions not prescribed by the Law, including consuming unclean foods and engaging in detestable acts and all deeds despised by the Lord, which are commonplace among sinners. 25 The virtuous, on the other hand, steer clear of everything that is abhorrent to the Lord. 26 He loves the righteous and will protect them from all their troubles, treating them as treasured possessions. 27 For they adhere to His Commandments and His Law and embrace all that He loves, whereas sinners fall under the dominion of Satan.

10

1 Fear the Lord who created you and has sustained you up to this day. Yet, you nobles and kings, do not follow the path of Satan. 2 Abide by the Law and Commandments of the Lord who reigns over all, and avoid the ways of Satan. 3 When the children of Israel approached Amalek to take possession of the lands of the Hittites, Canaanites, and Perizzites, remember how Balak, the son of Zippor, sought Balaam's curse: 4 "He whom you curse is cursed, and he whom you bless is blessed. Curse them for me, and through your curse, help me defeat them. I will reward you handsomely with silver and gold." Do not tread upon the path of Satan. 5 Driven by the prospect of reward for his sorcery, Balaam agreed, and Balak, the son of Zippor, showed him where the children of Israel were encamped. 6 For he acted on his malevolent intentions, offering sacrifices and slaughtering his fattened cattle and sheep, hoping to

curse and annihilate the children of Israel. 7 Yet, the Lord transformed the intended curse into a blessing, for He did not desire that they be cursed by His word. Therefore, do not follow the path of Satan. 8 "Since you are the people chosen by the Lord, and you are His dwelling that shall descend from Heaven, let those who curse you be cursed, and those who bless you be blessed," he proclaimed. 9 When Balaam blessed them in Balak's presence, Balak, the son of Zippor, was filled with sadness and intense vexation, insisting that Balaam should curse them. 10 But Balaam replied, "I cannot curse Israel, whom the Lord has blessed." 11 Balak, son of Zippor, then said to Balaam, "I had hoped that you would curse them for me. You have blessed them in my presence, but you did not curse them. If you had cursed them as I requested, I would have filled your house with silver and gold. But since you have only blessed them, you have not acted in my favor, and I will not reward you." 12 Balaam asserted, "I will only speak the words that the Lord has put in my mouth. I cannot dare to defy any command of the Lord. 13 I cannot bring a curse upon a people blessed by the Lord, for if I do so for the sake of wealth, the Lord will be displeased with me. I value my soul more than money. 14 The Lord promised their forefather Jacob, 'Those who bless you will be blessed, and those who curse you will be cursed.' I must not curse the blessed Jacob, for I do not value money over my soul," he continued. "As the Lord has decreed, those who bless you are blessed, 15 and those who unjustly curse you are cursed. Follow your path and fulfill your duties so that you may find favor with the Lord. 16 Do not be like those of the past who angered the Lord with their sins, whom He consequently abandoned. These are the ones whom He annihilated in the deluge. 17 Others He allowed to be destroyed by their adversaries. He brought upon them enemies, wicked people who inflicted great suffering upon them, capturing their rulers, priests, and prophets. 18 These captives were taken to a foreign land, unfamiliar to them. Their captors seized them completely, plundered their possessions, and laid waste to their land." 19 They tore down the defenses and walls of the revered city of Jerusalem, reducing it to a mere field. 20 Priests were taken captive, the Law was disregarded, and warriors who fought in battle fell. 21 Widows were seized, mourning for themselves but not for their husbands who had died. 22 Children cried, and the elderly felt shame; there was no respect shown either for the aged or for the elders. 23 Everything in the land was destroyed, with no consideration given to either the beautiful or the lawful. As the Lord grew angry with His people and decided to destroy His dwelling, the Temple, they were captured and taken to unfamiliar lands among foreign peoples. 24 Because they continually grieved their Creator, when the Lord finally turned away from the children of Israel, He allowed Jerusalem to be plowed over like a field. 25 His mercy towards them was for the sake of their forefathers; He did not annihilate them in one fell swoop. His love for their ancestors, Isaac, Abraham, and Jacob, who ruled justly and adhered faithfully to the correct Law before their Creator, was the reason for His forgiveness, not because of their own righteousness. 26 He bestowed upon them double honors and granted them two kingdoms: one on Earth and another in Heaven. 27 To you, kings and nobles dwelling in this transient world, just like your forefathers who lived righteously and are now your predecessors, you too are inheritors of the Kingdom of Heaven. Reflect on the legacy they left behind, how their names are revered by future generations. 28 Therefore, rectify your actions so that the Lord may establish your kingdom firmly and your name be remembered with honor, akin to the virtuous kings before you who served the Lord in the beauty of holiness and righteousness.

11

1 Reflect on Moses, the servant of the Lord, who never harbored anger while leading a multitude, exemplifying humility and devotion in his prayers. No one sought his harm, and he interceded with the Lord for his sister and brother who spoke against him, imploring, "They have sinned against You, O Lord; please forgive them and do not forsake Your people." Moses sought atonement for their sins, and the Lord took note of his unresentful spirit. 2 Moses pleaded, "I have transgressed against You, Lord. Forgive me, Your servant, a sinner, for You are Merciful and Forgiving. Please absolve them of their sins." 3 Thus, Moses also made amends for the sins of his sister and brother who had wronged him. 4 As a result, he was renowned for his innocence. 5 The Lord favored him more than all the children of priests, his brethren, appointing Moses to a role akin to His own among them. 6 Conversely, He caused the Earth to swallow Korah's children, who were insolent, sending them along with their livestock and tents into Sheol, as they boasted, "We are here, both in body and soul." As Moses was beloved by his Creator, the Lord, and did not deviate from His Commandments, all that he spoke came to pass as if it were the Word of the Lord. 7. Similarly, if you do not breach the Lord's Commandments, He will fulfill your desires, cherish your endeavors, and preserve your kingdom. 7 Similarly, if you do not breach the Lord's Commandments, He will fulfill your desires, cherish your endeavors, and preserve your kingdom. 8 Asaph and the descendants of Korah, who rebelled against Moses' authority, voiced their discontent when he instructed them to "direct your hearts to serve the Lord." 9 They protested, "Aren't we also the children of Levi, appointed to serve

as priests in the sacred Tent?" 10 They went on to burn incense, taking up their censers, but the Lord did not heed their offerings. They were consumed by the fire from their own censers, melting away like wax in the flames, leaving none of them alive. As was decreed, their censers, sanctified through the burning of their bodies, were the only things that remained, set apart for the Lord's dwelling, while neither their garments nor their bones were left intact. 11 Consequently, the Lord instructed Aaron and Moses, "Collect their censers and bring them to the Tent. They shall serve as instruments in My dwelling, which I have arranged in every detail, from the outer parts to the innermost areas." 12 Moses meticulously crafted the sacred Tent's instruments, fashioning rings, connectors, and a sea of imagery featuring Cherubim. 13 He created the bowls, curtains, and the base structures of the Tent for assembly, as well as the altar and the vessels used for sacrifices in the sacred Tent. 14 They offered various types of sacrifices according to their commitment: offerings for well- being, sin atonement sacrifices, vow offerings, and the regular morning and evening sacrifices. 15 Everything that the Lord had instructed Moses was relayed to the people for implementation in the sacred Tent, so they could carry out their duties there. 16 They did not disregard the command to serve their Creator, the Lord, allowing His name to be glorified through them in the Law, within the Tent of Meeting of their Creator, the Lord. He had promised to grant them the inheritance of their forefathers, a land flowing with milk and honey, as He had sworn to Abraham. 17 They faithfully followed the guidance of their Creator, the Lord, who made a covenant with Isaac and established His worship with Jacob, 18 and who established the sacred Tent for Aaron and Moses as a place where His worship would be preserved, 19 and who affirmed His worship through Elithe Lord and Samuel in the Temple and Tent that Solomon built, which ultimately became the dwelling place of the Lord in Jerusalem, a sanctuary for the name of the Lord, bringing honor to Israel. 20 This place serves as a site for supplication and sin atonement, a sanctuary where transgressions are forgiven for those who live righteously, including the priests. 21 It is a haven for those who abide by the Lord's Will, where He listens to their prayers, 22 and the embodiment of the Lord's Law, which brings glory to Israel. 23 This sacred place is where sacrifices are offered and incense is burned, creating a pleasing aroma to the Lord who has honored Israel. 24 It is here, upon the mercy seat, that the Lord speaks, offering forgiveness in the sacred Tent. The light of the Lord shines upon the descendants of Jacob, whom He has chosen, and upon those who faithfully adhere to His Law and Commandments. 25 However, those who disregard the Lord’s Law will face a fate similar to that of Korah's descendants, whom the Earth swallowed. In the same way, sinners are destined for Gehenna, a place of no return, where they will remain for eternity.

12

1 Woe unto you, nobles of Israel, who have failed to adhere to the Law as commanded in the Tent, following instead your own desires. This is manifest in arrogance, pride, greed, adultery, excessive drinking, and deceitful oaths. 2 My wrath against such transgressions will be as intense as a fire that burns chaff, as a flame that consumes a mountain, or as a whirlwind that scatters chaff across the earth and sky, leaving no trace behind. In the same way, my anger will utterly destroy you. 3 The Lord, who has favored Israel, proclaims, "I will likewise annihilate all who commit sin, remembering always the Lord who reigns over all, for whom nothing is impossible. 4 He cherishes those who love Him and for those who steadfastly follow His Commandments, He will absolve their sins and transgressions. Do not be obstinate or hard-hearted in disbelief. 5 Redirect your thoughts to serve the Lord faithfully and believe in Him, so that you may strengthen your spirit. I will deliver you from the hands of your enemies on the day of your distress." 6 "In the moment of your supplication, know this: I am with you to support and rescue you from the hands of your adversaries. Since you have placed your faith in Me, followed My Commandments, remained loyal to My Law, and cherished what I cherish," says the Lord, ruler of all, "I will not abandon you in your time of trial. 7 He cherishes those who love Him, for He is a Forgiver, kind and protective of those who observe His Law, treating them as precious trust. 8 He often restrains His wrath for their sake. Knowing they are but flesh and blood, He, in His merciful nature, does not wholly consume them in His reprimand. When their souls depart from their bodies, they return to their earthly origins. 9 As He is their Creator, having brought them forth from nonexistence, they remain unaware of their dwelling place until the Lord decides to resurrect them. Once their souls are separated from their bodies, the essence of Earth returns to its earthly form. 10 And once more, by His decree, He will bring them forth from nonexistence into existence." 11 Tseerutsaydan, in his denial of the Lord, intensified his arrogance towards Him. He elevated himself to grandiose heights until the day he turned away from the Lord. 12 "My reign shall last as long as the heavens, and I am the one who commands the sun. I shall live eternally," he proclaimed. 13 But before he could finish these words, the Angel of Death, known as Thilimyakos, descended and struck his heart. He died in that very hour. Failing to glorify his Creator, he was stripped of his opulent life and perished, consumed by his excessive pride and wicked deeds. 14 Meanwhile, the army of the Chaldean king, poised for battle in

the city and its surrounding areas at the time of his death, advanced and ravaged his lands. They seized all his livestock, and spared not even the elderly who witnessed the destruction of their defenses. 15 They looted all his wealth, taking even the smallest of his possessions, set his land ablaze, and then returned to their own country.

13

1 The five children of Maccabeus, steadfast in their faith, chose to sacrifice their lives rather than partake in offerings made to idols. 2 They understood that allegiance to the Lord was of far greater importance than yielding to human pressures, and that the wrath of the Lord was more to be feared than the anger of any earthly king. 3 Recognizing the transitory nature of this world and that earthly pleasures are not everlasting, they willingly embraced martyrdom in the flames, believing in salvation from the eternal fire in Heaven. 4 Aware that a single day of joy in the divine realm surpasses countless years in the mortal world, and that securing the Lord's forgiveness for even an hour is more valuable than many years of life, they surrendered themselves to the fire. 5 "What is our life but a fleeting shadow, akin to wax that melts and vanishes at the edge of a flame? Is it not so?" 6 "But You, O Lord, live eternally. Your reign is unending, and Your name will be revered by generations to come." 7 With these thoughts, the children of Maccabeus made their choice. Rejecting the abhorrent offerings, they firmly placed their faith in the Lord 8 With the firm belief that they would rise again alongside those who had passed before, and motivated by their devotion to the Lord, they understood that a final judgment would follow the resurrection. Therefore, they embraced martyrdom with courage and conviction. 9 To those who neither understand nor believe in the resurrection of the dead: realize that the life awaiting beyond is far superior to this transient earthly existence. This truth was embraced by the five children of Maccabeus, who, in their admirable youth and beauty, willingly faced death, fully aware of the resurrection to come. 10 Their faith in the Lord was unwavering, knowing that all earthly things are fleeting. They refused to bow to idols or partake in abominable offerings that provide no true sustenance. In sacrificing their lives, they sought to earn the grace of the Lord. 11 Anticipating the joy that the Lord would grant them in body and soul in the life to come, they disregarded the pleasures and pains of this world. Even those with families, understanding the promise of a resurrection in both flesh and spirit at the time of the Lord's return, willingly surrendered their lives. 12 With the conviction that those who faithfully uphold the Lord's Law, including nobles and kings who embrace and act kindly according to the Lord’s Word, 13 will reign for generations in the Kingdom of

Heaven—a realm devoid of sorrow, trouble, or death. Understanding in their hearts the glory that awaits beyond this life, as transient as wax in the midst of fire, 14 they courageously surrendered their lives. Believing firmly that their countenances in the hereafter will shine with a radiance surpassing even the sun sevenfold, and that they will bask in His Love when all rise again in both body and spirit, they embraced martyrdom 15

14

1 The beliefs of the Samaritans and the Jews, particularly the Sadducees who deny the resurrection of the dead, greatly trouble me and challenge my understanding. The Jews say, "We shall die tomorrow, so let us eat and drink today, for tomorrow we die. There is no joy or bliss to be found in the grave." 2 The Samaritans, on the other hand, argue, "Our flesh will turn to dust and will not rise again. 3 The soul, being invisible like the wind or the sound of thunder, exists here but is not tangible. Since it is intangible and cannot be seen or named, they reason that if the flesh dies, the soul cannot rise at the resurrection. Only then will we believe in the resurrection of our souls. 4 Our flesh, which can be consumed by beasts or decay in the grave, is visible to all. Eventually, it will turn to dust and ashes. 5 And those very beasts that consume it will also turn to dust, for they are like grass that withers and disintegrates as if they were never created, leaving no trace behind. Thus, they conclude that our flesh cannot and will not rise again." 6 The Pharisees believe in the resurrection of the dead, but they contend that God will reassemble souls with a different kind of flesh, not the one that decomposed on Earth, questioning, "Where can one find flesh that has decayed and rotted?" 7 The Sadducees, however, assert, "Once our soul leaves our body, there will be no resurrection for us. Both flesh and soul cease to exist upon death, and we shall not rise again." 8 In these ways, they are gravely mistaken, and their words of disrespect towards the sovereignty of the Lord deeply sadden me. 9 As they fail to put their faith in the Lord, who has blessed them, they have no hope of salvation. Their disbelief precludes them from the hope of dying and being resurrected to salvation. 10 "O Jew, whose understanding is clouded, you who were brought into being from nothingness and are as transient as a wisp of spit, how can you deem the Lord, who created you in His own image and likeness, to be unaware? Is it beyond the capability of the Lord who fashioned you to reunite your flesh with your soul? 11 You cannot evade the authority of the Lord. Do not entertain such thoughts. You will rise again, whether you desire it or not. The suffering that awaits you in Sheol, where you will be confined after death, will be inevitable and will be judged upon you, regardless of your wishes. 12 The sin that originates from demons, which they

implant in your mind, begins to work in you from the moment you are born and grows as you age. 13 These demonic influences embed themselves in your body at death, and they will bring upon you the consequences of the sins you committed. 14 Just as sin dwells in the hearts of those who succumb to it, so too do the families of sinners become entangled with demonic forces. 15 The souls of all sinners will be drawn from the edges of Heaven, where they currently reside, and your own sins will lead you into Gehenna, dragging your soul from its place. 16 After your body has been separated from your soul, the Lord's Dew of Mercy will resurrect you, purifying you sevenfold, just as He did with the flesh of our forefather Adam. 17 Those who lie in graves are also mistaken in their beliefs. Let it not seem to you that you are only deceiving others. By claiming, "There is no resurrection; those who have died will not rise," you lead others astray from the Lord's Commandments and into error. 18 The Lord will resurrect you to face the consequences of your actions, dispensing retribution according to the deeds you have done. Yet, who can spare you so that you might remain only as dust? 19 Regardless of your nature—whether like wind in the wind, water in the water, earth in the earth, or fire in the fire your reckoning will come. 20 If a soul that resided in you lived in Sheol, it will be summoned forth. 21 The souls of the righteous, basking in joy in the Garden, will also return. 22 But you, whether Jew, Samaritan, Pharisee, or Sadducee, will dwell in Sheol until judgment is pronounced upon you. 23 Then you will witness the Lord repaying you for your sins, as you have led others astray with your claims. 24 "The dead do not rise. Since we will die, let us eat and drink," you say. And by sitting in the seat of Moses yet leading others astray with your words, claiming "The dead do not rise," you will see the Lord mete out your punishment. 25 Your ignorance of the Torah, and your teachings from other books, have led you astray. It would have been better had you remained unlearned than to mislead others with your teachings. 26 It would have been far better had you not known the words of these books if you were going to mislead the Lord's people with your harmful teachings and futile words. 27 For the Lord shows no partiality based on appearances. He reserves His grace and glory for His friends, those who teach virtuous deeds. But you will receive recompense according to your actions and the words you have spoken. 28 There is no way to avoid the judgment of the Lord, who will recompense you according to your deeds. Both you and those whom you have misguided will face His judgment together. 29 Understand that the dead will rise. If they are those who followed His Law, they will be resurrected. Just as the Earth sprouts grass after the rains, as commanded by the Lord, so will they emerge from their graves.

Their decayed state cannot persist forever. 30 Like damp wood absorbs dew and sprouts leaves when nourished by rain, like wheat yields grain and seedlings bear buds, just as it's inevitable for them to produce their fruit, so too, if the Lord wills, the dead will rise, transformed and renewed. 31 Similarly, it is impossible for a pregnant woman to halt or prevent the process of childbirth when labor takes hold of her; she cannot avoid giving birth. 32 Just as dew descends by the command of the Lord, so too will she bring forth her child at the appointed time, once she hears the word of the Lord. In the same way, a grave cannot prevent the resurrection of those who rest within it. 33 The bodies will be reassembled at the very spots where they fell in death, their resting places will open, and the souls will reunite with the flesh from which they were once separated. 34 At the sounding of a trumpet, those who have died will rise instantly, as swiftly as the blinking of an eye. Upon their resurrection, they will stand before the Lord, who will then bestow upon them the rewards or consequences corresponding to their earthly deeds. 35 Then, you will witness yourself rising alongside the deceased, and you will be astonished at all the actions you undertook in this world. When you see all your sins laid bare before you, you will experience a profound but futile regret. 36 Understand that you, too, will rise with the deceased and face the repercussions proportionate to your actions in life.

15

1 Those who have earned their reward through virtuous deeds will rejoice in that moment. In contrast, those who have denied the resurrection, asserting "The dead will not rise," will be filled with sorrow when they witness the dead rising, along with the futility of their own wicked deeds. 2 Their own actions will stand as testimony against them, and they will come to the realization that their deeds condemn them, with no one left to argue in their defense. 3 On the day of judgment and lamentation, when the Lord returns, on the day when the final judgment is pronounced, those who have forsaken the Law of the Lord will find themselves standing where they must. 4 It will be a day of complete darkness, a day when the mists are drawn in, marked by flashes of light and the sound of thunder, 5 a day of earthquakes, terror, scorching heat, and icy cold, 6 On this day, the wicked who committed evil deeds will face their punishment, while the righteous will receive their reward for their pure actions. Those who neglected the Law of the Lord will suffer as sinners do, standing in the place designated for them. 7 For on that day, no distinction will be made between master and slave, nor between mistress and her servant, 8 neither will a king be more esteemed than a pauper, nor an elder more than an infant. A father will hold no greater honor than his

child, 9 and a mother no more than her offspring. The wealthy will not be more revered than the poor, the arrogant will not be esteemed above the humble, and the great will not be more respected than the small. 10 This is the day of judgment, the day when sentences and retributions are meted out, the day when everyone will face consequences commensurate with the sins they have committed. It is the day when those who have performed righteous deeds will receive their due rewards, and those who have sinned will bear the burden of their wrongdoings. 11 As this day brings joy to those who have secured their reward, those who have forgotten the Law of the Lord will find themselves fixed in their appointed place. Those who spread falsehoods and misguided others with claims that "The dead will not rise" will witness the reality of resurrection. 12 On that day, sinners of this world, who failed to perform righteous acts, will lament over their sins, engulfed in unending sorrow without any comfort. 13 Conversely, the righteous who have committed virtuous deeds will experience unceasing joy that lasts for eternity, for they acted righteously while in this world. 14 They lived with the knowledge that they would rise after death and did not stray from the Law of their Creator. 15 Because they remained faithful to His Law, they are set to receive dual blessings: their progeny flourished in this world, and their offspring were honored. 16 Moreover, they are destined to inherit the Kingdom of Heaven, a place of eternal bliss promised to their forefathers. This inheritance will be realized when the dead are resurrected, and the wealthy of this world see their fortunes reversed. 17 Those who committed sin, who lacked faith in the resurrection of the dead, who failed to adhere to the Law of the Lord, and who did not contemplate the Day of Resurrection, will be overtaken by grief. 18 In that moment, they will behold the relentless torment that awaits them—a state devoid of peace or relief, marked by an unending sorrow that offers no respite or solace to their minds. 19 They will encounter an unquenchable fire and incessant worms. 20 Where their bodies lie, there will be fire, brimstone, whirlwinds, freezing cold, hail, and sleet—all these elements will pour down upon them. 21 For those who denied the resurrection of the dead, the fiery pits of Gehenna await, a testament to their disbelief and disobedience.

16

1 Reflect upon the nature of your own body – consider the nails on your hands and feet, the hair on your head. They grow continuously, and when you trim them, they quickly grow back. Let this be a symbol to you of resurrection: that you possess reason, faith, and knowledge. 2 When you contemplate where the nails of your hands and feet, and the hair of your head, come from, recognize that it

is the Lord who has ordained their growth. This should serve as a reminder to you of the resurrection that awaits your flesh – a resurrection unique to your own body, affirming that you will rise again after death. 3 As you have led others astray by claiming, "There is no resurrection of the dead," when the dead indeed rise, you will face the consequences of your sins and wrongdoings. 4 Just as the seeds you plant – be it wheat or barley – do not remain dormant but grow, you will witness the reality of this on the day when you face the repercussions for your actions. 5 Similarly, the plants you cultivate do not resist growth. Whether it be a fig tree or a grapevine, its fruit and leaves will grow as intended. 6 If you plant grape seeds, they will grow into grapevines, not fig trees. If you plant fig seeds, they will grow into fig trees, not grapevines. Likewise, if you sow wheat, it will grow as wheat, not as barley. 7 Every seed, of each kind, produces its respective fruit, wood, leaves, and roots. They flourish and bear fruit, receiving the blessing of the Dew of Mercy from the Lord. Even if you sow barley, it will not transform into wheat. 8 In the same way, the grave will yield up bodies and souls as the Lord has planted them. The flesh and soul that the Lord placed in the earth will rise together. However, those who did righteous deeds will not be interchanged with those who committed evil, nor will the evil be interchanged with the righteous. Each will rise according to the nature of their deeds as sown by the Lord. 9 When the appointed time comes, signaled by the sound of a trumpet, those who have passed away will rise through the Mercy Dew granted by the Lord. Those who have performed righteous deeds will experience the Resurrection of Life, receiving their reward in the Heavenly Garden. This place, prepared by the Lord for the virtuous, is filled with joy and bliss, free from suffering and illness, and is the eternal abode of the pure, where death no longer has dominion. 10 Conversely, those who have committed evil deeds will face a Resurrection of Judgment, accompanied by the Devil who deceived them, 11 and his legions of demons, who desired that none of Adam's descendants would be saved. 12 These souls will descend into the depths of Gehenna, a place of utter darkness, characterized by gnashing of teeth and endless lamentation. It is devoid of love, forgiveness, and there is no escape, existing perpetually beneath Sheol. Their fate is sealed because they failed to perform virtuous acts while living in the flesh in this world. 13 Thus, judgment will be passed upon them when the flesh and soul are reunited at the resurrection. 14 Woe to those who do not believe in the resurrection of both flesh and soul, through which the Lord demonstrates the abundance of His miraculous power. 15 Everyone, without exception, will receive the reward or face the consequences according to their deeds and the efforts they have exerted in life.

17

1 A wheat kernel cannot sprout and produce fruit unless it first breaks down in the soil. But once the kernel is decomposed, it sends roots deep into the earth, sprouts leaves, forms buds, and eventually bears fruit. 2 From this single wheat kernel, multiple kernels are produced, exemplifying growth and multiplication. 3Similarly, the growth of this kernel is facilitated by the elements – water and wind – and the dew of the earth. For wheat to bear fruit, it requires sunlight, which acts as a source of energy, akin to fire. 4 Wind represents the soul, an essential element for the wheat's fruiting. Without wind, the wheat cannot produce fruit. Water nourishes the earth, quenching its thirst. 5 Once the earth, akin to ashes, absorbs the water, it develops roots, and its shoots grow upwards, bearing as much fruit as the Lord has blessed it to produce. 6 The wheat kernel serves as a metaphor for Adam, in whom resided a living soul created by the Lord. Similarly, a grapevine absorbs water, develops roots, and these slender roots draw up water to support the plant's growth. 7 The Dew of Mercy, provided by the Lord, nourishes the long tendrils of the grapevines, propelling water upwards to the very tips of the leaves. Warmed by the sun's rays and according to the Lord's will, the vine blossoms and bears fruit. 8 This fruit is delightfully fragrant, bringing joy to the mind. When consumed, it satisfies like water that quenches thirst and grain that appeases hunger. When pressed, its juice becomes the lifeblood of the grape. 9 As expressed in a Psalm, "Grapes gladden a person's heart." Drinking wine brings joy to the heart. When a carefree person opens his mouth to drink, he becomes intoxicated. He drinks deeply, filling his lungs, and the alcohol courses to his heart. 10 The inebriating effect of grapes can lead to disorientation, causing one to lose their senses. It transforms perilous pits and cliffs into seemingly harmless meadows, making the drinker oblivious to dangers, like thorns that might injure their feet and hands. 11 The Lord has created the fruits of the earth and the grapevine in such a way to illustrate His power and magnificence, so that His name may be praised by those who believe in the resurrection of the dead and who follow His commandments. 12 In the Kingdom of Heaven, He will bring joy and bliss to those who have faith in the resurrection of the dead and have lived according to His will.

18

1 Those who do not believe in the resurrection of the dead are deeply mistaken. When you are brought to a place unknown to you, you will experience regret, but it will be futile because you did not believe that the dead would rise again, united in both soul and flesh. And when you are cast into Gehenna, 2 you will

face the consequences of your actions, whether good or evil, for you have led others astray by claiming, "We know that those who

have died, turned to dust and ashes, will not rise again." 3 Your death will offer no escape from the punishment that awaits, and you will lack the strength to endure the trials you will face. Thus, you have misguided your companions by not acknowledging your standing before the Lord. 4 When His wrath is kindled against you, you will be consumed by fear. You failed to understand that you were brought into being from nothingness. As you spoke of the Lord's Law without truly understanding it, judgment will be passed upon you for your wickedness. 5 You are unaware of the Gehenna to which you are destined, because of your anger and corrupt deeds. You misled others according to the misguided inclinations of your thoughts, teaching falsely that "There is no resurrection of the dead," leading them astray. 6 In that defining moment, they will come to realize that the dead do indeed rise. They will acknowledge that judgment is upon them for their disbelief in the resurrection of all of Adam's descendants. 7 We are all children of Adam and have inherited death due to his transgression. The judgment of death has befallen us all from the Lord, as a consequence of our forefather Adam's mistake. 8 We will rise again alongside Adam to face the repercussions of our own actions, for the realm of death was ushered in through Adam's ignorance. 9 Adam's breach of the Lord's command brought hardship upon us all. Our bodies decomposed in the grave as wax melts away, our physical forms disintegrated. 10 The earth absorbed our essence. We vanished, and our beauty was lost in the grave. Our flesh was interred, and our eloquent words were silenced by the earth. 11 Worms emerged from our once bright eyes, and our faces decayed in the grave, turning to dust. 12 Where now is the beauty of the young with their attractive features and handsome stature, whose words were once heeded? What has become of the strength of warriors. 13 Where now are the mighty armies of kings, or the lordship of the nobles? What has become of the splendor of horses, the glitter of silver and gold, and the gleam of polished weapons? Have they not all perished and faded away? 14 Where is the sweetness of grape wine, and the savor of delicious foods? All these pleasures and signs of wealth and power have vanished, lost to the decay and oblivion of the grave.

19

1 Oh Earth, that has embraced nobles, kings, the wealthy, elders, beautiful women, and alluring beauties, woe stems from you. 2 Oh Earth, you have accumulated warriors, those with comely appearance, those with graceful legs, those endowed with reason and knowledge, and those whose

eloquent words were as melodious as the strumming of harps, lyres, and violins, 3 those whose laughter was as intoxicating as wine, whose eyes sparkled like the morning stars, 4 those skilled in crafting firm structures, whose right hands skillfully gave and took away, whose swift feet were a delight to behold, and who moved with the speed of spinning wheels, woe arises from you. 5 Oh death, that has torn apart the souls of the beautiful from their bodies, woe comes from you, for you act according to the will of the Lord. 6 You, Earth, have gathered many whom the Lord brought forth and to whom you have provided return. Woe arises from you. From you we came, to you we return, in accordance with the Lord's command. We rejoiced upon you by His decree. 7 You have become a resting place for our deceased bodies. We walked upon you, were interred within you, consumed your produce, and in turn, you consumed our flesh. 8 We drank from the waters that sprung forth from your soil, and in turn, you absorbed the lifeblood that flowed in our veins. We consumed the fruits grown from your earthliness, and you devoured the flesh of our bodies in return. 9 Just as the Lord ordained you, Earth, to provide us with sustenance, we partook of the grains nourished by your fertile lands and dew. You then reclaimed the beauty of our flesh, reducing it to dust to feed yourself, as was the command of the Lord. 10 Oh death, collector of nobles and mighty kings, woe comes from you. You showed no regard for their fame or terror, obedient only to the command of the Lord who created them. Oh death, woe comes from you, for you did not spare the afflicted. 11 You showed no kindness to those with fair appearances and did not relent for the mighty and the warriors. You did not discriminate between the poor and the rich, the kind and the wicked, children and the elderly, women and men. 12 You did not spare those who pondered good things and followed the Law, nor those who behaved like animals in their deeds, thinking only of evil. You were indifferent to the beauty of their features, the sweetness of their lives, and the eloquence of their words. Oh death, woe arises from you. 13 You, death, did not spare those whose words were filled with anger and curses. You have gathered souls from both darkness and light into your realm. Oh death, woe arises from you. 14 And the Earth has received the bodies of the living, whether they lay in caves or in the soil, waiting until the sounding of the trumpet, signaling the time for the dead to rise. 15 When that moment comes, as commanded by the Lord, those who have died will rise swiftly, as quickly as the blink of an eye, at the sound of the trumpet. Those who have committed evil deeds will face their punishments, measured against the extent of their sins. Conversely, those who have done good deeds will rejoice in their reward.

20

1 Believe me when I say that all our deeds performed in this world will neither remain hidden nor be forgotten when we stand before the Lord, filled with fear and trembling. 2 When we fail to prepare for our journey ahead, lacking provisions for the path, 3 when we find ourselves without clothing for our bodies, 4 when we have no staff in our hands or shoes on our feet, and we do not know the paths that demons will lead us on—whether they be slippery or smooth, dark or thorny, or whether they lead to deep waters or treacherous pits—believe me, our actions in this world will not remain concealed. 5 We will be unable to recognize the demons guiding us, nor will we comprehend their intentions. 6 As they are shrouded in darkness, their faces will be unseen to us. 7 As the prophet said, "When my soul parted from my flesh, Lord, my Lord, you knew my path. They set a snare along the way I traveled, and I saw no way to turn right. No one recognized me, and I had no means of escape." As these dark entities lead us, their faces will remain obscured from our view. 8 The prophet's words stem from his awareness that demons will mock and mislead him, guiding him on a path unknown. His lament reflects the realization that no matter which way he turns, left or right, there will be no one who recognizes him. 9 He finds himself alone among demons, isolated and without anyone to acknowledge him. 10 For the righteous, subtle Angels of Light are dispatched to receive the souls of the virtuous and escort them to a realm of Light, to the Garden where bliss abounds. 11 In contrast, demons and Angels of darkness are assigned to seize the souls of the wicked and transport them to Gehenna, a place designated for their punishment, in accordance with the sins they have committed. 12 Woe befalls the souls of sinners, led to their ruin, where no peace, rest, or escape from their afflictions exists, and from where there is no departure from Gehenna for eternity. 13 These sinners have followed the path of Cain, perished through the corruption of Balaam, and now find themselves bereft of righteous deeds. Woe to those sinners who sought to gain through usury and bribery, unjustly acquiring wealth that was not rightfully theirs. 14 They will face their retribution in Gehenna, suffering the consequences of their sins.

21

1 Where are those who amassed wealth that was not earned by their own labor, the wealth that belonged to others? 2 They acquired another person's wealth without effort, and they will be taken away, unexpectedly overtaken by the day of their death, leaving their ill-gotten gains to strangers. 3 Like their ancestors before them, they are part of a lineage of sinners, plagued by worry and seizing assets through unrighteous means, be it theft or robbery. Their children will

not find joy in the wealth accumulated through such violence. 4 Their ill-gotten wealth is as fleeting as mist, as ephemeral as smoke dispersed by the wind, as transient as withering grass, or as wax that melts away in the presence of fire. Just as these things vanish, so too will the illusory glory of sinners dissipate, leaving nothing of value for their descendants. 5 As David said, "I saw a wicked man, exalted and esteemed like the cedars of Lebanon, but when I returned, he was gone. I searched, but could not find any trace of him." Thus, no benefit or advantage will come from the wealth they accumulated. 6 Because they acquired wealth through violence, believing they would not face death, just as those who betray their peers should not take pride in their actions, so too will the downfall of sinners come suddenly and unexpectedly. 7 You who are indolent, realize that you will perish along with your wealth. Even if your silver and gold are abundant, they will eventually corrode and become worthless. 8 If you have many children, they will only inherit graves. If you build numerous houses, they will eventually crumble and fall. 9 You have failed to honor the covenant of your Creator, the Lord. Even if you acquire extensive livestock, they will be seized by your enemies. All the wealth you have amassed will disappear, for it was never blessed. 10 Whether stored in homes or hidden in forests, whether in wilderness or pasture lands, whether in vineyards or in grain fields, your wealth will vanish. 11 Because you have not adhered to the Lord's Commandments, He will not shield you and your family from calamities. You will be surrounded by sorrow from all your enemies and will not find joy in your offspring. 12 However, the Lord does not bring hardship upon those who have followed His decrees and Law. He provides for all who seek Him, blessing their children and the fruits of their lands. 13 He appoints them as leaders over the peoples in their regions, so they may govern rather than be governed. He bestows upon them all His abundance in their dwelling places. 14 The Lord blesses all that they have undertaken, including the fruits of their fields and their livestock. He fills them with joy over the children born to them. 15 He does not reduce their livestock and saves them from all forms of hardship, be it fatigue, sickness, destruction, or enemies, whether known or unknown. 16 The Lord defends them during times of dispute and rescues them from adversity and conflict, protecting them from all who oppose them. In earlier times, if there was a priest who diligently performed his duties in the Tent, adhered to the Law, and firmly lived in accordance with the Lord's Covenant, following the original ordinances and the entire Law, and received tithes and firstborn offerings, from humans to livestock, the Lord would deliver them from all tribulations. 17 As Moses instructed Joshua, son of

Nun, there were cities of refuge in their land. Whether the act was committed knowingly or unknowingly, judgments were passed for those accused and acquitted, 18 so that if someone accidentally caused a death, they could seek refuge and be saved. 19 They were instructed to carefully consider whether there had been a previous dispute, whether the death was caused by an axe, stone, or wood, and whether it was an accidental occurrence. If the person claimed the death was accidental, they were to be investigated and possibly saved. If the act was unintentional, efforts should be made to save them from death. 20 However, if the act was intentional, the perpetrator must face the consequences of their sin, and there would be no pardon. But if the death was truly accidental, a thorough investigation was needed to ensure their salvation and prevent an unjust death. 21 The ordinances were established to steer the people away from sin. Moses implemented these measures for the children of Israel to prevent them from straying from the Law of the Lord. 22 He instructed them to live faithfully according to the Lord's Commandments, avoiding idol worship, consuming meat from animals that died naturally or were killed without being properly bled, and refraining from all evil deeds. This guidance was provided to ensure that they would adhere to what was right and avoid all that was improper. 23 These commands were given as a reflection of the heavenly pattern, with the aim of preserving their bodies and securing their place alongside their ancestors. 24 As descendants of Seth and Adam, who were obedient to the Lord, those who believe in the Lord's Word and faithfully follow His Commandments will be recognized as the children of the righteous. 25 Being children of Adam, created in the Lord's Image and Likeness, we are called to perform all righteous deeds that bring joy to the Lord. He will not overlook those who do so. 26 The Lord will not forsake His faithful followers. Those who engage in righteous deeds will inherit the Kingdom of Heaven, where they will find bliss alongside others who have also committed themselves to goodness. 27 He has a deep affection for those who earnestly seek Him with pure hearts. He listens attentively to their prayers and accepts the repentance of those who truly repent and reform. He grants strength and power to those who uphold His decrees, Law, and Commandments. 28 Those who have abided by His covenant will rejoice in His Kingdom eternally, regardless of whether they were from earlier generations or arose later. They will offer endless praise to Him from this day forward and for all eternity. Let eternal glory be given to the Lord. Thus concludes the second book of Meqabyan. SELAH.

BOOK OF MEQABYAN III

1

1 Christ will bring joy to the people of Egypt when He comes in a future era. He will exact vengeance and defeat the Devil, who has harmed the kind and innocent, led people astray, and opposed the works of his Creator. 2 Christ will avenge and vanquish him, reducing his dominion to ruin and disgrace due to his prideful reasoning. 3 His power will be diminished as he boasted arrogantly, saying, "I will venture into the sea's heart, ascend to the heavens, explore the depths, and snatch up the children of Adam as easily as birds snatch chicks. Who is greater than I? 4 Because of me, they have strayed from the righteous Law of the Lord. I will exert my influence over those living in this world who do not follow the Lord's Covenant. No one will strip me of my power," he proclaimed. 5 "I will be the cause that leads them on an easy path, straight into Gehenna, to join me in damnation." 6 Those who love Him and adhere to His Law will despise me, but those who have strayed from their Lord's Law and have faltered will gravitate towards me. They will come to love me and keep my decrees. I will corrupt their reasoning and alter their thoughts to prevent them from returning to their Creator, the Lord. They will follow my commands as I have instructed. 7 When I expose them to the wealth of this world, I will divert their minds from the righteous Law. By presenting them with beautiful and alluring women, I will lead them away from the path of righteousness. 8 When I show them the glittering jewels of India, silver, and gold, I will also use these to draw them away from the righteous Law, enticing them to engage in my deeds. 9 When I display luxurious garments, fine red and white silk, linens, and exquisite fabrics, I will use these too to lure them away from the righteous Law and draw them towards my designs. When I make them see wealth and livestock as abundant as sand, I will use this to bring them into my fold. 10 When I incite jealousy through pride over women, stir anger and disputes, I will use all these means to sway them towards my ways. 11When I present them with omens and signs, I will implant these notions in the minds of their peers. I will embed a specific sign in each of their thoughts, showing them signs through words, leading them astray. 12 For those in whom I have established my presence, I will reveal signs, whether through the movements of the stars, the patterns of clouds, the flickering of flames, or the cries of animals and birds. Since they are under my influence, I will implant these signs in their minds through all these means. 13 They will speak and provide omens for their peers. Just as their skeptics have forewarned, I

will be ahead, serving as an omen for them. 14 I will carry out these verbal omens for them, causing those who investigate them to be deceived. This will lead people to compensate magicians and proclaim to their peers, "There are no experts like so-and-so, whose predictions come true, who discern prophecy, who can distinguish between good and evil, for whom everything happens as they say, and whose words always come to pass." 15 I will rejoice when they utter such declarations, for it means that more of Adam's descendants are led astray and doomed because of my influence. I was demoted from my former status by the Lord due to Adam, when I refused to bow to Adam, considering him inferior to myself. 16 I am determined to drag all those who steadfastly follow my commands down to destruction. I have a pledge from the Lord, the Creator, that all those I lead astray will join me in Gehenna. 17 When the Lord's anger towards me intensified and He ordered that I be bound and thrown into Gehenna, I pleaded with my Creator. I implored Him, saying, "As You are angered with me, and as You have reprimanded me with Your punishment, having chastised me in Your wrath, Lord, my Lord, allow me to say one thing before You." 18 My Lord responded to me, granting me permission to speak. I then began my plea, saying, "Since I have been stripped of my position, let those whom I have led astray share my fate in Gehenna, where I will endure suffering." 19 "Grant that those who resisted my temptations, who did not falter by my deceptions, who did not heed my commands, may serve Your Lordship. Let them follow Your Commandments, fulfill Your Covenant, and keep Your Word, for they did not succumb to my misleading ways and refused the paths I taught. When You favored me, let them receive the crown that was intended for me. 20 Award them the crown of the authorities, known as Satans, who accompanied me. Place them upon my former throne at Your Right Hand, which I and my hosts abandoned. 21 Let them sing praises to You as You desire. Let them be akin to my hosts and to me, for while You despised me, You cherished them, beings formed from dust and earth. As my dominion has fallen and their stature has risen, let them extol You as You desire." 22 My Lord responded, "If you led them astray while they were aware and conscious, and if you deceived them without their adherence to My Law, let them share your fate, conforming to your designs and words. 23 If they abandoned the Scripture and My Commandments, turning to you, and if your deceit caused them ruin which also grieved Me, then let them endure suffering in Gehenna, just like you," He told me. 24 "You will face suffering in Gehenna for eternity, and there will be no escape from Gehenna, forever, for both those you misled and for yourself."

2

1 "However, I will transfer your throne and dominion to those you failed to lead astray, such as my servant Job. The Lord of all declares, 'I will grant the Kingdom of Heaven to those you could not deceive.'" 2 "I continually challenge the children of Adam, attempting to lure them away if I can. I will not relent in trying to sway them from righteous actions. My antagonism extends to all of Adam's descendants, as I entice them with the fleeting pleasures of this world. 3 Whether it's through the love of food, drink, and clothing, or through the love of possessions, both in giving and withholding, 4 or through the enjoyment of sights and sounds, through the desire for touch and travel, or through increasing pride and material possessions, 5 or by promoting excessive drinking and revelry, by fostering quarrels and anger, encouraging idle talk and frivolous activities, 6 or by inciting conflicts and slander among peers, or by the allure of attractive women of this world, or by the seductive scent of perfumes, 7 I use all these means to lead them astray, hoping they will not find salvation. I strive to divert them from the Law of the Lord, leading them towards the same ruin that caused my fall from grace." 8 The prophet rebuked him, saying, "You who bring ruin to others, be doomed yourself. When you turned away from the Law of the Lord, committed transgressions through your stubborn reasoning and arrogance, and caused grief to your Creator by refusing to worship Him, how can you dare to defy God's creation? 9 When your Creator grew angry with you, He stripped you of your status due to your wicked deeds. Why then do you lead Adam, formed by God from the earth and fashioned as He pleased, into sin? Why do you corrupt the one set forth to glorify Him?" he questioned. 10 "You, who are cunning and were made from wind and fire, arrogantly claimed, 'I am the Creator.' 11 As you boasted of your false claim, the Lord saw your malevolent actions. When you and your hosts renounced the Lord, He created Adam to take your place in offering praise, so that His Name might be glorified ceaselessly. 12 Since you exalted yourself above all the angelic hosts similar to you, due to your pride, the Lord created Adam and his descendants to extol the Lord's Name, in place of the praises you once offered with your hosts, whom He now regards with disdain." 13 As a result, the Lord cast you out, separating you from all the chief angels like yourself, and your hosts that were created in unison with you. You all deviated from praising the Lord due to the baseless pride in your reasoning and the obstinacy of your thoughts. You became insolent against your Creator, not against someone else. 14 Therefore, He created Adam from the earth to be praised by those who are humble. He gave Adam a commandment and a law, instructing him not to eat from the tree of knowledge, warning that

eating its fruit would bring death. 15 He placed Adam in charge of all His creation and instructed him, saying, "Do not eat from that one tree which brings death, lest you bring death upon yourself. However, you may eat from all other trees in the Garden." 16 When you heard this decree, you sowed deceit in Adam through the words you spoke to Eve, who was created from a rib taken from Adam's side. 17 You led the innocent Adam into profound deceit, intending to make him a transgressor of the Law, just like yourself. 18 When you deceived Eve, who was like an innocent dove and unaware of your malice, you led her into betrayal with your successful, crooked words. After leading Eve astray, she in turn misled Adam, God's creation formed from the earth. 19 You caused Adam to falter, not because of your pride, but through your deceit, leading him to deny the word of his Creator. In your arrogance, you were responsible for Adam's downfall. 20 Through your wickedness, you estranged him from the love of his Creator. With your cunning, you banished him from the Garden of bliss and, through your obstruction, prevented him from enjoying its sustenance. 21 Since ancient times, you have been in conflict with the innocent creation, Adam, aiming to cast him into Sheol, where you suffer, to remove him from the love that brought him into being, and with your falsehood, you made him yearn for the Garden's waters. 22 Though Adam was earthly, God transformed him into a being as astute as an angel, fully capable of praising his Creator in body, soul, and mind. 23 The Lord instilled in him a multitude of thoughts, each resonating like a harp with its unique melody.

3

1 However, God bestowed upon you only one purpose: to offer ceaseless praise in the realm where your Creator assigned you. 2 In contrast, Adam was endowed with ten types of thoughts: five inclined towards evil and five towards goodness. 3 Additionally, Adam possessed a multitude of thoughts, as vast and varied as the waves of the sea, like a whirlwind stirring dust from the earth, or the tumultuous waves of the sea. His thoughts, numerous and uncountable in his heart, are akin to countless raindrops. 4 Your scope of thought is singular, as you are not of flesh and thus lack the complexity of human thought. 5 Yet, you chose to inhabit the reasoning of a serpent. Through malicious deception, you brought ruin to Adam, who was one with Eve. Upon hearing the serpent's words, Eve was swayed and acted as it instructed. 6 After she consumed the fruit of the forbidden tree, she went on to lead Adam, God's first creation, astray, bringing death upon both him and their progeny for defying the command of their Creator. 7 They were exiled from the Garden by the just judgment of the Lord. He placed them in a land where their descendants would

flourish, sustained by the fruits of the earth, yet they were not entirely removed from the strife of the Garden. 8 When you forced Adam and Eve out of the Garden, it was so they could cultivate plants and raise children, to find solace and rejuvenate their minds with the fruits of the Earth that it yields from its substance, and to be soothed by the Earth's produce as well as the fruits of the Garden that God had provided them. 9 God then granted them access to forests even more lush and verdant than those of the Garden, ensuring that Adam and Eve, whom you had banished from the Garden for their transgression, were fully consoled and freed from their grief. 10 The Lord, understanding how to pacify His creation, soothed their minds through their offspring and the crops that sprung from the Earth. 11 Sent into a world where nettles and thorns grow, they anchored their thoughts and found stability through the sustenance of water and grain.

4

1 "The Lord will redeem Adam and bring disgrace upon you. He will rescue the sheep (Adam) from the jaws of the wolf (the Devil). This act of salvation will humiliate you, who sought to dominate and corrupt. 2 You, however, will descend into Hell, dragging down with you those whom you managed to dominate and lead astray. 3 Those who adhered to their Creator The Lord's Law will rejoice with their Creator the Lord, who shielded them from wicked deeds. They are destined to become His treasured possession, joining in praise with the honorable Angels who, unlike you, did not violate their Creator the Lord's Law. 4 The Lord, who once elevated and favored you above all other angels like you, to praise Him alongside His servant Angels, stripped you of your exalted throne due to your arrogance. 5 You gained notoriety, being labeled as one who aspired to godhood, and your followers were branded as demons. 6 But those who loved the Lord will be considered His kin, akin to the esteemed Angels, Seraphim, and Cherubim who ceaselessly extend their wings in His praise." 7 "Your arrogance and negligence led to the loss of the praise you were meant to continually offer Him, along with your host and those created in your likeness. 8 To prevent the diminishment of the praise of the Lord, who created you as part of a tenth tribe, when you forgot to praise your Creator—thinking it impossible for Him to create another being like you—and to ensure His praise wasn't lessened when you broke away from the unity of your brethren, He created Adam to replace you. 9 But in the pride of your thoughts, you abandoned the praise of the Lord who made you. This angered Him, and He made a mockery of you, binding and casting you and your hosts into Hell. 10 Then, with His glorified Hands, He took Soil from the Earth, mixing it with fire, water, and wind, and fashioned Adam in His Image and Likeness. 11 He set Adam over all His creations, so that

the praise you once offered could be continued by Adam. This way, Adam's praise joined with that of the Angels, and their praises were aligned, maintaining balance." 12 "Due to the rigidity of your reasoning and your arrogance, you were stripped of your exalted position and, having turned away from the dominion of the Lord who created you, you brought about your own downfall. 13 Understand that His glorification did not suffer, for the Lord created Adam, who praised Him with the power of his mind, ensuring that the adoration due to the Lord remained unaltered. 14 God, who foresees all before it happens, knew of your existence even before your creation and that you would eventually defy His command. With a hidden plan in place before even the world was formed, when you rejected Him, He fashioned His servant Adam in His own Image and Likeness. 15 As Solomon stated, 'Before the formation of the hills, before the world was brought into being, before the creation of the winds which are the foundations of the earth, 16 before the establishment of hills and mountains, before the structuring of the world's framework, before the illumination of the moon and sun, before the management of times and stars was known, 17 before the alternation of day and night, before the sea was bordered by sand, before all of creation as we know it came into being, 18 before everything we see today existed, before the names we use today were spoken, He created me, Solomon', and just like the angels like you and you yourself, God's servant Adam was part of the Lord's divine plan." 19 "Adam was created so that God's exalted Name might be praised, especially when you rebelled. In your pride, God chose to be glorified through the praises of His humble creation, Adam, who was made from the earth. 20 Dwelling in the heavens, the Lord hears the cries of the poor and delights in the praises of the humble. He finds joy in saving those who revere Him, but He does not take pleasure in the strength of horses nor the legs of a man. 21The Lord does not concern Himself with the grandeur of the mighty. Their cries, born of sin, will go unheard. 22 Your opportunity for repentance was neglected. 23 Unlike you, Adam, formed from dust, turned back to God in genuine repentance, shedding tears of remorse for his transgression. 24 The pride in your heart and the stubbornness of your reasoning kept you from understanding acts of love and the essence of repentance. You failed to humbly seek forgiveness from your Creator, the Lord.25 In contrast, Adam, though merely dust and ashes, embraced repentance with a heart full of grief and humility, returning to a path of love and humility. 26 You, however, did not humble your thoughts or yourself before the Lord, who created you." 27 "The Lord will redeem Adam and bring disgrace upon you. He will rescue the sheep (Adam) from the jaws of the wolf (the Devil). This act of salvation will humiliate you, who sought to dominate and corrupt. 28 You, however, will descend into Hell, dragging down with you those whom you managed to dominate and lead astray. 29 Those who adhered to their Creator the Lord's Law will rejoice with their Creator the Lord, who shielded them from wicked deeds. They are destined to become His treasured possession, joining in praise with the honorable Angels who, unlike you, did not violate their Creator the Lord's Law. 30 The Lord, who once elevated and favored you above all other angels like you, to praise Him alongside His servant Angels, stripped you of your exalted throne due to your arrogance. 31 You gained notoriety, being labeled as one who aspired to godhood, and your followers were branded as demons. 32 But those who loved the Lord will be considered His kin, akin to the esteemed Angels, Seraphim, and Cherubim who ceaselessly extend their wings in His praise." 33 "Your arrogance and negligence led to the loss of the praise you were meant to continually offer Him, along with your host and those created in your likeness. 34 To prevent the diminishment of the praise of the Lord, who created you as part of a tenth tribe, when you forgot to praise your Creator— thinking it impossible for Him to create another being like you and to ensure His praise wasn't lessened when you broke away from the unity of your brethren, He created Adam to replace you. 35 But in the pride of your thoughts, you abandoned the praise of the Lord who made you. This angered Him, and He made a mockery of you, binding and casting you and your hosts into Hell. 36 Then, with His glorified Hands, He took Soil from the Earth, mixing it with fire, water, and wind, and fashioned Adam in His Image and Likeness. 37 He set Adam over all His creations, so that the praise you once offered could be continued by Adam. This way, Adam's praise joined with that of the Angels, and their praises were aligned, maintaining balance." 38 "Due to the rigidity of your reasoning and your arrogance, you were stripped of your exalted position and, having turned away from the dominion of the Lord who created you, you brought about your own downfall. 39 Understand that His glorification did not suffer, for the Lord created Adam, who praised Him with the power of his mind, ensuring that the adoration due to the Lord remained unaltered. 40 God, who foresees all before it happens, knew of your existence even before your creation and that you would eventually defy His command. With a hidden plan in place before even the world was formed, when you rejected Him, He fashioned His servant Adam in His own Image and Likeness. 41 As Solomon stated, 'Before the formation of the hills, before the world was brought into being, before the creation of the winds which are the foundations of the earth, 42 before the establishment of hills and mountains, before the structuring of the world's framework, before the illumination of the moon and sun, before the management of times and stars was known, 43 before the alternation of day and night, before the sea was bordered by sand, before all of creation as we know it came into being, 44 before everything we see today existed, before the names we use today were spoken, He created me, Solomon', and just like the angels like you and you yourself, God's servant Adam was part of the Lord's divine plan." 45 "Adam was created so that God's exalted Name might be praised, especially when you rebelled. In your pride, God chose to be glorified through the praises of His humble creation, Adam, who was made from the earth. 46 For, being in Heaven, the Lord hears the pleas of the poor, and He cherishes the praise of the humble. 47 He delights in saving those who harbor reverence for Him.Unlike His disregard for the strength of horses or the allure of physical charms, the Lord will overlook the entreaties of the proud. 48 Such individuals will lament their fate as they recall the sins they committed. 49 You missed the opportunity to seek forgiveness through repentance. 50 Unlike you, Adam, formed from dust, turned back to God in genuine repentance, shedding tears of remorse for his transgression. 51 The pride in your heart and the stubbornness of your reasoning kept you from understanding acts of love and the essence of repentance. You failed to humbly seek forgiveness from your Creator, the Lord. 52 In contrast, Adam, though merely dust and ashes, embraced repentance with a heart full of grief and humility, returning to a path of love and humility. 53 You, however, did not humble your thoughts or yourself before the Lord, who created you." 54 "Adam chose humility over pride, openly acknowledging and repenting for his sins. He did not allow pride to cloud his judgment. 55 You, on the other hand, have been a source of sin, leading Adam astray with your prideful ways towards destruction. 56 Before your creation, the Lord knew of your impending disobedience and the nature of your actions. He was aware that your downfall would stem from the pride in your heart.57 Yet, He guided Adam, who was free from such pride and malice, back to the path of repentance, filled with genuine mourning and sorrow. 58 One who sins and fails to seek repentance only compounds his wrongdoing. Your heart, swollen with pride, prevented you from seeking forgiveness. In contrast, those who earnestly repent and seek forgiveness from the Lord, 59 truly repent and find a path to salvation. They win the favor of the Lord through their humility and sincere repentance, moving away from their past transgressions. The Lord, in His grace, lightens their burden of sin, choosing not to hold their past against them and offering forgiveness." 60 If he refrained from reverting to his past sins and maintained this stance, then such behavior epitomizes true repentance. Adam consistently remembered his Creator, and never ceased to seek forgiveness from the Lord in a spirit of repentance. 61 And you, should seek forgiveness from the Lord in repentance, and avoid causing harm to those made of flesh and blood. For the Lord, their Creator, is fully aware of their frailties. Do not afflict those whom He has fashioned in His sovereign will. 62 Once their soul parts from the body, their corporeal form shall return to dust, remaining so until the Lord decrees otherwise.

5

1 Recognize the Lord who shaped you, for He crafted you in His Image and Likeness. As you are formed of earth, do not lose sight of the Lord who established and rescued you, whom Israel honors. He placed you in the Garden for delight and to cultivate the soil. 2 When you disobeyed His Command, He banished you from the Garden into this world, which bears nettles and thorns due to your actions. 3 Understand that you are of the earth, and unto the earth, you shall return. You are dust, nourished by the dust, and to the dust, you shall revert, remaining so until the Lord decides to resurrect you. At that time, He will evaluate your sins and all your wrongdoings. 4 Contemplate what you will say then. Reflect on your deeds, both good and evil, in this world. Determine whether your misdeeds predominate, or if your virtues do. Assess carefully. 5 If you engage in virtuous acts, it will be beneficial for you, bringing happiness on the day of resurrection. 6 However, if you commit evil deeds, woe unto you, for you will face the consequences equal to your actions and the wickedness of your thoughts. Should you harm your fellow beings or disregard the Lord, your suffering will match your misdeeds. 7 Betrayal of your peers, invoking the Lord's Name in falsehood, will lead to a just recompense for your actions. Deceit and treachery will not go unnoticed. 8 When you deceive others with lies disguised as truths, be aware that your falsehoods are known. 9 If you mislead those around you with deceitful claims and proliferate untruths, your punishment will be in accordance with your sins. Denying your promises to others, asserting intentions you never plan to fulfill, brings judgment upon you. 10 When you initially commit to giving with a sincere heart, evil forces may intervene, leading to forgetfulness or reluctance. These demonic influences are akin to persistent dogs, clouding your intentions. Be mindful that accumulating worldly wealth for selfish purposes offers no true gain or nourishment. 11 Furthermore, as stated, children of Adam who engage in deceit make use of unfair scales. Their drive for worldly wealth leads them from one act of theft to another. 12 O people, do not place your trust in corrupted scales and balances, in seizing another's money unjustly, in violently taking what belongs to your neighbor, or in defrauding

others for your own gain. 13 Engaging in such deceitful practices will bring consequences commensurate with your actions. 14 O people, sustain yourselves with the honest work of your hands. Do not covet or engage in theft. Unjustly consuming another's wealth will not bring true fulfillment. Upon death, you leave these ill-gotten gains for others, and even in abundance, they offer no real advantage. 15 If you amass wealth, do not let it corrupt your judgment. The wealth of sinners, fleeting as smoke from a griddle, swiftly disperses. A modest amount, earned honestly, holds greater value than the abundant but unrighteous wealth of sinners.

6

1 Contemplate the day of your demise. When your souls part from your bodies, relinquishing your wealth to others, and as you embark on an unknown journey, ponder the tribulations that await you. 2 The demons that will come for you are malevolent, with hideous appearances and terrifying splendor. They will not listen to your pleas, nor will you comprehend their speech. 3 Because you failed to abide by the Lord's commandments, these demons will ignore your entreaties and strike you with immense fear. 4 However, those who lived in accordance with the Lord's will need not fear; even demons dread them. Sinners, on the other hand, will face the scorn of these demons. 5 The souls of the virtuous will be enveloped in joy by angels, rewarded for their rejection of worldly temptations. Yet, it is the malevolent angels that will claim the souls of sinners. 6 Angels of Mercy are tasked with receiving the souls of the righteous and the kind-hearted, as they are sent by the Lord to bring peace to these souls. In contrast, the wicked angels, dispatched by the Devil, are assigned to seize the souls of sinners, subjecting them to mockery. 7 Sinners, lament for your fate before the inevitability of death overtakes you. When you stand before the Lord, 8 embrace repentance now, in your living years, before it's too late. This way, you can secure a future filled with happiness and freedom from suffering. Remember, once life has passed, there's no returning to rectify your errors. 9 Be wary of leading a life that distances you from the Lord, engrossed in self-indulgence and worldly pleasures. A soul satiated with excess will lose sight of the Lord's name, falling prey to the Devil's riches. Instead, let such earthly delights not ensnare you. 10 Reflect on Moses' words about Jacob, who indulged to his fill and grew prosperous, only to find himself distanced from the Lord who had created him.

7

1 Echoing David's words, "I have faith in the Lord. I shall not be afraid, for what can mere mortals do to me?" there is no fear or dread for those who have faith in the Lord. 2 Similarly, as he declared, "Even if I am surrounded by warriors, my

trust is in Him. I seek only one thing from the Lord, and that I will pursue," those who believe in Him are free from fear. A person with faith in Him will live eternally and shall not be terrified by any malevolence. 3 Who has ever been disgraced for placing their trust in the Lord? And who has forsaken Him for fleeting desires? 4 The Lord has stated, "I cherish those who love Me, and I will exalt those who honor Me. I will protect those who turn to Me in repentance." Thus, who has ever been dishonored for their belief in Him? 5 Uphold justice and defend the cause of the widow. Protect them so that the Lord may shield you from all adversaries and malevolence. Cherish them. As the offspring of the righteous are esteemed, they are blessed with prosperity, and the Lord will safeguard your progeny, ensuring they never lack sustenance.

8

1 Job's unwavering faith in the Lord was evident. He never ceased to praise his Creator, the Lord, which led to his salvation from all the afflictions that the adversary of humanity, the Devil, inflicted upon him. He proclaimed, "The Lord has given, and the Lord has taken away; blessed be the name of the Lord." His resilience and refusal to be disheartened by his ordeals won the Lord's favor. 2 Seeing Job's heart purified from sin, the Lord honored him greatly. 3 The Lord compensated him with wealth far exceeding what he had lost. Job's endurance through his trials and his healing from his afflictions were rewards for his steadfast faith in the face of adversity. 4 If you, like Job, can withstand the trials brought upon you by malevolent forces, you will be held in high regard. 5 Stand firm in your tribulations so that the Lord may be your stronghold and refuge against those who oppose you. May He also be a protective haven for your descendants and your children. Maintain your faith and do not let trials cloud your judgment. Trust in Him, and He will be your steadfast refuge. 6Pray to Him, and He will listen to you. Have hope and trust in His forgiveness. Call upon Him, and He will be as a Father to you;7 Remember Mordecai, Esther, Judith, Gideon, Deborah, Barak, Jephthah, Samson, 8 and others like them, who remained steadfast in their faith in the Lord, undaunted by their enemies. 9 The Lord is impartial and just; He does not show favoritism. Those who seek to indulge in sin bring suffering upon themselves. But all who revere Him and adhere to His laws will preserve their well-being. They will be cherished and honored by Him. 10 He will bless their comings and goings, in life and in death, in their rising and their resting. For He delivers and He shields. 11 He can cause sorrow, yet He also grants forgiveness. 12 He has the power to impoverish or to bestow honor. He can humble, yet also elevate to joy and honor.

9

1 Everything in Heaven and on Earth, both the subtle and the stout, exists within the framework of His Order. All that He owns, every aspect of His creation, abides steadfastly in His command. 2 Nothing has strayed from the Lord's Law and His Order, the Architect of all creation. Whether it be the trajectory of a vulture soaring in the sky, He guides it to its intended destination. 3 He directs the journey of a snake dwelling in the earth's caverns, and even the course of a ship navigating the sea is known only to Him. 4 Beyond the Lord, no one can fathom the journey a soul embarks upon after its separation from the body, whether the soul belongs to the righteous or the sinner. 5 Who can predict its course? Will it wander in the wilderness or rest upon a mountain? Might it soar like a bird, or descend like dew upon a mountaintop? 6 It could resemble the deep wind or mimic the straight path of lightning. 7 Perhaps it shines like the stars in the depths of the night or gathers like sand on the seashore. 8It might be as steadfast as a stone at the ocean's edge or as fruitful as a tree nourished by a water source. 9 Just as the reed, scorched by the sun's heat and carried away by the wind to unfamiliar lands, leaving no trace, so are the ways of the Lord beyond our comprehension. Who truly understands His work? Who can claim to be His counselor or to have been consulted by Him? 10 The thoughts of the Lord are veiled from humanity. Who can scrutinize and truly grasp His deeds? 11 He fashioned the Earth upon waters, securing it without any physical foundations. No one can fathom or uncover the depth of the Lord's counsel or His wisdom. 12 He crafted the heavens with sublime wisdom, anchoring them with winds, and extended the vast cosmos like a tent. 13 He commanded the clouds to pour rain upon the Earth, nurturing grass and producing innumerable fruits as sustenance for mankind. This abundance is meant for us to acknowledge and rejoice in the unity of the Lord. 14 The Lord is the giver of joy, abundance, and satisfaction to the children of Adam. He blesses them with fruits from the Earth, enabling them to be satiated and offer praise for His generosity. 15 He adorns them in exquisite garments and bestows upon them beloved riches, happiness, and joy, reserved for those who adhere to His will. 16 He grants love and honor in the dwelling He has prepared, in the Kingdom of Heaven, to the forefathers who were steadfast in His worship and law, never straying from His commandments. These faithful ones He exalted, ensuring they abide by His decrees and His law. 17 I have witnessed the Lord's deeds for His loyal followers in this world: He diminishes the power of their foes and preserves their well-being. 18 I have seen Him answer their prayers and fulfill their desires. Therefore, do not stray from the Lord; fulfill His will and commandments. 19 Do not stray

from His Command and His Law, or you risk provoking His anger, leading to your sudden destruction. Beware of departing from the path laid by your forefathers, as straying could result in an eternal sentence in Gehenna. 20 Adhere faithfully to the Law of your Creator, the Lord, especially as your soul parts from your body, so that He may bless you when you stand before Him. 21 The dominions of Earth and Heaven belong to Him, as do all power, kindness, and forgiveness. 22 He has the power to enrich or impoverish, to humble or exalt. Therefore, remain steadfast in observing the Lord's Law. 23 David spoke of His greatness, saying, "Man is fleeting, his time on Earth like a passing shadow." 24 He further proclaimed, "But the Lord endures eternally, and His Name is revered through generations." 25 And again, he acknowledged, "His reign encompasses the entire world, and His rule extends through generations." David witnessed the Lord's power in transferring the kingdom from Saul to himself. 26 No one can appoint or remove the Lord. He perceives everything, yet remains unseen. 27 His kingdom endures eternally, unchallenged, as He reigns over all. He sees all, but no one can behold Him. 28 Man was created in His image, to praise Him and acknowledge His sovereignty with clear and unquestioning understanding. He discerns the deepest thoughts and intentions. 29 Yet, they turn to worship inanimate objects made of stone, wood, silver, and gold, the creations of human hands. 30 They offer sacrifices to these idols, sending smoke to the heavens, compounding their sins before the Lord, yet they reject worshiping the Lord who created them. He will hold them accountable for their idolatry. 31 They have embraced idol worship, engaging in sorcery, astrology, and all manners of actions abhorred by the Lord, neglecting the Commands of the Lord they were meant to follow. 32 Their refusal to worship the Lord, which could have cleansed them of sin and iniquity through the intercession of His angels and their righteous deeds, has led them instead to praise wealth above the Lord, resulting in a lack of virtuous actions. 33 When all rise from their graves, where their bodies decayed, their souls will stand barren before the Lord. Those who were righteous will dwell in the Kingdom of Heaven, a realm prepared for the virtuous. 34 Conversely, the souls of sinners will inhabit Hell. At the resurrection, when graves open, those who have died will rise, their souls reuniting with their once-severed flesh. 35 They will stand before the Lord as naked as they were at birth, and every sin they committed, from early childhood to the end of their lives, will be laid bare. 36 They will bear the full weight of their sins on their bodies. Regardless of the extent of their wrongdoing, they will endure punishment proportionate to their sins.

10

1 The essence of life, originating from the Lord, will once again inhabit them, as it did before. For those skeptical about the resurrection, consider how nature revives each spring without the need for parental intervention. 2 It is by His divine command that they initially perish. 3 Though their bodies decay and decompose, they will be reborn and rise again as He wills. 4 Moreover, with the arrival of rain that replenishes the Earth, these creations will awaken to life, just as they were first formed. 5 Immortal beings with living souls in this world, and those brought forth by water, came into existence at His command. The Lord's power over the waters endows them with a living soul. 6 Created by His power and word, without earthly parents, how can you, blinded by your limited understanding, claim that those who have died will not be resurrected by the word of their Creator, the Lord? 7 Those who have passed away, reduced to ashes and dust in their graves, will be resurrected by the Lord's command. Therefore, repent and turn back to your faith. 8 As proclaimed earlier, they will rise through the Dew of Mercy granted by the Lord, and His word will rejuvenate the entire world and awaken the deceased as He desires. 9 Be aware that you too will rise and stand before Him. Do not be deluded by narrow-minded thinking into believing you will remain in the grave. 10 This is not the case. You will be resurrected and face the consequences of your actions, whether good or evil. Do not deceive yourself into thinking you will remain in the grave, for this Day is when retribution is meted out. 11 At the time of resurrection, you will bear the full weight of your sins committed throughout your life. There will be no excuse to justify your wrongdoings, and you cannot deny your sins as you might have done in the worldly realm. 12 Your skill in twisting falsehoods into truths in this world will be of no use in the afterlife. Your deceptions will not stand. 13 Every wrong deed you've done will be exposed before the Creator, the Lord. His Word will reveal your true nature, leaving no room for excuses. 14 In that moment, you will face disgrace for your sins. Instead of being praised among the righteous, you risk humiliation before both humans and Angels on the Day of Judgment. Seize the opportunity to repent in this life before it's too late. 15 Those who have glorified the Lord alongside the Angels will receive their just rewards, unashamed, rejoicing in the Kingdom of Heaven. But if you haven't committed righteous deeds in your earthly life, you will not share in their blessed fate. 16 Failing to act compassionately when you had the means and awareness, like not offering food to the needy despite having the resources, will lead to profound regret. Your inaction in life, when you had the chance to repent, will be lamented in vain. 17 You did not clothe the naked despite having clothes, nor did you defend the

wronged when you had the authority to do so. 18 You failed to guide the sinner towards repentance and knowledge, missing the chance to help them seek forgiveness for their past ignorance. You also did not confront the demons that challenged you, even though you possessed the strength to overcome them. 19 When you were capable, you did not fast or pray to subdue the desires of the flesh and align yourself with righteousness, which does not indulge in earthly pleasures like fine drinks, sweet foods, or luxurious clothing. 20 This righteousness is not concerned with earthly adornments, such as delicate garments or precious metals. 21 Since you neglected fasting and prayer to discipline yourself towards righteousness, which does not covet extravagant jewels like emeralds or topazes, you will face regret. True adornment for a person lies not in material possessions. 22 The real ornaments of a person are purity, wisdom, knowledge, and loving others appropriately without envy, jealousy, doubts, or quarrels. Loving your neighbor as yourself is the true measure. 23 By refraining from retaliating against those who wronged you, you demonstrate true love for one another, a quality essential for entry into the Kingdom of Heaven. This Kingdom is reserved for those who have persevered through trials, and there you will be rewarded for your faith in the Kingdom of Heaven, especially at the time of Resurrection, among those distinguished in knowledge and wisdom. 24 Do not fall into the trap of thinking, "After we die, we will not rise again." Such beliefs are sown by the Devil to sever people's hope of salvation at the Resurrection. Those who harbor such thoughts will only realize their mistake when the Day of Judgment arrives, finding themselves filled with regret for not believing in the possibility of Resurrection. 25 As a result, they will face condemnation proportionate to the wickedness of their deeds in this life, and they will witness the very Resurrection they once denied, rising again in the flesh. 26 At that time, they will lament not having performed virtuous acts during their earthly life. Their regret in this world might have spared them from the grief they will experience in Hell. 27 If we fail to weep out of our own volition in this world, demons in Hell will force us to weep against our will. Neglecting repentance in this life only leads to futile and vain lamentation in Hell. 28 Strive to perform righteous deeds, so you may transition from death to life, move from this transient world to the everlasting Kingdom of Heaven, and witness the celestial Light that eclipses any earthly light. 29 Shun the temporary pleasures of this world to revel in the boundless joy of the Kingdom of Heaven, a happiness that remains unfulfilled from now into eternity, shared with those who believe in the resurrection of the dead. Give eternal glory and praise to the

Creator, thus concludes the third book discussing the matters of the Meqabyans.SELAH

CONCLUSION

These are all the apocryphal books that added to the canonical 66 books of the Old and New Testaments, form the 1560 Geneva Bible in full and complete, without any exclusions.

BONUS

For completeness, we leave you a QR code to scan to receive and obtain the 66 books of the Old and New Testament, in PDF, downloadable, printable or readable online:

With the books you will find in the PDF, combined with all the apocryphal books you have just read, the 1560 Geneva Bible is COMPLETE with ALL the material.

Made in the USA
Columbia, SC
07 May 2024

2a250fba-e250-49c0-ad22-afff10b5028fR03